To Each
Its Own
Meaning

AN INTRODUCTION

TO EACH

TO BIBLICAL CRITICISMS

ITS OWN

AND THEIR

MEANING

APPLICATION

Revised and Expanded

STEVEN L. MCKENZIE AND
STEPHEN R. HAYNES, EDITORS

WESTMINSTER
JOHN KNOX PRESS
LOUISVILLE • KENTUCKY

Scripture quotations from the New Revised Standard Version of the Bible are copyright 1946, 1952, and 1971 by the Division of Christian Education of the National Council of the Churches of Christ in the U.S.A. and are used by permission. All rights reserved.

Grateful acknowledgment is made to the following for permission to quote from copyrighted material:

Kristine Batey, from her poem "Lot's Wife," which appeared in *Alive Now!* January/February 1988. Used by permission.

Zephyr Press, from "Lot's Wife," *The Complete Poems of Anna Akhmatova*, translated by Judith Henschemeyer, edited by Roberta Reeder. Copyright © 1990, 1992, 1997 by Judith Henschemeyer. Reprinted by permission of Zephyr Press.

Book design by Rohani Design, Edmonds, Washington
Cover design by Kevin Darst

Published by Westminster John Knox Press
Louisville, Kentucky

This book is printed on acid-free paper that meets the American National Standards Institute Z39.48 standard. ∞

PRINTED IN THE UNITED STATES OF AMERICA

04 05 06 07 08 — 10 9 8 7 6

Library of Congress Cataloging-in-Publication Data

To each its own meaning : an introduction to biblical criticisms and their
    applications / Steven L. McKenzie and Stephen R. Haynes, editors. — Rev.
    and expanded.
        p.   cm.
    Includes bibliographical references.
    ISBN 0-664-25784-4 (alk. paper)
     1. Bible—Hermeneutics.   I. McKenzie, Steven L., 1953–
II. Haynes, Stephen R.
BS476.T6 1999   99-28620

To our wives, Natalie and Vilma,
and to our children, Christina,
Bonnie, Christiana, and Matthew

The chief cupbearer told Pharaoh, "Today I remember my sins. When Pharaoh was angry with his servants and imprisoned me and the chief baker in the house of the chief of the bodyguard, he and I dreamt dreams on the same night, each dream with its own meaning. A Hebrew lad, servant to the chief of the bodyguard, was there with us, and when we told him our dreams he interpreted them for us, giving *to each its own meaning*.

—Genesis 41:9–12, editors' translation

CONTENTS

FOREWORD TO
THE REVISED EDITION

The introduction to the first edition outlined the need for a book of this nature. This has been confirmed over the last six years by the widespread use of this volume in college and seminary classrooms across the country. We have been extremely gratified by this reception and view it first and foremost as a tribute to the contributors. A survey of publishers' catalogs reveals that there is still nothing quite like this book available elsewhere—a single volume for a broad readership that aims to provide an introduction to biblical criticisms and their application by specialists in the various approaches. However, the landscape of biblical studies, like that of any academic field, is constantly changing. Thus we deemed it appropriate to produce a second, revised edition. As with the initial volume, the support and interest of the editors at Westminster John Knox Press convinced us that our perceptions were well aligned.

Over the past few years we have also received a number of suggestions about how to improve the volume. Such suggestions were usually directed toward a specific chapter (not always the same one), often by individuals who worked with the approach treated in the chapter. We perceive this as a sign of the diversity within the field of biblical studies. Not even those who work with a given method agree on just how to use that method. We gratefully acknowledge all who have provided their comments and recommendations for improvement. We have taken them seriously and offer this revision in hopes of addressing some of the criticisms of the book while enhancing its strengths.

The revisions represented here are of three kinds. First, it seemed to us best to allow our contributors the opportunity to revise and update their articles as they saw fit. They, after all, are the experts in these various approaches, and it was their work that brought the book its initial success. Hence, the contributors were asked to review their articles in light of their continuing research and subsequent developments in the field. Some chose to revise extensively, others not at all. Still others chose simply to update their bibliographies. As in the first edition, our objective was to offer a clear and up-to-date explanation of each method for readers who were new to the field of biblical criticism.

There were two instances where our primary objective necessitated a different kind of revision, or more accurately, replacement. The reasons in each case differed, and we wish to make it clear that they had nothing to do with the *quality* of either of the articles we chose to replace. Martin Buss's essay on form criticism in the first edition is a brilliant exploration of the philosophical assumptions behind the approach. However, our experiences and those of colleagues led us to believe that a rudimentary description of this important method was required before readers could appreciate the insights of Professor Buss's article. We therefore asked Marvin Sweeney to write such a rudimentary description. We would encourage readers to return to Buss's article in the first edition for a discussion and critique of the background to form criticism after having read Professor Sweeney's fine introduction.

The second case of replacement concerns the chapter on rhetorical criticism. The term is used for two types of approaches, one that analyzes biblical literature according to classical (especially Aristotelian) definitions of rhetoric, another that pays close attention to literary style and creativity. Yehoshua Gitay is a pioneer and the main practitioner of the former type, and his contribution to the first edition is a useful explanation of its techniques. As he makes clear, this approach focuses particularly on the prophetic literature of the Hebrew Bible. In part because of this narrowed focus, but also because of the long shadow of James Muilenburg, it is the second type of rhetorical criticism that has come more and more to be identified with that term. This development, to our minds, required replacing Professor Gitay's article with one that would treat rhetorical criticism in its broadest sense but also focus on its more prevalent form. Patricia Tull's contribution in this new edition does both of these things admirably and gives the reader a bonus in the bargain by discussing the increasingly popular technique of reading intertextually. Since intertextuality is recognized by both historical critics and literary critics, this new article fits nicely into the middle section of this book on "Expanding the Tradition."

The third kind of revision incorporated into this edition is the addition of an altogether new article. Ideological readings of the Bible have multiplied in recent years. Proper recognition of this trend and of the variety of ideologies driving such readings called for adding another example of ideological reading besides the first edition's chapter on feminist criticism. We are pleased that Fernando Segovia accepted our invitation to contribute. His chapter illustrates an ideological approach to the Bible (especially the New Testament) from the standpoint of Latin American liberation theology.

Scholars and scholarship in the field of biblical studies continue to diversify. The new and replacement articles in this edition reflect this development by enhancing the contributors' diversity in terms of identity, background, and location. As this process of diversification continues into the future, the need for dialogue between different approaches to the Bible and their practitioners will become more acute. It is our hope that this book will contribute to that dialogue by helping students of the Bible, both old and new, become more conversant with the many approaches used to understand it.

INTRODUCTION

"EVERYONE INTERPRETS THE
BIBLE IN THEIR OWN WAY."

This sentiment is often expressed during informal discussions on the nature of the Bible and the beliefs to which it gives rise. And the statement contains an element of truth. Different people certainly come away from the Bible with different understandings; no two people see it exactly the same way. Furthermore, the plethora of competing critical methods utilized by biblical scholars, often aimed at the very same texts, gives popular credence to the notion that, indeed, "everyone interprets the Bible in their own way." After all, if the "experts" cannot agree on how the Bible should be read, what hope is there for the rest of us in discovering meaning there?

But the statement above is also misleading, because it implies that there is no common ground for understanding the Bible, no way of evaluating a given interpretation, and that one person's guess about the meaning of a passage is as good as another's. Yet biblical scholars, who study the text professionally, work on the assumption that some interpretations of biblical texts are "better" than others. Still, the average reader of the Bible remains largely unaware of the techniques employed by professional biblical critics to arrive at meaningful interpretations. The distance from biblical scholarship felt by even the educated nonspecialist is exacerbated by two other factors. First, biblical scholars too often write only for one another, and thus their work is often filled with technical jargon. Second, while long on theoretical justification, their published writings tend to be short on practical demonstration.

The present volume seeks to address this state of affairs by introducing the most important methods of biblical criticism with special attention to the way in which they can be applied to specific biblical texts. Although theoretical questions are not ignored by the authors who have contributed these chapters, each has made a concerted effort to demonstrate how his or her method is actually applied, targeting the reader who is not an expert: the student, educated members of the clergy, and the nonspecialist who teaches the Bible.

Not surprisingly, the frustrating experiences of the editors are what is behind the conception of this volume. The idea for such a book was born in part from the struggles of an advanced graduate student trying to apply biblical criticism to the task of bringing the Bible to life for undergraduates. It did not take long for him to realize that these students were only likely to show interest in biblical criticism if its value could be demonstrated in action—if they could be convinced, that is, that biblical criticism sheds light upon texts that appear difficult or incomprehensible. When the graduate student became a fledgling college professor, he gained a new colleague who was trained as a biblical scholar and who made a living teaching introductory Bible classes. The biblical scholar had experienced his own frustrations in teaching the Bible to undergraduates. Among them was his inability to find an up-to-date text for a course introducing critical methods for understanding the Bible. After many discussions, the nonspecialist and the specialist joined forces to plan and edit this volume.

Despite our differences, then, we editors are united by the common, and often frustrating, experience of trying to show students how scholarship sheds light on the meaning of the Bible and thus helps bring it alive. Specifically, we share dismay at how little of what is written in the field of biblical scholarship addresses our goals for this volume. These goals are (1) to offer an up-to-date presentation of the principal methods of critical biblical study, including their assumptions and objectives; (2) to make the information about these methods readily accessible to students and other nonspecialists; and (3) to show biblical criticism in action by demonstrating how particular methods may be implemented in the interpretation and explication of specific texts. The surprising ease with which we were able to interest the editors at Westminster John Knox Press in our idea for a text that addressed these goals told us we were not alone in our perceptions of this gap in biblical scholarship.

The Current Shape of Biblical Studies

As editors we are hopeful that our markedly different approaches to the Bible are an additional factor that will distinguish this book. One of us has training in hermeneutics and literary theory and approaches biblical criticism from a "literary," and thus relatively nontraditional, posture. The other is trained in the techniques of modern biblical criticism and approaches the Bible primarily according to the more traditional "historical-critical method."

Significantly, our differing backgrounds and orientations are representative of an important division within biblical criticism itself. Increasingly over the last twenty years the hegemony of historical methods for interpreting the Bible has been challenged by biblical critics unhappy with either the results or the very assumptions of historical-critical scholarship. The division between critical methods that adhere to a historical paradigm for understanding texts and those that embrace a literary paradigm has been well documented in recent literature and is referred to in several of the chapters of this book. We offer here only a few comments on this critical split and the way it is reflected in the book's organization.

One fundamental disagreement between "historical" and "literary" methods of biblical criticism is found in their assumptions about the relationship between texts and history. This disagreement can be expressed in simple terms by saying that historical methods such as source criticism, form criticism, tradition-historical criticism, and redaction criticism emphasize the historical, archaeological, or literary *backgrounds* or roots of a text, and the development of the text *through time.* Thus historical-critical methods are sometimes referred to as "diachronic." On the other hand, literary methods such as structural criticism, narrative criticism, reader-response criticism, and poststructuralist criticism tend to focus on the *text itself* in its final form (however the final form might have been achieved), the relationships between a variety of textual elements (both surface and deep), and the interaction between texts and *readers.*

One methodological example of this difference in focus between historical and literary approaches may be particularly helpful to keep in mind while using this volume. Historically oriented biblical critics tend to regard an author's intention in writing as important for construing what a text meant originally, as well as what it means now. Scholars who depart from historical approaches in favor of more literary readings, however, often view authorial intention as irretrievable, or irrelevant to the interpretive process altogether. The latter even invoke the term "intentional fallacy" to argue that assumptions related to the author of an ancient text and his or her intentions are always dubious.

While we hope the preceding is helpful in communicating the distinction between historical and literary methods in general, we also realize that it is in some ways misleading. Easy distinctions break down even in an introductory text like this, where authors attempt to describe their methods in the simplest terms. For one thing, many scholars utilize a combination of historical and literary approaches in working with texts. Even scholars who think of themselves as theoretical purists (whether of the historical or literary variety) will often utilize insights from "the other side" when they prove illuminating. Also, some critical methods— social-scientific criticism, canonical criticism, and rhetorical criticism, for instance—simply do not fit easily under the rubrics "historical" or "literary." As the chapters that describe these critical methods demonstrate, they are in some ways typically "historical" and in others more characteristically "literary."

Finally, the literary/historical distinction becomes problematical when scholars use traditional (historical) methods in nontraditional ways. For instance, Patricia Tull uses the term "rhetorical criticism" to describe close attention to stylistic and ideological elements in a text, a method that is "literary" in its attention to the final form of a text and the interrelationships of textual elements. However, other forms of rhetorical criticism (for instance, the article by Yehoshua Gitay in the first edition of this book) scrutinize an author's persuasive intention as revealed in the rhetoric employed. The emphasis on recapturing an original "rhetorical situation" between author and audience in this form of rhetorical criticism places it within the domain of the historical paradigm.

The reader will recognize a comparable plurality of views *within* the confines of particular methods in other chapters—especially those on canonical criticism by Mary Callaway and social-scientific criticism by Dale Martin. These methods also have in common the fact that they simultaneously perpetuate and revise the historical paradigm. These chapters are found in the second section of the book, which we have chosen to call "the tradition expanded."

As one example of how the distinction between the historical and literary paradigms can actually become secondary for biblical studies, we include chapters on feminist criticism by Danna Nolan Fewell and socioeconomic criticism by Fernando Segovia. While Fewell's own orientation to the biblical text is "literary," this should not lead the reader to suppose that all feminist critics of the Bible have eschewed the historical-critical method. That this is not the case is clear from the works of feminist historical critics cited in Fewell's chapter, as well as the feminist concerns of scholars like Gail Streete (author of the chapter on redaction criticism), whose research falls within the historical paradigm. Similarly, while Segovia is concerned with the historical and material dimensions of the biblical text, he is also quite concerned with the ideological positions of texts and interpreters.

Fewell's chapter is titled "Reading the Bible Ideologically: Feminist Criticism"; Segovia's is titled "Reading the Bible Ideologically: Socioeconomic Criticism." These titles refer to the fact that feminist and socioeconomic approaches to the Bible are examples of "ideological criticism"—a method that is growing in importance and influence in biblical studies. But ideological critique is found throughout this volume—for example, in the articles by William Beardslee and David Gunn. In his discussion of narrative criticism, Gunn forays into both feminist and poststructuralist readings.

In many parts of the book, disagreement over the importance of historical investigation for understanding the biblical text is evident. For Daniel Patte, Gunn, Edgar McKnight, and Beardslee (authors of the chapters on structural criticism, narrative criticism, reader-response criticism, and poststructuralist criticism, respectively), the relationship between biblical texts and their historical origins or accuracy is of purely secondary importance, if it is considered at all. Conversely, for Pauline Viviano, Marvin Sweeney, Robert Di Vito, and Gail Streete (who introduce "historical" methods in section one), these questions are central, especially as they concern the development of texts through time. These larger assumptions regarding the relationship of history and biblical criticism are implicit throughout the book but are discussed explicitly in J. Maxwell Miller's introductory chapter, "Reading the Bible Historically: The Historian's Approach."

The Contributors

As editors we have sought to maintain a balance in a number of areas: between theory and application, usefulness for students and teachers, and, as should be clear by now, sympathy for historical and nonhistorical approaches to the Bible. Especially on the final point, such balance is rare in works by one author, and even in edited works, which often originate from one person or a group of persons with a similar critical orientation. The balance we have tried to achieve in this volume is evident in the nearly equal space devoted to "historical" and "literary" methods. But it has also been present in the process of editing itself, during which questions "from both sides" were directed strenuously at each chapter as the book took shape. In this sense, our respective weaknesses became strengths, as one of us was always able to articulate "dumb questions" the other had overlooked entirely. It also seems to us a sign of balance that, despite our friendship, we consistently disagreed on points of methodology raised in this book from start to finish.

We have also sought to achieve diversity, if not total balance, in the identities and backgrounds of our contributors. Five are women and nine are men. Seven are Hebrew Bible/Old Testament scholars, and seven work primarily in New Testament. Four are from Roman Catholic backgrounds, one is Jewish, and nine represent a variety of Protestant denominations. Seven of our contributors teach in seminaries or graduate divinity schools, while seven teach in college or university departments of religion.

Again in the interest of balance, some younger scholars were assigned chapters on more traditional methods, while more established scholars were asked to write chapters on newer methods. This was done in order to challenge the common misconception that literary and ideological methods are utilized only by the youngest generation of biblical critics, and that only those out of touch with current trends still practice historical methods of biblical criticism. The reality within the field of biblical studies is rather different. While it is finding increasing acceptance among important scholars, the literary paradigm has yet to make historical-critical investigation of the Bible obsolete. This book, therefore, challenges both the *evolutionary* picture of modern biblical criticism—according to which literary and ideological methods represent a movement out of a primitive stage of biblical criticism—and the *de-evolutionary* picture—in which literary criticism symbolizes a fall from the critical paradise in which confidence in objective certainties once reigned.

Although we have tried to produce a work that is both inclusive and ecumenical, some perspectives (for instance, Roman Catholic, Jewish, and feminist) are not represented according to their importance in the field of biblical studies at the present moment. It is important to understand that this book is not organized according to ideological *perspective* but according to critical *method*. This accounts for our inclusion of the standard methods of criticism while excluding, for example, various liberationist readings of the Bible that are extremely influential in the current scholarly milieu. On the other hand, liberationist perspectives have been formative for many of our authors, some of whom are clearly engaged in the kind of ideological criticism described in the book's final chapter.

Perhaps the most rewarding aspect of editing a volume like this one is that nearly every chapter has provided its own "a-ha" experiences. On several occasions in the process of reading and rereading these articles, we shared moments of revelation as a particular method was placed neatly within its intellectual or historical context or was applied to a passage in illuminating ways. We are grateful to the contributors for giving us these experiences and for enhancing our grasp of the methods they present. We are confident this book will prove helpful to others, partly because we believe it will have many readers like ourselves—those who, whether they are students or teachers, will benefit from observing practitioners of these methods as they explain and apply them.

Chapter Format

While the chapters in this book reflect differences in style as well as content, a general format has guided the writing of each chapter. This format was specified by the editors and was followed (more or less closely) by each of the contributors. The proposed chapter format was outlined in five parts and sent to each contributor as a general guide for her or his writing. With variations depending on the style of individual contributors and the methods they present, then, each chapter addresses five sets of issues:

1. Definition of the method, important terms and concepts, history of its development, assumptions made about the relationship of text and history, prospects for the future

2. The method in relation to others discussed in this book

3. The method in action, with reference to a particular text in either Genesis or Luke-Acts

4. The drawbacks of the method

5. Suggested reading for those who wish to pursue the method further

The Contribution

We believe that two aspects of this book's uniqueness lie in what we as editors asked each of the contributors to do. First, the critical method being dealt with is to be not only described, both in its own terms and in relation to other methods and intellectual currents, but also demonstrated in working with a particular text. In fact, this practical dimension generally takes up a quarter to a third of each chapter. Second, each contributor is asked to assess honestly the shortcomings of the critical method, suggesting the kind of texts on which it may not yield results.

Part of our format prescription found in point 1 above deserves further comment. A concern in our own discussions across the divide that separates historical from literary approaches to the Bible has been whether textual meaning is to be found "behind" a text (that is, in the historical events or sources that underlie it), "in" the text (that is, in the interaction of elements and structures that emerge in a close reading of the text in its final form), or "in front of" the text (that is, in the construction of meaning that takes place in the interaction between text and reader). It was not our expectation that this question would receive a definitive answer in the book. We only sought to provide a forum for each author to address it and provide his or her own version of an answer. The editors' attempt at an inclusive view would be that the best biblical criticism does not confidently announce what a text "means" but humbly assures us that the text can be "meaningful" by demonstrating one or more possible, if not convincing, meanings. This dialogical strategy suggests that we believe mutual enlightenment is in fact attainable through dialogue. This is at least our hope, and we pause to make it explicit because it is taken for granted less and less in scholarly circles. The balanced, dialogical format we have chosen also makes us hopeful that strawpersons will be more easily identifiable, as each method is described in detail by a practitioner.

This book itself has arisen from a dialogue between two persons who were raised in conservative Christian traditions, lost their precritical naiveté through engagement with critical study of the Bible, and found reorientation to this sacred text in different ways. While we are experienced enough to realize that rapprochement between the competing methodologies described here will not be easy, we remain naive enough to believe this is a legitimate goal, one toward which this book will, we hope, contribute.

CONTRIBUTORS

Stephen R. Haynes and Steven L. McKenzie
Rhodes College, Memphis, Tennessee
Introduction

J. Maxwell Miller
Candler School of Theology, Emory University, Atlanta, Georgia
Reading the Bible Historically: The Historian's Approach

Pauline A. Viviano
Loyola University of Chicago, Chicago, Illinois
Source Criticism

Marvin A. Sweeney
Claremont Graduate University, Claremont, California
Form Criticism

Robert A. Di Vito
Loyola University of Chicago, Chicago, Illinois
Tradition-Historical Criticism

Gail P. C. Streete
Rhodes College, Memphis, Tennessee
Redaction Criticism

Dale B. Martin
Duke University, Durham, North Carolina
Social-Scientific Criticism

Mary C. Callaway
Fordham University, Bronx, New York
Canonical Criticism

Patricia K. Tull
Louisville Presbyterian Theological Seminary, Louisville, Kentucky
Rhetorical Criticism and Intertextuality

Daniel Patte
Vanderbilt University, Nashville, Tennessee
Structural Criticism

David M. Gunn
Texas Christian University, Fort Worth, Texas
Narrative Criticism

Edgar V. McKnight
Furman University, Greenville, South Carolina
Reader-Response Criticism

William A. Beardslee
Process and Faith Center, Claremont Graduate University, Claremont,
California
Poststructuralist Criticism

Danna Nolan Fewell
Southern Methodist University, Dallas, Texas
Reading the Bible Ideologically: Feminist Criticism

Fernando F. Segovia
Vanderbilt University Divinity School, Nashville, Tennessee
Reading the Bible Ideologically: Socioeconomic Criticism

PART ONE

TRADITIONAL METHODS
OF BIBLICAL CRITICISM

1

READING THE BIBLE HISTORICALLY:
THE HISTORIAN'S APPROACH

J. MAXWELL MILLER

History and Historical Methodology

Although "history" is a much used term, it is not easily defined. Is history the sum total of past people and events? Or does it include only those people and events whose memory is preserved in written records? The available written evidence from ancient times is uneven in coverage, with some peoples and periods better represented than others. Moreover, the ancient documents provide very selective kinds of information. This information often is ambivalent, and sometimes the ancient sources make unbelievable or conflicting claims. Would it be more accurate, then, to say that history is the past as understood by historians, based on their analysis and interpretation of the available evidence but not necessarily identical with the claims made by ancient documents? What if the historians disagree? And does history belong to the professional historians anyhow? Perhaps history should be equated instead with the common consensus notions about the past held by the general public. These notions might be influenced by what professional historians say as well as by other factors, such as prevailing political, social, and religious attitudes. For that matter, are not professional historians themselves deeply influenced by prevailing attitudes?

It may be said, in any case, that historians seek to understand the human past and that they depend heavily on written sources for their information. Heavy reliance on written evidence is perhaps the main distinguishing characteristic of historical research as compared with other disciplines that also seek to understand the human past. This does not mean, of course, that contemporary historians concentrate solely on written evidence or that historical research is conducted independently of other disciplines. Contemporary scholars exploring the history of ancient Israel find themselves necessarily involved, for example, in Palestinian archaeology and sociology.

17

Historians seek objectivity. They are interested in discovering and reporting what really happened in the past, as opposed to collecting and passing on fanciful stories, writing "docudramas," or producing revisionist accounts of the past for propagandistic or ideological purposes. However, complete objectivity is a goal never reached. The historian's own presuppositions, ideology, and attitudes inevitably influence his or her research and reporting. Perhaps it is not an overstatement to say that any history book reveals as much about its author as it does about the period of time treated. If so, then a proper definition of history would suggest that it consists neither of the totality of past people and events on the one hand, nor of what we contemporaries know (or think we know) about the past on the other, but of an ongoing conversation between the past and the present. As we humans, individually and collectively, seek to understand the present, we naturally look to the past for bearings. At the same time, we constantly revise our understanding of the past in light of current developments, understandings, and attitudes.

Basic to modern historiography is the principle of analogy. Historians assume, consciously or unconsciously, that the past is analogous to the present and that one human society is analogous to another. Thus a historian's understanding of present reality serves as an overriding guide for evaluating evidence and interpreting the past, and the cultural patterns of a better-known society may be used as a guide for clarifying those of a lesser-known society. As an example of how this works in modern treatments of ancient Israelite history, note that the Bible presupposes a dynamic natural world into which God intrudes overtly upon human affairs from time to time. It is a world with waters rolling back so that the Israelites can escape Pharaoh's army, a world of burning bushes and floating ax heads. God hands down laws on Mount Sinai and sends angels to defend Jerusalem against the massive Assyrian army. Modern Western historians tend to perceive the world as being more orderly, however, and one of the standard tenets of modern historiography is that a natural explanation for a given historical phenomenon or event is preferable to an explanation that involves overt divine intervention. When speculating about the "actual historical events" behind the biblical account of Israel's past, therefore, what historians often do, in effect, is bring the biblical story into line with reality as we moderns perceive it. Surely the Assyrian army was not routed by angels, because angels, if they exist at all, do not play this sort of role in the world as we experience it. What other "more reasonable" explanation might there be for the rout of the Assyrians—"more reasonable" in the sense that it is more in keeping with our modern Western perception of reality? Possibly a plague broke out among the Assyrian troops, or maybe the narrator of the biblical account embellished the report. Either of these possibilities would be analogous to the world as we perceive it, but not angels. In effect, then, the modern historian offers explanations that do not involve miracles or "God talk" for historical developments reported in the Bible.

The analogy principle also is at work when historians draw upon knowledge of other societies, ancient and modern, in attempts to clarify aspects of Israelite and early Christian history. The Bible reports the names of court officials who served under David and Solomon, for example, but does not describe the duties of these various officials. Historians, assuming that the royal court in Jerusalem would have been similar to other royal courts of the day, search the records of neighboring kingdoms for information regarding the duties and responsibilities of such officials.

Another example pertains to the chronological data provided in the Bible for each of the Israelite and Judean kings following Solomon. Specifically, each king's accession to the throne is dated relative to the reign of his contemporary on the other throne, and also the length of each king's reign is recorded. The following verses are typical.

In the twentieth year of King Jeroboam of Israel, Asa began to reign over Judah; he reigned forty-one years in Jerusalem. (1 Kings 15:9)

Nadab son of Jeroboam began to reign over Israel in the second year of King Asa of Judah; he reigned over Israel two years. (1 Kings 15:25)

In the third year of King Asa of Judah, Baasha son of Ahijah began to reign over all Israel at Tirzah; he reigned twenty-four years. (1 Kings 15:33)

However, the figures provided do not always "add up." This may be due in part to copyists' mistakes in the transmission of the ancient manuscripts. But there are also other factors to be considered in view of the records of other ancient Middle Eastern kingdoms. It is known, for example, that some of these records presuppose a fall-to-fall calendar year while others presuppose a spring-to-spring calendar year. Some designate as the first year of a king's reign the year during which he ascended to the throne; others count only his first full year (i.e., the first full fall-to-fall or spring-to-spring year, depending on the calendar used). The possibility arises, therefore, on analogy with the practices of neighboring peoples, that the two Hebrew kingdoms, Israel and Judah, used separate and different calendars, employed different methods of reckoning their respective kings' reigns, and may even have changed calendars or methods of reckoning at one time or another. One or more of these factors may explain why the biblical figures seem to be internally inconsistent. It is hardly surprising, moreover, in view of the confusing biblical figures and the various factors to be taken into account, that historians rarely agree on exact dates for the Israelite and Judean kings.

Other than this principle of analogy, which is basic also to the other approaches treated in this volume, there is no specific methodology for historical research. Rather, the historian might be compared to an investigative lawyer who searches out and examines whatever evidence is available and relevant to a particular case, employs whatever techniques and methods of analysis apply to the evidence (often relying on the opinion of specialists), constructs a hypothetical scenario as to what probably happened, and then presents the case for this scenario to other historians and the public. The last step is as important as the first. The leading historians who have been able to influence academic and public opinion regarding the past have not only been outstanding scholars who demonstrated amazing coverage, competence, and creativity in research, but have been able also to present their ideas in an understandable and convincing fashion. Thus history is a search for "what really happened," but it is also what the historians can convince us really happened.

The Bible as History

The opening books of the Hebrew Bible, Genesis through 2 Kings, present a narrative account of people and events that extends from creation to the end of the Judean monarchy. Another sequence of books, 1–2 Chronicles, Ezra, and Nehemiah, presents an overlapping account that begins with Adam and concludes with Nehemiah's activities in Jerusalem under Persian rule. The so-called prophetical books (Isaiah, Jeremiah, Ezekiel, Hosea, etc.) make numerous references to national and international circumstances. The first part of the book of Daniel (chapters 1–6) describes events that supposedly occurred in the Babylonian court while Daniel and other Jews were exiled there. The latter part (chapters 7–12) reports a dream-vision that organizes world history into a sequence of four great empires and anticipates the culmination of history during the fourth. The Gospel of Luke dates Jesus' birth in relation to Roman history (Luke 2:1), and all four of the gospels narrate episodes in Jesus' ministry in what the reader is left to suppose is essentially chronological sequence. The book of Acts describes the emergence of Christianity from the immediate aftermath of Jesus' crucifixion to Paul's arrival in Rome for trial. Finally, the book of Revelation reports dream-visions similar to those of the book of Daniel and also presupposing a schematic view of history.

In short, the biblical writers were very conscious of history, and the Bible itself may be looked upon as largely historical in format and content. It is not history written for the sake of history, of course, and not history of the sort one would read in a modern history book. One might argue, in fact, that the biblical writers were more akin to contemporary theologians than to historians. Nevertheless, the theological messages that the biblical writers sought to convey are so thoroughly intermeshed with their perceptions of history that it is difficult to separate one from the other. The Bible itself, in other words, confronts us with history and raises historical questions that are difficult to ignore. It is only natural, therefore, that biblical scholarship through the ages has involved attention to historical matters.

Reflected to some degree in earlier biblical research, but becoming especially intense during the twentieth century, are differences of opinion regarding the trustworthiness and accuracy of the Bible as a source of historical information. At one extreme are those who, usually on theological grounds, insist that the Bible is literally accurate in all historical details, including the chronological data provided in Genesis–2 Kings that place the creation of the world approximately 6,000 years ago. Historical research for those who hold this extreme position involves harmonizing the information provided in different parts of the Bible—for example, the overlapping accounts of Genesis–2 Kings and 1 Chronicles–Nehemiah—and interpreting evidence from extrabiblical sources (other ancient documents and archaeology) to fit. Apparent contradictions within the Bible are viewed as being only "apparent," usually the result of the modern reader's failure to understand all of the surrounding circumstances. Conflicts between the Bible and extrabiblical sources also are explained away in one way or another.

At the opposite extreme are those who regard the biblical accounts as being so theologically and nationalistically tendentious and composed of such a hodgepodge of literary genera (myths, legends, etc.) that, except where extrabiblical sources shed some light, any attempt to reconstruct the history of ancient Israel is fruitless. This extreme is sometimes stated or implied by scholars who take essentially ahistorical approaches to the text such as structuralist, narrative, or reader-response criticisms (see especially part 3 of this volume).

However, it is very difficult to hold consistently to either of these extreme positions. The first, that of unwavering confidence in the historical accuracy of the biblical materials, is difficult to maintain in view of (1) the obvious tension between the dynamic and theocentric view of nature and history presupposed by the biblical writers and the more "scientific" or positivistic approach to reality that characterizes modern Western thought, (2) the mental gymnastics required to harmonize some of the apparent contradictions within the biblical narratives and to bring extrabiblical evidence into line, and (3) the results of close analysis of the biblical materials in accordance with source criticism, form criticism, tradition history, and other historical-critical methods.

As for the second position, that of extreme skepticism, it can hardly be doubted that there was an ancient Israel, that Israel had a history, or that the Bible is somehow relevant for understanding that history. Indeed, the very existence of the Bible, regardless of what one makes of its historical claims, is an undeniable item of historical evidence pointing to ancient Israel. It is difficult, moreover, regardless of the theory behind one's methodology, to approach an ancient document totally free of the influence of notions regarding the historical context from which it emerged. This is especially true with the Bible, which, as indicated above, is overtly attentive to history and makes such forceful historical claims. Close attention to the wording of their comments, therefore, often reveals that scholars who seem to take totally ahistorical approaches to the biblical materials nevertheless work with presuppositions regarding the history of ancient Israel that influence their overall understanding of the Bible if not their individual research.

Most biblical scholars, therefore, fall somewhere between the two extremes described above. On the one hand, they proceed with confidence that the Bible preserves authentic historical memory. On the other hand, they recognize that the Bible is not a monolithic document, that its different voices reflect different perceptions of ancient Israel's history, that these perceptions usually are heavily influenced by theological and nationalistic interests, and that some of the biblical materials were not intended to be read as literal history in the first place. The historian's task, therefore, is to separate the authentic historical memory from its highly theological and often legendary context.

Naturally, there is a wide range of views even within this middle ground between the extreme positions, with some scholars tending to place greater confidence in the historical accuracy of the biblical materials regardless of the theological, nationalistic, or legendary overtones and others tending to place less confidence in them. To see how this works out on a passage-by-passage basis, one might compare the *NIV Study Bible* (1985) with *The New Oxford Annotated Bible* (1991). The commentary and explanatory notes of the former were prepared by scholars who, although not biblical literalists, tend to take the biblical accounts of Israel's past as essentially historically accurate. Those of the latter were prepared by scholars who tend to be much more cautious on the matter.

Biblical Scholarship and the Study of Ancient Israelite History

Biblical scholarship and the study of ancient Israelite history are integrally related. On the one hand, most of our information about the history of ancient Israel prior to Roman times comes from the Bible. There are, to be sure, certain other ancient written sources and an ever increasing amount of archaeological data to be taken into account. As will become apparent below, however, these extrabiblical sources are useful primarily in that they shed light on the general cultural, social, and international circumstances of biblical times. Usually they tell us very little specifically about the people and events of Israelite history, except when interpreted in light of the biblical record. On the other hand, as observed above, analysis of biblical literature generally involves some knowledge of (or at least some notions about) the history of ancient Israel. This is particularly true insofar as the analysis is historical-critical in approach. Historical-critical analysis (including such specialized approaches as source criticism, form criticism, tradition-historical criticism, and redaction criticism) seeks to determine the historical contexts out of which the various biblical materials emerged and what changes occurred in these materials as they were transmitted from ancient times to the present. Even to speculate on such matters presupposes some knowledge of the history of biblical times.

It is not surprising, therefore, that modern histories of ancient Israel typically have been written by scholars deeply involved also in biblical research, and that their application of historical-critical methodology to the biblical materials has significantly impacted their treatments of Israelite history. This is noticeable especially when one compares histories of Israel written during the nineteenth century. H. H. Milman's *History of the Jews* (1829) represents the emerging spirit of critical biblical scholarship during the first half of the century. H. G. A. Ewald's *Geschichte des Volkes Israel bis Christus* (1843–55)[1] was based on a systematic source analysis of the Pentateuch, although not yet the classical "documentary hypothesis." While recognizing that the biblical traditions derive from a much later time than the period they describe and include imaginative elements, Ewald went to great lengths to explain that these traditions nevertheless preserve historical memory. He never clearly committed himself on what, if any, historical memory is preserved in the opening chapters of Genesis (which describe creation, the great flood, and the spread of population following the tower of Babel episode), but he regarded the patriarchs (Abraham, Isaac, Jacob) as personifications of tribal groups. Ewald was also noncommittal regarding the specific circumstances of the exodus but believed that it was a historical event in connection with which Moses inaugurated a Hebrew monotheistic theocracy that set the direction for the future of Israelite history.

Julius Wellhausen, so closely identified with the documentary hypothesis in its classical form, spelled out the radical implications of this and other late nineteenth-century historical-critical developments in his compelling *Prolegomena zur Geschichte Israels* (1878).[2] Since, according to the documentary hypothesis, none of the four sources that compose the Pentateuch predates the Israelite monarchy, neither these individual sources nor the Pentateuch as a whole is trustworthy for reconstructing history prior to that time. According to the hypothesis, moreover, the "Priestly" source, which accounts for the bulk of the narrative and legal instructions associated with Moses, actually reflects circumstances at the end of Judah's history, the time of the Babylonian exile and following. In Wellhausen's treatment of Israel's history, therefore, Moses becomes a very shadowy and virtually unknown figure, and the characteristic features of the Mosaic era as presented in the Pentateuch (monotheism, a highly developed priesthood, elaborate legal and cultic practices, etc.) are seen instead as characteristic of exilic and postexilic times.

During the present century, as other historical-critical methodologies (especially form criticism, tradition-historical criticism, and redaction criticism) have added their voices to source criticism, usually it has not been a question of whether treatments of Israelite history should presuppose a historical-critical approach to the Bible but of how much emphasis to place on the results of the analysis of the biblical literature itself as opposed to those of Palestinian archaeology or sociological models. This is illustrated by two widely used histories of Israel that were written during the 1950s and became widely influential during the 1960s and '70s—Martin Noth's *Geschichte Israels* (1950)[3] and John Bright's *A History of Israel* (1959).

Noth was one of the pioneers of tradition history, published comprehensive studies of the Pentateuch and the Deuteronomistic History,[4] and agreed with Wellhausen's conclusion that the Pentateuchal account of Israel's origins is an artificial literary construct composed largely of legendary materials. Thus Noth's history of Israel does not treat the patriarchs as historical figures, nor does he regard the exodus from Egypt or the conquest of Canaan as historical events. Drawing instead upon the sociological theories of Max Weber, the creative ideas of his teacher Albrecht Alt, clues from his own extensive tradition-historical studies of the Pentateuch, and what he thought were close parallels between early Israelite society and that of ancient Greek and Italian tribal leagues (known as amphictyonies), Noth argued that the ancestors of Israel probably were seminomads who ranged between the desert fringe and Canaan in search of pasture until they gradually settled down and took up agriculture. In stages, for which Noth believed there are clues in the Pentateuchal traditions, these tribal settlers formed an amphictyonic cultic league. Finally, under Saul and David, there emerged the Israelite monarchy, and it was only with the expansion of this monarchy under David that it is appropriate to speak of an Israelite conquest of Canaan.

Bright, while not ignoring the implications of historical-critical analysis, was inclined to give the biblical presentation of Israel's origins the benefit of the doubt, except where it seemed in serious conflict with extrabiblical evidence. Also, he was influenced deeply by the ideas of his teacher, W. F. Albright, who had been one of the pioneers in Palestinian archaeology and had advanced some rather appealing correlations between the biblical account of Israel's origins and archaeology. Thus Bright's *History* began with the patriarchs and followed the biblical outline fairly closely from that point on. Following Albright, he saw these as historical figures who lived approximately 2000 B.C.E. and probably were associated with Amorite movements that were believed to have been under way at the time. The exodus from Egypt occurred during the reign of Ramses II (ca. 1304–1237 B.C.E.), and the Israelite conquest of Canaan, which occurred near the close of the thirteenth century, was reflected in the pattern of city destructions that brought the Late Bronze Age to an end in Palestine.

While Noth's and Bright's histories of Israel still are widely read, the 1970s witnessed a decided shift in the discussion. This is reflected, for example, in a series of essays by an international team of scholars published under the title *Israelite and Judean History* (Hayes and Miller 1977). Before turning our attention to recent developments in this discussion, however, some observations are in order regarding epigraphy, archaeology, and sociology.

Epigraphical Evidence

In its broadest sense, epigraphy is the study of written documents recovered from ancient times. Over the past two centuries, thousands of such documents have been recovered and numerous languages deciphered from the peoples of the ancient Middle East. Among the major developments are the decipherment, beginning in 1822, of Egyptian hieroglyphic writing; the decipherment, beginning in 1846, of the cuneiform scripts of several Mesopotamian languages; the discovery in 1887, in the el-Amarna district of Egypt, of correspondence between Egypt and various Syro-Palestinian rulers during the late fifteenth–early fourteenth centuries B.C.E.; the decipherment in 1915 of royal Hittite archives discovered at Boghazköy (ancient Hattusas) in central Turkey; the discovery in 1929 at Ras Shamra (ancient Ugarit) on the Syrian coast of a mid-fourteenth to early twelfth-century B.C.E. archive of Canaanite documents, including mythical texts concerning the Canaanite god, Baal; the discovery, beginning in 1947, in caves along the northwest shore of the Dead Sea, of Hebrew documents from the first centuries B.C.E. and C.E., including manuscript fragments of most of the books of the Hebrew Bible; and finally, in 1975, the discovery at Tell Mardikh in Syria of royal archives of the ancient city of Ebla.

The recovery and decipherment of extrabiblical documents from the ancient Middle East understandably has had a major impact on biblical studies. The Israelites are not mentioned very often in these documents, however, which probably is to be explained on two grounds. First, epigraphical evidence from ancient Palestine is meager compared to the extensive archives that have been discovered in Egypt, Mesopotamia, Syria, and Asia Minor. Second, the Israelites rarely played a significant role in international affairs outside of Palestine, so that there was little occasion for them to be mentioned in the documents from ancient Egypt, Mesopotamia, and so forth.

A hieroglyphic inscription from the reign of Merneptah, an Egyptian pharaoh of dynasty XIX (thirteenth century B.C.E.), provides the earliest epigraphical reference to "Israel." Unfortunately, we learn very little about Israel from this inscription, and no other such references turn up in the epigraphical sources for the next three and a half centuries, until the time of Omri and Ahab in the ninth century B.C.E. This means that none of the characters or events that appear earlier than Omri and Ahab in the biblical narrative (Abraham, Isaac, Jacob, Joseph, Moses, the exodus from Egypt, Joshua, the conquest of Canaan, Saul, David, Solomon, etc.) are mentioned in any ancient sources outside the Bible. Another Egyptian inscription from the tenth century reports Pharaoh Sheshonk's military campaign into Palestine, an event that is mentioned also in 1 Kings 14:25–28 (where he is called Shishak). But while Sheshonk claims to have conquered some cities in Palestine, some of which presumably belonged at that time to the separate kingdoms of Israel and Judah, his inscription is conspicuously silent regarding these kingdoms.

Israel (the Northern Kingdom) seems to have enjoyed a brief period of national strength during the reigns of Omri and Ahab in the ninth century. But Assyria was beginning to expand westward during the same century and continued to grow in strength and to dominate much of the ancient Middle East for the next two centuries. Thus several kings of Israel and Judah are mentioned in the records of the Assyrian kings as having been subjugated by them or having paid tribute to them. Since these Assyrian rulers can be dated fairly securely, the points of contact between their records and the biblical account serve as valuable benchmarks for working out the chronology of the Israelite and Judean kings. With the collapse of Assyria and rise of Babylon, the Palestinian kingdoms (including Judah) that had survived Assyrian domination fell into Babylonian hands. One of the Babylonian Chronicles reports Nebuchadrezzar's conquest of Jerusalem in March of 597 B.C.E., and King Jehoiachin of Judah is mentioned in Babylonian lists of exiles in Babylon during Nebuchadrezzar's reign (604–561).

Of the epigraphical evidence from Palestine that pertains to the time of the Israelite and Judean monarchies, the following items are especially noteworthy. The Mesha Inscription reports the accomplishments of Mesha, king of Moab in the ninth century B.C.E. Mesha boasts that he rid Moab of Israelite domination and identifies Omri as the Israelite king who subjected Moab in the first place. Mesha himself figures in the narrative of 2 Kings 3:4–28. The Siloam Inscription commemorates the completion of a tunnel hewed out of solid rock for the purpose of transferring water from the Gihon Spring to the Siloam Pool in Jerusalem. Most scholars associate it with Hezekiah (cf. 2 Kings 20:20; 2 Chron. 32:30), although no king is mentioned by name on the surviving, legible portion of the inscription. Groups of ostraca (inscribed pottery fragments) from the ruins of several ancient cities in Israel and Judah contain administrative records and military correspondence.

There are no specific references to either the province of Samaria or of Judah in surviving records of the Persian rulers (who succeeded the Babylonians as masters of Syria-Palestine in 539 B.C.E.) or of the Ptolemaic and Seleucid rulers who dominated Syria-Palestine following Alexander the Great's conquest of the East. For the period following Alexander, the writings of Josephus, a Jewish historian in the latter half of the first century C.E., become our chief source of information for Samaritan and Judean affairs. Other Greek and Roman writers add further details and perspectives on the history of Palestine following Alexander. Also, occasional papyrus and manuscript discoveries from this time are useful for historical research. Included among these are the Dead Sea Scrolls, which provide insight into a Jewish sect around the time of the emergence of Christianity in the first centuries B.C.E. and C.E.

Archaeological Evidence

Artifactual evidence— that is, material remains of the sort usually associated with archaeology (city and village ruins, architectural remains, remnants of tools, potsherds, etc.)—is to be distinguished from epigraphical evidence, even though artifacts occasionally bear written messages (ostraca, scarabs, seal impressions, etc.) and many of the epigraphical texts discussed above were discovered in the course of archaeological excavations. With systematic analysis of the artifactual evidence surviving in a given area, archaeologists can learn a great deal about the settlement patterns and lifestyles of the people who lived there in times past. Since artifactual evidence typically is nonverbal, however, it usually is neither ethnic-specific nor very useful for clarifying matters of historical detail. If the people who lived in the cities, used the tools, and produced the pottery are to be identified in terms of their ethnic identity, in other words, or if any details are to be known about specific individuals and events of their history, the artifactual record must be coordinated with and interpreted in the light of written sources. The following is an example of how this works in the case of Palestinian archaeology and Israelite history.

Palestinian archaeologists recognize the end of the thirteenth century as a time of transition between two major cultural phases—that is, the end of the Late Bronze Age (ca. 1550–1200 B.C.E.) and the beginning of the Iron Age (ca. 1200–332 B.C.E.). Among the changes that marked the transition was the appearance of numerous Early Iron Age villages in the central Palestinian hill country, an area that had been only sparsely settled during the Late Bronze Age. Nothing has been discovered in any of the early Iron Age village ruins that identifies the settlers by name. Taking into account the Merneptah Inscription, however, which places Israel on the scene in Palestine at the end of the thirteenth century, and also the biblical narratives that associate the Israelite tribes specifically with the central hill country, it makes sense to suppose that the Israelites and the Early Iron Age settlements were connected in some way.

It is not always a simple task to locate the archaeological ruins of particular cities and villages mentioned in the Bible, or, from the other direction, to identify archaeological sites in terms of their ancient names. Places like Jerusalem that have been occupied continuously since ancient times pose no problem. But for many abandoned sites whose ancient names have long since been forgotten, archaeologists must turn to the Bible and epigraphical sources for clues as to which ruins represent which ancient cities. Following are some of the cities that figure prominently in the biblical narratives and, in parentheses, the modern Arabic names of their respective ruins: Jericho (Tell es-Sultan), Ai (et-Tell), Gibeon (el-Jib), Samaria (Sebastiyeh), Megiddo-Armageddon (Tell el-Mutesellim). When the ruins of biblical cities are excavated, naturally it is of interest to archaeologists and biblical scholars alike whether the archaeological findings corroborate the biblical record. In some cases, there seems to be a confirming fit. In other cases, there is obvious conflict. Often it is a matter of interpretation and debate. Research pertaining to the interface between biblical studies and archaeology sometimes is referred to as biblical archaeology.

Sociology

Historians necessarily work with conceptual models—hypothetical notions about how human society functions and what patterns of change tend to occur and under what circumstances. The Bible presents some very pronounced conceptual models and notions—for example, the idea that ethnic groups (Israelites, Moabites, Edomites, etc.) are extended families descended from individual male ancestors; that the direction of human history is guided by divine intervention; that Yahweh selected the Israelites as his special people and gave them the land of Canaan; and that the course of Israelite history was determined by Israel's fidelity or infidelity to Yahweh.

These notions undergird the Genesis–2 Kings narrative, which in turn has provided the basic outline for postbiblical treatments of Israel's history throughout the centuries, all the way from Josephus to Bright.

As mentioned above, the Alt-Noth reconstruction of Israel's origins and early history relied heavily on the sociological theories of Max Weber. Specifically, Weber distinguished four basic social structures in ancient Palestine (nomadic bedouin, seminomadic herders, peasant farmers, and city dwellers) and three basic types of societal authority (legal, traditional, and charismatic). The conceptual models undergirding the Alt-Noth scenario have been seriously challenged in recent years. Several studies have suggested that seminomadic herding normally exists in symbiotic relationship with a village farming economy rather than in competition with it and that seminomadic herding is more likely to have derived from sedentary agriculture in ancient Palestine than to have intruded from the desert fringe.

The most aggressive challenge to Alt and Noth argued that the early Israelite tribes did not enter Palestine from elsewhere but emerged from a revolt within the indigenous Canaanite population. This would have been a peasant uprising against the oppressive Canaanite city-states that resulted in an egalitarian tribal society. This notion of a peasant revolt also is influenced by a sociological model, specifically Marxism. The peasant revolt model was very influential from the late 1960s through the 1970s but receives little attention now. However, two aspects of this model remain influential—the idea that the early Israelite tribes emerged from the Canaanite population rather than entering the land from elsewhere and the recognition that any satisfactory explanation as to how this occurred must be well grounded in sociological research.

Recent Developments

Three major histories of Israel were published in the 1980s, all of them appearing about the same time. H. Donner's *Geschichte des Volkes Israel und seiner Nachbarn in Grundzügen* (1984–85) falls well within the Alt-Noth tradition. J. A. Soggin, in his *A History of Ancient Israel* (1984), finds the biblical presentation of Israel's history prior to the time of David as untrustworthy for the historian's purposes. Beginning with David, however, he places considerable confidence in the biblical narrative and follows it fairly closely. *A History of Ancient Israel and Judah* (1986) by J. M. Miller and J. H. Hayes also declines any attempt to reconstruct events prior to the establishment of the monarchy. Miller and Hayes are neither as reluctant as Soggin to speculate on the sociopolitical circumstances of the Israelite tribes from which the monarchy emerged, however, nor as trusting of the biblical materials pertaining to monarchical times. Specifically, Miller and Hayes argue that:

1. The clan was probably the basic sociopolitical unit among the early Israelite tribes, with the tribes themselves being essentially territorial groupings of clans whose sense of identity and mutual kinship developed in Palestine over a period of time.

2. The name "Israel" in premonarchical times probably referred specifically to the tribe of Ephraim and certain neighboring clans/tribes, such as Benjamin and Gilead, which Ephraim dominated.

3. This Ephraim-Israel tribal domain became the core of Saul's "kingdom," which itself remained essentially tribal in character.

4. Both Saul and David began their careers as military adventurers of a sort that may not have been typical of Ephraim-Israel but for which there was precedent nevertheless—that is, Saul and David followed in the tradition of Abimelech and Jephthah, who also had organized private armies with which they provided protection to their kinfolk in return for material support and engaged in raids on surrounding peoples.

5. David succeeded in carving out a territorial state that included as its core a southern grouping of tribes dominated by Judah, the city-state of Jerusalem, and the Ephraim-Israel tribes.

6. The biblical presentation of Solomon's "empire" is largely a literary fiction. Actually, his territorial domain probably was not any larger than David's, which did not even include some parts of Palestine (such as Philistia), much less all the lands between Egypt and the Euphrates.

7. Of the two kingdoms that resulted from the split at Solomon's death, the northern kingdom—which included the old Ephraim-Israel tribal domain and took the name Israel—emerged as the more powerful. Under the Omride dynasty, in fact, Israel achieved a level of commercial strength and international prestige superior to that achieved by either David or Solomon.

8. Beginning with the Omride period, moreover, and until Israel's defeat and annexation by the Assyrians, Judah often was little more than an Israelite vassal.

In yet more recent discussion about Israel's history the following positions have emerged. Some conservative biblical scholars continue to correlate an essentially literal reading of the biblical account of the Israelite conquest of Canaan with the available epigraphical and archaeological evidence. However, Albright's solution, which called for a thirteenth-century conquest, has been largely abandoned in favor of a conquest at the end of the fifteenth century. An opposite perspective is represented by scholars who regard the biblical materials as products almost entirely of exilic and postexilic Judaism and thus irrelevant for reconstructing the history of earlier periods. This means that we can know little about the history of earlier Israel beyond whatever information can be derived from epigraphy and archaeology and that, for all practical purposes, therefore, the history of Israel begins in the ninth century B.C.E.

Certain archaeologists have raised hopes that data from recent archaeological surveys and excavations will clarify such questions as whether the Israelites entered Palestine from elsewhere or emerged from the indigenous population, whether they were agriculturalists or pastoralists when they first settled in the hill country, and by what stages they spread throughout the land. Obviously, this new data is extremely important, but it is still inconclusive. For one thing, these archaeologists treat all of the Early Iron Age hill country settlements as Israelite and thus beg the question of what would have been meant by "Israelite" during premonarchical times and why the biblical narratives pertaining to this period distinguish between Israelite and non-Israelite villages in the hill country (cf. Judges 19:12). Also, the chief proponents of this approach have not yet reached agreement on their interpretation of the new data with respect to Israel's origins.

Yet other scholars are calling for a highly multidisciplinary approach to ancient Israelite history, involving close attention to the geographical features of Palestine, its various ecological zones, long-range settlement patterns as indicated by archaeological surveys, agricultural techniques and potentials, international trade patterns, and so on. Informed by the most up-to-date anthropological and sociological theories and models, archaeologists utilize all of this data to explain the process by which Israel came into being and gradually was transformed from tribal society into monarchy. One can only affirm the theoretical appropriateness of this approach; certainly all of the factors that these studies bring into consideration are relevant for understanding the history of ancient Israel. Perhaps their main contribution to this point, however, is that they raise new kinds of questions and warn against oversimplified answers. Thus far, in other words, it can hardly be said that this multidisciplinary approach has produced any notable breakthroughs or compelling clarifications—at least none that do not depend as much on the researcher's methodological presuppositions and working models as upon the various data compiled. An unfortunate characteristic of these studies is that they tend to use very jargonistic language—sometimes, it seems, belaboring the obvious. Also, they discuss such a wide range of factors at such an abstract and theoretical level that it is often difficult to understand what it all means with respect to the specific people and events of ancient Israel. The proponents of this approach tend to be deterministic in their social philosophy—that is, history unfolds in predictable fashion as determined largely by environmental circumstances; individual initiative plays a minor role in the course of human affairs, and specific events are incidental items in the broad sweep of social change.

Finally, the charge is being heard from several quarters that biblical studies in general, including historical-critical methodologies and treatments of ancient Israelite history, are biased to the core and should be approached from totally different perspectives. This bias begins, so the argument goes, with the ancient written sources, which tend to be male and elitist—that is, written records normally were produced by and for the powerful in ancient times (kings, priests, etc.). Even archaeology tends to present an elitist picture, since the substantial structures of the politically powerful naturally survive in greater proportion than the humble dwellings of the lower classes. This bias in the ancient sources has only been exacerbated by religious leaders in the Judeo-Christian tradition, it is charged, who usually have been men. Moreover, contemporary biblical scholarship in Western universities is decidedly Eurocentric—that is, culturally biased—in approach.

An increasing number of studies are appearing that attempt to redress the situation. Some attempt to do this by uncovering and correcting the old biases. Others, apparently liberated by the recognition of modern historians that complete objectivity is an unattainable goal anyhow, put aside even any effort in that direction and write essays on historical topics that unabashedly replace the old biases and ideologies with new ones.

Notes

1. English edition, *The History of Israel*, 3d ed. (London: Longmans, Green & Co., 1871–1876).

2. English edition, *Prolegomena to the History of Ancient Israel* (Gloucester, Mass.: Peter Smith, 1973).

3. English edition, *History of Israel*, trans. Peter Ackroyd (New York: Harper & Row, 1960).

4. The Deuteronomistic History is a term for the books of Deuteronomy, Joshua, Judges, 1–2 Samuel, and 1–2 Kings, which scholars generally regard as originally a single work.

For Further Reading

Avi-Yonah, M. *The Holy Land, from the Persian to the Arab Conquests (536 B.C. to A.D. 640): A Historical Geography*. Rev. ed. Grand Rapids: Baker, 1977. A well-documented summary of the political chronology and geographical boundaries of Samaria and Judea under the Persians, Greeks, and Romans.

Bartlett, J. R. *Jews in the Hellenistic World*. Cambridge Commentaries on Writings of the Jewish and Christian World, 200 B.C. to A.D. 200, vol. 1, part 1. Cambridge: Cambridge University Press, 1985. An introductory discussion of Josephus and other selected Jewish sources from the Roman period.

Bimson, J. *Redating the Exodus and Conquest*. Sheffield: Journal for the Study of the Old Testament, 1978. Taking the biblical account of Israel's exodus from Egypt and conquest of Canaan essentially at face value, Bimson seeks to demonstrate that this account is corroborated by archaeology. Read this as a balance to Van Seters's *In Search of History*.

Bowersock, G. W. *Roman Arabia*. Cambridge, Mass.: Harvard University Press, 1983. Although it focuses on the Transjordan, this book is especially helpful for understanding the political context of Palestine during the Roman period.

Clements, R. E., ed. *The World of Ancient Israel: Sociological, Anthropological, and Political Perspectives*. Cambridge: Cambridge University Press, 1989. A very useful collection of essays that explores the influence of sociology and anthropology on biblical studies in general and on the study of ancient Israelite history in particular.

Edelman, D., ed. *The Fabric of History: Text, Artifact, and Israel's Past*. Sheffield: Journal for the Study of the Old Testament, 1991. Essays on historiography and archaeology as related to the study of ancient Israelite history by six contemporary scholars.

Finkelstein, I. *The Archaeology of the Israelite Settlement*. Jerusalem: Israel Exploration Society, 1988. Provides a wealth of archaeological information about the Early Iron Age settlements in the central Palestinian hill country. However, readers should be cautious of the author's underlying assumption, reflected in the title of his book, that all of these Early Iron Age settlements were Israelite.

Hayes, J. H., and J. M. Miller, eds. *Israelite and Judaean History*. Philadelphia: Westminster, 1977. Reprinted London: SCM; Valley Forge, Pa.: Trinity Press International, 1990. Essays by an international group of scholars that signaled a move away from the Albright-Bright and Alt-Noth approaches to Israelite history. Especially useful is the opening chapter by Hayes, which surveys approaches and trends in the study of Israelite history from ancient to modern times.

Knight, D. A., and G. M. Tucker, eds. *The Hebrew Bible and Its Modern Interpreters*. Philadelphia: Fortress; Chico, Calif.: Scholars, 1985. A collection of essays that reviews scholarship pertaining to the Hebrew Bible since 1945. See especially the first three essays on "Israelite History" (J. M. Miller), "Syro-Palestinian and Biblical Archaeology" (W. G. Dever), and "The Ancient Near Eastern Environment" (J. J. M. Roberts).

Mazar, Amihai. *Archaeology of the Land of the Bible, 10,000–586* B.C.E. Anchor Bible Reference Library. Garden City, N.Y.: Doubleday, 1990. An up-to-date introduction to Palestinian archaeology (with coverage from prehistoric times through most of the Iron Age), with close attention to possible connections between Palestinian archaeology and Israelite history.

Meyers, C. *Discovering Eve*. New York: Oxford University Press, 1988. Seeks to give more adequate attention than do standard histories to the role and circumstances of women in ancient Israel. See also in this regard the collection of essays edited by P. L. Day, *Gender and Difference in Ancient Israel*. Minneapolis: Fortress, 1989.

Miller, J. M. *The Old Testament and the Historian*. Guides to Biblical Scholarship. Philadelphia: Fortress, 1976. Discusses more fully several of the issues raised in this chapter.

Miller, J. M., and J. H. Hayes, *A History of Ancient Israel and Judah*. London: SCM; Philadelphia: Westminster, 1986. A recent attempt to reconstruct the history of ancient Israel, which is concerned also to inform readers about the issues and uncertainties involved.

Pritchard, J. B., ed. *Ancient Near Eastern Texts Relating to the Old Testament*. Princeton, N. J.: Princeton University Press, 1955. See also the companion volume, *The Ancient Near East in Pictures Relating to the Old Testament* (Princeton, N. J.: Princeton University Press, 1954), and the supplement to both, *The Ancient Near East Supplement Relating to the Old Testament* (Princeton, N. J.: Princeton University Press, 1969). Still the most widely available and easily accessible collection of translated epigraphical texts relating to the Hebrew Bible.

Rogerson, J. *Atlas of the Bible*. New York: Facts on File, 1985. Useful for getting a grasp of the physical setting in which the history of ancient Israel and Judah unfolded and from which the Bible emerged. Another good atlas, written from a more conservative perspective, is B. J. Beitzel, *The Moody Atlas of Bible Lands* (Chicago: Moody, 1985).

Van Seters, J. *In Search of History: Historiography in the Ancient World and the Origins of Biblical History*. New Haven, Conn.: Yale University Press, 1983. An analysis of the biblical materials in comparison with other similar literature from the ancient world leading to a very skeptical view regarding its trustworthiness as a source for historical information. Read this as a balance to Bimson's *Redating the Exodus and Conquest*.

2

SOURCE CRITICISM

PAULINE A. VIVIANO

The historical-critical approach to interpretation has had a profound effect on the search for meaning in the biblical text. The new and often radical views of this century concerning the history of the biblical period and the formation of the Bible have been the direct result of the application of historical criticism to the Bible. This approach is not limited to one way of analyzing the text but employs many methods that try to answer such questions as, Who wrote it? When and where was it written? Why was it written and to whom? Each method has its own distinct concerns. But just as these questions are interrelated, so the concerns of the different methods overlap. The often complex answers given to these questions lead in turn to other questions dealing with multiple authorship, the variety of forms, numerous and conflicting purposes, and so on. One of the methods at the foundation of this process of questioning the text is source criticism.

Definition of Source Criticism

The historical approach presupposes that a literary work carries the imprint of the historical age in which it was produced and that the interpretation of a work is best served by situating it within its historical context and determining the intent of its author. A major difficulty in the application of the historical-critical method to the biblical text, however, is that neither authorship nor date, both essential for the method, can be ascertained readily. Indeed, complicating the issue is the fact that many books of the Bible give evidence of an extremely complex history of development, making questions of authorship and date virtually impossible to answer. Source criticism analyzes the biblical text in order to determine what sources were used in its formation. Once sources are isolated, the source critic considers issues of authorship, date, style, setting, and intent of each source. The primary focus of source criticism is the determination of

written sources. Although the determination of oral sources can theoretically be included in source criticism, it has become the provenance of form
criticism and tradition criticism and will not be considered here.

When source criticism emerged in the eighteenth century it was called
"literary criticism," and well into the twentieth century the terms have been
and continue to be used interchangeably.[1] Nevertheless, it is common today
to draw a distinction between "source criticism" and "literary criticism."
While both pay close attention to the literary features of a text, noting
stylistic characteristics, vocabulary usage, repetitions, contradictions or
inconsistencies, and other literary traits, their respective goals are different.
Source criticism tries to discover the sources behind the text by examining
its literary features. More recent literary criticism grounds meaning in the
literary or surface structure of a text; it focuses on the text as it is, not on
the text as it came to be. To avoid ambiguity, we will use the designation
"source criticism" for the method known to eighteenth- and nineteenth-
century scholars as "literary criticism."

The search for sources begins with a close examination of the biblical
text itself. It is clear that in certain instances sources were used in the compilation of various parts of the Bible,—for these sources are explicitly
mentioned, such as the Book of the Wars of Yahweh (Num. 21:14) and the
Book of Jashar (Josh. 10:13; 2 Sam. 1:18).[2] Apart from the titles of these
sources, nothing about them is known directly. But it is possible to draw
conclusions about their nature by studying the quotations taken from them
or the material in which those quotations are embedded. For example, the
Book of the Wars of Yahweh may have been just that, a collection of stories
of holy war, and the Book of Jashar may have been a collection of poems,
for the Old Testament quotes two poems from it (Josh. 10:12b–13a; 2 Sam.
1:19–27). The "chronicles" used in 1–2 Kings and 1–2 Chronicles (see n.
2) most likely were court records containing details of the reigns of the
kings of Israel and Judah.[3]

Although the study of explicitly mentioned sources is of some interest to
source critics, their primary concern is to detect and study sources that are
not directly mentioned in the Bible. It is assumed that the biblical authors
did not make up the stories they tell but that these stories were already in
circulation in their communities in oral or written form. While we should
not underestimate the creative genius of these ancient authors, source critics assume that they incorporated, rewrote, and reinterpreted traditional
material—whether they explicitly say so or not—to produce their versions
of Israel's past. Source critics also maintain that these versions were then
taken up by later authors or redactors who also incorporated, rewrote, and
reinterpreted Israel's past for their own audiences, and that this process continued until the text received its present form.

Source critics seek to retrace this process by isolating each redactional layer, thus revealing the sources that have come together to form the text as we now have it. In order to do this, source critics rely upon certain criteria that, when applied to the final form of the text, enable them to separate out its sources. Based on the assumption that authors exercise a certain consistency in the way they write, in the terminology they use, and in their perspective, source critics view marked differences in any of these areas as an indication that sources have been incorporated into a text. Likewise, it is assumed that single authors do not include contradictory material in their work and that such contradictions reveal multiple hands at work in the production of a text. Intrusions into a text—breaks in the sequence of events or interruptions in the progression of thought—are seen as evidence that works by various authors have been combined by later redactors. Multiple versions of the same basic story, as well as repetitions within a story, are taken as further proof that more than one author's work lies behind the present form of a text. These, then, are the criteria used by source critics to determine the presence of written sources behind the text: variations in style, vocabulary, and perspective; contradictions and inconsistencies in a passage or between passages; abrupt interruptions that break the continuity of a passage; and various kinds of duplications or repetitions.

Historical Background

As indicated above, source criticism is part of the historical-critical approach to biblical interpretation that emerged in the eighteenth century. The approach was already being used by classicists to deal with problems in interpretation of the Homeric epics. It was "borrowed" by biblical scholars who wanted to delve beneath the surface of the text to uncover information regarding authorship, date, provenance, and intent.

The area that received most attention in the application of source criticism to the Bible was the formation of the Pentateuch. Early source critics searched for the sources used by Moses in writing the Pentateuch, but eventually that search called Mosaic authorship itself into question. Challenges to Mosaic authorship of the Pentateuch had been raised prior to the eighteenth century,[4] but these challenges remained isolated until critics were able to offer a viable alternative to Mosaic authorship. That alternative was found in the Newer Documentary Hypothesis, articulated and defended most ably by Julius Wellhausen. Wellhausen's work was the culmination of a process whose origin can be traced to the work of Jean Astruc,[5] a French physician. In his *Conjectures on the Reminiscences Which Moses Appears to Have Used in Composing the Book of Genesis*,[6] Astruc sought to determine the sources used by Moses. Astruc himself did not deny Mosaic authorship, but his search for sources led inevitably in that direction. By dividing the text on the basis of the names of God found in the book of Genesis, Astruc posited two sources for this book, each using a different name for the deity. Source A used *Elohim*, translated "God" in English; Source B used *Yahweh*,[7] the personal name of Israel's God, often translated "LORD" in contemporary Bibles. Astruc's work was carried forward by J. G. Eichhorn in his *Introduction to the Old Testament*.[8] Eichhorn carefully analyzed the style and content of Astruc's two sources and set up additional criteria for the determination of sources, including repetitions or duplications, distinctive stylistic features, and characteristic terminology. Once the idea of more than one source or document in the Pentateuch was accepted, it remained to subsequent scholarship to determine the number and extent of the sources, their dates, and their interrelationship. In the process, the Newer Documentary Hypothesis emerged, but not before two alternate theories about the formation of the Pentateuch were developed: the Fragmentary Hypothesis and the Supplementary Hypothesis.

While the Documentary Hypothesis draws its strongest evidence from Genesis and the beginning of Exodus, the Fragmentary Hypothesis is based on evidence provided by the various law codes in the Pentateuch. A. Geddes,[9] credited with the origin of the Fragmentary Hypothesis, argued that fragments of varying lengths, rather than sources or documents, lay behind these law codes. He further argued that these fragments were put side by side without much consideration given to connecting links. The Pentateuch itself, like the law codes, was formed over a long period of time by the same process of combining fragments of varying lengths. According to J. S. Vater,[10] who accepted Geddes's position, the process of formation began with a collection of laws, now found in the book of Deuteronomy, dating from the time of David and Solomon but rediscovered during the reign of Josiah (621 B.C.E.).

Although the Fragmentary Hypothesis offered another way to account for the diversity in the Pentateuch, it did not account satisfactorily for the structural consistency of the Pentateuch, especially in terms of its chronology. While the Pentateuch has many diverse elements, it seems too unified to have been formed by the piecing together of fragments. The attempt to account for the extensive unity of the Pentateuch grew into the Supplementary Hypothesis, whose origin is attributed to H. Ewald.[11] Ewald maintained that the core of the Pentateuch was an "Elohistic" work that a compiler supplemented by drawing material from other sources. This Elohistic work was one connected strand, thus accounting for the Pentateuch's unity of theme and structure; the fragments, worked into this core, account for the diversity of style, vocabulary, and perspective.

Neither the Fragmentary Hypothesis nor the Supplementary Hypothesis found much support among scholars. Instead, the Documentary Hypothesis was revised and came virtually to control the field of source criticism in its formulation as the Newer Documentary Hypothesis. This process began with H. Hupfeld's *The Sources of Genesis and the Nature of Their Combination.*[12] Before Hupfeld, it was assumed that the Elohistic narrative, called the Foundation Document, was the oldest and most comprehensive of the Pentateuchal sources. Hupfeld showed that the Foundation Document was actually composed of two sources, both of which used the name *Elohim* for God. Thus the Elohistic work was divided in two, an early and a late Elohist. The third source was the Yahwistic source (J, based on the German spelling of Yahweh), which used the name *Yahweh* for God. In the later development of the Newer Documentary Hypothesis, Hupfeld's early Elohistic sources would be identified as the Priestly source (P).

The claim that the Deuteronomic Code (Deuteronomy 12–26) is not a compilation of the sources found in Genesis–Numbers (J, E, P) was advanced by W. M. L. de Wette.[13] De Wette maintained that this code was the law book discovered in the Temple during King Josiah's reform (2 Kings 22–23). De Wette dated the Deuteronomic Code shortly before 621 B.C.E., the date when it was discovered in the Temple and thus provided a fixed date around which to group the other sources. The dating of sources had been a major problem for source critics because the texts themselves give little evidence upon which to make a determination with respect to dates. Once the date of Deuteronomy was established, however, progress was made in dating the other sources. In *The Historical Books of the Old Testament*[14] H. Graf convincingly argued a suggestion made by his teacher, Eduard Reuss, that P was the latest of the sources. Graf maintained that the ceremonial and ritual laws found in the Pentateuch could not reflect Israel's early period but emerged only after the exile, after the prophets. In the books of Deuteronomy, Joshua, Judges, 1–2 Samuel, and 1–2 Kings, the ritual laws of Exodus, Leviticus, and Numbers are not presupposed and so must be later than Deuteronomy–2 Kings.

W. Vatke showed in his *The Religion of the Old Testament*[15] that ritualization is found at the end of a long process of religious development, not at its beginning. He maintained that J, E, 1–2 Samuel, and 1–2 Kings reflect the primitive period in Israel's development, which was replaced by one of ethical consciousness, emerging with the prophets and found in Deuteronomy. The latest stage of Israel's religious development was characterized by a more ceremonial religion that emphasized external rituals and is found in priestly law.[16] Vatke's position was based on Hegelian historical and philosophical assumptions, not on literary-critical grounds. Nevertheless, the conclusions drawn by Graf and Vatke revolutionized future scholarship and its understanding of the development of Israelite religion. By understanding Mosaic law as the latest development in the history of Israelite religion, they forced subsequent scholars to abandon a simplistic understanding of Israel's religious development. Now the history of Israel could be approached rationally and comprehensibly.[17]

It remained for Wellhausen to combine source analysis with the arguments of his predecessors. Wellhausen's *History of Israel*[18] is noted not so much for its originality as for the way in which he organized and built upon the work that had preceded him. In fact, the dominance of Wellhausen's view in all subsequent discussion of Pentateuchal sources is a testimony to his ability to synthesize and articulate the work of his predecessors. He showed the importance of the history of Israel's religious development as described by Graf and Vatke for dating the individual sources of the Pentateuch. Wellhausen also strengthened the foundation for the view that Mosaic legislation was postexilic. He made common property the view that there was a progressive development in Israel's religion from a spontaneous natural observance of religion to the reforms of the prophets, which were subsequently superseded by the ceremonial and ritual laws of the priests. Thus it was the prophets, according to Wellhausen, who established a truly ethical faith in Israel. Wellhausen's work became a standard in biblical criticism, not simply for the next generation but for generations to come.

The Newer Documentary Hypothesis as promulgated by Wellhausen maintains that four sources or documents were edited together to form the Pentateuch. The oldest of these is the Yahwistic source (J). It is linked to the period of intellectual growth and national consciousness under David and Solomon (ca. 950 B.C.E.). Its author, the Yahwist, used the name Yahweh for God from the beginning of its narrative (Gen. 2:4b). He tells vivid stories in a folkloric style and reflects a southern provenance (i.e., from the kingdom of Judah). The Yahwist provides the basic story line for Genesis and Exodus, beginning with creation in Gen. 2:4b; J material is also found in Numbers.

The work of the Elohist (E), a more or less fragmentary source, originated in the Northern Kingdom during the height of its power (ca. 850 B.C.E.). It is not found in the primeval history (Genesis 1–11) but begins with the Abraham story in Genesis 15.

The Deuteronomic source (D), generally believed to be confined to Deuteronomy 12–26, is a law code with a sermonic style characterized by stereotyped phrases. It is marked throughout by a sustained exhortation to obedience to the law. D is presumed to be of northern provenance and is dated prior to its discovery in the Temple during Josiah's reform (621 B.C.E.). The Deuteronomic source is thought either to have been written prior to the fall of the Northern Kingdom and brought south by refugees fleeing at the time of the fall (721 B.C.E.) or to have been written by northern refugees after they fled south and deposited in the Temple, where it was forgotten until Josiah's reform.

The latest of the sources is the Priestly work (P). This source provides the chronological framework of the Pentateuch and, as the name suggests, was primarily concerned with priestly matters: ritual laws, the origin of shrines and rituals, and genealogies. P has a formal, rigid, repetitive style. It is said to have emerged from priestly circles in Jerusalem during the period of the exile (ca. 550 B.C.E.). It begins in Gen. 1:1 and is juxtaposed to J and E, or intertwined with J and E throughout Genesis, Exodus, and Numbers. Leviticus is regarded as the work of P exclusively.

In Wellhausen's view, these four documents—J, E, D, and P—were combined to form the Pentateuch as we now have it. First, the Yahwistic source was supplemented by the Elohist, most likely after the fall of the Northern Kingdom. To this the Deuteronomic Code was added some time after 621 B.C.E. After the exile, the Priestly work was joined to the other sources. Since the final redaction bears the stamp of the Priestly author and carries the chronology of this source, it is supposed that the Priestly author himself or someone from the same priestly circles was the final redactor.

The generations following Wellhausen saw the emergence of a scholarly consensus regarding the Newer Documentary Hypothesis. Once this consensus was reached, source criticism in the Pentateuch turned to the task of examining the four documents and defining them more precisely. The only major change in the hypothesis was to view the documents as having undergone a long process of growth and therefore as being less unified than was once assumed. Attempts to trace the sources beyond the Pentateuch into Joshua–Kings have met with little success.[19] Successors of Wellhausen claimed to have discovered other sources beyond J, E, P, and D, but none of these additional sources has gained wide acceptance.

Despite refinements, the general contours of Wellhausen's view have remained dominant. Nearly every historical-critical scholar of the twentieth century, either explicitly or implicitly, has affirmed the Newer Documentary Hypothesis. Every critical introduction to the Old Testament written in this century has given prominence to the Newer Documentary Hypothesis, which has been considered an assured answer to the complex question of the formation of the Pentateuch and a firm basis for reconstructing the history of religious development in ancient Israel.

As early as 1924, it was suggested that source criticism had gone as far as it could and that it had no further problems to solve.[20] G. von Rad, a little over a decade later, agreed: "So far as the analysis of source documents is concerned, there are signs that the road has come to a dead end."[21] Other questions began to call for the attention of biblical scholars, and other methods, notably form criticism and tradition-historical criticism, were developing to address these new questions. Source criticism, it was felt, had done its job and had given such assured results that no change in the understanding of the formation of the Pentateuch was envisioned. The following statement by E. Kraeling is typical of the confidence concerning the achievements of source criticism.

> Universally it is conceded that Old Testament scholarship has given us a new, realistic and dependable picture of the way in which the literary materials of the Old Testament arose and of what they mean historically. While the future may bring many corrections, nothing that could be adduced along critical lines could change the situation very much in principle.[22]

The extent to which the Newer Documentary Hypothesis continues to dominate the field even today is evident in the spate of books and articles on the individual sources themselves.[23] This level of acceptance makes it hard for its critics to be taken seriously. Nevertheless, dissatisfaction with the Newer Documentary Hypothesis has persisted and in the last few decades has been growing in intensity. Criticism is directed not only against the Newer Documentary Hypothesis but also against source criticism itself, as we will see in the final section of this chapter.

Illustration of the Method

For purposes of illustration we will apply the source-critical method to Genesis 1–11.[24] This section of Genesis has the advantage of being manageable in size and a part of the Pentateuch about which there is some consensus regarding the presence and nature of its sources. We will begin with an application of the criteria used by source critics to discover sources behind a text: differences in style, vocabulary, and perspective; contradictions and inconsistencies; interruptions or abrupt changes; and duplications or repetitions.

Style

The most obvious stylistic characteristic of the opening chapter of Genesis is its repetition, which is a result of the framework surrounding each of the eight acts of creation: "And God said. . . . Let there be. . . . And it was so. . . . And God saw that it was good. . . . And there was evening and there was morning, X day." While not all elements of the framework are found each time, enough are present to characterize the style as formal and repetitive. This repetition gives a solemn, hymnic tone to the entire account. The repetitive style abruptly changes in Gen. 2:4b, which begins the first of several stories containing the usual elements of a narrative: characters and plot. In contrast to Gen. 1:1–2:4a, we find in Gen. 2:4b–4:26 a deity actively involved in shaping, breathing, and planting. There is interaction between creator and creature in a vividly told story filled with suspense and drama. Creation unfolds, not as the result of a series of commands but as an action taken by the deity with a kind of experimental flair. It is unclear what will happen once the man and the woman, the animals and the garden, have been created. Will God's will prevail, or will humans transgress the one command they were given? A new and unusual character, the serpent, is introduced, and the tension builds as the story moves from temptation to sin to punishment and on into Genesis 4. These narratives in Genesis 2–4 have all the elements of good storytelling: plot, characterization, action, dialogue, and suspense. The stories use an evocative vocabulary with poetic words such as "mists" and "deep sleep." They employ word plays: 'ādām (humanity)/'ădāmāh (ground), 'iššāh (woman)/'îš (man), 'ărûmmîm (naked)/'ārûm (cunning), qānāh (gotten)/ Cain. Such clever word plays hold the interest of the hearer or reader. Even in the genealogy of 4:17–26, where one would expect to find repetition, there are short narrative-like sections (4:17b, 19–24). In the genealogy of Genesis 5, a style that is repetitious as a result of a recurring framework, as in Gen. 1:1–2:4a, resumes. This repetitive framework is as follows: "When X had lived Y years he became the father of Z. X lived YY years and had other sons and daughters." Both Gen. 4:17–26 and Genesis 5 are genealogies, but their respective styles are very different. In Genesis 6–9 and 11:1–9 we find the same kind of vividly told stories that characterize Gen. 2:4b–4:26. There are characters and action as well as word plays: šēm (name)/šām (there), bālal (confuse)/Babel. In Genesis 10 and 11:10–32, repetition again comes to the fore, as in Genesis 1 and 5. Thus Genesis 1:1–2:4a; 5; 10; and 11:10–32 are consistent in style but different from the style of Genesis 2:4b–4:26; 6–9; and 11:1–9. Genesis 6–9, though similar in style to Genesis 2:4b–4:26 and 11:1–9, presents a special case, as will be clear when we examine its vocabulary, duplications, and inconsistencies.

Vocabulary

In comparing vocabulary, we will focus on different terms that have the same referent. For example, it is clear that *Elohim* and *Yahweh* are different terms for the deity. The same applies to terms such as "image and likeness"/"living being," "male and female"/"man and woman," and "create"/"form." The terminological distinctions in these early chapters of Genesis are illustrated in Table 2.1.

TABLE 2.1

Genesis 1:1–2:4a	Genesis 2:4b–25	Genesis 5
Elohim	Yahweh or Yahweh Elohim	Elohim
These are the generations of		These are the generations of
Image and likeness	Living being	Likeness of God
Male and female	Male and Woman	Male and female
Create	Form	Create

It is important to note that the vocabulary patterns in the chart occur elsewhere in Genesis 1–11. The name *Elohim*, used in Genesis 1 and 5, is found again in Genesis 6–9. The phrase "these are the generations of" (2:4a) is found again in Gen. 6:9; 10:1, 27; and 11:10, 27, and a similar phrase, "according to their generations," occurs in 10:32. The following phrases also recur: "the deep" (1:2/7:11), "male and female" (1:27/6:19), "in his image" (1:26–27/9:6), "be fruitful and multiply" (1:28/9:1, 7). In addition to Gen. 2:4b–25, the name *Yahweh* is found again in Genesis 3–4; 6–9; and 11:1–9, but not in the other chapters of Genesis 1–11. Furthermore, in Gen. 7:2 "man and woman" (NRSV: "the male and its mate") is the same as in Gen. 2:23–24, and the notion of the "ground" being cursed because of humanity repeats the motif of 3:17.

The fact that both *Elohim* and *Yahweh* are found in Genesis 6–9 is significant and calls for a closer examination of this section. In Gen. 6:5 Yahweh observes the "wickedness" of "humanity," in contrast to 6:12 where Elohim sees that the "earth" is filled with "violence," "corrupted" by "all flesh." In Gen. 6:7 Yahweh decides to "blot out humanity" from the "ground," whereas in 6:13 Elohim will make an "end" of "all flesh" and also of the "earth." In Gen. 7:12 we find "rain" rather than "the great deep" of 7:11. "Yahweh said in his heart" (Gen. 8:21) stands in contrast to "Elohim blessed Noah" (Gen. 9:1). The promise that Yahweh will "never again curse the ground" (Gen. 8:21) is paralleled by "I will establish my covenant" (Gen. 9:9, 11). Table 2.2 illustrates these differences.

Just as there are different styles in Gen. 1:1–2:4a; 5; 10; and 11:10–32, on the one hand, and Gen. 2:4b–4:26 and 11:1–9 on the other, so also 1:1–2:4a; 5; 10; and 11:10–32 have a distinctive and recurring vocabulary, different from that of 2:4b–4:26 and 11:1–9. There are different sets of vocabulary through Genesis 6–9, indicating a blend in these chapters of the

TABLE 2.2

Genesis 6:5, 7; 7:12; 8:21	Genesis 6:13, 22; 7:11; 9:1, 8, 11
Yahweh	Elohim
Wickedness	Violence, corruption
Blot out	Make an end
Humanity	All flesh
Ground	Earth
Rain	Great deep
Said in his heart	Blessed Noah
Never again curse the ground	Will establish my covenant

vocabulary from 1:1–2:4a; 5; 10; and 11:10–32 with that from 2:4b–4:26 and 11:1–9.

Perspective

In addition to stylistic and vocabulary differences, there are differences in perspective throughout Genesis 1–11. In Gen. 1:1–2:4a, God is presented as a majestic, transcendent being. The world is created by the mere power of God's word. In 2:4b–25, a different picture of the deity emerges. God is depicted in anthropomorphic terms. Here God is involved in creation, "getting his hands dirty," so to speak, as the deity forms clay like a potter and breathes life into that clay. This God is not distant but is as close as humanity's next breath. Far from the organized God of Genesis 1, this God seems to decide what to create in the very process of creating, and sometimes gets it wrong, as when the animals are formed as partners for the man before God discovers that they are not at all suitable. In Genesis 4, the deity interacts in a humanlike fashion with Cain. God is also described in human terms in Gen. 6:5–8: Yahweh is grieved by humanity's evil; Yahweh is sorry that humanity was ever created. Yahweh even shuts the door of the ark! But the transcendent, majestic figure of God resurfaces in the decree issued in 6:13–14 and the commands God gives Noah (6:3–22). The more human picture of God appears again in 8:20, where Yahweh smells the sacrifice; the more majestic God issues further decrees and establishes a covenant (Gen. 9:1–17). With Gen. 11:1–9 we return to the anthropomorphic presentation of the deity found in 2:4b–25. God is alarmed at the potential of humanity and has to "come down" to earth to find out what humanity is doing. We are forced to conclude that there are two very different images of God in Genesis 1–11: a majestic, transcendent God in 1:1–2:4a and a down–to–earth, humanlike God in 2:4b–4:26; 6–9; and 11:1–9. The God of 1:1–2:4a emerges again in Gen. 6:13–22 and 9:1–17.

Humanity is also viewed in very different ways in Genesis 1–11. In Genesis 1 humanity is created in the very image of God, suggesting an exalted view of what it is to be human and setting humans apart from animals. In Gen. 2:7 humanity is made from the dust of the ground and will be dependent upon the ground for food. Humans live because God breathes in them, and so humanity is dependent upon God for life. This dependent creature is much frailer and more vulnerable than humanity in Genesis 1. Humans and animals are both "living beings" (Gen. 2:7, 19); the only distinction given to humans is God's interest in them. Apart from the characterization of humanity as intent on evil, little can be said about how humanity is presented in the flood story. But in Gen. 9:6 it is affirmed that humanity is created in the image of God, and God gives the same command to humanity (9:1) as in Gen. 1:28: "Be fruitful and multiply." Thus in addition to two distinct styles and sets of vocabulary, Gen. 1:1–2:4a and parts of Genesis 6–9 differ in theological perspective from Gen. 2:4b–4:26, other parts of Genesis 6–9, and 11:1–9.

Contradictions/Inconsistencies

Careful analysis of Genesis 1–11 reveals several contradictions and inconsistencies between Genesis 1 and 2 and within Genesis 6–9. In Gen. 1:1–2:4a, animals are created before humans (1:24–25 and 1:26–27), but in Gen. 2:7 the human is created before the animals (2:19). In Gen. 1:2, water (the deep) is present and must be restrained by the creation of the firmament and the earth. But in Gen. 2:4b–5, the earth is a desert, and water must be brought to it in order to facilitate creation. In Gen. 6:19–20 and 7:15–16, one pair of every kind of animal is brought into the ark, yet 7:2 says that seven pairs of clean and one pair of unclean animals are to be brought into the ark. The flood is caused by rain in Gen. 7:4, 12, and 8:2b, but 7:11 and 8:2a speak of the fountains of the deep that burst forth, causing a reversion to the primeval chaos (the deep) of Genesis 1. In Gen. 7:4, 12, the rains lasts forty days, and it takes twenty-one days for the waters to recede (7:10; 8:8–12). But according to 7:24 and 8:2a, 3b, the flooding of the earth takes 150 days, and by the time the waters recede (8:13), a year and ten days have passed. In Gen. 8:5, the mountains have appeared, but in 8:9 the earth is still covered by water. The contradictions and inconsistencies between Genesis 1 and 2 and in Genesis 6–9, taken in conjunction with the differences in style, vocabulary, and perspective we have already noted, indicate separate stories of creation that have been juxtaposed and perhaps two separate flood stories that have been merged.

Interruptions

The first abrupt change that confronts the reader of Genesis 1–11 is that Gen. 2:4b begins again what has supposedly been concluded in 2:4a; in 2:4b God begins again to create. The story line of Gen. 2:4b–25 continues into chapters 3 and 4. Even the genealogy of Gen. 4:17–26, which introduces a shift in literary form from narrative to genealogy, is not as abrupt as the shift to the genealogy of Genesis 5 and 10. The genealogy of Genesis 4 is worked into the narrative, but in Genesis 5 it begins with a formal introduction that echoes Gen. 2:4a. The story of the flood is interrupted to give genealogical information (Gen. 6:9–10) and begins again in 6:11. The genealogy of chapter 10 is interrupted by the narrative of Gen. 11:1–9 and resumes in 11:10. These interruptions occur at the very points where changes in style, vocabulary, and perspective begin.

Repetitions/Duplications

Lastly, we draw evidence from the repetitions and duplications found in Genesis 1–11. Most repetitions are found in the Genesis flood story. God observes the malice of humanity in 6:5 and 6:12 and resolves to destroy humanity in 6:7 and 6:13. The flood is announced twice: 6:13, 17, and 7:4. Noah is ordered to enter the ark twice: 6:18–20 and 7:1–3. Noah obeys God's commands in both 6:22 and 7:5 and enters the ark twice: 7:7 and 7:13. Twice, the waters increase and raise the ark (7:17 and 7:18ff). All living creatures die in 7:21 and again in 7:22. The waters recede in 8:1 and again in 8:3b. God promises never again to destroy the earth by flood in both 8:21–22 and 9:8–17. Apart from these duplications, one notes that we have two accounts of creation (Gen. 1:1–2:4a; Gen. 2:4b–26), and the genealogy of Gen. 4:17–32 is repeated in a different order and with some variations in spelling in the genealogy of Genesis 5.[25] These repetitions and duplications support the view that two different stories of the flood have been merged, and, together with our other evidence, they indicate that Gen. 1:1–2:4a; 5; 10; and 11:10–32 can be attibuted to one source and Gen. 2:4b–2:26 and 11:1–9 to another. In Genesis 6–9 both sources have been merged.

Conclusions

On the strength of the differences in style, vocabulary, and perspective in Genesis 1–11, together with the abrupt shifts, contradictions, and repetitions/duplications in the same material, we may suggest that Genesis 1–11 is composed of two separate sources. Furthermore, each source can be identified on the basis of what we have discovered. Genesis 1:1–2:4a; 5; 10; and 11:10–32, taken apart from 2:4b–4:26 and 11:1–9, has a consistency of style, vocabulary, and perspective. When the two strands are separated from each other, duplications and contradictions are eliminated. Genesis 1:1–2:4a; 5; 10; and 11:10–32 have been attributed to the Priestly author, and Gen. 2:4b–4:26 and 11:1–9 to the Yahwist. It is more difficult to separate the stories intertwined in Genesis 6–9, but this can be accomplished by the same application of criteria. A consistency of style, vocabulary, and perspective, without contradictions or repetitions, is found in Gen. 6:1–8; 7:1–5, 7–8, 10, 12, 16b–17, 22–23; and 8:2b–3a, 6–12, 13b, 20–22 (J), on the one hand, and in Gen. 6:9–22; 7:6, 9, 11, 13–16a, 18–21, 24; 8:1–2a, 3b–5, 13a, 14–19; and 9:1–17 (P), on the other. Some slight variations may be found in the assignment of verses to J or P by different scholars, but there is agreement on those verses wherein the main contours of the story are found. Beyond Genesis 11 the same criteria can be applied. Although it is impossible to assign every verse or part of a verse with absolute certainty, J and P appear to continue throughout the Pentateuch, with E being introduced in Genesis 15 and D in Deuteronomy 12–26.

Critique of the Method

Now that we have seen the method in operation, it remains to consider the weaknesses of source criticism and its most prominent theory, the Newer Documentary Hypothesis. While the focus of our attention will be on that hypothesis, the issues raised below apply to any area of biblical study where source criticism has played a dominant role.

From the time when source criticism emerged as a critical method, there were questions about its validity. The Fragmentary and Supplementary Hypotheses, as we have seen, offered alternative ways to account for the evidence cited by proponents of the Documentary Hypothesis. Other scholars have continued to argue for the unity of the Pentateuch by explaining the stylistic peculiarities that led source critics to posit multiple sources as the result of oriental modes of thought[26] or by providing theological or stylistic justification for incongruities in the text.[27] But by and large these scholars have not been taken seriously, as scholars have generally regarded the evidence for multiple sources as compelling. If anything, the evidence suggests an even more complex process of formation than conceived of by the Newer Documentary Hypothesis. Although an overall unity may underlie the Pentateuch, its component parts are too disparate to assume the activity of a single author.

A more serious challenge was presented beginning early in this century by scholars who accepted the Newer Documentary Hypothesis but used other methods of inquiry. H. Gunkel,[28] a pioneer in form criticism, began to focus on smaller narrative units and their origin in oral tradition, separating them from their literary context. He sought to move behind the written text and emphasized the importance of the oral prehistory for the formation of the Pentateuch. Gunkel saw J and E less as authors than as inheritors of an oral tradition that was already formed. A. Alt[29] used a similar approach to demonstrate that even the oldest law was preceded by oral tradition. The effect of the approach taken by Gunkel and Alt was to cut loose both narrative and law from the chronological scheme of Wellhausen, thus giving a broader picture of Israel's religious development than source criticism had allowed. G. von Rad[30] moved beyond what he saw as the impasse created by source criticism when he used form criticism to understand the Hexateuch as a genre. By focusing on larger complexes of tradition and the process of their transmission, rather than on "documents," von Rad led attention away from individual sources. His work, coupled with that of M. Noth,[31] prepared the way for a tradition-historical approach that stands in tension with source criticism. R. Rendtorff,[32] a successor to von Rad and Noth, has now moved completely away from the Newer Documentary Hypothesis, providing an alternate description of the formation of the Pentateuch based on tradition-historical criticism. He maintains that individual traditions underwent a long process of development wherein smaller units grew into larger ones. These were combined into single continuous accounts, which in turn were combined into larger and larger continuous accounts, until the Pentateuch as we have it was formed. This process would have taken centuries, so that the formation of the Pentateuch as such is dated late. Thus Rendtorff explains the formation of the Pentateuch not on the basis of the Newer Documentary Hypothesis but in opposition to it. E. Blum adopts the approach taken by Rendtorff, his teacher, and has applied it in a detailed study of the patriarchal narratives[33] and more recently of the Pentateuch as a whole.[34] In Blum's reconstruction of the process of the formation of the Pentateuch, a D redactor has an expanded role in Genesis, Exodus, and Numbers, with the Pentateuch resulting from an integration of D and P. Future discussion of the formation of the Pentateuch has to take into account the methodological shift represented in the work of Rendtorff and Blum and the challenge that work poses to the Newer Documentary Hypothesis.

Scandinavian scholars since the middle of this century have also tended to emphasize the oral background of the text, objecting that the "book mentality" at the basis of the Newer Documentary Hypothesis—the notion that ancient authors "cut and pasted" from various documents—is more appropriate to modern culture than to that of the ancient world, which was primarily oral. In the background of the text, they hold, was an oral tradition that continued into the period of the exile and beyond. I. Engnell[35] maintained that there never were parallel continuous documents such as J and E. Variations in style, vocabulary, and perspective arose from the oral basis of the text, not from the splicing of documents. According to Engnell, contradictions and repetitions are to be expected given the cultural background of the Old Testament and the long period of time during which the text was in formation and passed on orally. During major crises, when there was a breakdown of normal communication, the need to commit traditions to writing arose. Then the tradition's oral form was replaced by a fixed written form.

In view of the ever-increasing knowledge of ancient Near Eastern culture, we are cautioned by these scholars against the application of modern literary categories to ancient literature. Nevertheless, the assumption that oral tradition dominated to the exclusion of written material is equally untenable. The many ancient texts uncovered as a result of archaeological excavation testify to a rich literary heritage dating back, not just centuries, but millennia before the biblical text. Biblical scholars need to be aware not only of the oral and written traditions of the ancient Near Eastern world but also of the interplay between oral and written forms in the development of a work like the Pentateuch.

The Newer Documentary Hypothesis has been significantly undermined by scholars who accept source criticism but dissent from the details of the hypothesis. For example, the fact that in most instances E cannot be extricated from J,[36] and that even when separated it does not yield a continuous narrative, has led some to challenge the existence of E as a continuous source.[37] In spite of recent attempts to save E,[38] it remains a fragmentary source and a problem for Pentateuchal analysis. Other scholars, however, have tried to divide J, E, D, or P even further on the basis of the same criteria that led to their initial identification. These critics see J, E, D, and P not as unified documents but as products of a "school" that generated more than one document and that shaped and reshaped these documents by further additions.[39] Still others have been led by further analysis of the Pentateuch to posit the existence of other sources: a Lay source (L), centered on matters of concern to laity as opposed to priests;[40] a Nomadic source (N), which contains a negative evaluation of civilized life;[41] a Kenite source (K), which deals with the life of Moses;[42] and a Southern or Seir source (S),[43] limited to Genesis. Finally, Noth[44] posited a "foundational source" or *Grundlage* (G), from which both J and E independently drew their content. In this way, Noth accounted for the similarity of J and E, finding the major themes of the Pentateuch already present in G.

The arguments for these various subdivisions and additional sources have not gained acceptance by many scholars beyond the recognition that the identification and formation of source documents are far more complicated than was once assumed. The multiplication of sources and the fragmentation of the original four sources into other documents have undermined the Newer Documentary Hypothesis itself. The more "sources" one finds, the more tenuous the evidence for the existence of continuous documents becomes, and the less likely it is that four unified documents ever existed. Even for those able to avoid skepticism and confusion in the face of the ever-increasing number of sources, the only logical recourse seems to be to move away from the Newer Documentary Hypothesis toward a position closer to the Fragmentary Hypothesis.

Another serious threat to the Newer Documentary Hypothesis is posed by problems of dating. Wellhausen based his dating of sources on the Hegelian view that progress in history occurs in an evolutionary manner from thesis to antithesis to synthesis. This Hegelian outlook contributed to the acceptance and popularity of the Newer Documentary Hypothesis, but critics were quick to show that it was unsatisfactory.[45] In fact, the generations of scholars following Wellhausen have abandoned the evolutionary scheme underlining the Newer Documentary Hypothesis as inappropriate to their philosophical frame of reference. Moreover, the scientific study of religious development in this century has produced no evidence to support Wellhausen's view that religions evolved from a primitive, spontaneous, personal stage to a rigid, formalistic, and ritualistic stage. The process of religious development is far more complex and uneven than Wellhausen imagined. Without his evolutionary assumptions, his dating of sources can no longer be accepted, and contrary views cannot be ignored. Several scholars over the past century have disagreed with Wellhausen's dates, especially for D and P.[46]

While the early date assigned to J has remained relatively unchallenged until recent years, J. Van Seters[47] has now dated J to the exile because of the similarity of its vocabulary to that of the Deuteronomistic History and Deutero-Isaiah. Likewise, H. H. Schmid[48] has critiqued the Solomonic date of J, maintaining that parts of the J narrative reveal the influence of later forms and theological development and so must be pushed to the exilic period. According to Schmid, the kind of reflection found in J only occurs when national history is at an end and can be reflected upon. Though Schmid accepts the existence of the sources, J, E, D, and P, his late dating makes the provenance, date, and form of these sources very different from what they are held to be by most source critics. The trend toward later dating is continued in the work of Blum, who argues for an exilic or post-exilic date for both P and D. Though he acknowledges the use of earlier written sources, he does not admit the existence of continuous "documents" passed down for centuries as in the Newer Documentary Hypothesis.[49]

While source criticism has always had its detractors, the past few decades have witnessed an escalation in the level of dissatisfaction with the method in general and in particular with its best-known representative, the Newer Documentary Hypothesis. The most sustained and vehement attack on the Hypothesis is found in R. N. Whybray's *The Making of the Pentateuch: A Methodological Study.*[50] Whybray draws together the arguments of his predecessors, highlighting the inadequacies of the Newer Documentary Hypothesis, its presuppositions, and the criteria upon which it is based. But he goes further in calling for an abandonment of the Documentary Hypothesis, and for its replacement with the view that a single ancient historian wrote about the origins of the world and the people of Israel, possibly as a preface to the Deuteronomistic History. According to Whybray, this historian used sources, but they were of recent origin and were reworked with substantial creative additions of the historian's own, according to the canons of historiography of his day. No attempt was made to eliminate inconsistencies, contradictions, and unevenness. Although most source critics are reluctant to discard the Newer Documentary Hypothesis as readily as Whybray, future source-critical analysis of the Pentateuch must take his work into account, while reevaluating its presuppositions in light of the ever-increasing knowledge of ancient literature and its formation.

The Pentateuch is a large and complex work, and the evidence it supplies is vast and conflicting. So it is not surprising that there are alternate explanations of its formation, none of which is completely satisfactory. Many more complex questions are involved in the determination of sources than was once thought. While it cannot be denied that the biblical authors used sources, serious questions have been raised about the possibility of recovering them. The criteria source critics use are inadequate for identifying sources. For instance, stylistic variation does not always indicate different sources, and variations in vocabulary could be necessitated by a change of topic. Inconsistencies and contradictions may simply result from the presuppositions of ancient authors who do not share our notion of "contradiction."

Source criticism and the Newer Documentary Hypothesis should not be discarded. Rather, both need to be reevaluated and reconceived. We are rightly admonished to exercise caution[51] in our reevaluation of the Newer Documentary Hypothesis, but a wholesale acceptance of the hypothesis that ignores its weaknesses is not advisable either. Certainly we can no longer use the hypothesis as a basis for reconstruction of the history of the religious development of Israel, nor even as a basis for Old Testament theology. Still, it has made a lasting contribution to our understanding of the Bible, moving scholarship away from a naive approach to the biblical text and opening up new possibilities of meaning. It has disabused us of "the notion that the Bible is through and through literal history."[52] For these reasons alone, if for no others, source criticism and the Newer Documentary Hypothesis merit our appreciation.

Notes

1. See, for example, Norman Habel, *Literary Criticism of the Old Testament* (Philadelphia: Fortress, 1971), which is on source criticism.

2. The narrator of 1–2 Kings refers to the Book of the Acts of Solomon (1 Kings 11:41), the Book of the Chronicles of the Kings of Israel (1 Kings 14:19; 15:31; 16:5, 14, 20, 27; 22:39; 2 Kings 1:18; 10:34; 13:8, 12; 14:15, 28; 15:11, 15, 21, 26, 31), and the Book of the Chronicles of the Kings of Judah (1 Kings 14:29; 15:7, 23; 22:45; 2 Kings 8:23; 12:19; 14:18; 15:6, 36; 16:19; 20:20; 21:25; 23:28; 24:5). First and Second Chronicles likewise makes reference to the Book of the Kings of Israel (1 Chron. 9:1; 2 Chron. 20:34), the Book of the Kings of Israel and Judah (2 Chron. 27:7; 35:27; 36:8), the Book of the Kings of Judah and Israel (2 Chron. 16:11; 25:26; 28:26; 32:32), the Commentary on the Book of the Kings (2 Chron. 24:27), and a book called Chronicles (Neh. 12:23).

3. The verbal similarity between 1–2 Chronicles, 1–2 Samuel, and 1–2 Kings suggests that the author of 1–2 Chronicles used 1–2 Samuel and 1–2 Kings as a source in addition to other "chronicles."

4. Already in the twelfth century, Abraham Ibn Ezra, a Jewish commentator, in discussing Gen. 12:6, had problems with the phrase, "When the Canaanites were in the land," noting that it must come from a time after Moses when the Canaanites were no longer in the land. Carlstadt, in *De canonicis scripturis libellis* (Wittenberg: Ioannes Viridi Montanus, 1520), pointed out that the Pentateuch contains Moses' death and burial (Deuteronomy 34) and that it is unlikely that he wrote of these events. Both T. Hobbes, *Leviathan* (London: Andrew Crooke, 1651) and B. Spinoza, *Tractatus theologico-politicus* (Hamburg: Henricus Künraht, 1670) raised questions about Mosaic authorship in the seventeenth century. Richard Simon, a French priest, likewise questioned Mosaic authorship in *Histoire critique du Vieux Testament* (Amsterdam: D. Elzevier, 1678) and was immediately censured by the Church.

5. H. B. Witter in *Jura Israelitiarum in Palaestinam* (Hildesiae: L. Schröderi, 1711) had come to similar conclusions based on the divine name, but his work remained unknown until discovered by A. Lods in *Jean Astruc et la critique biblique au XVIIIe siècle* (Strasbourg: Librairie Istra, 1924); and "Un précurseur allemand de Jean Astruc: Henning Bernhard Witter," *Zeitschrift für die alttestamentliche Wissenschaft* 43 (1925): 134–35.

6. J. Astruc, *Conjectures sur les mémoires originaux dont il paroit que Moyse s'est servi, pour composer le livre de la Genèse* (Brussels: Fricx, 1753).

7. Astruc used the term *Jehovah*, an archaic form of the name *Yahweh*. *Jehovah* resulted from reading the vowels of *'adonay* ("Lord") with the consonants of *Yahweh*. It was used often in the seventeenth and eighteenth centuries but has since been replaced by *Yahweh*.

8. J. G. Eichhorn, *Einleitung in das Alte Testament* (Leipzig: Weidmanns, 1780–1783).

9. A. Geddes, *The Holy Bible*, vol. 1 (London: J. Davis, 1792); *Critical Remarks on the Hebrew Scriptures*, vol. 1 (London, 1800).

10. J. S. Vater, *Commentar über den Pentateuch* (Halle: Waisenhaus, 1802–1805).

11. This is found in Ewald's review of J. J. Stähelin's *Critical Investigation of Genesis* (*Kritische Untersuchungen über die Genesis* [Basel: J. G. Neukirch, 1830]), in *Theologische Studien und Kritiken* 4 (1831): 595–606.

12. H. Hupfeld, *Die Quellen der Genesis und die Art ihrer Zusammensetzung* (Berlin: Wiegandt und Grieben, 1853).

13. M. L. de Wette, *Dissertatio critico-exegetica, qua Deuteronomium a prioribus Pentateuchi libris diversum, alius suiusdam recentioris auctoris opus esse monstratur* (1805).

14. H. Graf, *Die geschichtlichen Bücher des Alten Testaments* (Leipzig: T. O. Weigel, 1866).

15. W. Vatke, *Die Religion des Alten Testaments* (Berlin: G. Bethge, 1835).

16. B. Duhm (*Die Theologie der Propheten als Grundlage für die innere Entwicklungsgeschichte der israelitischen Religion* [Bonn: A. Marcus, 1875]) supported this view, demonstrating that the prophets do not presuppose P or D; rather, D depends on the prophetic movement, and P follows D.

17. The first to attempt a description of Israel's religious development that conformed to the chronology of Graf and Vatke was A. Kuenen, *The Religion of Israel* (*De Godsdienst van Israël* [Haarlem: A. C. Kruseman, 1869–1870]).

18. J. Wellhausen, *Geschichte Israels* (Berlin: G. Reimer, 1878). With the publication of the second edition (1883) the title became *Prolegomena zur Geschichte Israels*; in English it is known as *Prolegomena to the History of Ancient Israel* (Edinburgh: A. & C. Black, 1885).

19. Attempts were made by K. Budde (*Die Bücher Richter und Samuel, ihre Quellen und ihr Aufbau* [Giessen: J. Ricker, 1890)]) to carry the search for the four sources of the Pentateuch into the books of Judges and Samuel. See also R. Smend, "JE in den geschichtlichen Büchern des Alten Testaments," *Zeitschrift für die alttestamentliche Wissenschaft* 39 (1921): 181–217; I. Benzinger, *Jahvist und Elohist in den Königsbüchern* (Berlin: W. Kohlhammer, 1921); O. Eissfeldt, *Die Quellen des Richterbuches* (Leipzig: J. C. Hinrich, 1925) and *Die Komposition der Samuelisbücher* (Leipzig: J. C. Hinrich, 1931).

20. Cf. H. Gressmann, "Die Aufgaben der alttestamentlichen Forschung," *Zeitschrift für die alttestamentliche Wissenschaft* 42 (1924): 8.

21. G. von Rad, "The Form-Critical Problem of the Hexateuch," *The Problem of the Hexateuch and Other Essays* (Edinburgh and London: Oliver & Boyd, 1966), 1.

22. *The Old Testament since the Reformation* (New York: Schocken, 1969), 7.

23. On J see P. F. Ellis, *The Yahwist: The Bible's First Theologian* (Notre Dame: Fides, 1968); H. Bloom, *The Book of J* (New York: Grove Weidenfeld, 1990). On E and P, see A. W. Jenks, *The Elohist and North Israelite Traditions*, Society of Biblical Literature Monograph Series 22 (Missoula, Mont: Scholars Press, 1977); R. B. Coote, *In Defense of Revolution: The Elohist History* (Philadelphia: Fortress, 1991); J. G. Vink, "The Priestly Code," *Oudtestamentische Studiën* 15 (Leiden: E. J. Brill, 1969), to mention but a few. R. E. Friedman's *Who Wrote the Bible?* (New York: Harper & Row, 1987) is remarkable in the utter confidence with which the author expounds on the documentary hypothesis and, indeed, on the authorship of nearly every other book in the Old Testament.

24. For a fuller treatment of Genesis see Habel, *Literary Criticism of the Old Testament*.

25. The similarities between the genealogies can be seen in the following list. The numbers indicate the order in which the names appear; the first name in each unit is from Gen. 4:17–26, the second is from Genesis 5: 1. Adam/1. Adam; 8. Seth/2. Seth; 9. Enosh/3. Enosh; 2. Cain/4. Kenan; 5. Mehujael/5. Mahalalel; 4. Irad/6. Jared; 3. Enoch/7. Enoch; 6. Methusael/8. Methuselah; 7. Lamech/9. Lamech; 10. Noah/10. Noah.

26. B. Jacob, *Das erste Buch der Tora: Genesis übersetzt und erklärt* (Berlin: Schocken, 1934).

27. U. Cassuto, *La Questione della Genesi* (Florence: F. le Monnier, 1934); *The Documentary Hypothesis and the Composition of the Pentateuch*, trans. Israel Abrahams (Jerusalem: Magnes, 1961). Other scholars who have argued for the literary unity of the Pentateuch include Y. Kaufmann, *The Religion of Israel*, trans. M. Greenberg (London: Allen & Unwin, 1960); W. Möller, *Die Einheit und Echtheit der fünf Bücher Mosis* (Solzuflen, 1931); J. Dahse, "Naht ein Umschwung?" *Neue kirchliche Zeitschrift* 23 (1912): 748–56. More recently, the unity of the Pentateuch has been defended on other grounds; cf. Y. Radday and H. Shore, *Genesis: An Authorship Study in Computer-Assisted Statistical Linguistics* (Rome: Biblical Institute, 1985). But see also an evaluation of statistical data that leads to the opposite conclusion, by S. Portnoy and D. L. Petersen, "Statistical Differences among Documentary Sources: Comments on 'Genesis: An Authorship Study,'" *Journal for the Study of the Old Testament* 50 (1991): 3–14.

28. H. Gunkel, *Genesis* (Göttingen: Vandenhoeck & Ruprecht, 1901). The introduction of this book was published in English as *The Legends of Genesis*, trans. W. H. Carruth (Chicago: Open Court, 1901).

29. A. Alt, "The Origins of Israelite Law," *Essays on Old Testament History and Religion*, trans. R. A. Wilson (New York: Doubleday, 1968), 101–71.

30. Von Rad, "Form-Critical Problem of the Hexateuch."

31. M. Noth, *A History of Pentateuchal Traditions*, trans. B. W. Anderson (Englewood Cliffs, N. J.: Prentice-Hall, 1972).

32. R. Rendtorff, *The Problem of the Process of Transmission in the Pentateuch*, trans. J. J. Scullion, JSOT Supplements Series 89 (Sheffield: Journal for the Study of the Old Testament, 1990).

33. E. Blum, *Die Komposition der Vätergeschichte*, Wissenschaftliche Monographien zum Alten und Neuen Testament 57 (Neukirchen-Vluyn: Neukirchener Verlag, 1984).

34. E. Blum, *Studien zur Komposition des Pentateuch*, Beihefte zur Zeitschrift für die alttestamentliche Wissenschaft 189 (Berlin and New York: W. de Gruyter, 1990).

35. I. Engnell, *Gamla Testamentet: En traditionshistorisk inledning* (Stockholm, 1945).

36. This was noted by J. Pedersen in *Israel: Its Life and Culture* (London: Oxford, 1926).

37. For S. Mowinckel ("Der Ursprung der Bil'amsage," *Zeitschrift für die alttestamentliche Wissenschaft* 48 [1930]: 230–71), E is reduced to a series of corrective additions to J. P. Volz (*Der Elohist als Erzähler: Ein Irrweg der Pentateuch-kritik? Beihefte zur Zeitschrift für die alttestamentliche Wissenschaft* 63 [Giessen: A. Töpelmann, 1933]) and later W. Rudolph (*Der "Elohist" von Exodus bis Joshua*, Beihefte zur Zeitschrift für die alttestamentliche Wissenschaft 68 [Berlin: A. Töpelmann, 1938]) adopted a kind of "supplementary hypothesis" in which E ceases to exist as a continuous document and, at best, designates a series of additions to a single document that took place over a long period of time. More recently, J. Van Seters (*Abraham in History and Tradition* [New Haven, Conn.: Yale University Press, 1975]) has expressed doubt about the existence of E, preferring to speak about stages in the development of J, which he dates to the exile.

38. Cf. A. W. Jenks, *The Elohist and North Israelite Traditions* and R. B. Coote, *In Defense of Revolution: The Elohist History* (both cited in n. 23).

39. For example, R. Smend (*Die Erzählung des Hexateuch auf ihre Quellen untersucht* [Berlin: G. Reimer, 1912]) posited two separate strata of writing from the J "school," J[1] and J[2], and von Rad (*Die Priesterschrift im Hexateuch* [Stuttgart and Berlin: W.

Kohlhammer, 1934]) argued that the structure and theology of P shows it to be the combination of two sources, P^A and P^B, the latter being more complex and more priestly in perspective than the former.

40. O. Eissfeldt, *Hexateuch-Synopse* (Leipzig: J. C. Hinrich, 1922). Eissfeldt actually divided J into two sources, calling the earlier one L and the later one J.

41. G. Fohrer, *Introduction to the Old Testament*, trans. David E. Green (Nashville: Abingdon, 1968). Fohrer's N was akin to Eissfeldt's L. Despite its "nomadic" nature, N's theology was as highly developed as J's in Fohrer's view.

42. J. Morgenstern, "The Oldest Document of the Hexateuch," *Hebrew Union College Annual* 4 (1927): 1–138. Morgenstern dated his K source to the reign of King Asa, believing it was produced to support Asa's religious reform.

43. R. H. Pfeiffer, "A Non-Israelite Source of the Book of Genesis," *Zeitschrift für die alttestamentliche Wissenschaft* 48 (1930): 66–73; *Introduction to the Old Testament* (New York: Harper & Brothers, 1941). Pfeiffer dated S to the time of Solomon but believed that it had originated in Edom.

44. Noth, *History of Pentateuchal Traditions*.

45. For example, B. P. Eerdmans (*Alttestamentliche Studien*, 4 vols. [Giessen: A. Töpelmann, 1908–1912]), rejecting the evolutionary model adopted by Wellhausen, sought to show that Israel's religion was not primitive in its early stage. Eerdmans was not alone in attacking Wellhausen's Hegelianism; see also J. Pedersen, "Die Auffassung vom Alten Testament," *Zeitschrift für die alttestamentliche Wissenschaft* 49 (1931): 161–81.

46. A. Welch (*The Code of Deuteronomy: A New Theory of Its Origin* [London: J. Clarke, 1924] and "On the Present Position of Old Testament Criticism," *Expositor* 25 [1923]: 364–65) recognized archaic elements in D and argued that most of the P legislation was preexilic. E. Sellin (*Einleitung in das Alte Testament*, 5th ed. [Leipzig: Quelle & Meyer, 1929]) maintained that the narrative portions of P were as old as J and E. Y. Kaufmann ("Probleme der israelitisch-jüdischen Religionsgeschichte," *Zeitschrift für die alttestamentliche Wissenschaft* 48 [1930]: 23–32; 51 [1933]: 35–47) held that P was entirely preexilic. G. Hölscher ("Komposition und Ursprung des Deuteronomiums," *Zeitschrift für die alttestamentliche Wissenschaft* 40 [1922]: 161–255) went in the opposite direction, abandoning a preexilic date for D.

47. J. Van Seters, *Abraham in History and Tradition* (New Haven, Conn.: Yale University Press, 1975). See also his *Prologue to History: The Yahwist as Historian in Genesis* (Louisville, Ky.: Westminster/John Knox, 1992).

48. H. H. Schmid, *Der sogenannte Jahwist* (Zurich: Theologischer Verlag, 1976).

49. Blum, *Studien zur Komposition des Pentateuch*.

50. R. N. Whybray, *The Making of the Pentateuch: A Methodological Study*, JSOT Supplement Series 53 (Sheffield: Journal for the Study of the Old Testament, 1987).

51. E. W. Nicholson, "The Pentateuch in Recent Research: A Time for Caution," in *Congress Volume Leuven 1989*, ed. J. A. Emerton, Supplements to Vetus Testamentum 43 (Leiden: E. J. Brill, 1991).

52. D. McCarthy, "Twenty-five Years of Pentateuch Study," in *The Biblical Heritage*, ed. J. J. Collins and J. D. Crossan (Wilmington, Del.: Michael Glazier, 1986), 39.

For Further Reading

History, Description, and Application of Source Criticism

Barton, John. *Reading the Old Testament: Method in Biblical Study.* Philadelphia: Westminster, 1984.

Clements, Ronald E. *One Hundred Years of Old Testament Interpretation.* Philadelphia: Westminster, 1976.

Eissfeldt, Otto. *The Old Testament: An Introduction.* Trans. P. R. Ackroyd. New York: Harper & Row, 1965.

Habel, Norman. *Literary Criticism of the Old Testament.* Philadelphia: Fortress, 1971.

Hahn, Herbert F. *The Old Testament in Modern Research.* Philadelphia: Fortress, 1966.

Noth, Martin. *A History of Pentateuchal Traditions.* Trans. B. W. Anderson. Englewood Cliffs, N.J.: Prentice-Hall, 1972.

Petersen, David L. "The Formation of the Pentateuch." In *Old Testament Interpretation: Past, Present, and Future: Essays in Honor of Gene M. Tucker,* ed. J. L. Mays, D. L. Petersen, K. H. Richards. Nashville: Abingdon, 1995.

Wellhausen, Julius. *Prolegomena to the History of Ancient Israel.* New York: Meridian, 1957.

Critique of Source Criticism

Blenkinsopp, Joseph. "The Documentary Hypothesis in Trouble," *Bible Review* (winter 1985).

Nicholson, E. W. "The Pentateuch in Recent Research: A Time for Caution." In *Congress Volume Leuven 1989,* ed. J. A. Emerton. Supplements to Vetus Testamentum 43. Leiden: E. J. Brill, 1991.

Rendtorff, Rolf. *The Problem of the Process of Transmission in the Pentateuch.* Trans. J. J. Scullion. Journal for the Study of the Old Testament Supplement Series 89. Sheffield: Journal for the Study of the Old Testament, 1990.

Van Seters, John. *Abraham in History and Tradition.* New Haven, Conn.: Yale University Press, 1975.

Whybray, R. N. *The Making of the Pentateuch: A Methodological Study.* Journal for the Study of the Old Testament Supplement Series 53. Sheffield: Journal for the Study of the Old Testament, 1987.

3

FORM CRITICISM

MARVIN A. SWEENEY

Definitions

Throughout the twentieth century, form criticism has served as one of the primary exegetical tools in the scholarly interpretation of biblical texts. It is a method of linguistic textual analysis that may be applied both synchronically and diachronically to texts in either written or oral form. Insofar as its object is the interpretation of biblical literature, it functions in tandem with other critical methodologies, such as textual criticism, tradition-historical criticism, redaction criticism, philology, rhetorical criticism, the social sciences, and linguistics, within the broader context of literary criticism. Form criticism focuses especially on the patterns of language that appear within the overall linguistic configuration or form of a text and the role that these patterns play in giving shape and expression to the text.

Form criticism presupposes an intimate relationship between language and the social and literary settings in which it arises and functions. Such settings generate common or recurring conventions of language or genres to meet the needs for human communication and self-expression, and genres in turn influence the settings in which they originate and function. Although a genre arises in a particular setting, it may function in a wide variety of settings other than that in which it originates. It may also be further shaped or developed in relation to the various settings in which it functions. By focusing on the formal shape and content of the text and by correlating that concern with examination of its underlying genres and its social and literary settings, form criticism emerges as a fundamental exegetical method that enables the interpreter to come to an understanding of its communicative functions and effects.

Each text is unique and constitutes a singular event of communication, but the typical conventions of language that function within a specific social or literary context play an important role in achieving the goals of the

58

communication. This applies both to the contemporary and the ancient worlds. The credit card solicitation is a well-known example in which standardized modes of expression contribute to a unique communication that arises from the social context of sales and financing. It typically congratulates the recipient for exemplary management of finances, points out the advantages of consolidating all bills into one low monthly payment, and offers a low, fixed, introductory interest rate together with a hefty credit limit in an effort to entice the recipient to accept a credit card that reverts to relatively standard terms after six months or so. The contemporary novel arises from the social setting of literary artistry and communication. It employs a standard narrative form to develop a plot involving a set of fictional or semifictional characters, a situation that challenges the characters, and a means to overcome the challenge, in an effort to entertain, stimulate, and influence the reader.

The ancient world likewise employed standardized formal language features to facilitate communication. Prophetic speech uses a variety of formal features to validate and convey a prophet's message in an attempt to convince its audience to adopt a specific attitude or course of action because G-d* requires it. For example, the formula, "Thus says YHWH," typically introduces a discourse in which the prophet speaks a message concerning YHWH's expectations of the people. The "regnal reports" of Kings and Chronicles employ a standard form that reports and evaluates the reign of a king. The formulas concerning the beginning of a king's reign and his death and burial encase a report of his life's activities. Such reports provide the basis for an overall evaluation of his reign that contributes to a larger and distinctive interpretative presentation of Israel's or Judah's history that may call for increased observance of YHWH's requirements, the rebuilding of the land of Israel, or the like. In each case, typical genres of expression grow out of the social or literary setting to facilitate unique forms of communication, but they influence it as well by shaping the communication so that it will have some impact on those who read or hear it.

Form and genre are frequently confused, as both function together within various settings to produce communicative texts. Nevertheless, they must be distinguished. Form refers to the unique formulation of an individual text or communication, whereas genre refers to the typical conventions of expression or language that appear within the text. Since form criticism was developed initially by German-speaking scholars, German words are often used in form-critical studies: *Gattung* for "genre," *Sitz im Leben* for "setting in life" or "social setting," and *Sitz im Literatur* for "literary setting."

Editors' note: In accordance with Jewish tradition, Prof. Sweeney shows respect for the deity by not spelling out divine names but rendering them as G-d and L-rd.

Terminology for the method itself likewise appears frequently in German. Thus *Formgeschichte*, "the history of form," and *Gattungsgeschichte*, "the history of genres," designate the method insofar as it is concerned with the development of literary forms and linguistic genres. Otherwise, *Formkritik*, "form criticism," and *Gattungskritik*, "genre criticism," designate the method when it is concerned fundamentally with the synchronic critical analysis of forms and genres.

History of Form Criticism

Like all viable and dynamic currents of thought, form criticism has evolved considerably during the course of its development. Of course, the understanding and articulation of form criticism must be evaluated in relation to the intellectual and theological concerns and presuppositions of the individual form critics themselves and the contexts in which they worked. From the outset, form criticism has been concerned with the interpretation of biblical literature in its present form, particularly in relation to the forms, genres, settings, and intentions of biblical texts. But the history of form-critical research demonstrates a shift from an early focus on the short, self-contained, "original" oral speech unit to an emphasis on the literary and linguistic structures and modes of expression of the much larger textual compositions in which smaller formal units function. Such methodological evolution also entails a shift from a relatively limited and one-sided emphasis on the social realities that stand behind and generate a text to a much broader emphasis on the social and literary realities that generate a text and that are in turn created and sustained by that text. The theological background for such a shift lies in the general development of twentieth-century theological thinking, in which a largely Protestant concern with the origins of religion, specifically the Bible and the events on which it is based, has given way to greater appreciation for the creative role played by later religious traditions and institutions, based especially on the perspectives of Roman Catholicism and Judaism. The sociopolitical background of form criticism lies in the rise of the unified German state in the late nineteenth and early twentieth centuries and the recognition of its failures through the course of World War II and beyond, which prompted reconsideration of its romanticist conceptions of ideal central authority.[1]

The origins of modern form-critical research appear in the writings of Hermann Gunkel (1862–1932). At the outset of Gunkel's career, biblical scholarship was dominated by an interest in the source-critical work of Julius Wellhausen and others who labored to identify the earliest written sources or documents within the present text of the Bible in an attempt to establish the Bible's literary history. Wellhausen's work provided the basis for his reconceptualization of the development of Israelite religion from the emergence of the early Israelite state and its critique in prophetic monotheism to the moral and religious teachings of Jesus. Such concerns must be placed in relation to romanticist attempts to define the character of the emerging German nation by examining the folk traditions of the German people and the Hegelian concept of progressively evolving centralized leadership.

Influenced especially by concerns for establishing the history of a religious tradition and by the folklore research initiated by Wilhelm and Jakob Grimm, Gunkel argued that it is possible to push beyond the earliest written sources of the Bible into the realm of the oral tradition of mythology and folklore that stand behind the biblical text. Such an attempt was warranted by the common belief of the time that the purest and most creative religious expressions were to be found in the earliest stages of human development and that they could be reapplied as an authoritative basis for the advancement of religion in the modern age. To this end, Gunkel argued that the literary creation accounts in Genesis and the visions of the end time in Revelation derived largely from earlier orally transmitted mythological traditions that could ultimately be traced back to Babylonia.[2] In his later commentary on Genesis, he attempted to establish its character not as history but as saga and to trace its tradition history back to the originally oral stories about legendary figures that were told around the campfire by family or tribal units prior to the emergence of a unified Israelite state.[3]

Because of the prevailing view that primitive peoples were relatively simple minded and incapable of memorizing lengthy texts, Gunkel focused his research on the short, self-contained literary units of Genesis, believing that these would best point to the original, short, oral forms of the individual stories that circulated among the people. Gunkel believed that through the course of oral transmission, such short units were brought together in episodic chains to form longer narrative cycles or sagas that focused on a particular theme or subject, such as the establishment of the world (i.e., the primeval history in Genesis 1–11) or the lives of the patriarchs (i.e, the Abraham or Jacob-Esau cycles). Although Gunkel defined textual units by their brevity and self-sufficiency, insofar as they presented a complete plot or set of concerns he noted that various short units shared similar sets of common characteristics that enabled them to be classified as literary types or genres. Such genres include myths about the gods or divine action (Genesis 6–9); historical sagas, which reflect historical occurrences (Genesis 14); and etiologies, which explain the origins of tribal or national relations (Genesis 29–31), names (Genesis 32), ceremonies (Genesis 17), geological features (Genesis 19), and so forth. Gunkel's later research further developed the classification of narrative genres, especially folktales, as well as those of the psalms and prophetic literature.[4]

Throughout his life Gunkel continued to focus on the origins of biblical literature in the short, self-contained, oral unit and its function in the life of ancient Israelite society. But in his later writings and those of his student, Sigmund Mowinckel (1884–1965), a more sustained examination of the setting of textual units began to emerge. Gunkel wrote a commentary on Psalms followed by an introduction to Psalms that was completed after his death by his student, Joachim Begrich.[5] As in his Genesis commentary, Gunkel maintained that the psalms functioned specifically as oral texts in the social life of the Israelite people, particularly in cultic contexts in which the people expressed the various dimensions of their experience of the world and their relationship with YHWH. Gunkel identified several primary genres of psalmic expression: festival hymns, communal complaints, individual complaints, royal psalms, and thanksgiving psalms, each of which was employed in some form of worship service.

Mowinckel affirmed the basic validity of Gunkel's method, but went much further than his teacher in defining the setting in which such poetry functioned.[6] As a Norwegian, Mowinckel was heavily influenced by Scandinavian interest in comparative religions and religious anthropology. Such interest was prompted especially by the presence in northern Scandinavia, Finland, and Russia of the seminomadic Laplanders, whose religious and linguistic traditions demonstrated many similarities with those of various Asian and Native American populations. Mowinckel was less interested in the origins of biblical literature than in the process of oral transmission itself in the life of the Israelite people and therefore concentrated his research less on defining the genres of psalmic poetry than on establishing the setting in which they functioned. Based upon the comparative evidence of the Babylonian Akitu or New Year Festival in which the kingship of Marduk and the Babylonian monarch were simultaneously affirmed and renewed, Mowinckel argued especially for the cultic setting of many of the psalms in an analogous Israelite fall new year festival in which the psalms would have expressed YHWH's renewal of creation, defeat of enemies, and sovereignty. Likewise, his work on the prophets emphasized the role played by schools of prophetic disciples who orally transmitted and elaborated upon the work of the prophetic master until it was written down in the form of the prophetic book.[7] Thus Mowinckel's work is especially important for defining the institutional settings in which Israelite literature developed.

Similar concerns with institutional setting may be seen in the work of Albrecht Alt (1883–1956), another of Gunkel's students. Alt was primarily a historian who was intimately familiar with the geography and archaeological study of the land of Israel. In keeping with the sociopolitical currents in Germany throughout his lifetime, Alt was especially concerned with the formation of the Israelite state and the concentration of its political and religious authority. Alt argued that Israel emerged as various tribal groups peacefully moved into the highlands west of the Jordan River and later came into conflict with the inhabitants of the coastal plain.[8] He argued that Israelite religion emerged from an amalgamation of patriarchal ancestral cults and Canaanite cultic practices that were taken over and adapted by the later Israelite state.[9] His study on the origins of Israelite law[10] noted the distinction between two basic types of law in the Bible: the casuistically formulated laws that began by stating a legal case as a set of circumstances followed by a statement of legal disposition or consequence ("If X event takes place, then the course of legal action to be taken is Y") and the apodictically formulated laws, which state categorically what one shall or shall not do ("Thou shalt not X" or "Cursed is the one who does X"). Based upon the comparative evidence of ancient Near Eastern law codes, Alt argued that the casuistic laws represented a common ancient Near Eastern law form that was taken over by the Israelite tribes when they entered the land and that represented the disposition of actual legal cases in the "secular" Israelite courts. The apodictic legal formulations, however, were unique and represented the legal traditions that the tribes brought with them from the desert when they entered the land of Israel. They functioned especially in a cultic setting, in which YHWH's Torah was read to the people in order to familiarize them with YHWH's requirements and renew the covenant. Mixed forms ("If X takes place, then you shall do Y") represent attempts to combine the legal forms for application in the courts after settlement in the land.

As form-critical research progressed through the period of World War II, German scholars continued to be preoccupied with the underlying questions of state formation and the critique of political power, particularly against the background of the disastrous Nazi state. But they were also increasingly interested in the forms, settings, and functions of larger literary compositions in both oral and written forms. Overall, this resulted in the beginnings of a reconceptualization of form and genre, in that greater attention was paid to the role of genre in the formation of larger texts. Much of the discussion was centered around the work of Alt's students, Martin Noth (1902–1968) and Gerhard von Rad (1901–1971).

Von Rad is especially known for his work in Old Testament theology,[11] but his methodological basis lay in tradition-historical and form-critical research. His early work focused on the formation of the Hexateuch and its role in the development of ancient Israel's theological outlook.[12] Von Rad noted the presence of a number of short, self-contained creedal confessions, such as Deut. 26:5b–9; 6:20–24; and Josh. 24:2b–13, in which brief summaries of YHWH's actions on behalf of Israel pointed to the means by which Israel developed and expressed its theological understanding of history. These creedal statements provided the basis for the collection and organization of various traditions that ultimately were assembled into the Hexateuchal narrative. Von Rad argued that J served as the collector, author, and theologian who assembled the various elements of this material and shaped it into a coherent narrative that provided the basic historical and theological outlook of the newly formed Davidic monarchy. The J narrative was recited to the people in the context of the cultic observance of the festival of Sukkot as a means to establish the identity of the various tribes as a unified nation with a single history and G-d. Von Rad's later work focused on how the J narrative served as the basis for the continued development of the Hexateuch. Ultimately, he applied the model to the entire Bible to demonstrate how salvation history constituted the fundamental theological outlook of Israel and provided the basis for the present form of the Bible. In terms of form-critical methodology, however, he demonstrated how a short genre could expand to constitute a much larger genre and that textual interpretation should not, therefore, focus exclusively on the earliest levels of composition.

Noth was fundamentally a historian, but his research employed form criticism and tradition history.[13] His early work focused on the formation of Israel as a cultic amphictyony in which the twelve tribes united themselves around a cultic center,[14] but his later research focused on the formation of historical traditions and their historiographical perspectives. His study of the Deuteronomistic History noted the presence of various short, self-contained, historical summaries throughout the books of Joshua–Kings (e.g., Joshua 1; 23; 1 Samuel 12) that summed up Israel's historical experience of YHWH and showed great similarities in literary style and theological perspective.[15] On the basis of these and other observations, Noth argued that Joshua–Kings constituted a single "Deuteronomistic History," in which the historian (whom Noth called "Dtr") collected a wide variety of earlier material and assembled it into a single composition that attempted to explain the destruction of the Temple and Israel's exile from the land as YHWH's judgment of the people for their failure to adhere to the covenant as expressed in Deuteronomy. Similar work by Noth pointed to the "Chronicler's History" in the books of Chronicles, Ezra, and Nehemiah. Noth later attempted to define the formation of the Pentateuch as the coalescence at the preliterary stage of five separate tradition complexes centered around distinctive themes—exodus from Egypt, guidance into arable land, promise to the patriarchs, guidance in the wilderness, and revelation at Sinai—again in relation to the formation of Israel's identity as a unified state.[16] His results differed significantly from those of von Rad, but like von Rad he also identified larger literary units as genres and pointed out the creative, authorial role of later redaction.

Claus Westermann likewise has continued to examine the underlying concerns or intentions and generic (i.e., relating to genre) structures that generate biblical texts. His early work focuses especially on cultic laments and hymns of praise, whose surface structures he examines in an effort to define the word of G-d that prompted the psalmist to compose the work in the first place.[17] Similar concerns appear in his studies of Pentateuchal narratives and prophetic speech. His study of Genesis narratives identifies the promise to the patriarchs as a primary concern of the plot, but raises questions concerning the character of the promise as a genre.[18] Fundamentally, the promise is a basic motif of the Genesis narratives, but it can only be identified as a genre when the promise is germane to the resolution of tension in the plot. Otherwise, the narratives vary considerably in form, though the concern with promise remains constant. Finally, Westermann's study of prophetic speech forms points to the messenger speech form and the prophetic judgment speeches as relatively constant underlying features that are expressed in a variety of forms in the surface structure of individual texts.[19] Together von Rad, Noth, and Westermann note the distinction between form and genre and the role that genre plays in establishing form.

These studies stand well within the methodological framework of Gunkel's original program in that they demonstrate a concerted attempt to refine his earlier understandings of form, genre, setting, and intention. Nevertheless, the experience of World War II changed the field of biblical studies in general and form criticism in particular as intellectuals in various fields began to question the preoccupation with tracing the historical development of ideal centralized leadership and authority in both politics and religion. French thinkers in particular began to delve into the fields of linguistics, literature, and sociology, which focused on the masses of people and the function of language in society rather than upon elite leadership and central institutions. The result has been the emergence of methodological pluralism as scholars have experimented with new perspectives from which to interpret literature. Under the influence of such currents, form-critical scholarship and biblical scholarship in general have begun to focus more intently on the literary character of the Bible in its present written form rather than upon its ideal, original, oral forms, and upon the social context of the life of the people in which biblical literature was written, read, and interpreted. The foundations for such concerns were already present in the works of von Rad and Noth, who focused on larger literary compositions, albeit at the oral stage, and in the work of Westermann, who focused on the social and theological preoccupations that are expressed in biblical literature. But impulses from rhetorical criticism, semiotics and linguistics, and cultural anthropology have had a telling effect upon form-critical studies in the latter half of the twentieth century.

Rhetorical criticism is an especially important influence on form criticism in that it points to the unique formulation of each individual text and to its impact upon an audience. In his 1968 presidential address to the Society of Biblical Literature, James Muilenburg noted the limited nature of form criticism's preoccupation with the typical elements of biblical literature.[20] Instead, he highlighted the Bible's literary character and the individual literary formulation of each text that appears within the Bible. In addition, he called for recognition of the function of rhetorical devices within a composition, namely, how the text was formulated to accomplish its goals. Although generic forms may appear within or even constitute a text, each text is unique, and its individual characteristics as well as its typical elements must be examined in order to understand it fully. Recent rhetorical critics have focused especially upon the interaction of text and audience in an effort to understand the rhetorical function of biblical texts.[21] In a similar vein, studies of the performance of oral epic poetry demonstrate that each employs standardized or formulaic forms of expression to produce a unique text in interaction with its audience.[22] Such work has shown that Gunkel's focus on an original, self-contained, oral unit was mistaken.

Muilenburg's call for consideration of the unique formulation of a text coincided with a growing concern among European scholars with linguistics and semiotics and the role that the structures of language play in textual expression. Ferdinand de Saussure argued that each text is a communicative event in which the basic linguistic elements of *langue*, the common structures of expression in a linguistic system, and *parole*, the individual forms of expression in which a text appears, combine to produce the communication.[23] In his study of Russian folklore, Vladimir Propp further distinguished the roles of the "actant," who sends communication according to his or her own presuppositions and intentions, and the "receiver," who receives the communication and understands it in relation to his or her own linguistic and conceptual context.[24] When Klaus Koch applied these principles to form-critical research, *langue* and *parole* emerged respectively as the underlying genres that inform the composition of a text and the individual literary structure of its presentation.[25] The actant and the receiver correspond to the distinction between the intentions of an author and the understanding and subsequent interpretation of a redactor who redefines the meaning of the earlier text and places it into a new textual setting. Such a conception is important for the redaction-critical study of biblical literature as well, in that it provides a basis for distinguishing the concerns and understandings of an original author from that of a later redactor. Koch's commentary on Amos attempts to demonstrate these principles with a detailed analysis of the linguistic structure of the text coupled with analyses of the common structures of ancient Hebrew expression, the social settings of its oral and literary forms, and the preoccupations of its authors and redactors.[26]

Wolfgang Richter has further refined the linguistic basis for form-critical research by arguing that exegesis must be first and foremost a literary science.[27] He also contends that the exegete must be prepared to engage the text on the basis of its linguistic structures, including both its form and content, i.e., the outer form of its literary or linguistic expression (cf. *parole*) and the inner form or the deep structure of the concepts that it communicates (cf. *langue*). Richter distinguishes between the *Sitz im Leben* (social setting) of the linguistic system in which language functions and the *Sitz im Literatur* (literary setting) in which the text appears. The text must first be analyzed according to its syntactical, semantic, and pragmatic linguistic features in order to identify its underlying generic structures and concerns. Although Richter focuses largely on the synchronic level, a major goal of his research is to identify tensions within the text as a means to reconstruct its diachronic or redactional history. In large measure this focus is based on his definition of smaller, closed, linguistic units as the basis for exegesis and examination of their interrelationship within the larger text. Unfortunately, this definition unduly influences the interpretation of texts by introducing redaction-critical criteria at the outset of exegesis, that is, his focus on the short unit determines his view of the whole rather than vice versa. Indeed, redaction criticism is the final step in his obligatory sequence of methods. Richter's students have attempted to address the problem by focusing especially upon the syntactic and semantic forms of expression in the final form of the text as the basis for exegesis, although their concerns frequently return to redaction criticism.[28]

More recently, Rolf Knierim has pointed more forcefully to the synchronic dimensions of biblical literature and to the underlying conceptual structures that generate the present form of the text.[29] He does not abandon diachronic concerns. Rather, he argues that redaction criticism takes place at the outset of exegesis in that the interpreter is faced with the final redactional form of the text, in which earlier text forms have been subsumed by redactors, who select, modify, supplement, and reconceive earlier texts in accordance with their own purposes and presuppositions. But Knierim maintains that the text must be understood first in its final form prior to drawing conclusions concerning its literary history. The exegete cannot assume that earlier text forms appear in the present form of the text. Knierim presupposes the work of the structural anthropologist, Claude Lévi-Strauss, who argued that the deep structures of the human mind are based in the structure of language that in turn is derived from and defines the social structure of the society in which it functions.[30] Such deep structures play a role in creating genres, but different genres within a text are not to be identified as the deep structures; they are generated by the deep structures and preoccupations of the human mind, and individual texts employ them within their larger semantic and literary structure. The exegete therefore cannot be limited to the analysis of short, self-contained units, although they will appear as components of the larger text. Instead, the synchronic literary structure of the text must be analyzed first in its full form in order to identify the underlying conceptions and presuppositions or assumptions that both generate the text and are expressed in it. The larger structure of the text then enables the exegete to come to decisions concerning the place of smaller units within the whole. Redaction-critical concerns no longer determine the overall interpretation of the text. Like Richter, Knierim presupposes the inseparability of form and content, but he does not presuppose a literary history for the text. According to Knierim, redaction-critical reconstruction may proceed only if inner tension in the text points to a literary prehistory. In sum, Knierim emphasizes analysis of the text in and of itself, rather than a preconception of what the text should be, as the basis for establishing its presuppositions, intentions, and basic conceptual structure.

Under the influence of the text-linguistic and literary-synchronic approaches of Richter and Knierim, form criticism is well placed in the late twentieth century to address the synchronic interpretation of large literary units, such as the Deuteronomistic History, the prophetic books, or wisdom compositions such as Proverbs or Job. This is particularly important in relation to other critical methodologies, such as canonical criticism, narratology, and poetics. Insofar as biblical books appear in their final, edited forms, form criticism provides the basis for both the synchronic and the diachronic interpretation of biblical literature. Form criticism serves as the indispensable basis for redaction-critical study. It provides the tools by which the interpreter may assess the form, genres, settings, and intentions of the present biblical text in order to determine whether or not earlier text forms may be identified, and it enables the interpreter to assess any earlier text forms that may be reconstructed from the present text. Hence, the form critic must be prepared to consider multiple forms, genres, settings, and intentions in the interpretation of the biblical text throughout its literary history. This has tremendous implications for the concept of setting in form-critical scholarship, because it requires the consideration of various types of settings—sociological, historical, and literary—as well as multiple expressions of each. Although a text may be composed in relation to a specific context and set of concerns, it will be read in relation to later literary, historical, and social settings, according to the presuppositions and concerns that are operative in those later contexts. The present writer's commentary on Isaiah 1–39 attempts to address the interrelationship between synchronic and diachronic interpretation by assessing the formal characteristics of texts throughout four stages in the composition of the book of Isaiah.[31]

Form criticism is uniquely suited among the critical methodologies in biblical exegesis to address both synchronic and diachronic issues in the interpretation of the biblical text. Insofar as it is able to interact fruitfully with other critical methodologies, it will continue to serve as a fundamental method of biblical interpretation. In addition to studies cited above, current form-critical work appears in the Forms of the Old Testament Literature commentary series, as well as in the works of many scholars on different parts of the Bible.[32]

An Illustration of Form Criticism at Work

In order to understand the present state of form-critical study, it will be necessary to discuss its basic components—form, genre, setting, and intention—in relation to the interpretation of a specific biblical text. Genesis 15 provides an ideal example: It is a foundational text for understanding the covenant between YHWH and Israel through Abraham; various genres appear within the present form of the text; its presence in the Pentateuch indicates that it has gone through several stages of composition; and it has been understood by later readers to express important theological principles, such as justification by faith (Christianity) and possession of the land of Israel (Judaism).[33]

Form

The first component of a form-critical analysis is assessment of the form of the text in question, and textual demarcation is the essential first step in such an assessment. Basically this entails defining the boundaries of the text, i.e., determining where it begins, where it concludes, and why. A combination of factors relating to form and content play a role in this decision. Formulaic language that typically introduces or concludes a textual unit may mark its beginning. Examples include, "And it came to pass that . . ."; "In the year that . . ."; "Thus says YHWH . . ."; "These are the words of . . ."; and "A song of ascents . . ." Similar formulas may mark a text's end: ". . . and the land had rest for forty years"; ". . . and X slept with his fathers, and Y reigned in his stead"; ". . . utterance of YHWH"; "This is the Torah for . . ."; "In that day . . ." Motifs within the text, such as a change of character, event, setting, or the overall concern of the text, also play an important role in assessing its form. Although early form critics generally assumed that a well-defined, self-contained unit constituted an originally independent text, subsequent research has demonstrated that the interpreter cannot make this assumption, since such a self-contained unit may also constitute a component of a much larger whole.

Genesis 15 functions at several levels as a component of a larger narrative concerning the history of Israel through the exile (Genesis–Kings); this larger narrative includes the formative history of Israel, the ancestors of Israel (Gen. 11:27–50:26), and the Abraham/Sarah cycle (Gen. 11:10–25:11) or the narrative concerning the descendants of Terah (Gen. 11:27–25:11). Nevertheless, Genesis 15 is easily demarcated by its formal features and contents. The typical introductory formula, "After these things . . ." (cf. Gen. 22:1; 22:20; 39:7; 40:1; 48:1) introduces the beginning of a new episode in the context of the larger narrative by referring back to previous events. Likewise, the formula, "On that day," introduces the summation of YHWH's actions in verses 18–21 in a manner that commonly introduces the concluding segments of prophetic compositions (e.g., Isa. 2:20–22; 4:2–6; 11:10, 11–16; Ezek. 29:21; 30:9; 39:11–16; Zeph. 3:16–20; Zech. 3:10; 14:20–21). In addition, in Genesis 15 the narrative shifts from concern with Abram's rescue of Lot and other Sodomites in Genesis 14 to a concern with YHWH's promise to Abram. In Genesis 16, the narrative begins with a focus on Sarai (who had not been mentioned in Genesis 15) and the birth of Ishmael. Throughout Genesis 15, the concern is YHWH's promises of descendants and land to Abram. The summation in verses 18–21 ties both descendants and land together in YHWH's promise. Based upon form and content, Gen. 15:1–21 constitutes a coherent, well-defined textual unit.

The second step in form-critical analysis is an assessment of the literary structure of the text. Again this requires close attention to the formal features of the text in relation to its contents. Fundamentally, this includes the syntax or sentence structure of the unit and its semantic features, that is, the use and function of its words, phrases, expressions, and so forth. Genesis 15 is a narrative that conveys its action and ideas on the basis of a dialogue or, more properly, an action-response sequence in which two major characters, YHWH and Abram, each speak or act in response to the other. Earlier form critics argued that Genesis 15 comprises two basic structural subunits: verses 1–6, which take up the promise of descendants to Abram, and verses 7–21, which take up the promise of land.[34] Unfortunately, this determination was based in part on diachronic or redaction-critical criteria: verses 1–6 and 7–21 were seen to be two originally separate units within the text. Although there are ample grounds for these redaction-critical conclusions, the introduction of such diachronic criteria at this point unduly influences the synchronic analysis of literary structure. A synchronic analysis of the formal syntax indicates that the structure of Genesis 15 is based on a series of four verbs conjugated in the perfect tense that convey the successive stages of the narrative: "the word of YHWH was unto Abram" (v. 1); "and behold, the word of YHWH [was] unto him" (v. 4); "and he believed YHWH" (v. 6); and "On that day, YHWH cut with Abram a covenant" (v. 18). With the exception of verse 18, each perfect verb introduces a *waw*-consecutive sentence structure, a typical biblical Hebrew narrative form that conveys a sequence of action that follows from the initial finite (in this case, perfect) verb. Each verb in the sequence is formulated as a *waw*-consecutive imperfect conjugation: "and he said" (v. 2), "and he brought him out" (v. 5), and so forth. Verses 18–21 do not require a *waw*-consecutive verbal sequence as they do not convey further action beyond that of verses 1–17. Instead they present a statement by YHWH that summarizes the contents of verses 1–17. The result is a syntactical structure of four components: verses 1–3; 4–5; 6–17; and 18–21. The contents of each component or subunit define its role within the sequence of actions and motifs presented in the text as a whole. Further consideration of form and content within each subunit establishes its internal structure.

Genesis 15:1–3 introduces the text by stating its initial premises or tensions: YHWH's promise to Abram that his "reward" will be great and Abram's response that he is childless and therefore has no heir to whom to pass this "reward" after he dies. Verse 1 employs the perfect verbal statement, "the word of YHWH was unto Abram in a vision," to convey YHWH's promise of a "reward." The term "reward" (Hebrew, *śkr*) means "hire, fee, payment" and generally refers to wealth, but the text does not specify until later what this "reward" will be. Verses 2–3 convey Abram's response with two statements, each of which begins with a *waw*-consecutive imperfect verb, "and he [Abram] said." In the first statement (v. 2), Abram points out that he is childless, and that Eliezer of Damascus (the capital of ancient Aram or Syria) will be the "heir of my house." In the second statement (v. 3), Abram reiterates this problem by stating that YHWH has not given him "seed" (i.e., children) and that "a slave of my house" will possess or inherit his wealth. The statement in verse 3 employs the Hebrew verb *yôrēš*, a technical term that means "to inherit, take possession." The terms "heir of my house" and "a slave of my house" are difficult to interpret. "Heir of my house" is *ben-mešeq* in Hebrew, literally, "a son of *mesheq*." In the present context it is clearly a word play on Damascus, *dammešeq* in Hebrew, although the roots of the two words are not the same. Insofar as the meaning of *mešeq*, "heir," appears to be derived from an analogy with *mešek*, "possession," it likely serves as a technical term for an adopted heir. "A slave of my house" is literally "a son of my house," which also conveys the sense of adoptive heir, i.e., a son who is not born to Abram but who has entered his house by other means, such as adoption or purchase. Some take "son of my house" literally and argue that Abram asks a sarcastic question of YHWH, "shall my own son inherit (when I have no son)?" In either case, verses 1–3 lay out the tension that is at work in the narrative as a whole.

Verses 4–5 resolve the initial tension of verses 1–3 by presenting YHWH's promise of a son to Abram. The subunit begins with a statement in verse 4 based upon a perfect verbal conjugation, "and behold, the word of YHWH [was] unto him, saying . . ." which introduces YHWH's promise. In keeping with common Hebrew artistic style in parallel statements, the perfect verb "was" does not appear, since it is implied in the nearly identical verse 1. YHWH then makes an explicit promise that a natural son, not Eliezer, will inherit Abram's wealth. Verse 5 employs three *waw*-consecutive verbs to convey YHWH's actions and statements that validate and explain the promise that Abram's descendants will be as numerous as the stars of the heavens. Although verses 4–5 resolve the initial tension of verses 1–3, they also build toward the main subunit of the text in verses 6–17 in which YHWH promises the land of Canaan/Israel to Abram. Indeed, such large numbers of descendants require a land in which to live. In this respect, verses 4–5 leave open another question or tension from verses 1–3: what is Abram's "reward?"

In terms of both formal characteristics and content, Gen. 15:6–17 constitutes the literary "goal" of the chapter in that it is the largest subunit of the text and conveys YHWH's promise of land to Abram together with an implicit promise of descendants (v. 13). It begins with the statement in verse 6 of Abram's reactions to YHWH's promise of verses 4–5, formulated initially with a perfect verbal form ("And he believed YHWH and considered him [YHWH] to be right"). The balance of the subunit employs a *waw*-consecutive sequence to convey the exchange of words and actions between Abram and YHWH: YHWH identifies the divine self to Abram, and promises him the land in verse 7; Abram responds to YHWH, asking how he will know that this promise will be realized in verse 8; YHWH instructs Abram to prepare animals for a ritual that is commonly employed in the sealing of an ancient Near Eastern covenant or treaty in verse 9 (see further under genre); Abram does as he is instructed in verses 10–11; and YHWH states the future to Abram in a vision, including Israel's sojourn in a foreign land and Abram's peaceful death in old age, in verses 12–17. The term "deep sleep" (Hebrew, *tardēmāh*) in verse 12 frequently describes sleep or a trance state instigated by supernatural agency (Gen. 2:21; 1 Sam. 26:12; Isa. 29:10; Job 4:13; 33:15; Dan. 8:18; 10:9) and indicates the visionary context signaled in verse 1. The phrase, "know this for certain," in verse 13 is emphatic and validates YHWH's contentions. The "smoking fire pot and flaming torch" in verse 17 is a common representation of deities in Babylonian incantation texts; here it provides a symbolic image by which to represent YHWH passing through the pieces of the animals in a manner that will not compromise divine sanctity (cf. Ezekiel 1).[35] By passing through the pieces, YHWH signs or seals the covenant with Abram.

The role of Gen. 15:6 in relation to the structure and content of Gen. 15:6–17 requires further discussion. Verse 6 is normally taken as the conclusion to verses 1–5, but the initial perfect verbal form, "and he [Abram] believed YHWH," identifies it formally as the beginning of the unit in verses 6–17. Although Abram's response of belief in YHWH is a natural conclusion to draw from the preceding statement of YHWH's promises in verses 1–5, the placement of verse 6 at the head of verses 6–17 has several important interpretative consequences. First, verse 6b follows immediately upon verse 6a, in which Abram serves as subject. The failure to specify a subject in verse 6b indicates that Abram remains the subject of the verb. Second, verse 6 establishes the continuity of verses 1–3 and 4–5 with verses 6–17, indicating that in its present form Genesis 15 as a whole forms a coherent unit even if it does have a literary prehistory. Third, the statement in verse 6b, "and he reckoned it to him as righteousness," is frequently understood as YHWH's reckoning Abram righteous for his faith (Gal. 3:6–9; Heb. 11:8–12), but this is to read Paul's understanding of justification by faith back into the text of Genesis. Normally, righteousness, like purity, is "reckoned" or "imputed" to human beings in a cultic context (Deut. 24:13; Ps. 106:31; cf. Lev. 7:18; 13:17, 23, 28, etc.; 17:4), but the larger narrative framework of the Abraham/Sarah narratives must play a role in interpretation here. Throughout the Abraham/Sarah cycle, Abraham's righteousness is never questioned, but YHWH's is. Abraham does everything that YHWH requires, from moving to an unknown foreign land ((Genesis 12) to offering his son as a sacrifice (Genesis 22). YHWH, on the other hand, makes promises of descendants and land to Abraham, promises that come into question throughout the narrative as Sarah has no son up to Genesis 20, and YHWH demands the sacrifice of Isaac in Genesis 22. Indeed, Abraham must take the moral high ground in Genesis 18 when he demands to know if YHWH will kill the righteous with the wicked at Sodom. Fourth, if YHWH's granting of the land to Abram is conditioned on YHWH's deciding whether or not Abram is righteous, then one must conclude that YHWH's prior promises of land to Abram in the narrative (Gen. 12:7; 13:17) are not entirely sincere, which is the issue Abram raises in Gen. 15:2. Fifth, if verse 6 concludes verses 1–5 or verses 4–5, Abram's subsequent request for validation from YHWH suggests that in fact he does not believe YHWH. The placement of verse 6 at the beginning of a subunit in verses 6–17 indicates that verses 7–17 explain why Abram believes YHWH, i.e., YHWH gives Abram a sign. In the Hebrew Bible signs are a common means of validating a statement, especially a prophetic statement (cf. 1 Sam. 10:1–16; Isa. 7:1–25). The reader should bear in mind that the temporal sequence of Genesis 15 does not fully follow the narrative sequence; Gen. 15:1 states that YHWH speaks to Abram in a vision, but the visionary context is not evident until verses 12–17. Genesis 15:6 indicates Abram's perspective as a result of his encounter with YHWH, but at the outset of this encounter, the narrative provides ample evidence that Abram would have reason to question YHWH.

Finally, Gen. 15:18–21 discontinues the pattern of dialogue or action and response. Although YHWH speaks in verses 12–17, the text does not revert to Abram for his reaction; the reader already knows Abram's reaction from verse 6. Instead, it employs a narrative statement formulated with a perfect verb, "On that day YHWH cut with Abram a covenant, saying . . ." and a quote by YHWH to explain the meaning of what is presented in the preceding material, namely, YHWH cut a covenant with Abram to give him the entire land. The reference to the ten Canaanite peoples apparently is intended to represent all of the peoples who inhabited the land prior to Israel.

The form of Genesis 15 may be represented as follows:

Narrative Report of YHWH's Covenant with Abram   Gen. 15:1–21

    I. YHWH's promise of "reward" to Abram   1–3

        A. YHWH's word to Abram: expressed in vision   1

        B. Abram's response: no heir   2–3

           1. First response: I am childless   2

           2. Second response: "son of my house"
              (adoptive son) will inherit   3

    II. YHWH's promise of descendants to Abram   4–5

        A. First word: descendants from your loins will inherit   4

        B. Subsequent actions and statements concerning
           descendants:
           descendants will be like stars   5

    III. Abram's response to YHWH's promise of land:
        belief that YHWH is right   6–17

        A. Basic statement of Abram's belief in YHWH   6

        B. YHWH's promise of land to Abram   7

        C. Abram's request for confirmation   8

        D. YHWH's instruction to prepare for covenant
           ratification ritual   9

        E. Abram's compliance   10–11

        F. Report of ritual during Abram's "deep sleep" (trance)   12–17

Identifying this four-part structure of Genesis 15 leads to some important interpretive conclusions. The structure conveys four basic assertions in the text: (1) YHWH promises a "reward" to Abram but does not specify what the reward is or to whom it will be passed (vv. 1–3); (2) in verses 4–5 YHWH promises descendants to Abram, which resolves one of the tensions in verses 1–3; (3) Abram believes YHWH, based upon a sign presented to him in a vision (vv. 6–17); and (4) the encounter is identified as a covenant made by YHWH with Abram, which identifies the earlier "reward" as the land of Canaan/Israel. The literary structure of the text points to its "deep structure" or "conceptual structure," in which YHWH is obligated to provide Abram with descendants and land, but no obligations are defined for Abram. Descendants and land are clearly interrelated in the present form of the text; numerous descendants require a place to live, and a land requires people to tend to it. Furthermore, the structure of the text points to YHWH as the questionable figure in the relationship, as the reader is left to ponder whether or not YHWH will fulfill this covenant. Abram's role is clear—he believes YHWH and considers YHWH to be trustworthy.

Genre

The second stage in a form-critical analysis is to assess the genres that appear within the present form of the text. Essentially, this calls for the comparative identification of typical language forms in the text that appear elsewhere in biblical and ancient Near Eastern literature. It also calls for discussion of the typical social and literary settings in which such generic language functions as a basis for assessing its role within the present text. Of

course, attempts to reconstruct genres are constrained by the limited surviving textual base for ancient Near Eastern cultures and the inability to
observe directly the use of language in these ancient cultures.

Fundamentally, Genesis 15 constitutes a narrative that employs elements
of dialogue or personal interaction in its portrayal of YHWH's concluding a
covenant with Abram. In addition, it contains a number of generic forms
that function within the narrative context. The first is the formula, "the
word of YHWH was unto Abram, saying . . ." in verse 1. This formula is
known technically as the Prophetic Word Formula. It appears frequently in
narrative and prophetic literature as a typical means of introducing and
identifying a prophetic word or oracle (e.g., 1 Sam. 15:10; 1 Kings 6:11;
Jer. 7:1; 11:1; 33:19, 23). It may be formulated as a first person statement,
such as, "the word of YHWH came to me, saying . . ." (Jer. 1:4, 11; 2:1; Ezek.
6:1; 7:1). It also appears in the superscriptions to prophetic books as a
means of identifying the following material as prophetic oracles from
YHWH (Hos. 1:1; Joel 1:1; Micah 1:1; Zeph. 1:1). This formula presupposes the social setting of prophetic oracular reception and the reporting or
announcement of such oracles to some outside audience that either hears or
reads the announcement.

The presence of this formula in Genesis 15 is particularly striking in that
it presents Abram as a prophet or at least an individual who experiences a
prophetic vision. This, of course, ties in to the notice that Abram experiences the word of YHWH "in a vision" (v. 1). The term "vision" (Hebrew,
maḥăzeh), typically refers to prophetic oracular experience that includes
both visual and auditory aspects (Num. 24:4, 16; Ezek. 13:7). Here it points
to the vision experienced by Abram in verses 12–17, in which YHWH
appears to Abram while he is in a "deep sleep" or "trance," and informs
Abram of Israel's upcoming four hundred years of forced service in a foreign
land, YHWH's judgment of that nation and granting wealth to Israel,
Abram's peaceful death in old age and burial, and the return of the fourth
generation. In the context of the Pentateuchal narrative, this vision refers
to Israel's slavery in Egypt, YHWH's deliverance of Israel from Egypt
through Moses, Abraham's peaceful death at the age of 175 and his burial
at Machpelah, and the return of Israel to the land following the generation
of Joseph and his brothers. The language relating to the genre of prophetic
oracles or visionary experience functions as a means of pointing to the
future plot of the Pentateuch. It thereby aids in accomplishing two goals
within the present narrative. First, it validates YHWH's promises to Abram.
Of course, Abram will not see the full realization of this schema apart from
this visionary experience, but the vision provides sufficient basis for him to
accept YHWH's promises or covenant as valid, especially when he sees his
own son Isaac and lives to a full age. Second, the vision validates YHWH's

promises to the reader, who will in fact see the realization of the schema as she or he progresses through the Pentateuch. It thereby provides sufficient basis for the reader to accept YHWH's promises or covenant as valid.

The second example of generic language in Genesis 15 is the appearance of the salvation oracle genre in YHWH's initial statement to Abram, "Do not be afraid, Abram, I am your shield; your reward shall be very great" (v. 1). The typical reassurance formula, "Do not be afraid" ('al tîrā'), appears frequently throughout the Bible and the ancient Near East as the identifying phrase in oracles that promise salvation or reassurance (Isa. 7:4–9; 37:5–7; 41:8–13, 14–16; 43:1–7; Psalms 12; 35; 91; 121). The speaker can be a prophet (2 Kings 6:16; Isa. 10:24–27), YHWH (Gen. 26:24; Deut. 3:2; Josh. 8:1), or other people (Gen. 35:17; 42:23; Num. 14:9; 1 Sam. 22:23). The form appears to presuppose a situation of oracular inquiry (cf. Isa. 37) and therefore relates to the prophetic word formula discussed above. Again, this form plays a role in validating YHWH's promise by portraying Abram as the recipient of a prophetic or oracular vision.

The third example of generic language in Genesis 15 is the terminology that is bound up with the issue of Abram's descendants who will possess his "reward" (vv. 1–3, 4–5).[36] Here the language is not formulaic, but a number of technical terms appear that are related to the generic situation of inheritance in ancient Israel and the Near East. The key terms are various forms of the verb "possess" (yāraš), which refers to the inheritance of property (2 Sam. 14:7; Jer. 49:1; Micah 1:15; Prov. 30:23) and the terms "the heir of my house" (v. 2) and "a slave born of my house" (v. 3), which refer to the potential heirs of Abram's estate in the absence of a son. Ancient Israelite and Near Eastern law stipulates that the son or sons of a man shall inherit his property at death (Deut. 21:15–17; cf. Gen. 21:9–13; 27:1–40; 48:13–49:4; 1 Kings 1:15–21; Hammurabi Law Code, 165–176[37]). In the absence of a son, ancient Near Eastern legal codes allow a man to designate another as his heir, including a slave born in his extended household, which is precisely the situation in the present text. Obviously, this language aids in raising the issue of Abram's succession and the possession of the land that YHWH will grant him later in the text. Once again, this language addresses the validity of YHWH's covenant with Abram, for without children the covenant and the promise of land are entirely meaningless. Insofar as the reader knows that Abram's covenant stands as the basis for YHWH's relationship with Israel, the issue is the validity of YHWH's covenant. The identification of Eliezer of Damascus as a potential heir raises a question: In the absence of a people Israel, do the covenant and land then transfer to Aram/Syria? The present form of Genesis 15 asserts that they do not.

The fourth generic form in Genesis 15 involves the self-identification formula in verse 7, "I am YHWH who brought you out from Ur of the

Chaldeans to give to you this land to possess it." In biblical literature, this formula typically functions as part of the "prophetic proof saying," in which the identity of YHWH as the source of a prophetic oracle is established (1 Kings 20:13, 28; Isa. 41:17–20; 49:22–26; Ezek. 25:2–3, 6–7; 26:2–6). It functions in relation to the prophetic or oracular genres previously discussed and aids in validating YHWH's promise to Abram.

But the self-identification formula also relates to language pertaining to a fifth genre in Genesis 15. The expression in verse 18 reads literally, "On that day, YHWH cut with Abram a covenant." The expression "to cut a covenant" is a standard idiomatic form for expressing the making of a treaty in ancient Israel and the Near East.[38] The expression derives from the practice of sacrificing animals as part of the process of ratifying a treaty between two nations. Parties to a treaty walked between the halves of severed animals as a graphic portrayal of what would happen to them if they did not abide by the terms of the treaty ("As this calf is cut up, thus Matti'el and his nobles shall be cut up [if Matti'el is false]).[39] This practice apparently stands behind YHWH's instructions to Abram to cut several sacrificial animals in half so that YHWH, represented by the smoking fire pot and flaming torch, can pass between the pieces. In effect, YHWH "signs" or "affirms" the treaty, which validates YHWH's promises. Interestingly, Abram undertakes no action to ratify the covenant. The self-identification formula also plays a role in establishing the genre of Genesis 15, because suzerain kings typically identify themselves at the beginning of a treaty (e.g., "The treaty which Esarhaddon, king of the world, king of Assyria, son of Sennacherib, likewise king of the world, king of Assyria, with Rataia, city ruler of . . ."[40]) Furthermore, such treaties typically deal with the control of land as the suzerain monarch grants the right to a lesser vassal king, under specified conditions, to rule land without undue interference and to pass on the land to his sons as royal heirs.

Finally, YHWH's statement in verse 18, "To your descendants I have given this land from the River of Egypt to the great river, the River Euphrates," constitutes a standard oath, in which a party to a treaty binds itself to certain obligations. In the present instance, YHWH obligates the divine self to provide Abram's descendants with the land of Canaan/Israel. Again, the oath aids in validating YHWH's promise. Likewise, the formula "in that day" is a typical form employed in prophetic literature to announce a future event. This formula is part of the prophetic genres discussed above and aids in validating YHWH's promise.

In sum, a variety of expressions typical of genres from the spheres of prophecy, family property inheritance, and covenant or treaty making appear in Genesis 15. All of the genres combine in the present form of the text to validate YHWH's promise of descendants and land to Abram.

Setting

Although early form-critical scholarship emphasized the role of the social setting (*Sitz im Leben*) in the interpretation of biblical texts, more recent scholarship has recognized the roles of both literary settings and historical settings in the assessment of the social setting of a text. Indeed, the three settings are not to be equated, since each pertains to a specific set of questions concerning the context or matrix from which the text is generated and in which it functions. Nevertheless, the three are interrelated. Historical setting frequently plays a key role in defining the nature of the social setting. The social settings of the Israelite monarchy and priesthood, for example, appear to be very different in the tenth, eighth, and sixth centuries B.C.E. as the realities and roles of each institution changed over the course of time. Likewise, literary setting also plays a key role, especially since the basis for reconstruction of the social setting of a text must lie in the literature itself, which in turn functions in a literary context that has some bearing on how that literature is shaped and understood.

The preceeding discussion of genre established that Genesis 15 includes language from three major generic categories: oracular prophecy, family succession and property inheritance narrative, and treaties between nations in the ancient Near East. Each of these genres derives from a specific social setting that must be considered in the form-critical interpretation of Genesis 15.

The generic language pertaining to oracular prophecy raises the question as to whether Genesis 15 was generated in relation to the social setting of prophecy. Certainly, Abram is presented as receiving a prophetic vision while in a state of "deep sleep" or "trance." Typically, prophets might isolate themselves and deliver oracles in such a state of trance. Moses' speaking to YHWH in the wilderness tent of meeting (Exod. 33:7–11; 34:29–35), YHWH's revelation to Samuel in the Shiloh sanctuary (1 Samuel 3), and Ezekiel's breaking silence to deliver oracles to the Judean elders (Ezek. 3:22–27; 8–11; 14) are examples of such activity. Although the language portrays Abram in prophetic terms, there is little indication that the text itself derives from the social context of oracular prophecy. Specific prophetic concerns appear to play no role in the narrative, and Genesis elsewhere shows little interest in portraying Abram or the other ancestors in prophetic terms. The motif appears to function primarily as a means of signaling the future plot of the Pentateuchal narrative and of conveying YHWH's covenant with Abram. This language may derive from the social context of oracular prophecy, but it functions as a literary device in Genesis 15.

The terminology of inheritance and family succession in Genesis 15 appears to be the technical language employed in legal codes that define such matters, even though Genesis 15 is certainly not a legal text designed to set policy concerning inheritance and succession in the Israelite family. But issues of succession and inheritance do not pertain only to the family sphere in ancient Israel; they pertain to the monarchy and priesthood as well, in that both institutions employ a dynastic principle in determining succession to the throne or to priestly office. Abram is portrayed vaguely in priestly terms here, insofar as he receives oracular communication and prepares the sacrificial animals for the making of a treaty, but his role in this text and elsewhere does not appear to be primarily that of a priest. There are royal connotations in Abram's presentation, however, that must be considered.[41] Throughout the Genesis narrative, Abram is closely associated with the city of Hebron—indeed he is buried there—a city that served as the capital of the tribe of Judah and the seat of David's first kingdom (2 Samuel 2–5). Abram acts in a manner analogous to that of a king: He walks the length of his land and founds cultic sites (Genesis 12), allocates land to family members (Genesis 13), goes to war to protect them (Genesis 14), decides the fate of family members under his authority (Genesis 16; 21), stands up even to YHWH in order to maintain justice within his sphere (Genesis 18), arranges a marriage for his son with a foreign principal (Genesis 24), and enters into covenants (Genesis 15; 17).

The language pertaining to covenant making likewise points to a royal setting. As noted in the previous discussion of genre, the assignment of land, the ritual of passing through the pieces of slain animals, and YHWH's self-identification formula all derive from the sphere of ancient Near Eastern treaty making. The social setting, then, is that of international relations in the ancient world, and this again points to the monarchy as the principal party involved in the making of such treaties. Indeed, the most telling aspect of Abram's royal presentation is the definition of the land YHWH promises him as "this land from the River of Egypt to the great River, the River Euphrates," for this is also the definition of the land claimed for David in 2 Samuel 8 (cf. Numbers 34; Ezek. 47:13–20). The royal context is confirmed by the portrayal of the land as Abram's "reward," or spoil of war, and by the assignment of the land to Abram's "seed," a designation that also appears in the language of YHWH's promise to David of an eternal dynasty ("When your days are fulfilled and you lie down with your fathers, I will raise up your offspring [seed] after you, who shall come forth from your body, and I will establish his kingdom" [2 Sam. 7:12]). Genesis 15 portrays Abram in Davidic terms as the founder of a dynasty that will possess a land.

These considerations demonstrate that the social setting of Genesis 15 derives from the institutional setting of the royal house of David, inasmuch as it presents Abram as a precursor or model for the later Davidic monarchy. Like David, Abram is promised descendants and a land, and just as YHWH "makes firm" (*ne'man*) David's house (2 Sam. 7:16; 1 Kings 11:38) and expects David's descendants to hold faith (*he'ĕmîn*) with YHWH (Isa 7:9), so Abram believes (*he'ĕmîn*) in YHWH (Gen. 15:6).

This, of course, raises the question of the historical setting of Genesis 15. Based upon the identification of Genesis 15 as part of the J stratum of the Pentateuch, which is commonly dated to the time of the early Davidic monarchy in the tenth century, it would be easy to maintain that Genesis 15 is designed to justify the rule of the Davidic house over all Israel by pointing to Abram's covenant as a model for the claims of the Davidic house. But several factors call for caution. First, scholars persistently argue that E source elements, deriving from the Northern Kingdom in the eighth century, appear in the narrative, and many argue that J must be assigned to a date much later than the tenth century. Furthermore, the prophetic word formula appears especially frequently in literature that derives from the later period of the monarchy (Jer. 1:4, 11; 2:1; 7:1; 11:1; Zeph. 1:1) or even the exile and beyond (Ezek. 6:1; 7:1; Joel 1:1), and the influence of treaty language is especially pronounced during the eighth and seventh centuries B.C.E., when Assyria imposed its power and treaties on Israel and Judah. It was in the aftermath of the Northern Kingdom's and later Assyria's collapse that the Davidic monarchy under Hezekiah and later Josiah attempted to reassert Davidic claims to rule the entire land of Israel. Although it is possible to date Genesis 15 with its concern for Israelite/Davidic possession of the land to the period of the early monarchy, it is equally possible to read the chapter in relation to the interests of the Davidic monarchy in these later periods.

Finally, the literary context of Genesis must also be considered. As noted in the preceeding discussion, Genesis 15 functions within the context of the larger Abraham and Sarah cycle, in which the dominant motif is YHWH's promise of a son to Abram. The narrative highlights this fact at the very outset (Gen. 11:30) and returns to the theme of Abram's descendants repeatedly throughout (Gen. 12:1–3, 7, 10–20; 13:14–18; 16; 17; 18:9–15; 20; 21; 22). Indeed, the question as to whether YHWH will keep the promise to Abram is the basic motif of the entire Abraham and Sarah narrative from its outset in Genesis 11 to the threat of Isaac's sacrifice in Genesis 21. Such a question is pertinent to the early period of the monarchy as narrative tension concerning YHWH's promise to Abram would speak both to the narrative resolution of the issue and to the establishment of the Davidic house, especially at the succession of Solomon. These concerns would also be pertinent to the eighth and seventh centuries, when the Davidic house was attempting to reassert itself in the aftermath of Israelite and Assyrian collapse, and in the period of the exile, when the future of the Davidic house was in question. The relationship of the covenant in Genesis 15 to that in Genesis 17 is pertinent to this latter context. YHWH undertakes action to ratify the covenant in Genesis 15, whereas Abram does nothing; but in Genesis 17 Abraham undertakes the ritual of circumcision as a sign of his acceptance of the covenant. In the present form of the narrative the two texts must be read together, as they signify YHWH's and Abraham's entry into a covenant relationship. The fact that Genesis 17 presents Abraham in priestly terms, however, may speak to the realities of the exilic or postexilic periods, when the role of the royal house diminished and the priesthood became more prominent. The royal portrayal of Abram in Genesis 15 is now qualified by a priestly portrayal of Abraham in Genesis 17.

Intention

The concluding stage of form-critical analysis is the attempt to establish intention in the text. Intention in form-critical research refers to the meanings conveyed by a text on the basis of its unique literary form, the generic language that constitutes that form, and the settings from which the text derives and in which it functions. In other words, what does the text say based upon its formal features? Thus much of the intention of Genesis 15 appears in relation to the previous discussion of its form, genres, and settings.

Intention has become a very controversial feature of form-critical scholarship in recent discussions of exegetical theory. The controversy pertains to the identification of a text as a linguistic communicative entity and the interrelationship between its two primary communicative aspects—the "sender," who generates or employs the text in an attempt to communicate a message, and the "receiver," who interprets the text and thereby understands. The issue revolves around the fact that the messages sent by the sender and perceived by the receiver might not be the same. Furthermore, there can be multiple senders and receivers of a text, depending on the setting in which the text functions. These issues are particularly important in relation to redaction criticism and reader-response theory.

With regard to redaction criticism, exegetical theorists recognize that the intention of the author of a text may differ markedly from that of its redactor who reads and interprets it, edits it by adding or deleting material or by reworking the earlier text in some manner, or places it into another literary context. Authors and redactors are not the same; they do not share the same perspectives or worldviews, nor do they work in the same social, historical, or literary contexts. The result may be a text that is deliberately changed in the course of redaction as the later writers reformulate it to serve their own interpretative agendas and needs. The interrelationship between Samuel-Kings and Chronicles provides an example, since Chronicles appears to be a rewritten version of Samuel-Kings. The result of redaction may not be deliberate change in the text, but change in its sociohistorical or literary context that in turn influences its interpretation. The placement of the oracles of Isaiah ben Amoz in the later context of the book of Isaiah is an example. Whereas the original oracles of Isaiah, many of which appear in their original forms in Isaiah 1–39, speak to Israel's and Judah's experience in the Assyrian period, they are applied to the Babylonian and Persian periods when they are placed in the context of a book that contains the works of Deutero-Isaiah (Isaiah 40–55) and Trito-Isaiah (Isaiah 56–66) as well.

The issues surrounding intention pertain not only to ancient readers, but to modern ones also. Recent developments in reader-response theory point to the modern reader as interpreter and thus pose problems similar to those presented by redaction criticism. Every reader comes to a text with her or his own worldview, experience, and perspectives, and on the basis of those factors interprets the text with questions and presuppositions that derive from that worldview. Many reader-response critics question whether it is even possible to establish the original meaning of a text or the intentions of its author when that author is no longer available. Even if the author were available, the interrelationship of reader and text can render the author's intention irrelevant. Once the text is created, it exists as an entity unto itself that achieves meaning only when it is read. For many critics, meaning lies only in the reader, not in the text or the intentions of its author. Any construction of the author's intention necessarily represents the perspective and biases of the reader.

As these examples indicate, the interpretation of a text represents an interaction between the text and its interpreter, one that raises questions concerning the validity of attempts to reconstruct the intention or meaning of a text in relation to its sociohistorical setting or settings. Nevertheless, the form critic must keep in mind that, whatever the perspectives or biases of the reader, readings are based on a text that was written by an author or authors who wrote with well-defined intentions in specific sets of sociohistorical circumstances. Modern readers may have to identify their own perspectives and biases and those of earlier readers, and it may not be entirely possible to do so with full certainty, but attempting to do so is simply a necessary aspect of textual interpretation. The logical alternative is to give up the enterprise of textual interpretation altogether or to accept any interpretative assertion as valid regardless of the criteria, or lack thereof, employed to produce it. The interpreter must keep in mind that no interpretation is absolute; each interpretation is inherently hypothetical and must be made on the basis of a self-critical analysis of available data.

With these considerations in mind, analysis of the formal features of Genesis 15 points to an overall concern with the continuity of YHWH's covenant with Israel, including its identity as a people and its possession of the land of Israel. This is evident in the four-part formal structure of the passage, which points to (1) concern with possession of the land of Israel, based upon its identification as Abram's "reward" that will be passed to his heirs (vv. 1–3), (2) concern with the continuity of Israel as a people based upon its descent from Abram (vv. 4–5), (3) Abram's belief in the sincerity of YHWH's commitment to these promises based upon a sign that confirms YHWH's truthfulness and formal ratification of the covenant by YHWH (vv. 6–17), and (4) identification of the previous assertions and actions as a covenant in which YHWH obligates the divine self to provide Abram's descendants with the land of Israel defined according to the boundaries presented in the text (vv. 18–21). By highlighting Abram's belief in YHWH and considering YHWH to be righteous in the largest and most elaborate subunit of the passage (vv. 6–17), the text asserts that there is a basis for accepting YHWH's fidelity to the covenant as valid. Indeed, it is noteworthy that Abram does nothing but believe or accept YHWH's assertions in this text, thus emphasizing YHWH's credibility.

Furthermore, the generic language of the passage points to its social setting in the Davidic monarchy, which indicates that YHWH's promise of people and land must be understood in relation to the royal house of David. This social setting raises a number of interesting interpretative questions, since the concerns inherent in the text may be read in relation to a variety of historical and literary contexts. Much depends upon a redaction-critical analysis of Genesis 15, which is not possible in this article. Nevertheless, redaction critics have traced the composition of the book of Genesis through several layers from the tenth–ninth century J stratum of the Pentateuch to the fifth–fourth century P stratum. Hence, Genesis 15 might presuppose a secure Davidic state, such as that of Solomon, which justifies its existence and ideology by pointing to the patriarch Abram as the paradigm on which the Davidic monarchy is based. Or it might presuppose a situation in which the Davidic monarchy feels threatened by internal or external foes, such as the tenth century revolt of the northern tribes or the eighth century Assyrian invasions, and seeks to defend itself from criticism by pointing to Abram's covenant as a basis for its existence. It might also apply to resurgent Davidic states, such as those of Hezekiah or Josiah, which sought to reassert their claims over territory based upon Abram's covenant. The reference to Eliezer of Damascus would be particularly germane in the eighth century, when the Arameans played a key role in placing their allies on the northern Israelite throne, which resulted in Israel's challenge to Assyria and the Northern Kingdom's ultimate destruction. Finally, the social setting in the Davidic monarchy can also point to a situation of threat or disruption in which the Davidic monarchy had ceased to function and an attempt was made to revive it or to reinterpret the covenant. This might apply to the sixth century exilic period or the postexilic period from the late sixth century and beyond when attempts were made to revive the monarchy (Haggai), or to a situation in which the Davidic promise was applied to the people in general and not necessarily to a Davidic king (Isaiah 55). Indeed, Genesis 15 functioned in social settings and literary contexts well beyond the time of its composition, as shown by Paul's use of the passage to undergird his doctrine of justification by faith or by Judaism's understanding of it as a theological basis for the modern state of Israel.

Conclusion

Form criticism has clearly demonstrated its capacity for development and change over the course of its century-long history of research as it has interacted with a variety of other critical methods applied in biblical exegesis. Insofar as it provides the tools by which to assess the overall linguistic form and content of a biblical text while continuing to interact with other critical methods, form criticism is well positioned to serve as a fundamental method of biblical exegesis well into the twenty-first century.

Notes

1. For surveys of the development of biblical exegesis in general, see Robert Morgan with John Barton, *Biblical Interpretation*, The Oxford Bible Series (Oxford: Oxford University Press, 1988) and Hans-Joachim Kraus, *Geschichte der historisch-kritischen Erforschung des Alten Testaments von der Reformation bis zur Gegenwart* (Neukirchen-Vluyn: Neukirchener Verlag, 1969).

2. Hermann Gunkel, *Schöpfung und Chaos in Urzeit und Endzeit* (Göttingen: Vandenhoeck & Ruprecht, 1895).

3. See H. Gunkel, *Genesis*, 9. Auflage mit einem Geleitwort von Walter Baumgartner (Göttingen: Vandenhoeck & Ruprecht, 1977), first published as Handkommentar zum Alten Testament I/1 in 1901.

4. For example, H. Gunkel, *The Folktale in the Old Testament*, trans. Michael D. Rutter; Historic Texts and Interpreters in Biblical Scholarship (Sheffield: Almond Press, 1987); German edition, 1917.

5. H. Gunkel, *Die Psalmen*, Handkommentar zum Alten Testament II/2 (Göttingen: Vandenhoeck & Ruprecht, 1926); H. Gunkel and Joachim Begrich, *Einleitung in die Psalmen*, Handkommentar zum Alten Testament, supplement (Göttingen: Vandenhoeck & Ruprecht, 1933).

6. Sigmund Mowinckel, *Psalmenstudien I–VI* (Kristiania: J. Dybwad, 1921–24) and *The Psalms in Israel's Worship*, 2 vols., trans. D. W. Ap-Thomas (Nashville: Abingdon, 1962); Norwegian edition, 1951.

7. Cf. S. Mowinckel, *Prophecy and Tradition: The Prophetic Books in Light of the Study of the Growth and History of the Tradition* (Oslo: J. Dybwad, 1946).

8. Albrecht Alt, "The Settlement of the Israelites in Palestine," *Essays on Old Testament History and Religion*, trans. R. A. Wilson (Garden City, N.Y.: Doubleday, 1967), 173–221; German edition, 1925.

9. A. Alt, "The God of the Fathers," *Essays on Old Testament History and Religion*, 1–100; German edition, 1929.

10. A. Alt, "The Origins of Israelite Law," *Essays on Old Testament History and Religion*, 101–71; German edition, 1934.

11. Gerhard von Rad, *Old Testament Theology*, 2 vols., trans. D. M. G. Stalker (New York: Harper & Row, 1962–65); German editions, 1957–1960.

12. "Hexateuch" refers to the first six books of the Bible. Some source critics before and during von Rad's career traced the Pentateuchal sources into the book of Joshua as well. See G. von Rad, "The Form-Critical Problem of the Hexateuch," *The Problem of the Hexateuch and Other Essays* , trans. by E. W. Trueman Dicken (London: SCM, 1984), 1–78; German edition, 1938.

13. See, for example, Martin Noth, *The History of Israel*, trans. S. Godman (New York: Harper & Row, 1960); German edition, 1954.

14. M. Noth, *Das System der zwölf Stämme Israels*, Beiträge zur Wissenschaft vom Alten und Neuen Testament IV/1 (Stuttgart: W. Kohlhammer, 1930).

15. M. Noth, *Überlieferungsgeschichtliche Studien: Die sammelden und bearbeitenden Geschichtswerke im Alten Testament* (Halle: Max Niemeyer, 1943).

16. M. Noth, *A History of Pentateuchal Traditions*, trans. B. W. Anderson (Englewood Cliffs, N.J.: Prentice-Hall, 1972); German edition, 1948.

17. Claus Westermann, *The Praise of God in the Psalms*, trans. Keith R. Crim (Richmond: John Knox, 1965); German edition, 1961.

18. C. Westermann, "Arten der Erzählung in der Genesis," *Erforschung am Alten Testament*, Theologische Bücherei 24 (Munich: Chr. Kaiser, 1964), 9–91.

19. C. Westermann, *Basic Forms of Prophetic Speech, with a New Foreword by Gene M. Tucker*, trans. H. C. White (Cambridge: Lutterworth; Louisville, Ky.: Westminster/John Knox, 1991); German edition, 1960.

20. James Muilenburg, "Form Criticism and Beyond," *Journal of Biblical Literature* 88 (1969): 1–18.

21. Phyllis Trible, *Rhetorical Criticism: Context, Method, and the Book of Jonah*, Guides to Biblical Scholarship (Minneapolis: Fortress, 1994).

22. Albert B. Lord, *The Singer of Tales* (New York: Athenaeum, 1974); first published 1960.

23. Ferdinand de Saussure, *Course in General Linguistics*, trans. W. Baskin (New York: Philosophical Library, 1959); French edition, 1916.

24. Vladimir Propp, *Morphology of the Folktale*, trans. L. Scott (Austin: University of Texas, 1968).

25. Klaus Koch, "Linguistik und Formgeschichte," *Was ist Formgeschichte? Methoden der Bibelexegese*, 3d ed. (Neukirchen-Vluyn: Neukirchener Verlag, 1974), 173–97.

26. K. Koch et al., *Amos: Untersucht mit den Methoden einer strukturalen Formgeschichte*, Alter Orient und Altes Testament 30, 3 vols. (Neukirchen-Vluyn: Neukirchener Verlag; Butzon & Bercker, 1976).

27. Wolfgang Richter, *Exegese als Literaturwissenschaft: Entwurf einer alttestamentlichen Literaturtheorie und Methodologie* (Göttingen: Vandenhoeck & Ruprecht, 1971).

28. Cf. Harald Schweizer, *Metaphorische Grammatik: Wege zur Integration von Grammatik und Textinterpretation in der Exegese*, Arbeiten zu Text und Sprache im Alten Testament 15 (St. Ottilien: EOS, 1981) and Walter Gross, *Die Satzteilfolge im Verbalsatz alttestamentlicher Prosa*, Forschungen zum Alten Testament 17 (Tübingen: J. C. B. Mohr [Paul Siebeck], 1996).

29. Rolf Knierim, "Old Testament Form Criticism Reconsidered," *Interpretation* 27 (1973): 435–68; "Criticism of Literary Features, Form, Tradition, and Redaction," in *The Hebrew Bible and Its Modern Interpreters*, ed. D. A. Knight and G. M. Tucker (Chico, Calif.: Scholars, 1985), 123–65; and *Text and Concept in Leviticus 1:1–9*, Forschungen zum Alten Testament 2 (Tübingen: J. C. B. Mohr [Paul Siebeck], 1992).

30. Claude Lévi-Strauss, *Structural Anthropology*, trans. C. Jacobson and B. G. Schoepf (Garden City, N.Y.: Doubleday, 1967); French edition, 1958.

31. Marvin A. Sweeney, *Isaiah 1–39, with an Introduction to Prophetic Literature*, The Forms of the Old Testament Literature 16 (Grand Rapids and Cambridge: Eerdmans, 1996).

32. Among the most important such works for different parts of the Hebrew Bible are Suzanne Boorer, *The Promise of the Land as Oath: The Key to the Formation of the Pentateuch*, Beihefte zur *Zeitschrift für die alttestamentliche Wissenschaft* 205 (Berlin and New York: W. de Gruyter, 1992); Frank Crüsemann, *The Torah: Theology and Social History of Old Testament Law*, trans. A. W. Mahnke (Minneapolis: Fortress, 1996); German ed. 1992; Michael Floyd, "Prophetic Complaint about the Fulfillment of Oracles in Habakkuk 1:2–17 and Jeremiah 15:10–18," *Journal of Biblical Literature* 110 (1991): 397–418; and Christof Hardmeier, *Texttheorie und biblische Exegese: Zur rhetorischen Funktion der Trauermetaphorik in der Prophetie*, Beiträge zur evangelischen Theologie 79 (Munich: Chr. Kaiser, 1978).

33. For commentaries and studies of Genesis 15 see especially George W. Coats, *Genesis, with an Introduction to Narrative Literature*, The Forms of the Old Testament Literature 1 (Grand Rapids: Eerdmans, 1983); Gerhard von Rad, *Genesis, A Commentary*, Old Testament Library, trans. John H. Marks (Philadelphia: Westminster, 1972); Claus Westermann, *Genesis 12–36, A Commentary*, trans. J. J. Scullion (Minneapolis: Augsburg, 1985); David Carr, *Reading the Fractures of Genesis: Historical and Literary Approaches* (Louisville, Ky.: Westminster John Knox, 1996); and John Van Seters, *Prologue to History: The Yahwist as Historian in Genesis* (Louisville, Ky.: Westminster John Knox, 1992).

34. See the commentaries by Coats, von Rad, and Westermann.

35. See Ephraim A. Speiser, *Genesis*, Anchor Bible 1 (Garden City, N.Y.: Doubleday, 1964), 113–14.

36. On the background of this chapter in relation to ancient Near Eastern inheritance law, see especially Nahum Sarna, *Understanding Genesis* (New York: Schocken Books, 1966), 120–36.

37. "The Code of Hammurabi," trans. Theophile J. Meek, in James B. Pritchard, ed., *Ancient Near Eastern Texts relating to the Old Testament*, 3d ed. (Princeton, N.J.: Princeton University Press, 1969), 173–74.

38. For a discussion of ancient Near Eastern treaty practices, see Moshe Weinfeld, "The Covenant of Grant in the OT and in the Ancient Near East," *Journal of the American Oriental Society* 90 (1970): 184–203.

39. Sfire treaty IA, trans. Franz Rosenthal, in Pritchard, *Ancient Near Eastern Texts*, 660.

40. D. J. Wiseman, "The Vassal-Treaties of Esarhaddon," *Iraq* 20 (1958): 30.

41. Cf. Ronald Clements, *Genesis XV and Its Meaning for Israelite Tradition*, Studies in Biblical Theology II/5 (Naperville, Ill.: Allenson, 1967) and Van Seters, *Prologue to History*, 248–51.

For Further Reading

Form-Critical Theory and the History of Development

Hayes, John H., ed. *Old Testament Form Criticism*. Trinity University Monograph Series in Religion 2. San Antonio: Trinity University Press, 1974.
————. "Old Testament Form Criticism Reconsidered," *Interpretation* 27 (1973): 435–68.
Knierim, Rolf. "Criticism of Literary Features, Form, Tradition, and Redaction." In *The Hebrew Bible and Its Modern Interpreters*, ed. Douglas A. Knight and Gene M. Tucker. Chico, Calif.: Scholars, 1985.
Koch, Klaus. *The Growth of the Biblical Tradition: The Form-Critical Method.* Trans. S. M. Cupitt. New York: Scribner's, 1969.
Richter, Wolfgang. *Exegese als Literaturwissenschaft: Entwurf einer alttestamentlichen Literaturtheorie und Methodologie*. Göttingen: Vandenhoeck & Ruprecht, 1971.
Schweizer, Harald. *Metaphorische Grammatik: Wege zur Integration von Grammatik und Textinterpretation in der Exegese*. Arbeiten zu Text und Sprache im Alten Testament 15. St. Ottilien: EOS, 1981.
Steck, Odil Hannes. *Old Testament Exegesis: A Guide to Its Methodology*. Trans. James D. Nogalski. SBL Resources for Biblical Study 33. Atlanta: Scholars, 1995.
Sweeney, Marvin A. "Formation and Form in Prophetic Literature." In *Old Testament Interpretation: Past, Present, and Future; Essays in Honor of Gene M. Tucker*, ed. James Luther Mays, David L. Petersen, and Kent Harold Richards. Nashville: Abingdon, 1995.
Tucker, Gene M. *Form Criticism of the Old Testament*. Guides to Biblical Scholarship. Philadelphia: Fortress, 1971.

Forms of the Old Testament Literature Commentary Series

Coats, George W. *Genesis, with an Introduction to Narrative Literature*. FOTL 1. Grand Rapids: Eerdmans, 1983.
Collins, John J. *Daniel, with an Introduction to Apocalyptic Literature*. FOTL 20. Grand Rapids: Eerdmans, 1984.
De Vries, Simon J. *1 and 2 Chronicles*. FOTL 11. Grand Rapids: Eerdmans, 1989.
Gerstenberger, Erhard S. *Psalms, Part 1, with an Introduction to Cultic Poetry*. FOTL 14. Grand Rapids: Eerdmans, 1988.
Hals, Ronald M. *Ezekiel*. FOTL 19. Grand Rapids: Eerdmans, 1989.

Long, Burke O. *1 Kings, with an Introduction to Historical Literature*. FOTL 9. Grand Rapids: Eerdmans, 1984.

———. *2 Kings*. FOTL 10. Grand Rapids: Eerdmans, 1991.

Murphy, Roland E. *Wisdom Literature: Job, Proverbs, Ruth, Canticles, Ecclesiastes, Esther*. FOTL 13. Grand Rapids: Eerdmans, 1981.

Sweeney, Marvin A. *Isaiah 1–39, with an Introduction to Prophetic Literature*. FOTL 16. Grand Rapids and Cambridge: Eerdmans, 1996.

4

TRADITION-HISTORICAL CRITICISM

ROBERT A. DI VITO

What Is Tradition-Historical Criticism?

To think of tradition-historical criticism of the Bible as a "method" may be misleading. To begin with, the word "method" itself evokes thoughts of a commonly agreed-upon procedure for reading the text that will yield to every reader objective results, that is, "correct" interpretations of the text. On this understanding, the method controls the reading of the text and guarantees the validity of the results obtained, chiefly by eliminating those subjective intuitions and prejudices of the reader that are thought to falsify understanding. Obviously, the ideal here is that of the natural sciences with their goal of producing results that are always and everywhere valid for anyone who follows the same procedure. Yet it is not at all clear that such an ideal is appropriate for humanistic disciplines such as biblical criticism. The successful act of reading is precisely the one that engages a reader, in the way a great work of art does, in an interpretive enterprise that knows no end and is in principle new on each act of reading.[1]

In this sense, tradition criticism is no less "methodical" than any other form of biblical criticism. But there is another sense in which the application of the word "method" to tradition criticism can be a source of confusion. The traditional methods of textual criticism, source criticism, and form criticism present a more or less systematic body of specific procedures for analyzing a text according to certain guidelines. But tradition criticism lacks any generally accepted techniques or evaluative criteria of its own. Indeed, it cannot be viewed simply as one method among other methods of biblical criticism. Tradition criticism is at once less and more than other types of criticism. It is less because it is entirely dependent upon their procedures; but it is also more because it represents an approach to the biblical text that formulates investigative goals for synthesizing the manifold conclusions arrived at through "other" methods. Put simply, it formulates

the use of results obtained from the operation of several distinct methodologies, but above all from source- and form-critical studies.[2]

Although the word "tradition" can be so broad in its meaning as to
embrace the entire ongoing life, customs, and practices of a group or community over successive generations, it is used here in a narrower sense to
refer specifically to verbal tradition, that is, to words and texts transmitted
from one generation to the next orally and/or by means of writing.[3] Examples
include proverbs, riddles, songs, poems, epics, and various kinds of folk narratives. While theoretically originating with "someone," such traditions are
essentially anonymous in character, being developed and shaped over the
course of their transmission by the group or groups who have a direct interest in their preservation and for whom they play a vital role. In that sense,
whatever their origin, traditions become the common property of a community or a group, alive only as long as they are functional in meeting the
evolving needs of the group. Necessarily, then, traditions must change, or
develop, over the course of their transmission if they are to continue to be
viable. They can enjoy only a relative degree of stability over time.

The degree to which traditions change over the course of their transmission is variable for another reason. One must reckon with such factors
as, for example, whether the transmitted material is memorized verbatim
(which is the exception) or handed down in a freer form (the normal mode
of transmission), and whether written versions exist that can act, in some
fashion, as standards for its accurate transmission.[4] As a living process
engaging the interests and concerns of traditionists (those who hand on a
tradition), the only rule the transmission of tradition knows is change. Even
the wording of a memorized speech (e.g., a prayer or a song) varies over the
course of time, as does the degree of fixity that a written tradition can
achieve. For that, among other things, depends on the degree and kind of
authority a written tradition possesses.

Put simply, then, tradition-historical criticism seeks to reconstruct the
history of the transmission of the various individual traditions and tradition
complexes that are to be found in the Old Testament. Beginning with a
recognition of the historicalness of the Bible and its contents, it views the
Old Testament and its various component parts as a body of largely "traditional" literature. This means that unlike the free creation of an individual
author (in the modern sense of the word), the Bible is the product of a long
process of composition and transmission. Moreover, it is a process that quite
often did not begin simply with the writing of those texts that eventually
comprised the books of the Bible or even the earlier written sources utilized
in them. The process that tradition-historical criticism envisions and, in
fact, is most concerned with extends back beyond the written stage of the
Bible's formation to embrace stages that can be discerned in the preliterary

history of a textual unit. For many tradition historians it is really this oral stage of a tradition's composition and transmission that is of utmost importance for understanding its particular characteristics.

Tradition-historical criticism, in other words, deals with the entire sweep of history that a tradition passes through, from its earliest beginning as an independent tradition unit to its final elaboration and expression within the Bible. It embraces both the oral phase of a tradition's composition and transmission as well as its "recomposition" in writing and final literary redaction. For the Old Testament this can, of course, mean a history extending over the course of a thousand years. Nevertheless, the goal is to reconstruct within that long history the various stages a particular tradition, or tradition unit, passed through in its growth and development. Indeed, it may even include a tradition's "postliterary" history—that is, how it finally fits within broad intellectual currents that characterized the life of ancient Israel (e.g., the wisdom movement or the Deuteronomic movement).

To achieve such a comprehensive view of a tradition's history, tradition-historical criticism necessarily presupposes and utilizes the results of textual criticism, source criticism, form criticism, and redaction criticism. This is not difficult, because, for all their differences, each is always directly concerned with the course of the Bible's composition. So textual criticism seeks to recover as far as possible the earliest stages of a text's actual wording on the basis of extant Hebrew manuscripts and ancient versions. For its part, source criticism investigates the literary plan or structure of a text, its themes and language, with a view to determining its integrity (that it stems from a single author) or the degree of its compositeness. If the text turns out to be composite, source criticism attempts to discern the relationship of the compositional elements to each other (older/primary versus younger/secondary) and the nature of those elements (i.e., are they derived from other, perhaps larger written documents, as fragments, or are they redactional supplements to the text, such as introductions, conclusions, or explanatory glosses?).[5] Such an analysis of the written development of a textual unit might further be complemented by redaction criticism, with its particular emphasis on describing how these various compositional elements eventually came together to produce the text in its present form and what intentions or concerns guided those responsible for it. Nevertheless, the key role in tradition history is played by form criticism.

Form criticism represents the indispensable means of tradition history; it investigates precisely the crucial preliterary history of a text thought to contain ancient tradition, as well as traditional formulas that occur within it. Indeed, it is largely only through form-critical work that the tradition historian is able to identify a textual unit as a piece of tradition as opposed to the free creation of an author. This it characteristically accomplishes by recognizing that a given unit, whether prose or poetry, is an instance of an originally oral genre (e.g., historical tale, proverb, psalm, prophetic saying), with a characteristic content and the product of a particular kind of recurrent situation or situations (e.g., instruction, worship), which specifically shaped its intentions or goals. While a recognition of the genre to which a unit belongs does not in itself guarantee the antiquity of a particular unit, it goes a long way toward showing the possibility. And historically, form criticism has expended much effort in determining not only the genre to which a text belongs but also the earliest form, or forms, of the unit that might be recognizable over the course of its literary and especially preliterary (oral) transmission. Along with a determination of a unit's original setting-in-life (*Sitz im Leben*), this provides tradition history with the analysis and material necessary to reconstruct the history of a particular tradition or tradition complex. Such reconstruction is the comprehensive goal of tradition history.

Up to this point, we have restricted our discussion of tradition-historical criticism to one of the two facets of verbal tradition, namely, that of the viewpoint of the material handed down (*traditum*). But, as mention of a unit's *Sitz im Leben* suggests, tradition-historical criticism is also concerned with the process (*traditio*) by which this material is passed down from generation to generation.[6] Clearly, without an exploration of the forces and influences that exerted themselves on a tradition in the process of its transmission, little headway will be made in reconstructing the individual stages a particular unit of tradition went through. Under this rubric, tradition-historical criticism moves in several different directions,[7] among which three lines of research are particularly prominent.

First, form criticism's determination of the setting(s)-in-life of a particular tradition provides what is in many cases the only point of departure for ascertaining the group or the community responsible for the development and transmission of a tradition, the so-called traditionists. Quite simply, the more we know about such traditionists and their institutional commitments—the more we know about the social, political, and religious forces that operated through them and on them—the more we can understand the real meaning of a tradition and the vital role it played in the life of ancient Israel. Examples of such groups in ancient Israel are the priests at the local shrines or the Temple in Jerusalem, the bands of disciples of the great prophets, and the so-called "wise."

Second, the geographical area or location with which a tradition is associated is a topic of interest to tradition history. Through the localization of a tradition (e.g., the association of early exodus traditions with the north or messianic traditions with Judah), its interpretation acquires the kind of specificity and concreteness that allows us to appreciate a tradition's historical significance and function within the life of ancient Israel. The localization of tradition allows one to bring to bear on its interpretation whatever knowledge we possess of the various historical, geographical, economic, and cultural-political forces affecting a locale and its population. Such forces comprise the matrix that nourished the growth of tradition and shaped its ongoing formation.

A third line of research important to tradition-historical criticism is the study of the processes by which the creation and transmission of tradition take place. This means not only an investigation of "authorial" and scribal practices in the ancient Near East and the extent and nature of written communication but especially of the nature and dynamics of oral composition and oral transmission. For the latter, contemporary folklore studies, based on present-day oral cultures, have become absolutely indispensable, since the only access we have to oral tradition in the ancient world is filtered through written materials. Given how little we know about ancient society, a host of questions arises. For example, what kind of stability and longevity can be expected of oral tradition? Who is responsible for a society's oral memory? What techniques are used in the composition and transmission of oral literature? Are different kinds of materials handled in different ways? What are the role and extent of memorization and improvisation in the transmission of tradition? What is the relation between written and oral communication? What precipitates the writing down of an oral tradition and what changes does it undergo in the process? Such questions and many others have been hotly debated within tradition-historical research and will continue to be in the foreseeable future.[8]

As previously noted, there is little consensus today concerning the focus and methods of tradition-historical criticism. Some will argue that it already possesses, or must still develop, methods distinctly its own, or that the scope of tradition-historical criticism must be strictly limited to the preliterary, oral stages of a tradition's transmission.[9] The particular view presented here, however, is congruent with the history of the discipline's practice, and it would be helpful at this point to consider briefly some of the factors behind its emergence. By looking at the work of a few of its early practitioners, one achieves a better understanding of not only what tradition-historical criticism has been, but also, and as important, what issues and problems will shape its development in the future.

The Emergence of Tradition-Historical Study

The origin of the discipline may be found in an impasse that had been reached as a result of source-critical studies in the Pentateuch, culminating in Julius Wellhausen's classic formulation of the Documentary Hypothesis at the end of the nineteenth century. In Wellhausen's view, the four sources

that comprised the Pentateuch were substantially the product of the creative efforts of their authors, who worked much the same way as modern
authors. To be sure, legends about early times were at their disposal, but
these were unconnected to one another and were of only very limited value
as historical sources. The older they were, the more likely they were to be
simply the product of popular fancy.[10] As a result, the original sources
behind the present form of the Pentateuch provided the historian with little
or no access to the period before they were actually written, certainly not
to a period much before the time of David. Consequently, historical knowledge of the patriarchs was impossible, and very little could be known even
of the Age of Moses.[11]

By directly challenging Wellhausen's view of the role of the Pentateuch's
"authors," however, Hermann Gunkel was able to show a way behind the
written text of the Bible to earlier sources of Israel's history. In Gunkel's
view, the writers of the Pentateuch were not so much authors as they were
collectors ("redactors") of the traditions of their people, adding little of
their own to what they had received. And what they received was merely
the latest stage of a long process of these traditions' formation, in which
they had been passed down faithfully over many generations by word of
mouth. Over time, with each new telling, the originally independent, short
"sagas" or legends (which, for example, comprise the narrative cycles of
Genesis) changed and developed according to the needs of their hearers. As
they did so, however, they continued to bear with them authentic traces of
their origins as well as of their subsequent history. In this way, Gunkel
believed, a whole history of the religious, ethical, and aesthetic ideas of
ancient Israel can be derived from Genesis.[12]

Had Gunkel merely challenged Wellhausen's conception of the
Pentateuch's sources as written documents, his influence would probably not
have been so great. But Gunkel also developed a method congruent with
the nature of the Pentateuch's sources as "traditional" literature. That
method was form criticism, and by means of it, Gunkel found a way to
explore beyond the limitations of the written text, not only in Genesis but
throughout the Bible. Indeed, his goal was to recover by means of form-critical analysis the earliest form of a tradition or a tradition unit. The tradition
itself pointed the way, its variants, its inconsistencies, and its blind motifs
betraying earlier stages of a long development. In this way, one could hypo-
thetically describe a tradition's entire history on the basis of the tradition
itself, its "inner history," as Gunkel called it.[13] And for this realization, he is
justly recognized as the chief pioneer of tradition-historical criticism.[14]

While Gunkel himself did not regard the products of oral tradition
as appropriate material for specifically historical reconstruction,[15] a number
of scholars who followed in his wake took note of his insistence on the

antiquity of oral traditions behind the biblical narratives and on the fidelity of oral transmission. Confident of their ability to separate history from legend, they sought to reconstruct the earliest periods of Israel's history and religion. For example, on the basis of the sagas of Genesis, Albrecht Alt offered a description of the distinctive nature of patriarchal religion before the rise of Yahwism at the time of Moses.[16] In turn, his research had a particularly strong influence on two scholars whose names are more closely associated with tradition-historical criticism than even that of Gunkel himself—Gerhard von Rad and Martin Noth.

Gunkel had focused his form-critical attention on the smallest units of tradition, an emphasis that left largely unaddressed the question of the origin of the Pentateuch's/Hexateuch's larger thematic structures.[17] In texts such as Deut. 26:5–9; Deut. 6:20–24; and Josh. 24:1–18, von Rad found preserved what he considered to be nearly identical old summaries of Israelite belief, or "creeds," originating in Israel's worship at an ancient shrine (Gilgal).[18] As he saw it, these creeds formed the basis of the structure of the present Hexateuch, with whose outline they were essentially identical. Thus, rather than being something that has grown up on its own accidentally, "a casual recollection of historical events," the thematic structure of the Hexateuch itself rests on ancient tradition, a "canonical pattern . . . long since fixed as to its details."[19] Only the Sinai tradition of covenant making (Exodus 19–Numbers 10) was lacking in the old "creeds." However, von Rad concluded that it too derived from old tradition, having originated in a covenant renewal feast at Shechem. It was inserted by the Yahwist into the framework established by the old creeds, and this, along with the prefixing of the primeval history in Genesis 1–11, led to the creation of the present Hexateuch.

Although Noth states explicitly that the task of his history of Pentateuchal traditions is the investigation of its whole growth and formation from beginning to end, the critical period as far as he is concerned is the preliterary, which for him, even more than for von Rad, gave the Pentateuch its essential shape.[20] Moreover, Noth goes beyond von Rad in positing behind the earliest written sources of the Pentateuch, J and E, a common base from which both had independently derived and that *already* contained in a unified form what he identifies as the five major themes of the Pentateuch: the exodus, the guidance into the land, the promise to the patriarchs, the guidance in the wilderness, and the revelation at Sinai.[21] The last is noteworthy, for it was this tradition complex that von Rad had seen as an addition by the Yahwist. Consequently, aside from the primeval history, Noth is able to push the entire thematic structure of the Pentateuch back to the period of the Judges and the worship of the twelve-tribe confederacy.

Since each Pentateuchal theme is composed of its own block of individual traditions with its own history of development, however, still another stage of tradition formation must be imagined. During this stage, the individual themes and their associated traditions developed separately, only gradually growing together around the theme of the exodus from Egypt— the "kernel of the whole subsequent Pentateuchal tradition" and a "primary confession of Israel." With it, Noth believed he had reached "the bedrock of an historical occurrence."[22] In fact, for Noth, this attainment of the unique historical events giving rise to the Pentateuch's themes defined the real goal of his tradition-historical studies.[23] And to that end, in the course of detailed analyses of individual traditions that filled out the framework of the Pentateuch, he articulated various principles for separating out earlier traditions from later ones (e.g., the attachment of early traditions to specific places, the priority of cultic traditions over secular traditions, anonymity and typicality), which subsequently became major topics of tradition-historical discussions.[24] Though they have been severely criticized, they nonetheless highlight the kind of explicit criteria that will have to be found if tradition-historical criticism is going to succeed in its goal of reconstructing the history of tradition's transmission.

It is impossible here to consider further the lines of research opened up by von Rad and by Noth or by the numerous other scholars, particularly in Scandinavia, who took up the goals of tradition-historical research. They sought to apply its guiding insights to other parts of the Bible, such as the prophetic corpus or the wisdom books, as well as to investigate in a more systematic fashion the process of oral tradition itself.[25]

Problems and Issues in
Tradition-Historical Criticism Today

Today widespread disagreement remains concerning the specific object of tradition-historical research—whether it is restricted only to the phase of oral tradition or is all-inclusive—and concerning its methods of investigation, particularly as these relate to other forms of biblical criticism. Despite the best efforts of many scholars, this situation is likely to continue for some time into the foreseeable future, given the scope of the challenge tradition-historical criticism has posed for itself. Whether through naiveté or simple overconfidence, the magnitude of this challenge has not always been sufficiently recognized. We have only the written texts at our disposal; nevertheless, tradition-historical criticism has set itself the job of studying, if not actually recovering, nothing less than the entire prewritten phase of their composition!

It must be acknowledged that until the last fifteen years or so, much of the enthusiasm for tradition-historical studies came from their promise of breaking the methodological impasse created by Wellhausen's restriction of historical knowledge to the time in which the Bible's sources were actually written. This can be seen in Noth's tradition-historical work on the Pentateuch, which laid the groundwork for his efforts to reconstruct the history of ancient Israel.[26] Despite the rigor of many studies, numerous others failed to distinguish clearly between the history of a tradition and the question of its historicity. What was irreducible in a tradition was taken as historical; what was secondary was taken either as historically untrustworthy or as having an independent historical foundation.[27] But can "originality" itself settle the question of the historicity of these traditions? And what of the criteria used to decide primary and secondary elements of tradition? Noth, for example, had argued that the earliest traditions are formulated in small units in a concise style and that cultic traditions are earlier than comparable secular traditions.[28] Yet both criteria have been roundly rejected.[29]

In addition to skepticism regarding various criteria for judging the relative age of traditions, another issue central to penetrating the remote periods of Israel's history is the question of the very stability of tradition. While acknowledging that changes in the form and the content of traditions inevitably occurred in the course of transmission, Gunkel and those who followed him also insisted on the "fidelity" of the transmission process even over long stretches of time. But what exactly constitutes faithful transmission? Surely early studies exaggerated the role of memorization in the process of oral tradition, ignoring its restriction to a limited number of situations and forms; moreover, recent field studies in folklore emphasize that the transmission of oral tradition occurs largely through a process of recomposition, or re-creation, so that a text (even in poetry) never remains unchanged, even on the lips of the same person.[30] Thus the "fixity" of tradition over time can no longer be assumed but must be determined on the basis of tradition-historical investigations.

Perhaps more seriously, questions now are raised about our ability to reconstruct preliterary stages of a tradition on the basis of written documents.[31] After all, how does written Hebrew actually relate to spoken Hebrew? Although most scholars acknowledge differences between oral communication and written communication in general, what constitutes these differences is not always easy to determine. If, for example, one points to repetition as characteristic of spoken versus written communication, what is to be made of the unmistakable repetitive rhetorical style of Deuteronomy and the Deuteronomist? May not written language sometimes imitate spoken language? In fact, the issue of the "orality" of written texts is more pressing than it might at first appear, for it calls into question the very ability to discriminate between texts rooted authentically in oral tradition and those that are purely literary inventions.

Perhaps this discussion is sufficient to indicate some of the central issues facing tradition-historical research today. Of course, these concerns necessarily relate to the current practice of source criticism and form criticism. Tradition-historical criticism remains dependent on progress in these methods even as it will continue to reflect their limitations.

An Illustration of the Approach

A brief illustration of the applicability of tradition-historical criticism to a specific biblical text will draw together the various points made here and show concretely both the prospects and the limitations of its approach. The text to be considered is Gen. 32:22–32 (23–33 Heb.).

Anyone who has thoughtfully investigated the story of Jacob's encounter with the mysterious "man" in Genesis 32 can attest to the many obscurities with which it confronts the discerning reader. Yet if we follow the form-critical lead suggested by Gunkel for tracing the history of a tradition,[32] these obscurities are clear indications of the antiquity of the story and the long history of its transmission. Along with the presence of possible variant traditions, these indications provide the concrete means by which one may reconstruct the history of the tradition in question.

Such indications within the text of Genesis 32 include apparent vestiges of "primitive" religious conceptions, the narrative's lack of connection to the immediate context, the unevenness of the present form of the story, and its multiple etiologies and conclusions. Also a variant form of the tradition in Genesis 32 occurs in Hos. 12:3b–4a (4b–5a Heb.), where the prophet indicts Israel for following in the footsteps of its eponymous ancestor:

In his manly vigor he [Jacob] wrestled with a "god";
He [Jacob] wrestled a "god" and prevailed.
(The god) wept and besought his favor.[33]

On the basis of these two lines of evidence at least four stages in the growth of the tradition may be discerned.

Analysis proceeds by working "back" from the present narrative, beginning with the results obtained from source-critical study. Such study generally affirms the literary integrity of Gen. 32:22–32 and attributes the text to the work of the Yahwist.[34] The only exception concerns v. 32, along with its referent in v. 25b ("and Jacob's hip was put out of joint"). Verse 32 contains a strange dietary abstention on the part of Israelites (unknown elsewhere) and is the second of two successive etiologies, neither of which belongs to the essential story. Although older scholarship tended to regard the mere presence of an etiology as a sign of the etiological intention of an entire narrative, current scholarship recognizes that etiologies are often secondary additions, or redactional elements.[35] Consequently, a number of scholars have taken at least v. 32, along with v. 25b, as a postexilic, "midrashic" accretion to the text.[36] As the text stands, v. 25b is certainly puzzling in view of the man's cry in v. 26 ("Let me go"), and its loss would only help smooth the flow of the story.

At this last stage of the tradition, Gen. 32:22–32 has become an element in the composite created by the Priestly (P) redaction of earlier Pentateuchal sources. Although P probably introduced no changes into the tradition itself or into its position within the larger Jacob cycle, the new broader literary setting fabricated by P broadened and deepened the theological horizon. Genesis 32:22–32 now represents an episode under the auspices of the eternal covenant God established with Abraham to be the God of his descendants (chapter 17). As such, it falls within the third and penultimate historical age, according to the Priestly scheme of "salvation history."

The third stage of the tradition's development occurred with its inclusion in the Yahwist source. At this stage, a number of significant developments took place in the tradition, as perhaps it was reduced to writing for the first time. To begin with, the Yahwist is most likely responsible for the present "artful" position of Gen. 32:22–32 in the Jacob cycle, with which it has otherwise little in common. In the cycle, Jacob generally makes his way by trickery and cunning; here it seems to be a question of his strength. By inserting this text directly into the middle of the story of Jacob's perilous reunion with Esau (note the lack of an entirely consistent transition from 32:21 to 32:22), the story now forms a perfect counterpart to the theophany at Bethel (28:10–22). Thus Jacob's flight from Esau and his perilous return are both marked by special revelations of divine providence. The two incidents frame Jacob's "exile," otherwise lacking in religious color, and show it to have been under God's protection.

In addition, the Yahwist is probably responsible for the identification of Jacob's mysterious opponent with God. This is accomplished by the concluding etiology of the place name "Penuel" in v. 30, which puns on the meaning of the name ("For I have seen God face to face"). And it is probably indicated by the change of Jacob's name in v. 28, with the explanation given there of the name "Israel." In fact, it is likely that in the story inherited by the Yahwist, v. 29b ("and he blessed him") followed directly upon Jacob's demand in v. 26 (compare Hos. 12:4b–5a above) as the boon won by the hero's victory. In other words, the Yahwist is responsible for introducing the entire motif of the change of Jacob's name to Israel (vv. 27–29a), and with it, the effort to articulate the meaning of "Israel." (In Hos. 12:4a, there is a Hebrew pun on the name Israel, but no expansion of this into a change in the patriarch's name.) This becomes the center of attention, and to some extent it moves an identification of the text's genre, which continues to puzzle commentators, in the direction of an etiology of the name,[37] if not of the existence of Israel.[38] For the Yahwist, the struggle of the eponymous hero Jacob typifies Israel's spiritual struggles with God, a struggle that, as he sees it, constitutes Israel's destiny and deepest identity.

Identification of a second stage in the development of the tradition is perhaps warranted by the variant tradition appearing in Hosea. Were the Hosea tradition a true variant to Gen. 32:22–32 from the form-critical point of view rather than simply an allusion to a story, a reconstruction of the earliest form of the tradition could proceed on other than speculative grounds. Nonetheless, the tradition Hosea employs suggests a prior stage in the tradition of Jacob's struggle, less developed than the Genesis tradition. First, at this stage Jacob is not yet the eponymous hero of a united Israel, but only of the Northern Kingdom.[39] Second, Jacob's opponent is only identified as an "'ĕlōhîm," an identification that of itself need only indicate a supernatural, or superhuman, being (compare the usage in 1 Sam. 28:13, where it refers to the ghost of Samuel; see n. 33). Third, although the Hebrew in Hos. 12:5a (4a Eng.) contains a pun on the name "Israel," (yiśar'ēl), "he wrestled God/a god"),[40] the pun is not developed into an etiology for the change of Jacob's name. If this is the case, at this stage of the tradition's transmission, the narrative as a whole would lack any strong etiological thrust, further suggesting an identification of the unit's original genre as that of folktale. Finally, in the tradition the prophet utilizes (albeit negatively, as an example of the eponymous hero's brazen daring) the depiction of Jacob's extraordinary feat of strength is clearly cast in a heroic mode. Jacob successfully wrestled with this superhuman being and won from it some kind of blessing. In this incident, which was clearly a source of popular pride, there is little hint of its later "spiritualization." Most likely the tale circulated as merely one of a number of such folktales about the eponymous hero of the Northern Kingdom, perhaps part of the "stock in trade" of professional storytellers who roamed the countryside entertaining the populace wherever a crowd might be likely to gather.

Although it is merely speculation, one can conjecture a still earlier stage of the tradition's development. Perhaps to this stage belong originally those elements of the story such as the motif of the "magic touch" (v. 25a) or of the demonlike creature whose power is restricted to the night and who seeks to block the hero's passage. Given the ubiquity of such stories in folklore (cf. Ex. 4:24–26), there is no reason to think the story in this original form even concerned the eponymous hero Jacob or had its present localization. Surely the delightful pun on the name "Israel," in evidence at the second stage of the tale's transmission, is in no way essential to the action of the basic story. It probably was introduced later, as part of the

"Israelitizing" of the tale when it became associated with the figure of Jacob. So, too, perhaps came the introduction of the river's name, "Jabbok," which in Hebrew puns on the name Jacob, as well as on the word for "wrestle."

Enough has been said to indicate the lines of the tradition's possible transmission and development, up to and including its final redaction in Genesis. By seeking to uncover the richness of this intriguing text's long and complicated history, tradition-historical criticism reveals something of the riches of biblical narrative, which could take a popular tale about a hero and transform it into a profound statement of the vocation and destiny of Israel. At the same time, we also learn something about the historical development of Israel's religious beliefs and spiritual sojourn, as Israel walks in the footsteps of its ancestor Jacob. Like Jacob, Israel too only discovers along the way that the Mysterious Presence with whom it has had to struggle continually in its history bore the name of its God.

Notes

1. For a penetrating examination of this question, see H.-G. Gadamer, *Truth and Method* (New York: Seabury, 1975).

2. So Gene M. Tucker, *Form Criticism of the Old Testament*, Guides to Biblical Scholarship (Philadelphia: Fortress, 1971); John Barton, *Reading the Old Testament* (Philadelphia: Westminster, 1984), 10; and K. Jeppesen and B. Otzen, "Status Quaestionis," *The Productions of Time: Tradition History in Old Testament Scholarship*, ed. K. Jeppesen and B. Otzen (Sheffield: Almond, 1984), 129. Klaus Koch, (*The Growth of the Biblical Tradition*, trans. S. M. Cupitt [New York: Scribner's, 1969], 53) regards tradition history as simply a branch of form-critical work. Of course, this is not the self-understanding of many who have been and are proponents of tradition history. See, for example, Douglas A. Knight, *Rediscovering the Traditions of Israel*, Society of Biblical Literature Dissertation Series 9 (Missoula, Mont.: Scholars, 1975), esp. 193–94.

3. Knight, *Rediscovering the Traditions*, 1.

4. R. C. Culley, "An Approach to the Problem of Oral Tradition," *Vetus Testamentum* 13 (1963): 115–17.

5. Rolf Knierim, "Criticism of Literary Features, Form, Tradition, and Redaction," in *The Hebrew Bible and Its Modern Interpreters*, ed. D. A. Knight and G. M. Tucker (Philadelphia: Fortress, 1985), 130–34.

6. For the distinction, cf. Knight, *Rediscovering the Traditions*, 5–20.

7. Ibid., 5–10.

8. For a valuable discussion of the problem in relation to Old Testament studies, see, in addition to Culley ("An Approach to the Problem of Oral Tradition," 113–25) mentioned above, Burke O. Long, "Recent Field Studies in Oral Literature and Their Bearing on OT Criticism," *Vetus Testamentum* 26 (1976): 187–98.

9. For example, O. H. Steck, "Theological Streams of Tradition," *Tradition and Theology in the Old Testament*, ed. D. A. Knight (Philadelphia: Fortress, 1977), esp. 183–85; see also the review of methodological positions in Knierim, "Criticism of Literary Features," 146–48.

10. Julius Wellhausen, *Prolegomena to the History of Ancient Israel* (Gloucester, Mass.: Peter Smith, 1973), 296, 326. Wellhausen's work was first published in German in 1878, with a second edition in 1883.

11. Ibid., 318–19.

12. Hermann Gunkel, *The Legends of Genesis* (New York: Schocken Books, 1964), 99.

13. Ibid., 100–102.

14. Knight, *Rediscovering the Traditions*, 72.

15. Gunkel, *Legends of Genesis*, 1–12

16. Albrecht Alt, "The God of the Fathers," *Essays in Old Testament History and Religion* (New York: Doubleday, Anchor Books, 1968), 3–100.

17. John Van Seters, *Abraham in History and Tradition* (New Haven, Conn.: Yale University Press, 1975), 142.

18. Gerhard von Rad, "The Form-Critical Problem of the Hexateuch," *The Problem of the Hexateuch and Other Essays* (London: SCM, 1984), 1–78.

19. Ibid., 2, 8.

20. Martin Noth, *A History of Pentateuchal Traditions* (Englewood Cliffs, N.J.: Prentice-Hall, 1972), 1.

21. Ibid., 38–41.

22. Ibid., 49–50.

23. Bernhard W. Anderson, "Introduction: Martin Noth's Tradition-Historical Approach in the Context of Twentieth-Century Biblical Research," *A History of Pentateuchal Traditions*, xviii–xxi.

24. See Anderson's (ibid., xxiii–xxviii) formulation of these principles.

25. For the contribution of the so-called Scandinavian School to tradition-historical criticism, as well as for examples of other studies, see the excellent survey of Knight, *Rediscovering the Traditions*, 177–92, 217–399.

26. M. Noth, *The History of Israel* (New York: Harper & Row, 1958).

27. T. L. Thompson, "The Joseph-Moses Traditions and Pentateuchal Criticism," in *Israelite and Judaean History*, ed. J. H. Hayes and J. M. Miller (Philadelphia: Westminster, 1977), 170–71.

28. Anderson, "Introduction," xxiii–xxiv.

29. R. Polzin, "Martin Noth's *A History of Pentateuchal Traditions*," *Bulletin of the American Society of Oriental Research* 221 (1976): 113–20, esp. 115–16.

30. R. C. Culley, "Oral Tradition," 119–50.

31. R. Lapointe, "Tradition and Language: The Import of Oral Expression," in *Tradition and Theology in the Old Testament*, 125–42, esp. 131–34.

32. Gunkel, *Legends of Genesis*, 99–100.

33. The scripture translations in this chapter are the author's own. The reconstruction of the Hebrew text for the first colon of v. 4 follows the one proposed by S. L. McKenzie, "The Jacob Tradition in Hosea XII 4–5," *Vetus Testamentum* 36 (1986): 312–14. I depart in taking the subject of the second colon to be Jacob's opponent, which I understand as an unspecified type of supernatural being. Compare the use of the word "god" (*'ĕlōhîm*) for the shade of Samuel in 1 Sam. 28:13.

34. Claus Westermann, *Genesis 12–36: A Commentary* (Minneapolis: Augsburg, 1985), 515.

35. See Brevard Childs, "A Study of the Formula 'Until This Day,'" *Journal of Biblical Literature* 82 (1963): 179–92.

36. So Westermann, *Genesis 12–36*, 520.

37. George W. Coats, *Genesis*, The Forms of the Old Testament Literature 1 (Grand Rapids: Eerdmans, 1983), 230.

38. Tucker, *Form Criticism*, 49.

39. W. D. Whitt, "The Jacob Traditions in Hosea and Their Relation to Genesis," *Zeitschrift für die alttestamentliche Wissenschaft* 103 (1991): 22–24.

40. McKenzie, "Jacob Tradition," 313–14.

For Further Reading

Cross, Frank M. "The Epic Traditions of Early Israel: Epic Narrative and the Reconstruction of Early Israelite Institutions." In *The Poet and the Historian: Essays in Literary and Historical Biblical Criticism*, ed. Richard E. Friedman. Harvard Semitic Studies 26. Chico, Calif.: Scholars, 1983.

Culley, Robert C. "An Approach to the Problem of Oral Tradition," *Vetus Testamentum* 13 (1963): 113–25.

Gunkel, Hermann. *The Legends of Genesis: The Biblical Saga and History*. New York: Schocken Books, 1964.

Knight, Douglas A. *Rediscovering the Traditions of Israel*. Society of Biblical Literature Dissertation Series 9. Missoula, Mont.: Scholars, 1975.

Koch, Klaus. *The Growth of the Biblical Tradition*. New York: Scribner's, 1969.

Long, Burke O. "Recent Field Studies in Oral Literature and Their Bearing on OT Criticism." *Vetus Testamentum* 26 (1976): 187–98.

Noth, Martin. *A History of Pentateuchal Traditions*. Trans. with an introduction by Bernhard W. Anderson. Englewood Cliffs, N.J.: Prentice-Hall, 1972.

Rast, Walter E. *Tradition History and the Old Testament*. Guides to Biblical Scholarship. Philadelphia: Fortress, 1972.

Van Seters, John. *Abraham in History and Tradition*. New Haven, Conn.: Yale University Press, 1975.

von Rad, Gerhard. "The Form-Critical Problem of the Hexateuch." In *The Problem of the Hexateuch and Other Essays*. Trans. E. W. Trueman Dicken. London: SCM, 1984.

5

REDACTION CRITICISM

GAIL P. C. STREETE

The Method and Its History

R edaction criticism, a translation of the German *Redaktionsgeschichte* (history of redaction), is the technical term for what is arguably the most significant advance in Gospel scholarship in this century. Also known as composition criticism or composition history, redaction criticism is a method of analysis that has been applied primarily to the Synoptic Gospels. It fully acknowledges that the Gospel writers, albeit inheritors of both common and specific traditions, were also creative authors and theologians and not mere transcribers or collectors. New Testament scholar David Barr has forcefully acknowledged the impact of this method of interpretation on biblical scholars: "The excitement many of us felt on our first exposure to redaction criticism is due to the ability of this method to take seriously the differences between the gospels, to explain the differences without explaining them away."[1]

The appeal and acceptance of the redaction-critical method has been such that few introductions to the New Testament fail to include a description of it, however cursory, in their surveys of modern biblical criticism. Indeed, their analysis of the Gospels in virtually every case relies upon the perspective of redaction criticism, whether or not they acknowledge this debt. Other fields of New Testament scholarship that attempt to interpret the New Testament writers as theologians or as writers with a specific ideological bent depend upon the basic insight offered by redaction criticism— that each evangelist is a uniquely creative theologian as well as an inheritor of a repertory of traditions. In the United States in particular, this perspective has been true for methods of literary criticism. These literary-critical approaches (see Part 3 of this book), especially the more recent ones, include structuralist and poststructuralist analysis, rhetorical criticism, narrative criticism, reader-response criticism, and to some extent ideological criticism. According to critic Stephen D. Moore, narrative criticism and reader-response criticism have tended to be identified with American biblical scholars using the literary-critical approach.[2] German scholars, however, according to Rolf Rendtorff, mean something very different by literary criticism than do their American or British colleagues.[3] As Norman Perrin, the foremost American exponent and practitioner of the redaction-critical method, has put it:

> Once it was recognized that the final author was in fact an *author* and not merely a transmitter of tradition, it became natural and inevitable to inquire into his [sic] purpose and theology, not only into his redaction of previously existing tradition. In this connection redaction criticism shades over into general literary criticism, especially in redaction critical work carried on in America, where the influence of general literary criticism is strong on New Testament scholars.[4]

But even when it began to be developed and utilized in German scholarship following World War I, redaction criticism was not regarded either as an exclusive or a standard method, nor was this terminology applied to the method until 1954.[5] It both depended upon and intersected with the insights of form and source criticism and belonged under the general category of the historical-critical method, which it advanced. As Perrin has it, the method was born out of research on the so-called "Marcan hypothesis."[6] This research was itself generated by the pioneering "historical Jesus" work of David F. Strauss (*The Life of Jesus Critically Examined*, German ed., 1835–1836). His followers reasoned that Mark, which they noted was the briefest and most unadorned of the Gospels since it lacked what they called "mythical elements," was therefore the earliest Gospel and thus the most "historical," or the closest to the historical Jesus. Hermann Gunkel's form criticism of the Hebrew Bible had taught biblical scholars that in the oral tradition from which the written works were assembled, units of oral tradition called *pericopes* could be isolated and analyzed with a view to discovering the "life-setting," or *Sitz im Leben*, of the communities in which they arose.

It would be several years before these insights could be combined with those of redaction criticism by Martin Dibelius (*From Tradition to Gospel*, English translation [ET] 1935) and Rudolf Bultmann (*History of the Synoptic Tradition*, ET 1963). They were employed, however, along with close attention to the literary structure of Mark, by Wilhelm Wrede in 1901 to produce his epochal work on Mark's theology, *The Messianic Secret in the Gospels* (*Das Messiasgeheimnis in den Evangelien*, ET 1971). Based on his close and careful analysis of Mark and a comparison with parallels in Matthew and Luke, Wrede noted in Mark especially the paradox of the simultaneous exposure and deliberate concealment of Jesus' messianic nature, primarily in connection with his performance of miracles (e.g.,

Mark 1:43–45). Reasoning from numerous such examples, Wrede concluded, in contradistinction to previous scholarship, that while Mark may have been the earliest Gospel, it was no more historically accurate than the others, nor did it have any fewer "mythical elements." Indeed, the recurrent theme of the "messianic secret," uniquely emphasized by Mark, pointed, in Wrede's view, to the existence of the evangelist's own "dogma."[7]

This idea of Mark as a theologian was later developed and delineated by Willi Marxsen in his redaction-critical study *Mark the Evangelist* (*Der Evangelist Markus*, 1956; ET 1969). It is probably thus fitting that Marxsen should have been the first New Testament scholar to use the technical term *Redaktionsgeschichte* (history of redaction or editorial history) to describe the method he and others had begun to use.[8] Following the work of Dibelius and Bultmann, who combined form-critical with redaction-critical perspectives,[9] three significant treatments of the Synoptic evangelists appeared in postwar Germany: the previously mentioned work by Marxsen on Mark; the study of Matthew by Günther Bornkamm, G. Barth, and H. J. Held, *Tradition and Interpretation in Matthew* (ET 1963); and Hans Conzelmann's influential study of Luke-Acts, *The Theology of St. Luke* (ET 1954).

Much of the work in redaction criticism, like that in the form criticism on which it depends, was pioneered in Germany. But English-speaking redaction critics, though initially few in number, have also developed the discipline, often in ways significantly different from those of German scholars.[10] Both Perrin and Barr credit R. H. Lightfoot's Bampton Lectures of 1934 with "anticipating" the later work of Marxsen, Conzelmann, and Bornkamm; indeed, Perrin calls Lightfoot "the first redaction critic," preceding Bornkamm by fourteen years.[11] In the United States, Perrin has been the foremost redaction critic, using the insights of the method to write his own introduction to the New Testament (*The New Testament: An Introduction*, 1974). As has been previously noted, however, American biblical scholars have tended to focus upon various literary-critical methods, either in addition to, as a result of, or in reaction against the redaction-critical method. Nevertheless, according to Barr, a practitioner of narrative criticism, these same interpretive techniques are largely reliant upon the insights offered by redaction criticism and its "attempt to understand the gospels as unified stories."[12] Rendtorff observes that, while many modern interpreters reject the older "diachronic" methods of analyzing biblical texts according to "levels, sources and the like," the same persons interpret the text "as we have it before us, in its given form."[13] Although Rendtorff was speaking of Hebrew Bible critics, his analysis leads to the rather ironic conclusion that redaction criticism, while belonging to the older "diachronic" methods, nevertheless remains the first modern method of biblical criticism that treats the text "as we have it before us."

Distinctiveness and Current Applications of the Method

Joachim Rohde has offered a stringent definition of the method of redaction criticism: "The method . . . is in principle applicable only to the Synoptic Gospels, including the Acts of the Apostles, and not to the Epistles. An exception may at the most be made for the Epistle of James."[14] The insights into evangelistic creativity offered by the redaction-critical perspective have nevertheless also lent themselves readily to other, more recent methods of biblical criticism, including sociological and sociohistorical criticism. Despite Rohde's limitation of the application of the method to the Synoptic Gospels, the method has also been fruitfully applied to such noncanonical documents as the *Gospel of Peter* and the *Secret Gospel of Mark* (see John Dominic Crossan, *Four Other Gospels: Shadows on the Contours of the Canon*, 1985; and *The Cross That Spoke*, 1988). Indeed, redaction criticism may be particularly valuable in connection with the study of such noncanonical works, helping to shed light not only on the various versions of Jesus' teaching and the traditions about Jesus that were circulating in the early Christian world, but also upon the selection process involved in, and the interests that lay behind, the shaping of the present canon. Here the insights of redaction criticism intersect with those of canonical criticism. Based upon his use of form, source, redaction, and literary criticism, Crossan has actually concluded that the noncanonical *Gospel of Peter* may be the *earliest* of the Gospel passion narratives.[15] Such a contention revolutionizes the study of the canonical Gospels and brings us back almost to the point at which redaction criticism began: the question of which traditions are closest to the "historical Jesus," and in what ways those traditions have been altered. Even the concept of "Synoptic Gospels" has changed and expanded, furthering redaction-critical studies of the canonical Synoptics. The *Gospel of Thomas*, discovered in a complete Coptic edition in the Nag Hammadi Library in 1945, has initiated a number of redaction-critical, source-critical, and canon-critical studies, including Bertil E. Gärtner's *The Theology of the Gospel according to Thomas* (ET 1961). Work on "Q," (German *Quelle*, or Source), believed to have been a written "sayings" Gospel used as a source by the canonical evangelists Matthew and Luke, has also employed an enhanced redaction criticism (e.g., John S. Kloppenborg, *The Formation of Q*, 1987; Burton Mack, *The Lost Gospel: Q and Christian Origins*, 1993). The idea of the existence of layers of oral and written tradition and contributions made to that tradition by authorial and community interests has moreover been applied to studies of the apocryphal Acts, using the canonical book of Acts as a means of comparison (e.g., Dennis R. MacDonald, *The Gospel and the Apostle*, 1982, which also applies the method to the study of Paul). Redaction-critical work on the book of Acts itself has been done by Conzelmann (*The Book of Acts*, ET 1963) and Ernst Haenchen (*Acts*, ET 1971). In fact, Luke-Acts has been the focus of many recent redaction-critical studies, including those by J. C. O'Neill (*The Theology of Acts*, 1961), Leander Keck and J. Louis Martyn (*Studies in Luke/Acts*, 1966), and Charles H. Talbert (*Literary Patterns, Theological Themes, and the Genre of Luke-Acts*, 1975).

Finally, the redaction-critical method has either been readily presupposed to be foundational (and therefore dismissed) or regarded as superseded and ultimately rejected by approaches that spurn the "intentional fallacy," the idea that one can discover from the text itself the intention of its "author."[16] David J. A. Clines has also suggested that methods like redaction criticism, which speak of biblical writers as "authors," may be outmoded by at least three decades.[17] Redaction-critical studies nevertheless continue to abound, perhaps given the "discovery" of Gospels such as *Thomas* and the continuing "recovery" of Q. The existence of the Redaction Criticism and the Two-Gospel Hypothesis Group as a program unit of the Society of Biblical Literature is one indication of the method's continuing vitality and viability for biblical studies, particularly for studies of the Gospels.

Another important contribution of the method to recent New Testament scholarship has been analysis of the "authenticity" of certain sayings of Jesus, a task first undertaken in the United States by Perrin (*Rediscovering the Teachings of Jesus*, 1976), in some sense a response to Rohde's redaction-critical introduction to the New Testament (*Rediscovering the Teachings of the Evangelists*, ET 1969). Perrin's foundational work, which presents three criteria for isolating "authentic" Jesus material in the sayings—dissimilarity, coherence, multiple attestation—has had a profound influence on Gospel scholarship in the United States, including the work of the Jesus Seminar, a two-hundred member group of biblical scholars who are widely regarded as engaged in a renewed quest for the historical Jesus, attempting for the past decade to determine the relative authenticity of sayings attributed to Jesus by the canonical Gospels. The group has produced a number of works, including *The Five Gospels* (1993) and *The Complete Gospels* (1995), which acknowledge the insights contributed by form, source, and redaction criticism.[18] Such insights into gospel formation are also employed by Helmut Koester's comprehensive study, *Ancient Christian Gospels* (1990).

Other works to which redaction criticism has contributed include studies of early Christian "titles" for Jesus and studies of early Christologies, such as H. E. Tödt's *The Son of Man in the Synoptic Tradition* (ET 1965) and R. H. Fuller's *The Foundations of New Testament Christology* (1965). Redaction criticism has been interwoven with feminist criticism by Elisabeth Schüssler Fiorenza in her landmark feminist reconstruction of Christian origins, *In Memory of Her: A Feminist Theological Reconstruction of Christian Origins*

(1983). Such undertakings are further evidence of the value of redaction criticism, not merely in providing yet another chapter in historical Jesus research, but in investigating the scope and variety of early Christian beliefs about Jesus.[19]

Application of the Method in Practice: Luke 4:16–30 (Jesus' Sermon at Nazareth)

The best way to demonstrate the validity and richness of the redaction-critical approach to the study of the Gospels is to show it in the actual analysis of a pericope.

When attempting to explain the method to first-year students, I often compare it to studying the art of quilting. Quilts are made from available scraps of already-existing material, which are pieced together, beginning with individual blocks. The blocks are then combined, usually in a traditional pattern (Wedding Ring, Log Cabin, Broken Dishes, etc.), to create a new article. Several different quilts may thus employ the same design, but they will vary according to the materials used, and each will be a unique finished piece. Indeed, I like to think of the *Gospel of Thomas* as rather like a "scrap quilt," consisting of pieces connected apparently at random, yet producing its own integral pattern. Quilters, like evangelists, thus deal with preexisting materials (traditional sources), put them together first in blocks (pericopes), and then unite them in a kind of overall structure (the Gospel framework). Like the evangelists, quilters create something subtly, or not so subtly, different from the given materials each time. Like the evangelists also, quilters come from communities for whom certain patterns or designs are meaningful. Those patterns or designs also help to determine the origins of the quilts, since their creators, like the evangelists, are often anonymous. Redaction criticism, like studying quilts, involves looking at the pattern, determining the traditional "pieces," and examining the resulting "new" article as a unique creation, intended for a specific use.

Of course, just as there are numerous books on the art of making and analyzing quilts, so there are also ways to assist the interpreter with the analysis of a selected pericope as part of the pattern within a Gospel. The first step is usually to see the shape of the pericope—the quilt block—by determining its logical beginning or introduction and its end. Next the "form" of the pericope and the *Sitz im Leben* (life-setting) in which it arose are to be determined, as if one would ask of a quilt piece, Did it come from a blouse? A skirt? A shirt? Does its fabric indicate use for formal occasions? Work? What signs of wear does it show? When I was learning exegesis from my German-trained professors, Bultmann's *History of the Synoptic Tradition* proved invaluable in this first form-critical step.[20]

The pericope then is translated from the original language, paying attention to textual variants (or several English translations are compared), noticing "lead" or "key" words that may also be included in other pericopes within the Gospel, as possible clues to the evangelist's point of view. The interpreter may find that the *Theological Dictionary of the New Testament* (*TDNT*) assists with this step, always keeping in mind that such "word studies" have limited value. The "fit" of the passage into the overall outline or pattern of the Gospel then needs to be determined. (For this outline I have found Perrin's *The New Testament: An Introduction* [1974], as helpful a guide today as in the past, although it is dated and does not include apocryphal Gospels such as *Thomas*.) The next step in the process is to compare the specific passage with its versions in other Gospel and Gospel-related materials. This task has been considerably enhanced by the work of the Jesus and Q Seminars, resulting in the publication of Robert Funk's two-volume *New Gospel Parallels* (1985), which expands the earlier *Gospel Parallels* by Burton Throckmorton (1967), combining Gnostic, apocryphal, and patristic parallels with those of the canonical Gospels; John Dominic Crossan's *Sayings Parallels* (1986); and John S. Kloppenborg's *Q Parallels* (1988). The exegete at this stage will want to compare studies of the passage from various commentaries, particularly as they may illuminate difficult or puzzling language. All of these steps help illuminate the traditions inherited by the evangelist, how the evangelist transformed these traditions according to an individual theological purpose, and how that purpose differed from those of other early Christian "authors."

This rather mechanical and formulaic approach nevertheless essentially replicates the steps taken by redaction critics in determining, from the "composition history" of the Gospel, the various theological perspectives of early Christian communities. However, such a process, it is now recognized, may never contribute to the achievement of Perrin's overly optimistic hope for the writing of a complete "theological history" of early Christianity.[21]

Let us now use as an example of the method the passage in Luke's Gospel in which Jesus preaches his first sermon in the synagogue at Nazareth: Luke 4:16–30.[22] According to Perrin, this passage is the one in which the purpose of Jesus' ministry is set out by Luke.[23] It thus serves as an illustration of the theological concerns of Luke, who, in Perrin's opinion, usually remains "reasonably true, in our sense of the word, to his sources," unless he has theological reasons, in which case he alters his received traditions considerably.[24] This passage should therefore provide an excellent example of how analysis of a redactor/author's use of sources helps to reveal theological interests.

In terms of its position within the Gospel, Luke 4:16–30 falls within the first half, prior to the turning point—Jesus' decision to go up to Jerusalem

(9:51)—and at the beginning of Jesus' ministry, which will culminate in Jerusalem with his death. The introduction to the Gospel (1:1–4) indicates Luke's consciousness of himself as a deliberate narrator, an "I" who is different from the "others." The Gospel also reflects a sense of definite arrangement of "the things that have been accomplished among us" and has an identified recipient, one Theophilus, whose Greek name suggests that he is a representative of the Gentiles or Gentile "God-fearers" (Jewish proselytes) who were most likely Luke's primary audience.[25]

This introduction is followed by 1:5–4:13, a section that comprises the "prehistory" of Jesus' ministry by anticipating even the birth of Jesus with that of the last of the prophets, John the Baptist, in whom the dormant spirit of prophecy is revived (1:17).[26] The activity of the Spirit is also evident in Jesus' birth from the Spirit (1:35) and in the prophecies of Zechariah (1:68–79), Simeon (2:29–32), and Anna (2:36–38). The centerpiece of this section of spirit-filled activity, however, is the Song of Mary (1:46–55). It is linked in terms of language and theme to Hannah's song of rejoicing over the unexpected conception of Samuel (1 Sam. 2:1–10), and, by Luke's use of the term "female slave" (*doulē*) for Mary, to the theme of the outpouring of the Spirit on "all flesh" prophesied by Joel. This prophecy is quoted by Peter in Acts 2:18, as the followers of Jesus receive the Spirit: "And I will pour out my spirit in those days even upon your male and female slaves." Most important, however, the Song of Mary sets up the theme echoed throughout the Gospel of Luke of the reversals of status that occur through the hand of God, providing another thematic and literary link to Hannah's song in 1 Samuel (Luke 1:51–55). This unexpected good news to the excluded and outcast, which is in turn unexpected woe to others, is the theme also of Jesus' first sermon (4:18) and of his Sermon on the Plain, Luke's version of Matthew's Sermon on the Mount, which departs from their common Q tradition in having not only blessings promised to the poor but woes pronounced upon the rich (Luke 6:20–49).

This preliminary section of Luke ends after Jesus' receipt of the Spirit in visible form at his baptism (3:21–22) and the incarceration of his baptizer, John (3:20). With the departure of Jesus' antagonist in the temptation story, called "the devil" rather than "Satan" by Luke (4:13), until an "opportune moment" (which occurs with the devil's entry into Judas [22:3], initiating the end to Jesus' ministry), the stage is set for the Spirit-inaugurated ministry of Jesus to begin. It is thus fitting that Jesus begins his first sermon with a reading from Isaiah about the "spirit of the Lord" resting upon him (Isa. 61:1–2).

Proceeding to the way the passage itself is structured, we shall compare Matthew's and Mark's versions to that of Luke in order to reveal Luke's own unique concerns. Form-critically, the entire Lukan passage is a narrative, serving as the framework for two distinct units defined as "aphorisms" by

Crossan: "The Prophet's Own Country" (4:24), which appears in the Synoptic tradition, and "Physician, Heal Yourself" (4:23).[27] Within the framework of the narrative is a "biographical apophthegm" on Jesus' family, adapted from Mark,[28] and a logion or "dominical saying" (defined by Bultmann as a pronouncement of Jesus as "lord of the church") on Jews and Gentiles (4:25–27), unique to Luke.[29] Traditional also is the introduction to the passage (4:16), which has parallels in Matt. 13:53–54a and in Mark 6:1–2a, indicating that Luke has probably taken it from Mark, whose general outline of Jesus' ministry he follows. Yet, as we shall see, comparisons with similar passages in Mark 6:1–6 and Matt. 13:53–58 will show how freely Luke alters traditional material to suit his purposes. To summarize, the material inherited by Luke consists of v. 16, the introduction; v. 22, a Lukan adaptation of Mark 6:2b–3; and vv. 23–24 (the two aphorisms on "the Physician" and "the Prophet"), which are combined in this way only by Luke. Verses 17–21, the reading and interpretation of Isaiah, are unique to Luke, as are vv. 25–27, Jesus' teaching on the ministry of the prophets Elijah and Elisha, and vv. 28–30, the unexpectedly violent reaction of the audience, which had initially been favorably impressed by Jesus.

Let us begin with verse 16: "And he came to Nazareth, where he had been raised, and entered the synagogue according to his custom, on the day of the Sabbath, and he got up to read." Judging from the parallels in Mark 6:1–2a and Matt. 13:53–54a, Luke got from Mark the tradition of Jesus' going to the synagogue in his native region, and on the Sabbath. Luke adds, "as was his custom," in a characteristically Lukan emphasis on Jesus' fulfillment of Jewish custom, which Luke has already established in the birth narratives (2:21–24, 27, 41–42). Barr points out the further linkage of Jesus with Jewish custom through his being "called up" to read from the scroll of the prophet.[30] The reading from the Isaiah scroll (Isa. 61:1–12; 58:6), which is a combination of two verses, not in sequential order, and the subsequent interpretation of the reading (Luke 4:18–21) emphasize entirely Lukan themes: Jesus is the "one anointed" (*echrisen*, v. 18), the Messiah who is to "preach good news to the poor" and to announce the "acceptable (*dekton*) year of the Lord," which in Luke's understanding means the coming of the rule of God, initiating reversals of the present situation that will prove welcome for some, catastrophic for others (cf. 1:46–55; 6:20–49).[31]

The reaction to this announcement—which Perrin sees as Luke's own, to announce the good news to the poor and oppressed[32]—is astonishment. This astonishment echoes the reaction of the "crowd" in the synagogue in similar passages in Mark 6:2b–3 and Matt. 13:54b–56, but in Luke it is a reaction to a *specific* pronouncement. It prepares the reader for the crowd's further unexpected reaction: fury at Jesus' delineation of the purpose of God, not only as including in his care those who have been excluded—

Gentiles particularly—but the idea that God may even *prefer* them and has always done so (vv. 25–27). When the people of Nazareth hear Jesus' interpretation of the prophet's words, they try to "locate" him, to make him theirs: "Is this not the son of Joseph?" (v. 22). Whereas in the Marcan and Matthean versions Jesus' entire family is included in the question, Luke mentions only Joseph, as if to point out the irony of their question, having already in the Temple episode (2:49) established the fact that Jesus' true "father" is God. Thus the crowd, confounded by its own presuppositions, is disposed to misunderstand Jesus' role from the outset. Further, at this point in Mark's and Matthew's narratives, the crowd has already taken offense at Jesus for his presuming to teach them, prompting the saying on "the prophet in his own country." Luke postpones their taking offense and Jesus' quotation of the saying on the prophet in order to underscore the opposition between Jesus' "own" (and God's own) and those outside, an opposition that in Luke's scheme provokes the wrath of the audience because it inverts their expectations, casting Jesus as an "outsider" to them and casting them as outsiders, even antagonists, to the rule of God that Jesus is sent to preach (vv. 28–30).

In Luke's version, the saying, "Physician, heal yourself" (v. 23), one with no parallels in the Synoptic tradition, is the preface to an anticipated request: "The things which we have heard were done in Capernaum—do them here, in your own native country." This implied request for miracles, not contained in Mark or Matthew, perhaps furnishes Luke's explanation of Jesus' nonperformance of miracles—his unwillingness—rather than his being unable to do them because of the lack of faith among "his own" people, as in Mark 6:4 and Matt. 13:57. The request is also the occasion for Jesus' saying in Luke about the prophet's own country (v. 24): "Truly I tell you that no prophet is acceptable (*dektos*) in his own country." Luke alters the Markan version of the saying (followed by Matthew), "A prophet is without honor (*atimos*) in his own country," perhaps as a play on words with the prophetic proclamation of "the acceptable (*dekton*) year of the Lord" in v. 19. Through this wordplay, Luke implies that neither the anointed prophet (Messiah) nor his message is "acceptable."[33] As the stories of Elijah and Elisha will also show, prophets often perform miracles outside their own country, being chosen by God for that very purpose (vv. 25–27).

At this point in the Marcan and Matthean versions of the narrative, the audience has "taken offense" (*eskandalisen*) at Jesus because of his "local-boy" presumption, and he is therefore unable to do any "mighty work" because of their lack of faith in him (Mark 6:5–6; Matt. 13:58). The lack of faith in Mark and Matthew provides an occasion for the saying on the prophet, but Luke's version does not end at this point, nor with this saying. For Luke, the reaction of the crowd is not a mere unspecified "taking offense," nor is Jesus' reaction an inability to perform miracles, although he does talk about prophets performing miracles. The offense in Luke is deeper. In vv. 25–27, which follow thematically the saying on the prophet, Jesus mentions two of the mightiest prophets in Israelite history: Elijah, whose miracle of resurrection, alluded to by the mention of the Sidonian widow, is replicated by Jesus' raising of the widow's son at Nain in Luke 7:11–17, and Elisha. Luke's choice of words here indicates not merely that these Israelite prophets had dealings with Gentiles (Elijah with a widow from Sidon, Elisha with the Syrian leper Naaman), or that a prophet's ministry should be to the poor and outcast (a widow, a leper), but that God's *intention* is to send his prophets to such persons. In this case, the excluded are pointedly Gentiles, the prophets being sent to them even though there were plenty of widows and lepers in Israel. The use of the passive voice indicates that the prophets, like Jesus, are *God's* instruments to reach the outcast: Elijah is "sent out" and Naaman "is cleansed."

The audience's reaction to this story, which Bultmann believes is an independent piece in the tradition, itself a prophetic saying,[34] appears to be out of proportion to Jesus' words. But in the context of Luke's purpose, it is entirely appropriate. Not only is offense taken, but great offense indeed. All are "filled with anger," and they intend to throw Jesus off the brow of the hill at Nazareth (vv. 28–30)—an attempt of Jesus' "own" to cast him out. The startling reaction of the crowd, which echoes their astonishment at his initial words, is perhaps intended by Luke to make his readers question why the crowd is so angry with Jesus that they want to kill him. In Bultmann's view, the saying in vv. 25–27 "may well be a secondary community construction, introduced into the anti-Jewish polemic of the Gentile Christian Church."[35] The crowd's reaction may also belong to the same construction, indicating the Lukan community's view that Jesus as Messiah was sent to the Gentiles (themselves) from the beginning, and not just after his rejection by Israel as in Matthew and Mark, where the rejection occurred *because* of his sending. Without adopting Bultmann's certainty as to the location of Luke within purely Gentile Christianity, we might consider the fact that Luke, unlike Mark and Matthew, has no saying of Jesus in reply to the Gentile woman's importunity on taking the "children's" (i.e., Israel's) bread and throwing it to the "dogs" (i.e., Gentiles; cf. Mark 7:24–30; Matt. 15:21–28). This saying is prefaced in Matthew with Jesus' assertion that his mission is only "to the lost sheep of the house of Israel" (Matt. 15:24). Thus we may conclude that even if Luke does not reflect a directly anti-Jewish polemic in vv. 25–27, he does show not only that God had always intended the inclusion of the excluded, especially Gentiles, but also that his activity is specifically directed to them. Luke's Gentile Christians may thus consider themselves rather than the Jews to be God's elect.

What has our redaction-critical analysis of this particular passage shown us about Luke's activity as a theologian? In the first place, his setting of this passage as a "programmatic statement" of the purpose of Jesus' ministry shows us what Luke believed that ministry to be. Jesus' messiahship ("anointing," 4:18) through the "spirit of the Lord" is a prophetic mission of proclamation of God's "acceptable year," which includes "good news to the poor," "release to the captives," and "restoration of sight to the blind" (4:18). It includes more than just pronouncement, however: The anointed one, as God's agent, is also "to send forth in liberty those who have been oppressed." The ministry of Luke's Jesus is thus portrayed as a prophetic call not only to proclaim but to inaugurate God's "acceptable year" by summoning to inclusion those who have been excluded. Those who do not accept the excluded are themselves "unacceptable" to God and in turn find themselves outsiders. To them, this is not "good news" at all, yet for Luke God's rule is located in this activity, "in the midst of you" (17:23). God's intention according to Luke, fulfilled by Jesus and carried on by the apostles, is for his message to reach those for whom it is not expected, including the Gentiles. Mere inclusion of the Gentiles, moreover, is not the point, since the Messiah is *sent* to the Gentiles *because* they have been excluded from the good news of God's kingdom. By these means Luke also explains the "problem" of Israel's rejection of Jesus as the Messiah by putting it in the framework of the unexpected, radical reversals that are the hallmark of God's saving activity. The rejection is part of God's plan and even hastens the inauguration of God's rule.

Limitations and Drawbacks of the Method

The foregoing redaction-critical analysis of a specific passage in Luke's Gospel has offered a method for gaining insights into the unique theological contributions of "Luke" to early Christianity. This is not to say that the method does not have significant drawbacks, which current trends in biblical scholarship have recognized and critiqued. The primary drawback to this method is that crediting individual "evangelists" with distinct personal perspectives is an example of what some modern literary critics, who maintain that an author's intentions cannot be known or are irrelevant to the text, call the "intentional fallacy." That is to say that, when positing an evangelist as an "author," the critic thereby assumes that this "author" is speaking from a definite viewpoint that can be determined with some degree of reliability from evidence offered by the text and that this viewpoint governs the text's meaning at later stages in its transmission. Traditionally, redaction critics have tried to distinguish characteristic language and recurrent themes or "leading ideas" (leitmotifs) and to isolate certain passages in the Gospels themselves as the "key" to the author's "life-setting" and hence intention. Marxsen, for example, understands the "Little Apocalypse" of Mark 13 as the "key" to Mark's situation; indeed, it is in connection with this passage that Marxsen speaks of Mark's intent.[36]

Marxsen's analysis of Mark, Conzelmann's study of Luke-Acts, and Bornkamm, Barth, and Held's treatment of Matthew—three landmark redaction-critical studies—have tended to dominate subsequent views of the respective evangelists' intentions. This intentional approach, unless used with extreme caution, may result in an interpretation that ignores its own presuppositions, often including Eurocentric and androcentric biases, thus taking the path of circular argumentation. The technique may also therefore be incompatible with other forms of contemporary biblical criticism, especially postmodern critical methods such as deconstruction. As Terence J. Keegan, in his overview of postmodernism's impact on biblical criticism, observes, the tenets central to postmodern critiques clash with those of traditional critical methods: "Any attempt to conceive of a literary text as a structure with a determinate meaning leads to indeterminacy."[37] Postmodern criticism challenges the assumption that one can know the intention or purposes of an author, or that such knowledge is crucial to the interpretation of a text. Nevertheless, while the privileging of a single voice in a text has proven highly problematic for contemporary methods of biblical scholarship, the redaction-critical method helped lead to the notion of such privilege. Perhaps the technique of redaction criticism has called for its own deconstruction. Indeed, Moore has named the German-identified type of literary criticism that includes source, form, and redaction criticism "deconstruction's elderly uncle," and claims that it is much more like deconstruction than modern American literary criticism, especially narrative criticism.[38]

Another drawback to redaction criticism is that it has been most often applied to the New Testament (but see chapter 4), and until quite recently exclusively to the Synoptic Gospels. This limitation is understandable, given the fact that redaction criticism developed out of work on the "Synoptic problem," and because the Synoptic Gospels (and the *Gospel of Thomas*) are associated with the name of an "author," and may be readily compared with one another form-critically. Thus layers of tradition, interpretation, and the redactor's (or author's) own contributions are most easily recognizable here. The method is less readily applied, therefore, when it is more difficult either to discern layers of tradition or to compare the author's work with that of another inheritor of the same tradition. Nevertheless, redaction criticism has been applied to the Gospel of John (J. Louis Martyn, *History and Theology in the Fourth Gospel*, 1968), often in combination with source criticism (Raymond Brown, *The Gospel according to John*, 1966; Robert Fortna, *The Gospel of Signs*, 1970). Burton Mack (*The Lost Gospel*,

1993) and John Kloppenborg (*The Formation of Q*, 1987) have even applied the technique to analysis of Q, positing three different layers, each with its own particular theology, for a Gospel whose existence remains, however well-supported, hypothetical.

Nonetheless, although redaction criticism throws into high relief the idea of individual "authors," paradoxically it does not work as well with one of the known and most prolific authors of the New Testament, Paul. This may be because Paul, while at times giving a nod to the "things I received" (cf. 1 Cor. 13:3–8), was for the most part consciously battling any visible reliance upon "tradition," especially that coming from Jerusalem (cf. Gal. 1:14–2:11). Although it is conceivable that studies of Paul as a redactor of inherited traditions could be undertaken, a more fruitful approach, like that of MacDonald in *The Gospel and the Apostle*, considers Paul's followers (the "authors" of the Deutero-Pauline and Pastoral epistles) as redactors of the tradition that *they* received from Paul and handed on to their own communities, with their own "necessary" alterations to the tradition.

Despite its drawbacks, the redaction-critical method, as a part of the historical-critical paradigm, attempts not to straitjacket interpretation but to discern both layers of tradition in the Gospels and the distinct contributions of the evangelists as theologians located within specific early Christian communities.

Notes

1. David Barr, *New Testament Story* (Belmont, Calif.: Wadsworth, 1987), 144.

2. Stephen D. Moore, *Literary Criticism and the Gospels: The Theoretical Challenge* (New Haven, Conn.: Yale University Press, 1989), xx–xxi.

3. Rolf Rendtorff, "The Paradigm Is Changing: Hopes—and Fears," *Biblical Interpretation* 1 (1993): 50–51.

4. Norman R. Perrin and Dennis Duling, *The New Testament: An Introduction*, 2d ed. (New York: Harcourt Brace Jovanovich, 1982), p. 236.

5. Joachim Rohde (*Rediscovering the Teaching of the Evangelists* [Philadelphia: Westminster, 1968; ET of *Die Redaktionsgeschichtliche Methode*], p. 10) attributes the first use of this term to Willi Marxsen, in the *Monatschrift für Pastoraltheologie* 6 (1954): 254.

6. Perrin, *What Is Redaction Criticism?* Guides to Biblical Scholarship, New Testament Series (Philadelphia: Fortress, 1969), 3. Rohde (*Rediscovering the Teaching*, 10) credits Günther Bornkamm's research on Matthew in 1948 with the first use of the method, although the term was first applied by Marxsen to Hans Conzelmann's study of Luke-Acts.

7. Wilhelm Wrede, *Das Messiasgeheimnis in den Evangelien* (Göttingen: Vandenhoeck & Ruprecht, 1901), 131; cited in Perrin, *What Is Redaction Criticism?*, 3.

8. Perrin, *What Is Redaction Criticism?*, 1; cf. Rohde, *Rediscovering the Teaching*, 10.

9. Dibelius, however, referred to the redaction-critical method as "composition criticism" or "composition history" (*Kompositionsgeschichte*), as did Ernst Haenchen in his 1966 study of Acts; cf. Perrin, *What Is Redaction Criticism?*, 1.

10. See, for example, Rendtorff, "The Paradigm Is Changing," 50–51.

11. Barr, *New Testament Story*, 144; Perrin, *What Is Redaction Criticism?*, 22–23. According to Rohde (*Rediscovering the Teaching*, 10), Bornkamm's 1948 article, "Die Sturmstillung im Matthäusevangelium" ("The Stilling of the Storm in Matthew's Gospel," reprinted in Günther Bornkamm, G. Barth, and H. J. Held, *Tradition and Interpretation in Matthew*, [Philadelphia: Westminster, 1963]) was the first study to use the method.

12. Barr, *New Testament Story*, 145.

13. Rendtorff, "The Paradigm Is Changing," 51.

14. Rohde, *Rediscovering the Teaching*, 9.

15. John Dominic Crossan, *The Cross That Spoke* (San Francisco: Harper & Row, 1988), 21ff.

16. The term "intentional fallacy" was defined as a fallacy in literary and aesthetic criticism by W. K. Wimsatt Jr. and Monroe C. Beardsley in an article entitled "The Intentional Fallacy," *Sewanee Review* 54 (1946): 468–88.

17. David J. A. Clines, "Biblical Interpretation in an International Perspective," *Biblical Interpretation* 1 (1993): 86.

18. Robert W. Funk, Roy W. Hoover, and the Jesus Seminar, *The Five Gospels*, (New York: Macmillan, 1993), 21–22.

19. Cf. Helmut Koester, "The Structure and Criteria of Early Christian Beliefs," *Trajectories in Early Christianity*, ed. James M. Robinson and Helmut Koester (Philadelphia: Fortress, 1972), 205–31.

20. John Dominic Crossan's *Sayings Parallels* (Philadelphia: Fortress, 1986) also helps in the classification of these "forms."

21. Perrin, *What Is Redaction Criticism?*, 39.

22. Scripture translations in this chapter are the author's own.

23. Perrin, *What Is Redaction Criticism?*, 63.

24. Ibid., 28.

25. Cf. Barr, *New Testament Story*, 207–8, for possible interpretations of the introduction and Luke's "intended" audience.

26. Conzelmann's study of Luke-Acts (*The Theology of St. Luke*, trans. Geoffrey Buswell [New York: Harper & Row, 1961]) divides Luke's two-volume work into three eras of salvation history: the "time of the prophets" up to the birth of the Baptist; the "time of Jesus" up to the end of the Gospel; and the "time of the Church," beginning with the receipt of the Spirit by the apostles at Pentecost in Acts 2. All three eras, according to Conzelmann, are initiated by and filled with the Holy Spirit.

27. According to Crossan (*Sayings Parallels*), this latter aphorism appears in the Thomas tradition (*Gospel of Thomas* 31; Papyrus Oxyrhynchus 1, 31) and in Genesis Rabbah 15c, but not in Mark or in Q, the two sources common to Matthew and Luke. The aphorism is thus not "Synoptic."

28. Rudolf Bultmann, *History of the Synoptic Tradition*, trans. John Marsh (New York: Harper & Row, 1963), 31.

29. Ibid., 116, 227.

30. Barr, *New Testament Story*, 212, 215. Luke's constant explanation of "Jewish custom" is also an indication that he is writing largely for Gentiles, probably those who had little or no knowledge of Jewish practice.

31. Cf. Elisabeth Schüssler Fiorenza, *In Memory of Her: A Feminist Theological Reconstruction of Christian Origins* (New York: Crossroad, 1983), for Luke's scheme of

reversal. Schüssler Fiorenza, like other liberation theologians, regards Luke as an evangelist to the poor and outcast, without emphasizing the fact that Luke's Jesus promises "woes" not only for the rich and the powerful but also on others who perceive themselves favored by God: i.e., the Jews. This perspective thus inadvertently ignores Luke's anti-Judaism.

32. Perrin, *Rediscovering the Teaching of Jesus* (New York: Harper & Row, 1967), 63.

33. Cf. Conzelmann, *Theology of St. Luke*, 36–37, for a different perspective on Jesus' nonperformance of miracles.

34. Bultmann, *History of the Synoptic Tradition*, 116.

35. Ibid., 116, 127.

36. Willi Marxsen, *Mark the Evangelist*, trans. James Boyce et al. (Nashville: Abingdon, 1969), 167.

37. Terence J. Keegan, "Biblical Criticism and the Challenge of Postmodernism," *Biblical Interpretation* 3 (1995): 3–4.

38. Stephen D. Moore, *Poststructuralism and the New Testament* (Philadelphia: Fortress, 1994), 65–81.

For Further Reading

Introductions and Overviews

Bultmann, Rudolf. *History of the Synoptic Tradition*. Trans. John Marsh. New York: Harper & Row, 1963.

Dibelius, Martin. *From Tradition to Gospel*. Trans. B. L. Woolf. New York: Scribner's, 1935.

Lightfoot, R. H. *History and Interpretation in the Gospels*. Bampton Lectures, 1934. New York: Harper & Row, 1935.

Perrin, Norman. *What Is Redaction Criticism?* Guides to Biblical Scholarship, New Testament Series. Philadelphia: Fortress, 1969.

Rohde, Joachim. *Rediscovering the Teaching of the Evangelists*. Philadelphia: Westminster, 1968.

Studies of Specific New Testament Books

Bornkamm, Günther, G. Barth, and H. J. Held. *Tradition and Interpretation in Matthew*. Trans. Percy Scott. Philadelphia: Westminster, 1963.

Conzelmann, Hans. *The Theology of St. Luke*. Trans. Geoffrey Buswell. New York: Harper & Row, 1960.

Crossan, John Dominic. *Four Other Gospels: Shadows on the Contours of Canon*. Minneapolis: Winston-Seabury, 1985.

Edwards, Richard A. *A Theology of Q*. Philadelphia: Fortress, 1976.

Gärtner, Bertil E. *The Theology of the Gospel according to Thomas*. Trans. Eric J. Sharpe. New York: Harper & Row, 1961.

Martyn, J. Louis. *History and Theology in the Fourth Gospel*. New York: Harper & Row, 1968.

Marxsen, Willi. *Mark the Evangelist: Studies in the Redaction History of the Gospel.* Trans. James Boyce et al. Nashville: Abingdon, 1969.

O'Neill, J. C. *The Theology of Acts in Its Historical Setting.* London: SPCK, 1961.

Suggs, M. Jack. *Wisdom, Christology, and Law in Matthew's Gospel.* Cambridge, Mass.: Harvard University Press, 1970.

Talbert, Charles H. *Literary Patterns, Theological Themes, and the Genre of Luke-Acts.* SBL Monograph Series. Missoula, Mont.: Society of Biblical Literature, 1975.

PART TWO

EXPANDING THE TRADITION

6

SOCIAL-SCIENTIFIC CRITICISM

DALE B. MARTIN

N o title given to this chapter will please every scholar whose work is discussed within it. Some scholars are content to define themselves as social historians, seeing their own work as a continuation of traditional historical criticism of the Bible, except that they explore social aspects of biblical issues that have traditionally been analyzed from a theological point of view. Other scholars explicitly call their work "social-scientific," indicating that they self-consciously appropriate concepts and models from sociology and anthropology and attempt to explain ancient Israelite and early Christian developments by use of those models. Still others resist the labels of "sociologist" or "social historian" entirely, and prefer to characterize their work as "cultural anthropology" or "ethnography of ancient Israel or early Christianity." All these approaches will be considered in this essay as attempts to interpret early Christian literature and history through categories borrowed from the social sciences, sociology, and anthropology in particular.

Although social-scientific criticism as a subspecialty within biblical studies has a relatively brief history, beginning only about twenty years ago, it owns what may be called a long "prehistory" within historical criticism of the Bible. Indeed, as Elisabeth Schüssler Fiorenza insists, modern historical research has always had social interests: "I don't think there is a historical method without a social or sociological awareness and conceptualization. For example, historiography as a discipline has been conceptualized as one of national states and their identity, and that is a social or sociological concept."[1] In fact, the discipline of sociology in its inception owes something to nineteenth-century biblical scholarship, since Max Weber, one of the pioneers of sociology, was influenced by Rudolph Sohm's debates with Adolf von Harnack, as well as by Julius Wellhausen's analysis of the development of ancient Israel.[2] Around the turn of the century, Marxist scholarship took the lead in the social analysis of early Christianity. In 1894 Frederick Engels argued that early Christianity was a social movement of the dispossessed with remarkable similarities to modern working-class movements, while in 1925 Karl Kautsky expanded the thesis to present an account of early Christianity from a (rather simplistic) Marxist point of view.[3] Such arguments affected even mainstream biblical scholarship of the time, as scholars such as Ernst Troeltsch and Adolf Deissmann tried to broaden the scope of traditional theological analysis to pose questions about the social significances of the New Testament.[4] Although the early Marxist account of incipient Christianity has generally been rejected by historians, including most Marxists, their interests in the social locations of early Christians and the social and political ramifications of Christian language live on in all contemporary social-scientific approaches to the New Testament.

Other movements of early twentieth-century scholarship—the history of religions school, form criticism, and the so-called Chicago School of social analysis—may also be seen as precursors to social-scientific criticism. The history of religions school includes those scholars who made connections between New Testament concepts and practices and religious elements from the surrounding (primarily Greco-Roman) environment.[5] Early form critics, notably Martin Dibelius and Rudolf Bultmann, wanted to isolate sections of the New Testament text, reconstruct their *Sitz im Leben* or "setting in life," and show how those originally oral units functioned in early Christian contexts of preaching, worship, prayer, or other social activity.[6] The "Chicago School," represented mainly by Shailer Mathews and Shirley Jackson Case, also addressed social issues, such as why Christianity succeeded among Gentiles when it did not among Jews, and the social level of early Christians.[7]

Several contemporary scholars have pointed out, however, that none of these precursors of the current social-scientific approach had a direct influence on the rise of similar concerns in the 1960s and 1970s. As Wayne Meeks puts it, "The *religionsgeschichtliche Schule* [history of religions school] pursued a history of ideas and mythology, lacking any kind of sociological dimension. And the form critics, who talked about *Sitz im Leben*, did not use anything that resembles sociological method in order to define what the typical life settings were."[8] John Elliott says much the same thing about the Chicago School: "Nobody out of that school is responsible for stimulating any of us when we revived [the social-scientific approach] in the sixties and seventies. Though we can look back and see interesting insights [in the Chicago School], the approach was quickly dropped."[9] Recent social-scientific criticism of the New Testament in its multiple embodiments thus dates from the 1960s and 1970s. From a variety of perspectives, scholars began to ask social questions about the New Testament. The discussion below sketches the beginnings of that recent history by mentioning the foundational works (though not necessarily the most recent or ultimately most important) of four scholars who led the way in social-scientific methods and the New Testament. Although the account offered here is necessarily selective and partial, it is nonetheless representative of the various ways in which New Testament scholars became interested in social-scientific criticism.

In 1967–68 John Gager was teaching an introductory course on the study of religion at Haverford College, in which he had students read the works of Clifford Geertz, Evans Pritchard, Max Weber, Peter Berger, and Edmund Leach, among others. At that time New Testament scholars generally made no use of such sociologists and anthropologists for their own work. The result of Gager's attempt to do so was the publication in 1975 of *Kingdom and Community*, in which he applied different social-scientific theories and methods to early Christian texts.[10] For example, Gager analyzes early Christianity as a "millenarian movement" that developed in ways similar to modern movements expecting an imminent end to the present world order. When the *parousia* failed to occur in the first century, early Christians experienced "cognitive dissonance," a psychological tension resulting from a discrepancy between two constructions of reality, in this case their expectation of Jesus' return and the nonoccurrence of that event. They reacted to that dissonance by renewed missionary activity, as have modern groups documented by sociologists of religion. Gager's work provoked great controversy and disagreement, a reaction that testifies to the far-reaching impact of *Kingdom and Community* on biblical studies.

In the mid-1960s John Elliott was involved in the civil rights movement, first in St. Louis and then in San Francisco. Later, through his participation in protests against the Vietnam War, his attention turned increasingly to the social and political ramifications of religious belief and action. Moreover, his political activity brought him into contact with others, such as Old Testament critic Norman Gottwald, who were pursuing ways to combine social analysis with historical study of the Bible. For Elliott, the result was an analysis of 1 Peter, *A Home for the Homeless*, the manuscript of which was completed in 1978.[11] Originally, Elliott called his study a "sociological exegesis" of 1 Peter but has since decided that the term is inappropriate since it excludes reference to anthropology, which provides important theoretical scaffolding for his claims. Elliott appropriates Bryan Wilson's typology of sects to argue that the Christians reflected in the text of 1 Peter saw themselves—or the author saw them—as "resident aliens," living in but opposed to the dominant Greco-Roman culture.[12] Recognition of the sectarian nature of the community illuminates the possible social functions of elements of the letter, such as the household code of 1 Peter 2:18–3:7. By reading 1 Peter with social-scientific concerns, Elliott suggested a possible historical reconstruction of one community of early Christianity.

Although most social-scientific criticism has taken place in North America, few scholars anywhere have been as influential in this field as

Gerd Theissen, a German. Influenced by sociological "functionalism," Theissen first analyzed the early "Jesus movement" by applying concepts derived for the most part from Max Weber and his later American disciple Talcott Parsons. Functionalism conceives of societies as something like organisms whose different elements (religious practices, belief structures, mechanisms for dealing with conflict, etc.) interact with one another to integrate different members and groups into the whole organism, diffusing conflict through repression and/or change. Conflict is often considered by functionalism a natural element in the development or evolution of a society, but it is usually seen as resolving itself within the modified but coherently "functioning" unity. In an important article first published in 1973, Theissen used the Gospel texts to reconstruct the prehistory of Palestinian Christianity, arguing that many Gospel sayings reflect a social role of the "Itinerant Radical" who, due to socioeconomic tensions and problems in first-century Palestine, abandoned normal social structures such as job and family to wander about preaching Jesus' message. Other early Christians in Palestine remained in their traditional social roles and provided support and communal structures for these "wandering charismatics." Theissen's ideas were later expanded in a book, *The Sociology of Early Palestinian Christianity*, and in several essays on Paul and the Corinthian church. Although Theissen's work is repeatedly criticized, it continues to have enormous influence on all branches of social-scientific criticism of the New Testament.[13]

One of the disseminators of Theissen's work on this side of the Atlantic has been Wayne A. Meeks, who, like other pioneering practitioners of social-scientific methods, became interested in them through a combination of pedagogical and research concerns. Meeks began teaching at Indiana University in 1966. Becoming more and more disenchanted with exclusively theological categories for teaching New Testament studies to undergraduates, he searched other disciplines for (in his words) "some sense of reality" not provided by a traditional history-of-religions approach. Unimpressed by most psychological models and many sociological ones, Meeks eventually settled on what may be identified as a moderate Weberian functionalism, although his work also shows strong influences from the "sociology of knowledge" theories of Peter Berger and Thomas Luckmann and from the cultural anthropology of Clifford Geertz. Meeks's most important work to date is *The First Urban Christians*, an analysis of Pauline Christianity using various social-scientific models and typologies. But the early piece that launched Meeks's social-scientific voyage and influenced many other scholars was "The Man from Heaven in Johannine Sectarianism," an examination of Johannine Christianity using concepts of sectarianism borrowed from the sociology of knowledge.[14] According to Meeks, John's portrayal of Jesus as one rejected

by his own people reflects the social rupture between the Johannine community and the synagogue:

> One of the primary functions of the book, therefore, must have been
> to provide a reinforcement for the community's social identity, which
> appears to have been largely negative. It provided a symbolic universe
> which gave religious legitimacy, a theodicy, to the group's actual iso-
> lation from the larger society.[15]

In 1973 these diverse initiatives in the social analysis of the New Testament converged, at least in North America, with the establishment by the
Society of Biblical Literature of a working group on "The Social World of
Early Christianity," chaired by Meeks and Leander Keck. In the following
years a split, reflected in the discussions of this working group, occurred
among scholars interested in social analysis. At the risk of oversimplification,
one may identify a break between those who are content to consider their
work to be "social history" and others who more self-consciously practice a
"social-scientific" method. The "social historians" (among whom one might
include John Gager, Wayne Meeks, William Countryman, and Howard Kee)
see themselves as using traditional historical-critical methods to explore the
"social world" of early Christianity. The "social scientists" (John Elliott,
Jerome Neyrey, Bruce Malina, Antoinette Wire, among others) argue, to the
contrary, that the task of cross-cultural analysis necessitates a more self-conscious use of anthropological or sociological models, made explicit at the
outset and tested thoroughly by application to the data mined from historical texts. The latter group has formed its own organs of dialogue and
research, the most visible of which is the current Society of Biblical Literature Section on "Social Sciences and New Testament Interpretation."

It would be a mistake, however, to paint a picture of two distinct groups
of scholars using opposing methods. Rather, in reading the numerous pub-
lications that use the term "social" somewhere in their self-descriptions and
in talking to scholars engaged in such research, one senses a spectrum of
opinion about what precisely a social-scientific method should be. Much of
the debate, as is already obvious from the discussion thus far, centers on the
use of "models" derived from the social sciences. Malina defines "model" as
"an abstract, simplified representation of some real world object, event, or
interaction constructed for the purpose of understanding, control, or pre-
diction . . . a scheme or pattern that derives from the process of abstracting
similarities from a range of instances in order to comprehend."[16] The problem with the term "model," however, is that it may refer to a classification
system as abstract, rigid, and universalizing as Mary Douglas's "group-grid"
construction, or to a conceptual construction as culturally specific, freely

used, and content-oriented as patron-client systems or societal perceptions of honor and shame.[17] Few historical critics, if any, doubt the usefulness of knowledge about ancient patron-client structures for interpretation of early Christianity. Many scholars, on the other hand, have found the "group-grid" model to be too rigid or uninteresting, if not downright incomprehensible, when applied to New Testament texts.[18] Thus the debate over method becomes complicated by different uses of the term "model," which sometimes refers to an explicit appropriation of a carefully defined research practice or taxonomy, sometimes to a flexible appropriation of social-historical categories, and sometimes simply to the presuppositions of the exegete. The disagreement really centers around what particular models are used and how they are used.

Reflecting on social-scientific criticism of the New Testament, Wayne Meeks, for example, agrees that scholars need to be clearer about their methodological presuppositions but expresses reservations about some uses of models:

> Once one has a model, one is tempted to use it no longer as a pattern for sorting data or a heuristic model to look through, but as material to fill in gaps where we do not have evidence. One is tempted to reify things, not only models, but types, and treat them as real things in the world. I am not satisfied, however, that any of the models is comprehensive enough to account for all the historical material; some are too bound to a particular cultural setting, usually ours, and whether they fit the ancient setting is often very difficult to tell.[19]

John Elliott, on the other hand, has criticized scholars for not recognizing that their own presuppositions are actually "models":

> I think another word for "presupposition" is "model," if by that we think of how we imagine the structure, population, activities, and dynamics of the first-century world. That is a very large, abstract model. We have to be clear to ourselves what implicit models we are using, then indicate what they are to one another so we can more adequately communicate with one another, then finally get to the critical point where we can evaluate one another's work.[20]

As Meeks's comments imply, some scholars feel that models have too often been anachronistically employed, thus imposing modern sociological categories on ancient texts. William Countryman, for example, admits that "one should pay attention to social models in the hope that they will break up one's preconceptions." But he continues with more reticence: "I don't think models evolved to explain modern society will always explain ancient society. There is no society, in my opinion, that completely matches up with the ancient Mediterranean world, though there may be some that are more closely related than others."[21] Jerome Neyrey responds, however, that the very point of using self-conscious models is to avoid anachronism. "I take these [models] and test them. Do they apply to the first century? By and large I find that, yes, the honor and shame system described by anthropologists does apply to the ancient texts. This is not anachronistic, imposing a twentieth-century phenomenon. The same applies to patron-client models and structures."[22]

Often debate about the use of models is linked with concern over the "scientific" reliability or respectability of social approaches to the New Testament. In a recent survey, Bengt Holmberg raises the issue of the "scientific maturity" of the approach, criticizing, for example, the theory of "relative deprivation" used by John Gager on the grounds that it is too "psychological," cannot be objectively verified, and resembles "metaphysical" speculation rather than "scientific precision."[23] Indeed, some scholars sound as if they believe that the use of social-scientific models that have been "tested" in the laboratory of anthropological research can deliver them from the dangers of ethnocentrism; they seem confident that the models will enable them to see things the way ancient Mediterraneans saw them.[24] Thus John Elliott, when asked whether he views his work as "scientific," answers, "Definitely yes. That is the reason I want to clarify the models, because if I can demonstrate that one abstract conception is more useful than another, I have been able to advance research. I don't want simply to say something interesting, but to advance the whole state of research in a particular area."[25]

Such a view, however, does not characterize all the scholars who use social-scientific methods. Susan R. Garrett describes her method not as "scientific" but as "hermeneutic." She explains,

> There is an insistence by some people that by formulating hypotheses and testing them one will be able to escape ethnocentric bias, and I think that is an illusion. One cannot escape it, and the very formulation of the hypothesis, of questions to apply to the data is already ethnocentrically biased. The data generated and collected is biased from the beginning, and there is simply no way out of that trap.[26]

Even John Gager, who is well known for his use of explicit models, resists the label "scientific":

> I am very much a humanist. I have no idea what the term "scientific" would mean in this context. The people who talk in terms of science sometimes also talk in terms of provability or demonstrability, and I

am sufficiently a postmodern thinker that I do not believe that the notion of demonstrability or provability has any value at all in our field. It's just a red herring. If you talk to anthropologists these days, they don't put much weight on notions of demonstrability either but are more interested in aspects like the cogency, coherence, and persuasiveness of an account.[27]

As these diverse sentiments indicate, there is currently much debate over what constitutes a social-scientific method for biblical studies, and much of the debate centers around profound theoretical differences, particularly epistemological ones. Nonetheless, these various scholars share the belief that all language is ineluctably social, that religion is to be interpreted as woven into the complex fabric of social structures and symbolic matrices, and that sociology and anthropology can provide useful perspectives and methods for interpreting the function of religion in society.

Examples of Social-Scientific Criticism in Luke-Acts

Ready examples are at hand that illustrate these various social-scientific approaches in studies of Luke-Acts. Three such examples demonstrate how different scholars, with somewhat different theoretical presuppositions, use social-scientific methods for exegesis. The first is the analysis of "magic" from a cultural-anthropological perspective embodied in Susan R. Garrett's *The Demise of the Devil: Magic and the Demonic in Luke's Writings*.[28] The second comes from Philip Francis Esler, who uses a concept of "legitimation" derived from the sociology of knowledge practiced by Peter Berger and Thomas Luckmann. The third example is an article by Douglas E. Oakman, that is the most explicit and rigorous in its use of a specific social-scientific model.

In *The Demise of the Devil*, Garrett does not claim to employ any explicit model. Indeed, beginning with a discussion of anthropological studies of "magic," she criticizes an older model that differentiated "magic" from "religion" or "science" and that spoke of certain cultures as evidencing a "magical world view." Scholars who adopt this model consider magic to be "instrumental and goal-oriented" in its attempts to manipulate forces through ritualistic activities that practically guarantee results. Religion, on the other hand, is understood as a relationship among beings, communication rather than manipulation, and carries with it no assurance of "automatic efficacy."[29] According to this view, the anthropologist should be able to analyze how an activity is performed and decide whether the phenomenon falls under the category "magic" or "religion."

Garrett notes that such an approach is "etic," meaning that the activity is described from the anthropologist's, rather than from the native's, point of view, using categories of description and analysis that come from outside the cultural sphere being examined. Garrett characterizes her analysis, on the other hand, as balancing etic categories with "emic" ones. Instead of attempting to decide whether an action portrayed in the New Testament is "really" magical or religious, she tries to perceive the activity from the point of view of the "native," in this case, the writer and early readers of Luke-Acts. Borrowing language from cultural anthropologists such as Clifford Geertz, Garrett states her working presupposition:

> Like language, ritual acts are socially transmitted and contextually dependent. Hence, they have "meaning" only as it is attributed to them by actors and observers (enemies *and* supporters), whose various interpretations are guided by their respective social locations and by the shape of their own cultural world."[30]

This means that for Garrett's purposes, whether (for example) an action of Paul in Acts would have been considered magical or religious has little connection with what Paul actually did, but rather would have been decided by intricate social conventions of labeling and by the perceptions of the people who occupied Paul's own cultural, or subcultural, world. Garrett sees her role as something like an "interpretive ethnographer" of the "culture" of Luke-Acts, who, as a member of another culture, questions the text to ascertain "the symbolic forms—words, images, institutions, behaviors—in terms of which . . . people actually represented themselves to themselves and one another."[31] The fruitfulness of Garrett's approach is demonstrated by her exegesis of various passages in Acts, including the problematic text of Acts 13:4–12. The crux of the problem is this: If Luke wants to contrast Christianity with magic, surely one of his goals, why does he portray Paul as "cursing" Bar Jesus—a deed that appears, at least to modern persons, just as "magical" as any action of Bar Jesus? What is the function of this conflict in Luke's narrative and worldview?

By comparing ancient Jewish and Christian works that speak of magic or cursing, Garrett demonstrates how references to magic function in Luke's overarching story as signals of the activity of Satan. Magic and religion cannot be differentiated on the basis of a phenomenological understanding of the activity itself. "In portraying Paul's curse of Bar Jesus, Luke reveals that he shared with ancient magicians . . . the presupposition that words backed up with sufficient authority could wreak terrible damage."[32] But in Luke's view, Paul's actions cannot be magic because magic is satanic, and Luke portrays Paul as "*conquering* magical-satanic powers." Of course, opponents of Christianity could easily construe the situation oppositely, seeing the healings and exorcisms of Luke-Acts as magic.

In her discussion of the Bar Jesus incident and others (including, for example, Acts 8:4–25 and 19:8–20), Garrett's interests are primarily exegetical: She is concerned with the inter- and intratextual connections in Luke-Acts and related documents. *The Demise of the Devil*, therefore, is for the most part a traditional exegetical study in the historical-critical, philological tradition. Her use of social-scientific methods consists in her adoption of an ethnographic posture. In other words, she listens to the text of Luke-Acts and other ancient documents with the ears of an ethnographer; she attempts to trace unspoken connections, assumed meanings and references, underlying but unacknowledged myths. Other social-scientific critics, on the other hand, exhibit what might be called primarily historical interests. Although they are interested in exegesis, their ultimate concern is to reconstruct structures, conflicts, and developments of early Christian communities. Their concentration on the texts of early Christianity has as its goal more to ascertain the function of a particular document within the social history of early Christian groups than to explicate literary problems internal to the documents themselves. An example of this latter approach is Philip Francis Esler's *Community and Gospel in Luke-Acts*.[33]

Esler begins by criticizing the view that Luke wrote his work to apply a previously developed theological position to social and political issues, i.e., that Luke's theology came first and only derivatively had social or political significance. As Esler responds, "What if Luke did not sharply differentiate the theological realm from the social and political, but saw them, in fact, as closely inter-related? What if social and political exigencies played a vital role in the formation of Luke's theology, rather than merely constituting the areas in which it was applied?"[34] Of course, one traditional interpretation maintains that Luke-Acts is directly concerned with political questions, namely, that it is an apology for Christianity directed to a non-Christian Greco-Roman audience—or, alternatively, for the Roman Empire and the dominant Greco-Roman culture directed toward Christians. Esler rejects such readings of Luke-Acts, insisting that its function is not apology but "legitimation." Luke wanted to legitimate Christianity to his contemporary fellow Christians, both Jews and Gentiles, including some Romans, who "needed strong assurance that their decision to convert and to adopt a different life-style had been the correct one."[35]

Taking his model of legitimation from Peter Berger and Thomas Luckmann's writings, Esler defines legitimation as "a process which is carried out after a social institution has originated in the first place. In essence, legitimation is the collection of ways in which an institution is explained and justified to its members."[36] Legitimation appeals to other beliefs, assumptions, myths, or elements of the audience's "symbolic universe," a concept that is very important for the sociology of knowledge. As Esler explains:

> A symbolic universe is a body of theoretical tradition which integrates different provinces of meaning and encompasses the institutional order in a symbolic totality. . . . Within such a universe, the members of the institution have an experience of everything in its right place and also of the various phases of their biography as ordered. . . . Over the institutional level as well, symbolic universes operate as sheltering canopies. The symbolic universe also orders history; it locates all collective acts in a cohesive unity that includes past, present and future.[37]

Having set forth his theoretical assumptions, Esler proceeds to investigate several traditional exegetical conundrums of Luke-Acts. In the last chapter Esler explores a problem that has vexed many interpreters of Luke-Acts: the stance of the author toward the Roman Empire. Surely one of Luke's purposes is to portray Christianity as politically innocuous, as a movement that should be tolerated if not welcomed by Romans. Why, then, does Luke retain aspects of the tradition that could make Christianity appear revolutionary or at least socially problematic, such as the experiences of Jesus and Paul before Roman courts, the obvious corruptness of Roman officials such as Felix and Festus, and Christianity's concern with the poor and oppressed? What precisely is Luke's position toward the Roman government, and whom does he want to influence with his depiction of it?

First, Esler argues that Luke modifies much of his inherited tradition to show that even though the new religious movement might appear politically dangerous, Jesus and his disciples were repeatedly pronounced innocent of breaking any Roman law. Furthermore, when the Christians found themselves in trouble, it was through the instigation of unbelieving Jews, whose occasional successes against the Christians were due to the weakness or self-aggrandizement of individual Roman officials, not to any problem with the system of Roman jurisprudence itself. Indeed, the Roman system often saved Christians from local, and in Luke's view, unfounded hostility.[38]

But why does Luke go out of his way to portray the Romans this way?

> There is only one answer which offers a satisfying explanation for the political theme in Luke-Acts, that among the members of Luke's community were a number of Romans serving the empire in a military or administrative capacity, and that part of Luke's task was to present Christian history in such a way as to demonstrate that faith in Jesus Christ and allegiance to Rome were not mutually inconsistent.[39]

Esler has thus come full circle in his book to return to the theme of legitimation. He concludes,

> Luke's two volumes may be described as an exercise in the legitimation of a sectarian movement, as a sophisticated attempt to explain and justify Christianity to the members of his community at a time when they were exposed to social and political pressures which were making their allegiance waver. Luke represents traditions relating how the gospel was initially proclaimed by Jesus and later preached throughout the Roman East in such a way as to erect a symbolic universe, a sacred canopy, beneath which the institutional order of his community is given meaning and justification.[40]

Garrett and Esler are scholars who use social-scientific approaches rather freely, eclectically appropriating sociological or anthropological perspectives when they seem heuristically useful. A different practice is exemplified by *The Social World of Luke-Acts: Models for Interpretation* edited by Jerome Neyrey. The book includes articles by several scholars who meet regularly and collaborate in their use of explicit social-scientific models and methods.[41] This particular collection of essays by the "Context Group," as the scholars call themselves, includes studies of Luke-Acts centering on "honor and shame," personality in the first century, urban social relations of the preindustrial city, sickness and healing, and patron-client relations. One feature setting this collection of essays apart from most other social approaches to the New Testament is that each of the authors begins with a clearly expressed social-scientific model and proceeds to apply that model to the text of Luke-Acts. Some of the essays are more successful than others in blending social-scientific methods with textual interpretation, but the collection nevertheless serves as a valuable resource, even if only to spur theoretical and methodological discussion among biblical scholars.

An especially interesting article in *The Social World of Luke-Acts* is that by Douglas E. Oakman, "The Countryside in Luke-Acts."[42] Oakman begins with a conflict model of social interaction, as opposed to a structural-functionalist model. (Conflict models tend to analyze social structure and change by concentrating on the way different groups within a society pursue their own interests; the approach thus emphasizes the conflicts between different worldviews and ideologies rather than accepting the functionalist view of society as a self-maintaining organism. The opposition between these two approaches was important in sociological theory in past years, but the clean demarcation between them has now been generally blurred.) Oakman also outlines an agrarian social stratification model to demonstrate the way land and its resources are controlled in preindustrial, peasant economies. By carefully noting how Luke portrays the countryside and peasant activity in Luke-Acts, Oakman is able to address a concern that we already have seen dealt with in Esler's book: the political implications of Luke's writings. Oakman notes that although Luke does seem concerned about the poor, his apparent solutions to social inequalities center on voluntary charity within the church, never on a questioning of the land distribution system that sustained the economic injustices of the Roman Empire. Therefore, what might initially appear to be Luke's revolutionary inclination against the oppressive nature of early imperial economy turns out to be politically conservative. As Oakman concludes,

> What was originally a radical social critique by Jesus and his followers of the violent and oppressive political-economic order in the countryside under the early empire becomes in Luke's conception a rather innocuous sharing-ethic ambiguous in its import for rural dwellers. The countryside is apparently idealized by Luke as a place particularly receptive to this message. . . . No dramatic social reconstruction— such as the elimination of the preindustrial city or Roman imperium—is to be expected or is necessary.[43]

Oakman's article demonstrates the interesting results that can be obtained by combining detailed social-scientific models with historical and exegetical research.

A tight consensus, it is evident, does not exist among social-scientific critics regarding epistemology or methodology. Thus it is difficult to predict what the future will bring for this much-divided subdiscipline of biblical studies. Some opine that, due to the scarcity of data and evidence, we have *already* said most of what can be said about the social history of early Christianity. But most scholars believe that new directions in scholarship will emerge more from new questions and perspectives on the part of scholars than from new "raw" data (if such can theoretically be said to exist). Antoinette Wire, for example, points out that feminist scholarship has long led the way in understanding that "historical research reflects its own time." So the future of social-scientific criticism "depends on our history and what the trends are in our world."[44] As Andrew Overman puts it, "In all areas of academic study, especially religion, there is a synergistic relationship between our contemporary reality and the research we do on antiquity. Our reading is nuanced and sometimes changed radically, based on changes in our contemporary world." Of course, more historical discoveries and a better knowledge of the materials we do possess would be welcome. "A broader and more sophisticated use of the Roman world—archaeology, epigraphy, realia—needs to come about to fill out this approach," Overman concludes.[45]

Beyond the question of data, however, I would like to note a few new theoretical directions being taken in the field. First, most scholars engaged in social approaches to the New Testament claim to find sociologists less and less helpful and anthropologists and ethnographers more and more interesting.[46] Second, many scholars recognize the importance of various literary methods and are attempting in their study of the New Testament to combine insights of literary critics with those of social critics. This movement in biblical studies perhaps reflects the burgeoning of "cultural studies" in many universities.[47] Third, the studies by Esler and Oakman mentioned above share a concern to analyze the social and political ramifications of religious language, texts, and movements. Such studies may be the harbingers of a growing interest in what may loosely be called "ideological criticism." Now that scholars have some social-historical material in hand, it may be time to interrogate that evidence more carefully to ascertain what structures and operations of power are reflected in the early church's texts. How do the theological debates of the New Testament relate to ideological conflicts or struggles for power among early Christians? What are the social and political positions of various Christian groups in relation to the dominant Greco-Roman culture or to the Roman Empire? With several literary-critical circles turning to ideological issues (I have in mind various forms of poststructuralist criticism, the "New Historicism," feminist criticism, gay and lesbian theories, besides the many different embodiments of Marxist analysis), it is to be expected that biblical scholars, especially those just emerging from university graduate schools, will bring similar interests to their study of early Christianity.

Whatever the future may bring, it is clear that after a twenty-year deluge of articles and books employing social-scientific methods for the study of the Bible, the approach has now arrived at a certain maturity. Different schools of thought even within this subdiscipline of biblical studies vie for the attentions and approval of the guild as a whole. Social-scientific criticism, which only recently enjoyed the reputation of a maverick among methods, is now a staid and respectable (and predictable?) member of the neighborhood. Whether it continues to provoke controversy and interest probably depends more on the ingenuity of its practitioners than on any specific characteristic of the method itself.

Notes

1. Interview, May 23, 1991. This essay is based on a series of telephone interviews as well as published documents. Between May 22 and 27, 1991, the following people were interviewed, with transcriptions of those interviews providing the sources for many of the quotations in this essay: L. William Countryman, John H. Elliott, Elisabeth Schüssler Fiorenza, John Gager, Susan R. Garrett, Wayne A. Meeks, Jerome H. Neyrey, Andrew Overman, and Antoinette Wire. The reader should keep in mind that these

quotations are from oral interviews and therefore should not be expected to display the polished prose that characterizes the written works of the scholars quoted.

2. For the theological influences on Weber, see Gilbert A. Greggs Jr., "Priest, Prophet, and Apocalyptic: The Authoring of Religious Identity in the Period of the Restoration," (Ph.D. dissertation, Yale University, 1991), 74–114; see also Peter Burke, *Sociology and History* (London: Allen & Unwin, 1980), 20, 24; Fredric Jameson, "The Vanishing Mediator: Or, Max Weber as Storyteller," in *The Ideologies of Theory: Essays 1971–1986*, vol. 2 of *The Syntax of History* (Minneapolis: University of Minnesota Press, 1988), 23–34.

3. Frederick Engels, "On the History of Early Christianity," in *Marx and Engels on Religion* (Moscow: Progress Publishers, 1957); Karl Kautsky, *Foundations of Christianity* (New York: International, 1925).

4. Ernst Troeltsch, *The Social Teaching of the Christian Churches* (Chicago: University of Chicago, 1976); Adolf Deissmann, *Light from the Ancient East* (New York: George H. Doran, 1927).

5. See Werner George Kümmel, *The New Testament: The History of the Investigation of Its Problems*, trans. S. McLean Gilmour and Howard C. Kee (Nashville: Abingdon, 1972), 206–324.

6. Martin Dibelius, *The Message of Jesus Christ: The Tradition of the Early Christian Communities* (New York: Scribner's, 1939); Rudolf Bultmann, *The History of the Synoptic Tradition*, 2d ed. (Oxford: Basil Blackwell, 1968).

7. Shailer Mathews, *The Social Teaching of Jesus: An Essay in Christian Sociology* (New York: Macmillan, 1897); Shirley Jackson Case, *The Evolution of Early Christianity* (Chicago: University of Chicago, 1914); *The Social Origins of Christianity* (Chicago: University of Chicago, 1923).

8. Wayne Meeks, interview, May 22, 1991.

9. John Elliott, interview, May 24, 1991.

10. John Gager, *Kingdom and Community: The Social World of Early Christianity* (Englewood Cliffs, N.J.: Prentice-Hall, 1975).

11. John H. Elliott, *A Home for the Homeless: A Sociological Exegesis of 1 Peter, Its Situation and Strategy* (Philadelphia: Fortress, 1981).

12. Bryan R. Wilson, *Sects and Society: A Sociological Study of the Elim Tabernacle, Christian Science, and the Christadelphians* (Berkeley, Calif.: University of California Press, 1961).

13. Gerd Theissen, "Itinerant Radicalism: The Tradition of Jesus' Sayings from the Perspective of the Sociology of Literature," *Radical Religion* 2 (1975): 84–93, originally published in German in *Zeitschrift für Theologie und Kirche* 70 (1973): 245–71; see also *Sociology of Early Palestinian Christianity* (Philadelphia: Fortress, 1978); *The Social Setting of Pauline Christianity: Essays on Corinth* (Philadelphia: Fortress, 1982). The essays in the latter were written from 1973 to 1975. For a survey of critiques of Theissen's work, see Bengt Holmberg, *Sociology and the New Testament: An Appraisal* (Minneapolis: Fortress, 1990), 44–54, 119–25, 140, and the works there cited.

14. Wayne A. Meeks, "The Man from Heaven in Johannine Sectarianism," *Journal of Biblical Literature* 91 (1972): 44–72.

15. Ibid. 70.

16. Bruce Malina, "The Social Sciences and Biblical Interpretation," *Interpretation* 37 (1982): 231.

17. The "group-grid model," articulated by Mary Douglas, plots social groups on a chart depicting four quadrants arranged around two axes, one horizontal ("group") and one

vertical ("grid"), based on the worldview of the group and the members' attitudes toward issues such as purity, ritual, the body, and boundaries. The axis called "group" gauges the pressures put on individual members to conform to the group's norms and the degree to which individuals submit to those pressures. The "grid" axis measures the degree to which the society utilizes, on the one hand, a shared system of values and beliefs or, on the other hand, whether classification systems are "privatized." See *Natural Symbols: Explorations in Cosmology* (New York: Vintage, 1973; originally published in 1970), esp. 82–86.

18. For use of the group-grid model see Bruce Malina, *Christian Origins and Cultural Anthropology: Practical Models for Biblical Interpretation* (Atlanta: John Knox, 1986); and Bruce Malina and Jerome Neyrey, *Calling Jesus Names: The Social Value of Labels in Matthew* (Sonoma, Calif.: Polebridge, 1988). For criticism, see Susan R. Garrett, review of *Christian Origins and Cultural Anthropology, Journal of Biblical Literature* 107 (1988): 532–34; and "Sociology of Early Christianity," in *The Anchor Bible Dictionary* (New York: Doubleday, 1992), vol. 6, 88–89.

19. Wayne Meeks, interview, May 22, 1991.

20. John Elliott, interview, May 24, 1991.

21. William Countryman, interview, May 25, 1991.

22. Jerome H. Neyrey, interview, May 23, 1991.

23. Bengt Holmberg, *Sociology and the New Testament: An Appraisal* (Minneapolis: Fortress, 1990), 18, 66. The latter terms are embedded in a quotation of James Beckford, *The Trumpet of Prophecy: A Sociological Study of Jehovah's Witnesses* (New York: Wiley, 1975), 154–58.

24. Almost every essay in a recent book on Luke-Acts makes such a claim: Jerome H. Neyrey, ed., *The Social World of Luke-Acts: Models for Interpretation* (Peabody, Mass.: Hendrickson, 1991), 64, 95, 128, 149 et passim.

25. John Elliott, interview, May 24, 1991.

26. Susan R. Garrett, interview, May 22, 1991.

27. John Gager, interview, May 27, 1991.

28. Susan R. Garrett, *The Demise of the Devil: Magic and the Demonic in Luke's Writings* (Minneapolis: Fortress, 1989).

29. Ibid., 29, citing several different theories in a brief section.

30. Ibid.

31. Ibid., 35; she is quoting Clifford Geertz, *Local Knowledge: Further Essays in Interpretive Anthropology* (New York: Basic Books, 1983), 58.

32. Ibid., 86.

33. Philip Francis Esler, *Community and Gospel in Luke-Acts: The Social and Political Motivations of Lucan Theology* (Cambridge: Cambridge University Press, 1987).

34. Ibid., 1.

35. Ibid., 16

36. Ibid., 16–17. See Peter Berger and Thomas Luckmann, *The Social Construction of Reality: A Treatise in the Sociology of Knowledge* (Garden City, N.Y.: Doubleday, 1967); see also Berger, *The Sacred Canopy: Elements of a Sociological Theory of Religion* (Garden City, N.Y.: Doubleday, 1969).

37. Ibid., 18.

38. Ibid., 204–5.

39. Ibid., 210.

40. Ibid., 222.

41. See note 24.

42. Douglas E. Oakman, "The Countryside in Luke-Acts," in Neyrey, ed., *Social World of Luke-Acts*.

43. Ibid., 177.

44. Antoinette Wire, interview, May 23, 1991.

45. Andrew Overman, interview, May 23, 1991.

46. In interviews this sentiment was expressed explicitly by Wayne Meeks, Susan Garrett, and Jerome Neyrey, but a perusal of studies also gives the impression that particularly sociological (as opposed to anthropological or ethnographic) theories are on the wane among scholars of early Christianity.

47. See, for example, Jeffrey C. Alexander and Steven Seidman, eds., *Culture and Society: Contemporary Debates* (Cambridge: Cambridge University Press, 1990).

For Further Reading

Alexander, Jeffrey C. and Steven Seidman, eds. *Culture and Society: Contemporary Debates*. Cambridge: Cambridge University Press, 1990. An interesting anthology of different authors from anthropology, sociology, literary studies, and social history, showing how various disciplines have approached what is known in some circles as "cultural studies."

Bauman, Zygmunt. *Thinking Sociologically*. Oxford: Basil Blackwell, 1990. Very readable introduction to the basic issues in traditional sociology.

Burke, Peter. *Sociology and History*. Controversies in Sociology 10. London: Allen & Unwin, 1980. Entertainingly written, brief discussion of the intersection between sociological and historical methods.

Elliott, John H., ed. *Social-Scientific Criticism of the New Testament and Its Social World. Semeia* 35 (1986). A collection of essays primarily by New Testament scholars who use the more rigorous social-scientific approach concentrating on explicit models.

Garrett, Susan R. "Sociology of Early Christianity," *Anchor Bible Dictionary*, vol. 6, pp. 89–99. New York: Doubleday, 1992. An in-depth introduction to social-scientific methods in New Testament studies, addressing the theoretical issues underlying differences in method.

Holmberg, Bengt. *Sociology and the New Testament: An Appraisal*. Minneapolis: Fortress, 1990. A critical survey of the field, especially useful for its attention to German and Scandinavian scholarship. This book covers many important subjects but is rather shallow in its handling of theoretical issues.

Kee, Howard C. *Knowing the Truth: A Sociological Approach to New Testament Interpretation*. Minneapolis: Fortress, 1989. A brief survey of the field with suggestions for further work; a prolegomenon for a future book on possible theological significances of New Testament sociology.

Osiek, Carolyn. "The New Handmaid: The Bible and the Social Sciences." *Theological Studies* 50 (1989): 260–78. An excellent, brief survey of the relevant literature.

7

CANONICAL CRITICISM

MARY C. CALLAWAY

One significant factor distinguishing biblical texts from similar ancient Near Eastern writings is that they were not dug up from the ground by archaeologists, but have been interpreted and handed on from the beginning by communities who define themselves by them. Tradition history has demonstrated that Israelite traditions were transmitted and reinterpreted by successive generations to respond to new situations, and the Bible is the result of layer upon layer of these resignified traditions and stories. At certain historical moments, notably the sixth century B.C.E. and the first century C.E., the process of shaping traditions ceased and the finished text became canonical. However, even when the boundaries were fixed, the form of the text remained fluid for centuries, as text critics have shown. Further, the process of recontextualizing and actualizing traditions that had been informing Israel since at least the tenth century B.C.E. continued unabated in Israel's heirs, Judaism and Christianity. Although we know very little about how canonization occurred, it is clear that the canon represented formalization of an ancient phenomenon: a core of traditions that was continually contemporized for the benefit of the community.

It is this dynamic quality of scripture in interactive formation with the believing communities that canonical criticism addresses. In its narrow sense "canon" refers to lists of authoritative books, found in both Judaism and Christianity from the beginning of the first century C.E., and a concern with what is included in the boundaries of the official text and what is excluded. But the Dead Sea Scrolls, the Septuagint, and the New Testament all bear witness to the diversity of canons in the first century C.E. Even today the major faiths for whom the Bible is of central importance represent five different canons. Canonical criticism does not address the history of these lists or the councils that may have formalized them; those concerns properly belong to the history of canon. Canonical criticism begins instead with the assumption that biblical texts were generated, transmitted, reworked, and preserved in communities for which they were authoritative and that biblical criticism should include study of how these texts functioned in the believing communities. Source, form, and redaction criticism focus on stages in the development of the biblical text prior to its final form, whereas canonical criticism analyzes the text as it was received in its final form. The emphasis may be on the function of the fixed text in the first communities to receive it, or on the process of adaptation by which the community resignified earlier traditions to function authoritatively in a new situation and thereby produced the final text. In either case, the focus of canonical criticism is on the two-way process by which the tradition functioned to define the communities and communities continued to shape the traditions. Hence the emphasis is on communities, rather than individual authors or sources, and on the final form rather than on earlier stages in its development. Canonical criticism understands the exegetical task to be constructive as well as descriptive.

Historical Background

A brief sketch of three factors giving rise to the canonical approach may help clarify its relation to biblical criticism. First, the attempts to write a biblical theology, ongoing since at least the 1940s, began to unravel in the early 1960s. The task of biblical theologians had been to find the locus of biblical authority in a single, controlling theological construct of the scriptures. Two criteria were essential: The idea must be distinctive to the scriptures (i.e., not found in the literature outside Israel) and the Bible must be so suffused with it implicitly or explicitly that at least a tinge of it could be detected in every book. Like a variety of garments dyed various shades of the same hue, the books of the Bible could be unified by their tincture with a unifying theological concept. For Walther Eichrodt this concept was covenant, for Oscar Cullman the biblical idea of time, for Gerhard von Rad salvation history.[1] But the multiplicity of theories, and the failure of any of them to construct a roof wide enough to cover all of the idiosyncratic residents of the Bible, began to suggest that the search for the unifying idea of scripture was ill-conceived. The recalcitrant books of the Bible were made of different fabrics and would not all take a single dye.

Brevard Childs responded to this situation in his *Biblical Theology in Crisis* (1970), in which he suggested that exegesis should not stop with relating a pericope to its original historical context but should explore the dialectic between individual text and full canonical context. At the same time, he was working on parts of the Old Testament seen by others as intrusions into the text, such as Psalm superscriptions, asking how these "late" additions functioned, and what they could tell scholars about the ways in

which the earliest communities unified their diverse authoritative traditions.[2] The development of the canonical approach moved the quest for the
locus of biblical authority from the Bible's content to its shape.

A second factor influencing the development of canonical criticism was
growing dissatisfaction with the results of historical-critical scholarship.
What had promised to be an objective analysis of the biblical texts in their
original settings had proved impossible because it was based on the assumption that the scholar could stand outside of history in order to analyze it. A
review of critical work over a period of years shows how emphases change
because the exegetes' own historical contexts inevitably color their work. It
is easy from a distance to see the effect of Darwin's theory on Wellhausen's
reconstruction of Israel's religion, of existentialist philosophy on Bultmann's
reading of the New Testament, or of anti-Semitism in some Christian Old
Testament scholarship. The growing suspicion that value-free, objective historical work is impossible has posed one of the most serious challenges to
the historical-critical method.

Symptomatic of this problem was the hidden assumption of many biblical
critics that authority rested in the earliest version of a biblical tradition. The
work of later tradents and redactors was called "accretions," a term suggesting
hardened deposits encrusting and distorting the original text, implicitly
understood to be of lesser authority than the earliest tradition. The judgment
that certain verses were "not genuine" ostensibly referred to their provenance
but functionally came to mean "not authoritative." Authority was located in
individuals, such as the Yahwist, Isaiah of Jerusalem, or Jeremiah, over against
the communities that preserved, interpreted, and shaped the traditions about
the individuals. Such a bias toward the earliest over the later and the individual over the community represented the values of Western post-
Enlightenment societies read back into early Israel. Ironically, both liberals
and fundamentalists based their reading of scripture on the shared assumption
that the individual author represents the authoritative voice of the text.

By focusing on the early communities that preserved and shaped the
traditions, canonical criticism resisted the unspoken hermeneutical assumption of historical criticism that biblical authority resided at the level of the
"original author." On the other hand, canonical criticism was also a logical
development of historical-critical work, whose history was a movement from
smaller (sources) to larger (redaction) units of tradition. Canonical criticism can be understood as the next logical step after redaction criticism,
moving from the last stage of redaction to the early stages of reception as
scripture. James Sanders notes the necessity of canonical criticism by arguing that "criticism had skipped over the crucial link, jumping from
redaction to conciliar decision."[3] Canonical criticism attends to this rich
stage in the formation of the Bible.

Converging with growing disenchantment in the academy was the disillusionment in the churches that methods promising to make the Bible accessible had in fact locked it in the past. Further, by fragmenting the text into ever smaller units that could only be read diachronically, some thought that biblical scholars had made the Bible virtually unreadable and unpreachable. In the words of a one-time colleague of both Childs and Sanders, scholars had effectively "decanonized" the Bible.[4] By reading the Bible as scripture, which meant emphasizing the continuity between the reading of canonizing communities and contemporary believing communities, canonical criticism tried to bridge this gap. Sanders refers to canonical criticism as "the beadle who carries the critically studied Bible in procession back to the church lectern from the scholar's study."[5] The origins of canonical criticism, then, lie in both the academic and the ecclesiastical communities. Its history is germane to an understanding of its nature, which can be characterized as a hermeneutical approach, grounded in the historical-critical method.

Canonical Context and Canonical Hermeneutics

Canonical criticism has been defined by the work of two scholars, Brevard Childs of Yale University and James Sanders of Claremont Graduate School, whose approaches differ in significant ways.[6] The very term "canonical criticism" embodies the problem and is a good place to begin the discussion. The term was coined by Sanders in 1972 in *Torah and Canon*, in which he raised the question of why the Torah ends with Deuteronomy rather than Joshua. Since the most ancient traditions appear to have been a story of God's promise to the fathers and its fulfillment in the conquest of Canaan, the omission of Joshua—the fulfillment of the promise—is a startling reinterpretation of Israel's foundational story. In its final, canonical shape, the Torah in effect reinterprets Israel's story. Tradition history and form criticism have recovered the lineaments of the original story, climaxing with Israel's entry into Canaan (see, e.g., Ex. 15:1–18; Deut. 26:5–9; 33:1–29); yet the authoritative version preserved in Israel ends with Israel encamped in the enemy territory of Moab, leaderless after the death of Moses. The results of redaction criticism indicate that the final editing of the Torah was accomplished by Priestly editors in sixth-century Babylon. The work of canonical criticism begins with the results of redaction criticism, asking how the *shape* of the Torah resignified the traditions embedded within it. In Sanders's analysis, the canonical shaping of Israel's story into the Torah produced a radical new interpretation of the promise-fulfillment tradition by truncating the original story. For the exiles in Babylon who had lost the land, the Torah offered a new reading of traditions that must have seemed dead, for it situated the fulfillment of the promise in the future. Further, the Torah moved the focus from the land, which Israel had lost, to the law, which it could never lose.

Sanders used the term "canonical criticism" purposely to underscore the nature of canonical criticism as a critical pursuit, building on tradition history and comparative midrash. Its goal is to recover the hermeneutics of those who interpreted older traditions into what became the authoritative version. Using the metaphor of inflected languages, Sanders refers to the canon as a paradigm by which the believing community can learn to conjugate the verbs of God's activity. Scripture does not offer eternal truths or theological doctrines but a set of stories, along with the various ways in which the believing communities have found life in those stories. The very nature of canon is to be simultaneously stable and adaptable, a fixed set of traditions infinitely adaptable to new contexts by successive communities of believers. Hence, for Sanders, it is not the final form of the text but the process by which the community arrived at that form that is canonically significant. Canonical criticism helps close the gap between what it meant and what it means by retrieving canonical hermeneutics, the underlying theological presuppositions by which ancient communities applied old traditions to new situations.

Brevard Childs, on the other hand, rejects the term "canonical criticism" precisely because it implies that here is another technique that can take its place alongside source, form, and redaction criticism. Canonical criticism for him is "a stance from which the Bible is to be read as sacred Scripture."[7] Childs uses the term "canon" to emphasize "that the process of religious interpretation by a historical faith community left its mark on the literary texts which did not continue to evolve and which became the normative interpretation of those events to which it bore witness."[8] Characterizing scripture as canon also avoids the idea of an authoritative text whose meaning resides in the mind of God, for canonical texts imply an authority resulting from transmission and reception of traditions that have been shaped in the communities of faith.

Unlike redaction criticism, which investigates the editorial processes leading up to the final form of the text, canonical criticism seeks to understand the effect of redaction on the final form of the text and to investigate its theological dimensions. Childs has shown, for example, how the canonical context of Isaiah 1–39 within Isaiah 1–66 shifts the original emphasis of Isaiah's message of doom for Jerusalem to a movement from judgment to salvation.[9] Although the historical context of First Isaiah is important for exegesis, for Childs this context has been subsumed into the larger literary context of the canonical book of Isaiah. While an exegetical understanding of First Isaiah begins with eighth-century Judah, a canonical reading proceeds from there to analyze how the words of the eighth-century prophet first functioned as scripture when they were preserved on a scroll with the words of the anonymous prophet of sixth-century Babylon. Significant for Childs is the way the original oracles are "loosed from their historical moorings" and thereby made available for successive generations. Reading the oracles of First Isaiah canonically, therefore, means reading them synchronically in the literary and theological context of the whole book of Isaiah. For Childs the focus is not the process of reinterpretation or the hermeneutic leading to the final form of the text, but its *theological shape*. The term "canonical" signifies both the historically final as well as the normative form of the text.

From these two approaches it is possible to distill some basic features characterizing the emerging discipline of canonical criticism. First, while using literary and historical methods, canonical criticism is primarily theological in its nature. Its underlying concern is to find the locus of authority in the biblical texts by analyzing the ways in which the texts were authoritative for the believing communities that received them as scripture. Second, canonical criticism focuses on the dynamics by which the communities of faith and the developing traditions shaped each other. The biblical text is seen as the product of the believing community, but at the same time the community's identity has been shaped by reflection on its religious traditions. The voices of individual authors preserved within the text are of less significance than the "voice" of the text received by the community. Third, canonical criticism assumes that hermeneutics by which the scriptures can be appropriated need not (indeed, should not) be imported from philosophical or theological systems, but are to be found within the scriptures themselves. The discipline of canonical criticism attempts to tease them out, either in the hermeneutics of the communities adapting the tradition (Sanders) or in the shape of the canonical text (Childs). Childs expresses this succinctly when he says "There is no one hermeneutical key for unlocking the biblical message, but the canon provides the arena in which the struggle for understanding takes place."[10]

Fourth, canonical criticism insists that authority resides only in the full canon, which is the context in which every biblical text finally must be read. The voice of a particular tradition is heard canonically against other voices and points of view; no position is absolute. Canonical criticism views scripture not as a treasury of stories but as a lively discussion in which theological ideas are constantly being reformulated in response to new data. Childs notes:

> One of the important aspects within the shaping process of the Old Testament is the manner by which different parts of the canon were increasingly interchanged to produce a new angle of vision on the

tradition. The canonical process involved the shaping of the tradition not only into independent books, but also into larger canonical units, such as the Torah, Prophets and Writings. For example, law was seen from the perspective of wisdom; psalmody and prophecy were interrelated; and Israel's narrative traditions were sapientialized. . . . The canonical process thus built in a dimension of flexibility which encourages constantly fresh ways of actualizing the material.[11]

Reading in a Canonical Context

Genesis 1–2 offers an opportunity to explore how canonical criticism relies on the results of historical criticism yet approaches the text with a different set of questions. Source criticism has demonstrated that Genesis 1–2 is a composite work, comprised of Priestly traditions in Gen. 1:1–2:4a and Yahwistic traditions in Gen. 2:4b–25, while redaction criticism suggests that P has subordinated the J tradition by subsuming it under the framework established by Genesis 1. P's editorial technique here appears to be asyndetic, setting one text alongside another without any link. As a result scholars refer to "the two creation accounts" in Genesis 1–2, and are interested in differentiating the two accounts by their reliance on earlier traditions, theological presuppositions, and their relation to the purposes of J and P.

But the shape of the biblical text before the reader does not suggest that it is offering two contradictory accounts of a single event. The canonical approach tries to make sense of the text as it appears (i.e., the Masoretic text) and to hear in it a single voice, while at the same time affirming that literary-historical analysis has recovered two independent traditions. Since the believing communities transmitted only the text as we have it, scholarly reconstructions of earlier authoritative traditions embedded in the text are pertinent to the prehistory of the text but not to an understanding of its canonical meaning. The canonical text speaks with a single voice, and that is not the voice of the earliest tradent, nor of the redactor, but a new voice that transcends even the intentions of the final redactor.

A canonical approach can legitimately seek the unity of the text in this new voice. Hence Gen. 2:4b, "These are the generations of the heavens and the earth," can be understood not as the end of the P creation account, forming an inclusion with Gen. 1:1, but rather as the introduction to the J account.[12] In this reading, J's account is absorbed into P's and read as an elaboration of it. The creation of heavens and earth in Genesis 1 points to the creation of human beings and their intimate relation to YHWH in the garden. Whatever the striking shift in language and literary style from Genesis 1 to Genesis 2 may suggest about original sources, it now functions to alert the reader to the relationship between the two chapters. Similarly, by reading Genesis 2 as an elaboration of the creation of the heavens and the earth in Genesis 1, the reader is encouraged to hear the language of Genesis 2 as figurative rather than literal.

In wrestling with the problem of the two names for the deity, the ancient rabbis determined that whenever the text said *Elohim* (God), it referred to the just aspect of the deity, and whenever it said *YHWH* (Lord), it referred to the deity as merciful. They did not posit two sources behind the text of the Torah, but they did hear two opposing tendencies, and drew from them the lesson of the inscrutability of the Holy One, paradoxically both just and merciful. Reading the text as a unity, the rabbis nevertheless heard the echoes of two voices and tried to maintain their distinctive emphases even as they harmonized them. One of the benefits of canonical criticism is its recovery of the history of interpretation as a legitimate aid to exegesis.

A somewhat different way of reading canonically is to highlight the multivalence in the final shape of the text. If Gen. 2:4a is read as an inclusio with Gen. 1:1 and is the end of the Priestly tradition, then a distinctive shift in perspective occurs at 2:4b. As has often been noted, P's term "the heavens and the earth" signifies primary interest in the cosmos and its order, while J's "the earth and the heavens" indicates emphasis on the earth and its inhabitants. The different semantic fields and literary forms employed by the two chapters strengthen the perception that here are two different perspectives. Finally, the different sequence of events and mode of creation in each chapter might well lead a reader to ask why the canonical form of the creation story is so confusing and contradictory. The canonical shape of Genesis 1–2 encourages the reader to attend to the peculiar diction and timbre of each voice in turn. To read Genesis 1–2 canonically is to allow the play of perspectives without insisting on a resolution. Perhaps the "canonical intention" is to remind the believing communities that creation is God's business. One account standing by itself could encourage a literal reading, leading the community to believe that it had the facts of how God created the world. Two conflicting accounts set back to back suggest that all language about the process of creation is figurative.

This understanding of Genesis 1–2 is supported when we broaden the canonical context to include the entire canon of the Hebrew Bible. Most other creation texts are poetic, and often highlight the very aspects notably absent from Genesis 1. The battle between the creator god and the waters/dragon of chaos, so prevalent in the literature of Israel's neighbors, does not occur in Genesis 1. The absence of the traditional battle is particularly noticeable because the text opens with uncreated waters and darkness, and God spends the first two days of creation separating off and containing these forces. The creation of light and of the firmament seems to deal with problems posed by preexistent "stuff" whose presence impedes the created order. Of course, no battle takes place; God speaks, and the light and the firmament appear to cordon off the darkness and the waters. Yet P's insistence that God was alone at creation and met no opposition is challenged by poetic traditions (Pss. 74:2–17; 89:5–11; Job 38:8–21) and again in the eschatological visions of the prophets (Isa. 51:9–11) and the apocalyptic belief that the ultimate battle will recapitulate God's victory at creation (Isa. 27:1; most vividly apparent in Revelation 12). The canon bears witness to a variety of creation traditions, some describing a bloody battle between YHWH and chaos, others picturing a calmly majestic artist calling the world into being.

Another creation text, Prov. 8:22–31, provides an alternative to the solitary deity of Genesis 1–2. In Proverbs, Wisdom (Hebrew: *hokmāh*, Greek: *sophia*) helps YHWH draw up blueprints for the cosmos and delights in the newly created works day by day. She is "the first of YHWH's works," preceding the creation of the world, yet Genesis 1–2 is silent about her. The figure of Wisdom is minor in the canon of the Hebrew Bible, yet becomes indispensable in the development of christological formulations about the preexistence of the Logos and its role in creation (e.g., in John 1:1–3 and Col. 1:15–17).

Genesis 1–2 reflects the ambiguity of the larger canonical treatment of creation, suggesting that no version of creation can be read as absolute. Since scripture is a canon and not a compendium, a faithful reading cannot select the text most conducive to the reader's own predisposition, but must maintain the multiplicity of traditions in all their ambiguity and contradiction. The most significant theological contribution of canonical criticism is the axiom that no voice of the canon should be privileged over others; there is no text by which all other texts must be interpreted. Biblical texts only become the Word of God in their full canonical context.

Canonical Hermeneutics

Reading Genesis 1–2 for its canonical hermeneutics illuminates another significant dimension of the text. The tradition that creation followed a bloody battle between a young deity and the primordial waters of chaos, portrayed as the dragon Tiamat, dominated Babylonian theology. The story of Marduk's victory over Tiamat and his subsequent creation of the world and enthronement as king was read in public celebration at the Babylonian New Year festival. A comparison of this story with Genesis 1 suggests that P incorporated the Babylonian cosmology and some of its storyline into the Israelite creation account, but with a distinctive shift in emphasis. By presenting the waters as a neutral, nameless presence, without history or power, P has transformed the old story into a monotheistic one. But the monotheizing hermeneutic creates the theological problem of theodicy. If there is no Tiamat, who is responsible for the evil we experience in creation?

Genesis 1 maintains a careful, ambivalent stance toward the waters. They have been drained of personality and divine status; nevertheless they remain in their appointed places. On the one hand, they had to be dealt with before God could create the world. On the other hand, they could be contained by the power of the divine word—contained, but not exterminated. The waters remain, albeit in check behind the firmament and under the earth, a potential threat to creation. This ambivalence toward the power of the waters is seen in P's version of the Flood narrative (Gen. 7:11), in which God temporarily allows the primordial waters to reclaim their original power, devastating the whole creation except the occupants of a single boat designed to withstand the waters. P calls attention again to the hostile nature of the waters in the Noachic covenant, when God promises never again to let the waters destroy the earth. Yet they remain, encircling the world from above, on the other side of the firmament, and from below, lapping at the pillars supporting the earth.

Elsewhere in the canon the menacing nature of the waters is graphically evoked. The use of the deep as an image of peril in the Psalms (Pss. 18:1–19; 69:1–3; 130:1) and the description of wicked enemies as "waters" (Isa. 17:12–14; S. of Sol. 8:7) testifies to the link made between the primordial waters and the human experience of evil. The interpretation of the ancient Babylonian story with a monotheistic hermeneutic results in a text in which the potential for evil in a good creation becomes a way of describing the freedom of God. It turns the question of theodicy around to view it from God's perspective, and what we are shown is the impenetrable mystery of the uncreated waters checked by the divine word.[13]

For those in Babylon who had lost their land and for whom God's promise seemed dead, the question of evil was not an academic one. The book of Lamentations and Psalms 74 and 137 eloquently bear witness to the genuine despair that threatened to overcome the exiled Judeans whose theological framework was inadequate to contain their experience. Either God had been defeated by Marduk or he had ruthlessly abandoned his people and promises. Even the theological explanation that eventually dominated, construing the exile as punishment for Judah's sins, was not wholly adequate. In the exile, apparently, the innocent had been swept away with the guilty.

In the context of this experience of cognitive dissonance between the official theology and the experience of the exile, the hermeneutics by which the ancient traditions were resignified in Genesis 1 are significant. Our reading suggests that theirs was a hermeneutic that above all presupposed the freedom of God. Not only is God not bound by any other powers in the universe, he is not even bound by Israel's theology. By placing Genesis 1 at the beginning of the Torah, the canonical shapers provided a lens through which the ensuing stories could be read. God is God, and is not limited by any human understanding of what a deity ought to do. The unthinkable had happened to Israel, and it threatened Israel's most cherished doctrines about God. In this context of devastation, P fashioned a new way of reading the old stories, teaching the Judeans that their understanding of God had been inadequate; they needed to do a new reading of their entire history.

The Limits of Canonical Readings

Canonical criticism is in the formative stages, and its originators are still the most significant practitioners, but even at this stage misreadings demonstrate that reductive understandings are a serious problem. Some critics mistakenly construe canonical criticism to be akin to the New Criticism in literary analysis, an interest in the literary text without reference to any historical context. This misunderstanding arises from focusing on Childs's emphasis on interpreting the text in its final form and fails to grasp the importance of the believing communities as the context in which the text has been shaped.[14]

A second misunderstanding sees in canonical criticism an attempt to return to precritical reading, casting aside the gains of historical-critical work. This reductive view fails to see the foundations of historical-critical exegesis on which canonical criticism is based, and the tendency of canonical criticism to favor multiple readings of every biblical text. It is ironic that canonical criticism is attacked by some as akin to fundamentalism and by others as leaning toward deconstruction. And there may be cause for concern. Childs's work is extensive and highly nuanced. But in lesser hands canonical criticism could become simply a way of avoiding the arduous process of exegesis and returning to precritical reading of scripture.

An unresolved theological problem resulting from the hegemony of the historical-critical method is the relation of history to the biblical witness. Canonical criticism assumes that scripture resulted from the believing communities' reflection on Israel's religious traditions. Because the act of shaping loosened the traditions from their original moorings, the original historical contexts of passages recoverable by historical-critical methods have been subordinated to the canonical context in which they have been preserved. The actual events that gave rise to the religious traditions in the first place are not only for the most part unrecoverable, but are secondary. It is the witness of the believing community that is canonical, not the historical event itself. Canonical criticism resists dethroning the biblical witness as only one source of historical information among many. Here, canonical criticism has raised a most significant theological issue: What is the relation between historical-critical study of the Bible and its use as religious literature?[15]

On the other hand, canonical criticism as practiced by Childs tends to absolutize the historical moment crystallized in the final form of the text without much regard for the historical factors that may have influenced its formation. The moment of canonization, like earlier moments in the development of the text, was motivated by immediate concerns of the community; it was not directed at unborn generations centuries away. The canonical shapers of Isaiah may have loosed the oracles of First Isaiah from their historical moorings to attach them to the oracles of an anonymous exilic prophet, but they did so in response to a particular historical situation. Any move away from understanding the biblical writings in their historical context, at any stage in their development, opens the risk of absolutizing the words at the expense of the Word.

Another potential danger in canonical criticism is the tendency to read texts as a unity and therefore to prefer harmonization to dissonance and uncertainty. Reading a biblical book canonically is like walking a tightrope, because it means attending to the subordinated voices even while hearing them in the context of the dominant voice. When a canonical-critical reading subordinates earlier sources to later ones, it risks flattening out the text in order to make it more accessible to the reader. Yet it is precisely in the nature of the canon to protect the ancient voices and to create dissonances within the texts. The canon has a peculiar double effect, encouraging the reader to find unity in the texts, yet at the same time checking those attempts by its plurality of voices. Even if earlier traditions are intentionally recontextualized and subsumed in the final form of the text, they still remain part of its fabric. Sometimes the "fabric" of the text works against its final shape; in such cases the tension is a critical part of the authoritative voice of the text, transcending the agenda of any one historical group, including the canonical shapers, but preserving them all.[16] The sum is truly greater than the parts, but it will not tell the truth unless the parts function in it. Because of this peculiar nature of the canon, "the Bible contains its own self-corrective apparatus."[17] Further, "with its affirmation that many have been given glimpses of God's purpose and none has the entire, complete and final answer, the canon calls us to continue to study the text."[18]

Perhaps here is the genuine theological issue of canonical criticism as a hermeneutical approach to the text. Childs says that "the use of the term 'canonical integrity' is not to be identified with literary, historical, or conceptual unity. It refers rather to the effectiveness of the literature to function coherently within a community of faith."[19] Elsewhere he says:

> I do not wish to suggest that the canonical shaping provides a full-blown hermeneutic as if there were only one correct interpretation built into every text which a proper canonical reading could always

recover. The canonical shaping provided larger contexts for interpretation, established the semantic level, and left important structural
and material keys for understanding. Nevertheless, exegesis also
involves the activity of the interpreter who from his modern context
must also construe the material. There is an important dimension
of "reader competence" which reacts to the coercion exercised by
the text itself."[20]

Ideally, canonical shaping provides a guide to interpretation, not the
assumption of a single "correct" reading. In practice, however, by finding a
hermeneutical key in the final shape of the text, canonical criticism gives
the impression of offering at least the parameters of a theologically definitive reading. The frequency of the term "normative" in canonical criticism
further encourages the conclusion that the readings of canonical criticism
are somehow authoritative ones. The variety of possible readings of Genesis
1–2 proposed above attempts to show that canonical criticism properly leads
not to one normative reading but to a variety of canonical possibilities in a
text. Perhaps the future of canonical criticism lies in the work of staking out
the parameters within which a multiplicity of readings can function for the
believing communities.

Notes

1. For a discussion of the relation between biblical theology and canonical criticism
see James Barr, *Holy Scripture: Canon, Authority, Criticism* (Philadelphia: Westminster,
1983), 130–44; Childs's response to Barr, in *Interpretation* 38 (1984): 66–70; and James
Sanders, *From Sacred Story to Sacred Text* (Philadelphia: Fortress, 1987), 155–63.

2. Brevard Childs, "Psalm Titles and Midrashic Exegesis," *Journal of Semitic Studies* 16
(1971): 137–50.

3. Sanders, *From Sacred Story to Sacred Text*, 165.

4. Gerald Sheppard, cited in Brevard Childs, *Introduction to the Old Testament as
Scripture* (Philadelphia: Fortress, 1979), 79, and Sanders, *From Sacred Story to Sacred
Text*, 158.

5. James Sanders, *Canon and Community: A Guide to Canonical Criticism*
(Philadelphia: Fortress, 1984), 20.

6. For an interchange between Childs and Sanders see *Horizons in Biblical Theology* 2
(1980): 113–211.

7. Childs, *Introduction to the Old Testament as Scripture*, 82.

8. Childs, *Interpretation* 38 (1984): 68.

9. Childs, *Introduction to the Old Testament as Scripture*, 325–33.

10. Brevard Childs, *Old Testament Theology in a Canonical Context* (Philadelphia:
Fortress, 1985), 15.

11. Ibid., 3.

12. Childs, *Introduction to the Old Testament as Scripture*, 148–50.

13. For a fuller exploration of the relation between the motif of the waters and the problem of evil, see John Levenson, *Creation and the Persistence of Evil* (San Francisco: Harper & Row, 1988).

14. John Barton's *Reading the Old Testament* (Philadelphia: Westminster, 1984), in which he presents canonical criticism as essentially a form of literary analysis, is a prime example of such a misunderstanding.

15. See Childs's remarks in *Journal for the Study of the Old Testament* 16 (1980): 58, and *Introduction to the Old Testament as Scripture*, 5.

16. A careful reader of 1 Samuel 7–31 cannot help seeing that the voice of the "early source," which is pro-Saul, cannot be readily harmonized with the redactor's voice, which is pro-David. Because the early Saul traditions and Saul's demise are so intertwined with David's rise, the canonical shape of the text suggests something of the dark side of God. As Childs repeatedly insists, a canonical reading is not coterminous with the agenda of the last redactors.

17. Sanders, *Canon and Community*, 46.

18. Donn F. Morgan, *Between Text and Community: The "Writings" in Canonical Interpretation* (Minneapolis: Fortress, 1990), 147.

19. Childs, *Interpretation* 38 (1984): 55.

20. Ibid., 69.

For Further Reading

Childs, Brevard. *The Book of Exodus: A Critical, Theological Commentary.* Philadelphia: Westminster, 1974.

———. *Introduction to the Old Testament as Scripture.* Philadelphia: Fortress, 1979.

———. *Old Testament Theology in a Canonical Context.* Philadelphia: Fortress, 1985.

Sanders, James. *Canon and Community: A Guide to Canonical Criticism.* Philadelphia: Fortress, 1984.

———. *From Sacred Story to Sacred Text.* Philadelphia: Fortress, 1987.

8

RHETORICAL CRITICISM
AND INTERTEXTUALITY

PATRICIA K. TULL

Rhetorical criticism, like many forms of biblical interpretation, is understood in a wide variety of ways by scholars of both the Hebrew Scriptures and the New Testament. This variety in approaches is related not only to the diverse kinds of writings in the Bible, but also to scholarly differences in understanding the nature of language itself. These differences reflect deep divisions that have arisen in recent discussions in the wider field of literature and literary criticism, divisions often having to do with whether, and to what extent, a text may be viewed as a single whole, relatively self-contained, or whether a text must be viewed in relation to its surroundings. Some critics attend primarily to stylistic features or rhetorical devices of the text itself, while others attend in various ways to factors that lie beyond the immediate text. These factors may include the text's having been situated in a dissonant rhetorical environment, the stances that the text anticipates and attempts to address in its audience, and even the text's interactions with subsequent readers and environments unanticipated by the author. Because relationships among texts are so central to many forms of rhetorical criticism, this chapter will include a discussion of the development in current literary theory known as "intertextuality."

Rhetoric as a Historical Category

From classical times until the eighteenth and nineteenth centuries, rhetoric was considered the foundation of Western education. Among ancient Greeks, rhetoric was the art of effective communication, often particularized as persuasive public speech. Various handbooks teaching rhetorical technique began to appear by the fifth century B.C.E. In the late fourth century B.C.E., Aristotle cataloged types of rhetoric (judicial, epideictic, deliberative), modes of persuasion (logos, ethos, pathos), and steps in the compositional process (invention, arrangement, style, memory, and delivery). His structures became the basis for the teaching of rhetoric for many centuries.

This tradition passed into the Roman world, was developed particularly by Cicero in the first century B.C.E. and in turn deeply influenced many Christian patristic writers who had themselves been educated in the rhetorical tradition. Most notable among these was Augustine, who in his *On Christian Doctrine* borrowed from Cicero to develop his own theory of Christian rhetoric, and interpreted the letters of Paul as having drawn upon classical rhetorical style.

The subject of rhetoric developed throughout the Middle Ages. The category of "style" in particular became a subject of great interest as rhetoricians amassed lengthy lists of stylistic devices and ornaments intended to beautify speech. As the Enlightenment progressed, however, interest in rhetoric declined. This was partly due to the increasing focus on style to the neglect of argumentation, which led to a view of rhetoric as chiefly ornamental.

The downfall of rhetoric was due primarily, however, to the rise of scientific inquiry and the consequent drive to view knowledge as founded upon observable fact rather than upon logic or persuasion. Whereas classical rhetorical studies had always preserved the insight that language "invented" (or in more recent terminology, "constructed") perceptions of reality, during the Enlightenment scientific language came to be privileged as referential speech conveying certain knowledge about a world objectively perceived. Nonscientific language was relegated to categories of poetry, self-expression, and propaganda (thus the modern phrase, which the ancients would not have understood: "mere rhetoric"). Rhetoric came to be understood as a subcategory describing the stylistic features of language that were subjective or persuasive, and therefore inferior to scientific language. As a result, by the beginning of this century rhetoric had been dropped from university curricula altogether or relegated to courses on writing skills offered by English departments to college freshmen.

No more than a generation after its demise, rhetoric began to be resurrected by theorists such as Chaim Perelman, Kenneth Burke, I. A. Richards, and Richard Weaver. These scholars sought to restore the term "rhetoric" to its ancient fullness as characteristic of all speech, not merely the poetic and ornamental. Yet whereas classical rhetoric concentrated on prescriptions for effective speaking, the "new rhetoric," as it is called, deals more broadly with theories of discourse and epistemology, investigating the relationships among language, persuasion, knowledge, and social control.

Many have attended to the question left open by ancient rhetoricians regarding the nature of the links between language and knowledge. In doing so, they have come to view rhetoric and persuasion as inherent in all forms of communication—as the means by which common understanding and knowledge are both achieved and transformed within a society. This has allowed the critique of forms of discourse that purport to be nonrhetorical, universal statements, and has led to a recognition of speech as inevitably value-laden. Naturally this work has involved investigations not only of scientific and political language but also of religious truth claims.

In addition, great emphasis has been placed on the dialogical interaction of language with its rhetorical contexts. I. A. Richards, for instance, claimed that words are meaningful only within a wider discourse (not in isolation), and that people understand them only in reference to their previous experiences of the same expressions. When contexts change, interpretation is altered. These concepts developed by twentieth-century rhetoricians are crucial for understanding the range of studies that fall under the umbrella of rhetorical criticism in biblical studies.

Rhetoric as Literary Artistry

The entrance of the term "rhetorical criticism" into biblical studies is related only indirectly to the fortunes of the discipline of rhetoric. The birth of interest in rhetorical criticism in biblical studies arose not from a revival of classical rhetoric or interaction with the "new rhetoric," but from dissatisfaction with historical criticism of the Bible.

James Muilenburg was a form critic whose interest in the particular compositional structure of individual Old Testament texts led him to look beyond what he perceived as limitations in the practice of form criticism. In his presidential address at the annual meeting of the Society of Biblical Literature in 1968, Muilenburg pointed out that in their quest to analyze texts according to catalogs of conventional speech genres, form critics had neglected the texts' own unique qualities.[1] As an antidote to this problem he suggested that "the circumspect scholar will not fail to supplement his form-critical analysis with a careful inspection of the literary unit in its precise and unique formulation."[2]

Muilenburg emphasized analysis of the structural patterns of literary units and discernment of "the many and various devices by which the predications are formulated and ordered into a unified whole."[3] Although he frequently used the term "stylistics" to describe this enterprise, he adopted the term "rhetorical criticism" as an overall designation for his proposed program.[4] Muilenburg called attention to chiasms and inclusios, repetition of key words, strophic structure, repetitions of particles and vocatives, and rhetorical questions, all of which contributed to his perception of Hebrew poetry as unified and carefully wrought, "often with consummate skill and artistry."[5]

While Muilenburg himself viewed rhetorical criticism as a subcategory of form criticism, his suggestions lent official sanction and voice to a movement already gestating within biblical studies. This new trend worked toward a kind of literary analysis that was completely different from what previous generations of Old Testament scholars had meant by "literary criticism" (that is, source criticism—see chapter 2), but much nearer to the sort of "close reading" that had been practiced in English departments for years. Studies of the stylistic, aesthetic features of biblical texts proliferated very rapidly and came to be known variously as literary criticism, narrative criticism, poetics, and, especially among followers of Muilenburg, rhetorical criticism.

Such work took many of its cues from the earlier, parallel movement in secular literary analysis known as "New Criticism," which similarly resisted appeal to factors beyond a text such as historical or authorial context, and gave close attention to the text's structural and stylistic features. Many practitioners of the new literary criticism in biblical studies followed New Critics in taking a polemical stance against historical criticism and excluding from their discussion all factors lying beyond the immediate text. Extremists among these critics would view the field of biblical studies as bifurcated into a diachronic and synchronic polarity.

As a result of Muilenburg's description of it in terms of stylistics, rhetorical criticism is still viewed in many circles as synonymous with literary criticism.[6] This is particularly true in studies of Hebrew scriptures. Several of Muilenburg's students, most notably Phyllis Trible and Jack Lundbom, have refined and clarified the enterprise of rhetorical analysis, each building upon his insights in differing ways.

Trible, for instance, has written *Rhetorical Criticism: Context, Method, and the Book of Jonah*, an entire book describing and exemplifying her method.[7] The foundation of her method is this statement, adapted from Muilenburg: "Proper articulation of form-content yields proper articulation of meaning."[8] Stressing the organic unity of form and content, she describes close reading of the parts and whole of a text as full rhetorical analysis. Trible does not bracket out the findings of historical-critical, sociological, or intertextual analysis when they are useful, but views rhetorical criticism as focusing primarily on an "intrinsic reading" of the text. In her instructions for rhetorical study of a text, Trible recommends attention to these details of textual construction: the beginning and ending of the text; repetition of words, phrases, and sentences; types of discourse; design and structure; plot development; character portrayals; syntax; particles.

Jack Lundbom's 1973 dissertation, *Jeremiah: A Study in Ancient Hebrew Rhetoric*,[9] was republished in 1997 along with an introductory essay, written in 1991, entitled "Rhetorical Criticism: History, Method and Use in the Book of Jeremiah."[10] In his essay Lundbom attends not only to the work of Muilenburg but also to the discipline of rhetoric as developed in universities in the past century. In his estimation, "the Muilenburg program appears somewhat narrow"[11] in comparison with the rhetorical criticism practiced in the universities, since it does not concern itself with the audience or persuasive qualities of speech. "Most of the effort is expended doing close work on the biblical text," Lundbom comments, making the enterprise "little more than an exercise in textual description."[12]

The dissertation itself, which is not revised in the 1997 edition, examines instances of inclusio and chiasm in the book of Jeremiah and discusses in depth the structure of these stylistic devices. Occasionally these discussions include consideration of a passage's function in Jeremiah's rhetoric, or the possible effects of the rhetoric on Jeremiah's audience. Although anticipating the shift to the more audience-oriented discussion of rhetoric that was soon to come, Lundbom's work on Jeremiah concentrates, in the Muilenburg style, primarily on stylistic concerns.

Muilenburg's impact upon biblical studies cannot be overestimated. His 1956 commentary on Isaiah 40–66 drew much-needed attention to the literary coherence, aesthetic beauty, and structured argumentation of texts that in the hands of other interpreters were being characterized as artless deposits of layers of untidy tradition, awaiting sophisticated and methodologically obscure systems of sorting to rescue them from their own redactors.[13] Muilenburg's thorough familiarity with historical criticism through a lifetime of study enabled him to articulate its shortcomings in convincing ways.

Moreover, the very fact that a well-respected form critic and president of the SBL would point out the excesses of his own discipline and suggest such new directions conferred much-needed legitimation upon literary interests. This legitimation facilitated the acceptance of methods that attended to the biblical texts themselves, leading to a sense of literary appreciation and even pleasure that could be shared by nonspecialists and scholars alike. Ironically, Muilenburg's use of the term "rhetorical criticism" to refer to stylistic analysis reflected the very reduction that had helped signal rhetoric's eclipse in earlier centuries. Still, his reintroduction of the concept of rhetoric into biblical studies soon directed attention both to classical rhetoric and to the work of twentieth-century rhetorical theorists.

Rhetoric as Persuasion

According to Aristotle, rhetoric is "the faculty of observing in any given case the available means of persuasion."[14] Muilenburg's use of the term "rhetorical criticism" has inspired many biblical scholars to reexamine such classical definitions of rhetoric. Consequently, many have begun to direct attention to the hortatory nature of much of the Bible—that is, its effort to persuade audiences not merely to appreciate the aesthetic power of its language but, even more importantly, to act and think according to its norms. Thus while rhetorical critics often begin with textual, literary questions reminiscent of the approaches of the Muilenburg school, many also inquire about the ways in which a text "establishes and manages its relationship to its audience in order to achieve a particular effect."[15]

George Kennedy summarizes the task of New Testament rhetorical criticism as follows: Rhetorical criticism "takes the text as we have it, whether the work of a single author or the product of editing, and looks at it from the point of view of the author's or editor's intent, the unified results, and how it would be perceived by an audience of near contemporaries."[16] In distinction from methods that bracket historical setting, this form of rhetorical criticism draws attention to the contexts in which texts arose and were read. Scholars who view rhetorical criticism in this way are generally more attentive to classical formulations of rhetoric. Consequently, like many traditional interpreters from Augustine on, several contemporary scholars understand parts of the New Testament as having been directly informed by Greek and Roman rhetorical practices. Others do not posit direct relationships to classical rhetoric, but understand it to provide categories that are useful for assessing a text's persuasive features.

George Kennedy begins his book on rhetorical criticism of the New Testament by differentiating his approach from those who investigate stylistics. He emphasizes the orality and linearity of biblical texts as well as the particularities of religious rhetoric (characterized by immediacy, metaphor and imagery, absoluteness and urgency, and authoritative truth claims rather than the logic of inference). In his opinion, the writers of the New Testament may not have received formal training in rhetoric, but they had enough cultural contact with a world dominated by classical rhetorical education to be aware of its norms and practices. Moreover, because the classical formulations were intended to describe not merely Greek practice but all rhetorical categories humanly available, they are apt templates for analysis of texts from all over the world, including the Bible.

For Kennedy, rhetorical analysis involves, first, a determination of the rhetorical unit to be studied; and second, a determination of the rhetorical situation, that is, the condition or situation that invited this utterance, with the particular problem that the author is seeking to overcome. Next comes study of the material's arrangement and its stylistic devices, and finally, a review of the unit's success in addressing the rhetorical problem. Kennedy and others who draw from the classics in analyzing biblical rhetoric tend to focus primarily on the displays of persuasive intentionality within texts. Sensitivity is shown to the text's strategies of argumentation (including stylistic devices) and to the ways in which the author, through the text, posits, persuades, and even rhetorically manipulates the intended audience.

Yehoshua Gitay, in his discussion of Second Isaiah, follows Kennedy in paying close attention to classical models.[17] For Gitay, rhetoric is the art of pragmatic persuasion—that is, persuasion with a specific pragmatic goal in mind. In his analysis of each of ten units in Isaiah 40–48, Gitay follows classical categories closely, not because he thinks the prophet employed them, but because he sees them as useful for examining and evaluating rhetoric. Each section of Gitay's work begins with structural arguments for viewing a particular passage as a rhetorical unit. Next he analyzes the unit on the basis of its invention, organization, and stylistic features. Many of the details he notes are similar to concerns raised by Muilenburg, but Gitay's focus on pragmatic persuasion leads him to inquire into the intended effects of Second Isaiah's arguments on its audience.

Though he does not appeal to classical categories, Meir Sternberg also sets out to demonstrate the persuasive strategies of biblical authors in relation to their intended audiences.[18] Sternberg's work on narrative, in which he seeks to describe the unique narrative rules governing the Hebrew Bible, displays literary virtuosity in its intricate assessment of the aims and effects of narrative details. In Sternberg's view, the author not only persuades but actually manipulates the audience into accepting certain views of the stories and the characters within them. The narratives display "foolproof composition"; that is, they are created in such a way as to make it "virtually impossible to counterread" them.[19] Readers' responses are controlled by the narrator throughout the reading process.

To Sternberg, biblical narrative is regulated by three principles coexisting in "tense complementarity" with one another: ideology, historiography, and aesthetics. Although one might conclude that these principles would drive the discourse in contradictory directions, Sternberg is convinced that the Bible's ideology is reinforced and underscored by its aesthetic choices. In Sternberg's view, the most important rhetorical goal of biblical narrative is to inculcate in its readers a divine system of norms: By appearing to serve the readers, the narrator seeks the readers' subjugation to God and God's ways. In intricate retellings of biblical stories in which every word and every silence counts, Sternberg shows how the reader is ineluctably drawn into the narrator's ideological orbit—that is, if the reader first lays aside his or her own opinions to "play by the Bible's rules of communication."[20]

As the authors of *The Postmodern Bible* point out, however, most readers do not easily lay aside their own opinions.[21] When Sternberg labors to demonstrate that the biblical narrator has shown Levi and Simeon in a sympathetic light even as they were slaughtering the Shechemites (Genesis 34), these critics observe that Sternberg

> puts forth his formidable powers of persuasion to persuade us (Sternberg's readers) that the biblical narrator is a skillful persuader who puts forth his own formidable powers to persuade us (readers of

Genesis) to side with the sons. But if the narrator is so rhetorically powerful, why are there so many readers he has failed to persuade? There is at least the suspicion that the one who wants to persuade readers of Genesis 34 to take a certain view is not the biblical narrator, but Sternberg himself.[22]

Sternberg's equating of his own interpretation with the narrator's intent, and of narrative intent with narrative effect, points to some important issues in rhetorical criticism that cannot be addressed by analysis of the text alone. First, rhetorical criticism (or for that matter any exegetical method) is not simply a kind of criticism; it is also a kind of rhetoric. That is to say, it is essential to take seriously the rhetorical, persuasive, value-laden nature of *all* discourse. The very practice we are analyzing, we are also ourselves exercising, since any stance that an interpreter takes concerning the text is by nature a rhetorical stance. Those of us studying the Bible as rhetoric should be aware of the persuasion that we are practicing as we "present" the persuasive interaction of biblical writers.

Second, the very fact that interpreters must work hard to persuade others of their views should make it clear that not all readers are the ideal readers we may see the text as projecting, nor even the alert and obedient readers the actual writer may have had in mind. In describing the effects of a biblical text upon audiences, Gitay and Sternberg reconstruct from the signals within the text an intended, or authorial, audience, and assess the text's success in persuading this ideal audience. Other scholars who agree on the importance of the audience-directed and persuasive nature of biblical texts do not posit such obedient audiences or unobstructed paths to rhetorical success. According to them, no text, not even the Bible, enters an ideological vacuum waiting expectantly to be filled. Rather, even in the most submissive of readers, even in the readers closest to the authors' own contexts, texts meet assumptions, experiences, questions, and demands that the authors could not have anticipated. Echoes of the claims and language of previously heard texts compete with the new text. Its words, forms, and cadences are recognized from previous encounters in other texts, and this makes them understandable. Yet the connotations imported from other texts by means of these particulars are also what color, bend, and even determine what is heard in the next text.

In other words, many scholars see rhetoric as an open, dialogical, intertextually laden practice, filled with ideological commitments and charges. Without neglecting the style and structure of biblical passages and their persuasive elements, many rhetorical critics also attend to issues lying beyond the boundaries of the text immediately in front of them. Within this category are interpreters with widely diverse methods, goals, and insights.

What they share is a view of texts as arising within, and being read within, contexts in which there is rhetorical tension, contexts filled not only with voices that are similar to that of the text, but also with those that may con-tradict it. This dialogical atmosphere influences not only the argumentation of the text but also the ways in which it is received by its readers.

Some interpreters train attention on a text's rhetorical environment in order to bring to clearer focus the dialogues into which the text is entering. Others point out the elements in the text that create problems for a unified, assured interpretation or that expose tensions or fissures in the author's own assumptions. Still others note the questions that a less-than-submissive audi-ence may bring to a text. Or, reading from a social location different from that of the author's intended audience, they may offer an ideological critique of the text. Or, by reframing questions asked of the text, they may suggest that the text itself offers critique of some dominant interpretive tradition. In one way or another, such rhetorical critics examine the nature of the text's com-plex intertextual relationships. To understand better the basis of their work, it is necessary first to explore what is meant by the term "intertextuality."

Intertextuality as a Property of Texts

Learning a language involves a process of associating new sounds, words, phrases, and grammatical patterns—which at first appear meaningless and opaque—with what is already known. The first time a completely new word is heard it has no meaning; it is only a sound, sometimes indistinctly heard. Upon subsequent hearings it becomes meaningful only insofar as it can be associated with previous recognitions. After several encounters, the sound and its meaning merge so that the concept is called up whenever the word is heard. At that point the brain has so thoroughly connected the sound with the idea that they seem to be naturally, intrinsically connected. But they are not; if they had been, the word would have been recognized on first hearing.

Although most of us do not remember, acquisition of our first language depended upon a structure of associations that built on one another and that were practiced until the associations became so habitual that they were no longer noticed. Every word we acquired was learned within a context that rendered it understandable by association with other words, gestures, and facial expressions. Similarly, every word we recognize in a new text came to us first in another context. Every text we hear or read becomes intelligible by means of association with what has already been heard or read. Moreover, every text we write or speak is constructed from the build-ing blocks of previous texts.

This is true not only on the level of words and grammatical constructions but on the level of much larger complexes of ideas as well. When readers come to this book on biblical interpretation, for instance, they come with a previously developed concept of what it means to read the Bible. They understand that the Bible is to be studied and interpreted, that study of the Bible occurs in complex and systematic ways, and that total strangers are engaging in similar enough processes with similar enough goals that reading their suggestions could be useful. More basically, they come with the knowledge of how to open a book and begin to read, of how to associate certain squiggles on the page with certain sounds and concepts and how to associate squiggles that have no known association with the same squiggles in a dictionary. In other words, we all approach books (or any text, whether written or oral) filled with presuppositions and associations based upon previous experience, without which a new book would be as indecipherable as the rows of wedged-shaped indentations on an ancient Sumerian tablet.[23] Similarly, all new texts, including this one, are formed from the building blocks of other texts—from the use of previously learned words to the restating of information received from elsewhere to the direct quoting, with citation, of other books.

This property of texts, that is, their inseparability from associations with other texts, is known as "intertextuality." In a general sense, intertextuality simply refers to the interconnections among texts. These connections can be as general and indirect as shared language, or sound as specific and direct as the footnoted quotation of one text in another.

What makes intertextuality interesting, however, is that the shared webs of meaning and association that enable communication between people are never fully and completely shared. Five people in a room simultaneously hearing the word "rhetoric" may all have heard something intelligible, but may each, because of different previous associations, have heard something different. Even the concept of intertextuality itself is subject to such dispute: Some associate it with general, untraceable intelligibility; others with direct, traceable literary borrowing or allusion. Still others (including myself) view it as a phenomenon that manifests itself on all levels from the general and untraceable to specific quoting.

Thus, even with a shared term, tension arises over how it ought to be used, who is right, and to which authorities (intertextually related texts) appeal will be made. Rhetoric begins with the reality of shared texts—it is not possible without them—but it arises because texts are not fully shared. It arises in the desire to make one's own internalized text (one's own view of the subject) a text that an audience will internalize as well.

This brings us back to the issue of how rhetorical criticism is understood. In the opinion of some, many of the forms of rhetorical criticism we have considered so far fail to take seriously enough what it means to call texts and their intertextual environments "rhetorical." In an attempt to delimit the task of interpretation, these approaches analyze texts as if they were self-contained depositories of information that, if appropriately received by audiences (that is, received in the way the current interpreter receives them), would persuade of their beauty and truth or, in other words, would be rhetorically effective.

But if rhetorical contexts influence both writing and reading, consideration of texts in isolation from the rhetorical contexts of authors and readers yields interpretation that is truncated and incomplete, maybe even irrelevant. In fact, to ignore one's own rhetorical context is to offer interpretation that is unconsciously overdetermined by one's reading practices.

Like many other concepts in biblical interpretation, intertextuality is more helpful in providing an angle of vision on the nature of biblical texts than in prescribing a precise set of procedures for producing an interpretation. Attention to intertextuality and rhetoric calls forth certain ways of posing questions, and benefits from both imagination and disciplined analytical skills. In order to describe ways in which the insights of intertextuality may affect biblical interpretation, I will draw upon the work of Russian theorist Mikhail Bakhtin.

Mikhail Bakhtin's Dialogism

Julia Kristeva, who first coined the term "intertextuality" to describe the intrinsic interrelationship of texts, credited Bakhtin with introducing this concept into literary theory. Addressing the previously puzzling question of the stylistic qualities of prose fiction, Bakhtin suggested that novelistic prose is characterized by its dialogical quality—that is, the propensity of prose fiction to lack a unified voice of its own, but rather to mirror, emulate, and even set side by side a variety of the kinds of language found in the author's own world.[24] Bakhtin's criticism of "stylistics" as a useful category for describing prose fiction has been found equally applicable to literature in general and to biblical studies in particular:

> Stylistics has been . . . completely deaf to dialogue. A literary work has been conceived by stylistics as if it were a hermetic and self-sufficient whole, one whose elements constitute a closed system presuming nothing beyond themselves, no other utterances. . . . From the point of view of stylistics, the artistic work as a whole—whatever that whole might be—is a self-sufficient and closed authorial monologue, one that presumes only passive listeners beyond its own boundaries. . . . Stylistics locks every stylistic phenomenon into the monologic context of a given self-sufficient and hermetic utterance, imprisoning it, as it were, in the dungeon of a single context; it is not able to

exchange messages with other utterances; it is not able to realize its own stylistic implications in a relationship with them; it is obliged to exhaust itself in its own single hermetic context.[25]

In other words, Bakhtin accuses literary critics of assuming that when readers read, communication proceeds in a simple, direct, and uniform line from text to reader: The reader does not protest against or contribute insights to the text, no other texts are appealed to by the text or recalled by the reader, and the text itself is the only influence on the reader's interpretation. In sum, the text is assumed to speak in monologue to the reader. In opposition to such assumptions, Bakhtin calls attention to three loci where some sort of dialogue is operative. All three are points of intertextual exchange affecting the text and its reception by the reader. The first is the existence of a variety of other, foreign, even competing utterances already present in the environment into which the text enters, that attach themselves to the subject about which the text wishes to speak; the second, an internal dialogism operating within the text as it responds to the utterances in its environment; and the third, the active, sometimes competing responses of the audience.

Dialogue in the Text's Rhetorical Environment

According to George Kennedy, the "rhetorical environment" is the situation that calls forth the text; it is the question seeking an answer. Bakhtin's understanding of rhetorical environment is more complex, for it involves competing answers to the same question, competing constructions of the same event, competing views of the same world, differing characterizations and valuations of the same idea, and a profusion of other voices already speaking before the text adds its voice:

Between the word and its object, between the word and the speaking subject, there exists an elastic environment of other, alien words about the same object, the same theme, and this is an environment that is often difficult to penetrate. . . .

Indeed, any concrete discourse (utterance) finds the object at which it was directed already as it were overlain with qualifications, open to dispute, charged with value, already enveloped in an obscuring mist—or, on the contrary, by the "light" of alien words that have already been spoken about it. It is entangled, shot through with shared thoughts, points of view, alien value judgments and accents. The word, directed toward its object, enters a dialogically agitated and tension-filled environment of alien words, value judgments and accents.[26]

For Bakhtin, then, the rhetorical environment is the plurality of other discourse—not simply the plurality of questions but the plurality of other answers. Nor can it be thought of as the plurality of wrong discourse, for if these other voices were not in some measure persuasive there would be no need for the new voice to compete with them, declaring them unpersuasive. Thus before a discourse begins to describe its object, that object is already in the midst of being described and imagined in other ways, some slightly different, some extremely different. To reflect on the object of this very chapter, if I had been able to declare the first word ever uttered on rhetorical criticism, I could have assigned it a single definition—my definition, *the* definition—and it would have been persuasive, because there would be no other contestants. But alas, before I began writing, "rhetorical criticism" was a term already subject to dispute, overlain with differing definitions and characterizations, charged with the values of diachronic and synchronic exegesis, enveloped in the obscuring mist of diverse allegiances: some claiming descent from form criticism, some claiming cohesion with Aristotle, others declaring fidelity to Muilenburg, and still others desiring to clear the field and start over.

The disputed rhetorical environment surrounding many biblical texts, especially in the Hebrew scriptures, is difficult for us to perceive because we no longer have access to many of the voices to which these texts were responding. Nevertheless, the idea of rhetorical environment has been useful in comparing texts with obvious precursor texts, such as Chronicles with Samuel-Kings, or Matthew and Luke with Mark. In his monumental treatise on interpretive texts within the Hebrew scriptures, Michael Fishbane pays particular attention to Chronicles as an exegetical revision of Samuel-Kings, reflecting later practices and sensibilities.[27] In his view, Chronicles was not meant to supplement but to replace Samuel-Kings as a depiction of history. But modern readers with access to both texts can attend to the similarities and differences between them to arrive at a fuller understanding of the Chronicler's rhetorical agenda. Transformations in divine speech—for example, from "go before me" (1 Kings 8:25) to "go in my Torah" (2 Chron. 6:16)—show a concern to present the postexilic ideal of devotion to Torah as one that the kings in Israel's past knew and lived. Knowing that the author deliberately altered a text in this way helps train the exegete's attention to other ways in which the role of Torah has been enhanced. This may help the interpreter understand more precisely the unique features and trends of the Chronicler's setting and ideas.

Earlier discussions of Chronicles tended to dismiss it as a tendentious and inaccurate revisionist history, inferior to the text upon which it depended. Such dismissals were related to a nineteenth-century preference for the "original" and disdain for writings that were clearly derivative. But as

Fishbane pointed out, Samuel-Kings was a product of exegetical revisions of previous texts too, and was far from pristine in its presentation of facts. Like Chronicles—and in some sense like all texts—Samuel-Kings is a derivative text. What is significant is not the mere fact that these books used earlier material, but the way in which earlier material was used for a new rhetorical purpose. It is less pertinent to say that the texts are influenced by previous texts and more accurate to note the ways in which the new texts *appropriate* previous material, establishing a complex system of relationships of opposition, agreement, partial agreement, and reformulation. In his discussion of the web of relationships among works of art, Michael Baxandall concocts a virtual thesaurus of reutilization that applies to biblical texts as well. In relation to an older work of art, he says, a new work may

> draw on, resort to, avail oneself of, appropriate from, have recourse to, adapt, misunderstand, refer to, pick up, take on, engage with, react to, quote, differentiate oneself from, assimilate oneself to, assimilate, align oneself with, copy, address, paraphrase, absorb, make a variation on, revive, continue, remodel, ape, emulate, travesty, parody, extract from, distort, attend to, resist, simplify, reconstitute, elaborate on, develop, face up to, master, subvert, perpetuate, reduce, promote, respond to, transform, tackle. . . . Everyone will be able to think of others.[28]

Moreover, the clarity of the Chronicler's reutilization of Samuel-Kings can sensitize interpreters to the presence of inner-biblical transformations even when a precursor text no longer exists or has not been directly copied, and helps alert us to what can be learned by attending to such transformations. As the next section will show, even markers within texts can be clues to the rhetorical struggle the author is engaging and attempting to win.

Dialogism within Texts

One of the Chronicler's techniques in reshaping the story in Samuel-Kings was to expunge problematic material, such as the story of Bathsheba and Uriah. Without knowledge of the precursor text, the existence of that story and of its later repression would not have been known. Undeniably, many such revisions occurred during the long centuries of writing and rewriting through which the Bible came into existence. As 1 Chron. 20:1–3 indicates (compare 2 Sam. 11:1–12:31), materials may disappear without a trace and be replaced by other materials that tell a very different story. Without Samuel-Kings we would not be aware of some of the less complimentary views of King David that circulated in ancient Judah.

Yet it is not always the case that dissonant voices are so easily silenced. To suppress a textual voice is one rhetorical technique; to acknowledge it and organize against it is often a more effective one. In order to respond to a plurality of viewpoints, a text often actively voices approval of some and rejection of others. Thus it is the "tension-filled environment," not simply the conventions of artistry, that shape and define a text and that may be detected in the text's own content. Bakhtin describes the text's entrance into this rhetorical environment with these words:

> The word, directed toward its object, enters a dialogically agitated and tension-filled environment of alien words, value judgments and accents, weaves in and out of complex interrelationships, merges with some, recoils from others, intersects with yet a third group: and all this may crucially shape discourse, may leave a trace in all its semantic layers, may complicate its expression and influence its entire stylistic profile.[29]

In order to achieve credibility, a new text must show that the pertinent issues are being considered—that the author knows what people are saying about the subject and can argue a new viewpoint in relation to the other voices. This means that even rejected ideas may be acknowledged and disputed rather than ignored. Often they will even be given a chance to speak within the text, if only within the most severe quotation marks.

Here the self-reflective example should be obvious. In order to create a description of rhetorical criticism that responds to and organizes other descriptions and allows them what I consider their proper place in my universe of discourse, I must quote them and describe them, give them voice, group them, allow them to speak to one another, and respond to them myself. While the rhetorical environment in 1998 does not absolutely determine the kind of chapter that I write, it does shape it in important ways.

In terms of the Bible, internally dialogized texts are much easier to find than direct, or even indirect, relationships among texts. In every part of the Bible the speech of others is quoted, organized, and laid open to dispute. Second Isaiah, for instance, presents viewpoints disputed by its author in the form of quotations:

> Now therefore hear this, you lover of pleasures,
>   who sit securely,
> who say in your heart,
>   "I am, and there is no one besides me;
> I shall not sit as a widow
>   or know the loss of children"—

both these things shall come upon you
   in a moment, in one day:
the loss of children and widowhood. . .
                         (Isa. 47:8–9a, NRSV)

But Zion said, "The LORD has forsaken me,
   my Lord has forgotten me."
Can a woman forget her nursing child,
   or show no compassion for the child of her womb?
Even these may forget,
   yet I will not forget you.
                         (Isa. 49:14–15, NRSV)

In these passages, the prophet is quoting the symbolic figures "Virgin Daughter Babylon" and "Daughter Zion." Their words can in no wise be understood as representing the prophet's own understanding; rather, these figures are given voice in order to sharpen the contrast with the divine words that follow. Furthermore, since both of these female entities are symbolic figures, it should be clear that the prophet is projecting imaginative, not actual, conversations between God and these women. Yet through dialogue the prophet presents what he apparently considers fair representations of the (faulty) opinions of groups represented by these figures: that is, real Babylonians and real Judeans. In this way, competing interpretations of current events are highlighted, organized, and placed in relation to the prophet's own message. Over against any claims to the contrary, YHWH's ascendancy over Babylonian arrogance is asserted; YHWH's sustained attention to Jerusalem is affirmed.[30]

Narrative can also contain internal dialogism, reflecting a disputed environment. The words and attitudes of characters, even if they are fictionalized, reflect words and attitudes encountered in the author's world. Giving these characters voice and body in a story, the author is able to comment upon their words and attitudes using the narrator, the other characters, or the chain of circumstances that befall them. For instance, in Luke 16:19–30, Jesus tells a story to illustrate his dire warning to those who "were lovers of money" and "ridiculed him" (16:14). The parable of the rich man and Lazarus enables Jesus to comment indirectly upon his opponents by casting them as the ones doomed to torment. On yet another level the parable enables the author of Luke to comment upon those in the authorial context who are wealthy detractors of the faithful. The rich man's own words, directly quoted, allow readers to gaze ironically upon his arrogance, as he continues to assume—even in Hades—that Lazarus's purpose in life and in death is to serve him and his five brothers. Through the voice of

Father Abraham, the narrator communicates to the audience that the law and the prophets, though sufficient, are of no help to those who refuse to live by them.

But direct quote is only one form of internal dialogism. Bakhtin also describes the double-voiced quality of speech that adopts within it the cadences of another while retaining its own control. In doing so, it in effect winks at the audience even as it weaves in and out of others' speech. Job, for instance, mocks the inflated self-opinion he perceives in his three friends, and through Job's voice the narrator undercuts wisdom's spokespersons. Answering a lengthy and rhetorically overblown description of Job's future should he repent of whatever sins he has committed, Job says, "No doubt you are the people, and wisdom will die with you" (Job 12:1). Note the complexity of dialogism here: The narrator's own viewpoint is communicated through Job's anguished sarcasm, which echoes and magnifies his tormenters' pompous message.

Although the internal dialogism of biblical texts usually moves toward resolution, privileging one viewpoint over others, there are texts in which the competing discourses are allowed to remain in tension. The book of Job, as many have noted, begins and ends with prose narrative that contrasts with the poetic dialogue of the rest of the book not only in genre but also in linguistic sophistication and, more surprisingly, in theological outlook. One voice gets most of the lines; yet the other is allowed to begin and, more importantly, to end the story. Together these voices create tensions for those trying to decide what Job is finally saying. Though it is tempting to try to collapse these tensions into one dominant message, Carol Newsom has suggested that the struggle among dissonant messages is an essential feature of the book's meaning, deepening the reader's engagement with the mystery of human suffering:

> By leaving the tension between the two parts unresolved, the book as a whole allows the frame story and the dialogue to explore different dimensions of the complex question of the moral basis for divine-human relations. That dissonance both recognizes and refuses the reader's desire for closures to the story and a definitive resolution of the issues it has raised.[31]

Many other studies have pointed out the profit to be gained from taking seriously the dialogical dissonance within biblical books. Mieke Bal's work on Judges reveals both the violence in the social order that the book reflects and the continuing inclination, exemplified by scholarly commentaries, to ignore and hence to perpetuate this violence, particularly as it is expressed against women.[32] In that way the book of Judges becomes a mirror reflecting the danger-filled experiences of real women.

Dialogism in the Audience

The presence of many differing voices and opinions in a text's environment not only necessitates that the author engage and manage these voices, but also that audiences themselves, even before coming to the text, are already managing and organizing a variety of perspectives and pronouncements upon the same subject. Effective orators anticipate this process and the obstacles it may create within their listeners. Preachers, for instance, should be aware that their sermons on the Prodigal Son are likely to be the twentieth or thirtieth their parishioners have heard, and that elements of previous interpretations linger in their minds and influence what they hear. Bakhtin noted the ways in which a text is shaped by such anticipation:

> Every word is directed toward an *answer* and cannot escape the profound influence of the answering word that it anticipates.
>
> The word in living conversation is directly, blatantly, oriented toward a future answer-word: it provokes an answer, anticipates it and structures itself in the answer's direction. Forming itself in an atmosphere of the already spoken the word is at the same time determined by that which has not yet been said but which is needed and in fact anticipated by the answering word. Such is the situation in any living dialogue.
>
> All rhetorical forms, monologic in their compositional structure, are oriented toward the listener and his answer. This orientation toward the listener is usually considered the basic constitutive feature of rhetorical discourse.[33]

In other words, a text responds to other texts not simply to correct the previous record, but in order to persuade an audience of its author's view of the world. To do so, the author must envision the desired audience and anticipate its responses, even to the point of defusing possible objections before they are made.

Stanley Kent Stowers, in his 1981 dissertation, *The Diatribe and Paul's Letter to the Romans*, studies Paul's use of classical forms that anticipate audience response. He identifies the "diatribe" as a "type of discourse employed in the philosophical school [that] . . . presupposes a student-teacher relationship."[34] Paul employed this style in his letter to the Romans, addressing his readers as if they were his pupils, and making rhetorical use of a form he knew his audience would recognize. More specifically, the imaginary interlocutor against whom Paul argues in Romans anticipates many of the questions and objections Paul expected in his actual audience. Stowers shows the ways in which Paul shaped his letter to the Romans, tailoring his theological message to the specific philosophical needs of the Gentiles he envisioned reading it.

Insofar as the author can assess an audience, their dialogical context and concerns shape the text's creation. But even more significantly, the audience's dialogical context shapes the way the text, once composed and delivered, is actually received. As reader-response critics have pointed out (see chapter 11), different audiences in different contexts will receive the same text in a variety of ways. It is not simply that some choose to disagree with the obvious meaning of a text, or that "everyone else" is misinterpreting. Rather, in different environments the same text *means* differently.

This is especially important in terms of biblical reading and reception. The canonization of biblical books in the Jewish and Christian traditions has meant that generations of audiences in different settings have read texts written without them, their needs, questions, or intertexts in mind. Whenever a text is handed on with its interpretation, that interpretation predisposes the next audience to view the text from an angle that may not have been anticipated by the original author. Theologies of the "living word" are ways of articulating the notion that this is acceptable, that biblical texts are reactualized by succeeding generations in new ways that become part of the text's expanding afterlife.

For instance, Isa. 52:13–53:12, the famous "suffering servant" passage, has been appropriated in very different ways throughout the course of its history. Paul's failure to discuss this passage as a reference to Christ's suffering is consistent with the Jewish background from which he came, in which none of the previous interpretations or reutilizations of the servant passages had to do with messianic expectations.[35] In fact, a brief survey of New Testament texts shows a degree of latitude in appropriation of Isaiah 53, even when it is used in reference to Jesus. Matthew 8:17 associates Isa. 53:4 ("He took our infirmities and bore our diseases") not with Jesus' suffering, but with his healing ministry. Acts 8 links the "sheep led to the slaughter" of Isa. 53:7 to Jesus, without providing an explicit interpretation of this link. First Peter 2:18–25 refers the passage to Jesus' passion in order to show how slaves should obey their harsh masters.

Over the first several centuries of the church's existence, however, Christian interpretation of Isa. 52:13–53:12 crystallized. As the passage's importance as an allusion to Jesus' sufferings took shape, its perceived usefulness as Christian apologetic grew. For both John Chrysostom and Augustine in the fourth century, Isaiah 53 served as a proof text predicting and confirming the crimes of the Jews against Jesus.[36] By the Middle Ages, the passage was used to supply lurid details to retellings of Jesus' passion. For instance, based on the reference to sheep shearers in Isa. 53:7, the idea spread that Jesus' hair and beard were completely pulled out by his persecutors, who in paintings and popular sentiment were synonymous with contemporary Jews.[37] Christian frustration that Jews have not read

Isaiah 53 as proof of Christian claims about Jesus continues to be voiced to this day.

In contrast to this trajectory, beginning very early and continuing throughout the Middle Ages and into the present, the servant in Isaiah has been seen in Jewish interpretation not as a messianic figure, but as a representative of Israel or of the faithful in Israel. In fact, it was often in the face of Christian persecution that this passage became significant as a model for Jewish faithfulness to God. Rabbi Abraham of Cordova (c. 1600), for instance, turned the Christian message completely on its head, asserting that the servant was Israel, while the ones persecuting him were the ones who claimed that the servant was Jesus:

> The chastisement and penalty which should have been ours [speaking for the heathens] for having invented the fiction of the advent of our Messiah, fell upon Israel instead during the long years of his bitter captivity, although he always steadily adhered to the truth, and would never acknowledge our errors; hence we never ceased to afflict him, imagining that by his stripes which were produced when, in zeal for our own lying belief, we visited him with the rod of our anger.[38]

A rhetorical critic examining the interactions of the Isaiah passage with a variety of social contexts would note the ways in which the passage and its interpretations are affected by the particular rhetorical needs of interpretive communities to produce disparate and even contradictory interpretations. Knowledge of the diversity of interpretive possibilities that have operated in the past not only opens unexplored vistas on the passage itself, but also helps readers understand the sources of their own assumptions. Explorations of the history of biblical interpretation have helped recent exegetes become more critically aware of the ideological interests that have influenced not only the text but its interpretations as well.

Conclusion

The concept of intertextuality has helped rhetorical critics recognize that a text is more than the sum of its words. As important as stylistic analysis is for attending to particulars, it does not sufficiently account for all that texts do and come to mean. Arising out of a writer's desire to communicate a particular viewpoint in relation to other relevant viewpoints, a text is designed to maximize its persuasive powers. Although originally addressing particular intended audiences, biblical texts encounter a wide variety of readers in different settings, readers who ask—and see answered—questions that the original writer may never have imagined. Rhetorical criticism helps interpreters attend to the persuasive intents and effects of biblical texts and to the long history of theological interpretation that has shaped our own reception and reading.

Two recent studies, one dealing with Proverbs and the other involving Romans, are particularly commendable as illustrations of the sort of rich rhetorical interpretation that proceeds from integrating attention to rhetorical environment, textual dialogism, and the positioning of intended and real readers. Carol Newsom's study of Proverbs 1–9 appeals intertextually to Genesis, Job, and Ecclesiastes; points out the author's use of a variety of voices, including voices quoting voices; and explores the crisis that results for the text when the actual audience differs from that envisioned by the author.[39] Stanley Stowers's A *Rereading of Romans: Justice, Jews, and Gentiles* attends to four intertextual perspectives: (1) interpretations of Romans in different places and times throughout Christian history; (2) rhetorical conventions and generic conceptions available to readers in Paul's time; (3) cultural codes and interrelated texts available to Paul's readers; and (4) the audience and author as textual strategies in Romans.[40] Both of these works successfully employ a variety of rhetorical and intertextual clues to produce fuller readings of biblical texts than can be achieved from observation of the text alone, in isolation from the contexts in which it is written and read.

Rhetorical Criticism in Action: Genesis 1

In this chapter I have discussed several angles of vision that rhetorical criticism might open. In this final section I will briefly illustrate how the constellation of rhetorical approaches might illuminate Genesis 1.

Stylistic analysis would attend to the unfolding repetitions of the creation story: the repetitions of God's words that speak the universe into being, of creative actions that proceed from those words, of God's positive responses to what God sees, and of the cycles of day and night. Within this basic framework, each day is described in increasingly complex detail as the number of created entities proliferates. Two verses describe the first day, but the sixth day requires a climactic eight verses, before the seventh day reverts to the simplicity and brevity of the first.

A critic viewing this text in terms of pragmatic persuasion might be hampered by a lack of direct clues for understanding the viewpoints the text is opposing. Here some subtle intertextual features become useful. For instance, references to the "great sea monsters" in verse 21, along with references in verse 2 to the "deep," and in verses 9–10 to the making of boundaries for the sea, whisper echoes of an earlier ancient Near Eastern tradition in which creation comes about through a divine battle against the sea or a sea monster (see Isa. 51:9–10; Ps. 89:9–10; Ps. 74:14–15; Mark

4:37–41; Rev. 21:1). In opposition to those texts, Genesis 1 depicts even the sea monster (which remains, like the sun and moon, unnamed) as God's creation, and God as powerful enough to create by fiat rather than through battle.[41] Similarly, the reference to God's "image" in verse 27 echoes texts in which idols are called "images" of other gods or even of the people making them (see especially Num. 33:52; 1 Sam. 6:5; 2 Kings 11:18; Ezek. 16:17; Amos 5:26). This twist on the language of image-making, in which it is the god who forms the human, becomes especially noticeable in view of Isa. 46:1–7. In that text the Babylonian gods Bel and Nebo ride helplessly into captivity, unable to save the worshipers who made them, while God is depicted as the one who made, bears, and will save Israel.

Critics interested in Genesis 1's interactions with a variety of subsequent communities might note the very different concerns the text has been made to address over the centuries. Modern creationism is by no means the first attempt to use Genesis 1 for purposes it was never intended to fulfill. Very foreign to our modern sensibilities, yet much closer to the original text, for instance, is its retelling in the pseudepigraphic book of Jubilees from the second century B.C.E., which emphasizes the Sabbath day and commandments related to it, and draws a parallel between the Sabbath as a sacred day and Israel as a sacred people. In fact, the entire book of Jubilees is structured around a delimitation of time sequences based on the Sabbath.

Throughout history, the minutest details of Genesis 1 have been used to support various ideological programs. In the mid-second century C.E., Justin Martyr used the phrase "let *us* make *man* after *our* image and likeness" to argue that God was speaking to the preexistent Christ.[42] The great eleventh-century commentator Rashi (Rabbi Solomon ben Isaac) used the absence of a single unnecessary consonant in the word "subdue" in verse 28 to argue that "the male controls the female in order that she may not become a gadabout; teaching you also that to the man, whose nature is to master, was given the divine command to have issue, and not to the woman."[43] In both cases, details of the text that can be interpreted in a number of ways are used to buttress the interests of a commentator's own community. Rhetorical analysis of the Genesis text side by side with its commentaries can illuminate the creativity of biblical interpreters and the danger of overlooking their inventive additions.

As this brief survey has shown, rhetorical criticism can address a variety of questions related to the persuasive powers of texts. When exercised in relation to other critical methods such as textual criticism, form criticism, social-scientific criticism, or ideological criticism, rhetorical criticism can sharpen our picture of a text and its world in remarkable ways. Rhetorical criticism's attention to the constructed, persuasive nature of all communication can offer a much-needed reality check for all who are involved in the interpretive enterprise. As with other forms of criticism, its chief limitations lie with the imagination, analytical faculties, and intellectual honesty of the exegete.

Notes

1. This address was subsequently published as "Form Criticism and Beyond," *Journal of Biblical Literature* 88 (1969): 1–18.

2. *Ibid.*, 7.

3. *Ibid.*, 8.

4. *Ibid.*

5. *Ibid.*, 18.

6. See, for example, the 1974 Festschrift for Muilenburg compiled by his students: *Rhetorical Criticism: Essays in Honor of James Muilenburg*, ed. J. J. Jackson and Martin Kessler (Pittsburgh: Pickwick, 1974); and Duane F. Watson's "Notes on History and Method" in Watson and Alan J. Hauser, *Rhetorical Criticism of the Bible: A Comprehensive Bibliography with Notes on History and Method* (Leiden: E. J. Brill, 1994).

7. Phyllis Trible, *Rhetorical Criticism: Context, Method, and the Book of Jonah* (Minneapolis: Fortress, 1994).

8. *Ibid.*, 91.

9. This work was first published in 1975 by Scholars Press.

10. Jack Lundbom, *Jeremiah: A Study in Ancient Hebrew Rhetoric* (Winona Lake, Ind.: Eisenbrauns, 1997).

11. *Ibid.*, xxviii.

12. *Ibid.*

13. James Muilenburg, "Isaiah 40–66," *The Interpreter's Bible*, vol. 5 (New York: Abingdon, 1956), 381–773.

14. Aristotle, *Rhetoric*, trans. W. Rhys Roberts (New York: Modern Library, 1954), 1.1.1355b.

15. Dale Patrick and Allen Scult, *Rhetoric and Biblical Interpretation* (Sheffield: Sheffield Academic Press, 1990), 12.

16. George Kennedy, *New Testament Interpretation through Rhetorical Criticism* (Chapel Hill, N.C.: University of North Carolina Press, 1984), 4.

17. Yehoshua Gitay, *Prophecy and Persuasion: A Study of Isaiah 40–48* (Bonn: Linguistica Biblica, 1981).

18. Meir Sternberg, *The Poetics of Biblical Narrative: Ideological Literature and the Drama of Reading* (Bloomington, Ind.: Indiana University Press, 1985).

19. *Ibid.*, 50.

20. *Ibid.*, 37.

21. George Aichele et al., *The Postmodern Bible* (New Haven, Conn.: Yale University Press, 1995).

22. *Ibid.*, 182.

23. "Intertextuality is the defining condition for literary readability. Without intertextuality, a literary work would simply be unintelligible, like speech in a language one has not yet learned" (L. Jenny, "The Strategy of Form," in *French Literary Theory Today: A Reader*, ed. T. Todorov [Cambridge: Cambridge University Press, 1982; French original, 1976], 34).

24. Mikhail M. Bakhtin, *The Dialogic Imagination*, ed. Michael Holquist (Austin, Tex: University of Texas Press, 1981; Russian original, 1975).

25. *Ibid.*, 273–74.

26. *Ibid.*, 276.

27. Michael Fishbane, *Biblical Interpretation in Ancient Israel* (Oxford: Clarendon Press, 1985).

28. Michael Baxandall, "Figures in the Corpus: Theories of Influence and Intertextuality," in J. Clayton and E. Rothstein, eds., *Influence and Intertextuality in Literary History* (Madison, Wis.: University of Wisconsin Press, 1991), 6.

29. Bakhtin, *Dialogic Imagination*, 276.

30. For a detailed discussion of Second Isaiah's use of such previously known figures as Daughters Babylon and Zion, see Patricia Tull Willey, *Remember the Former Things: The Recollection of Previous Texts in Second Isaiah*, SBL Dissertation Series 161 (Atlanta: Scholars, 1997).

31. Carol Newsom, "Job," *The New Interpreter's Bible*, vol. 4 (Nashville: Abingdon, 1996), 634.

32. Mieke Bal, *Death and Dissymmetry: The Politics of Coherence in the Book of Judges* (Chicago: University of Chicago Press, 1988).

33. Bakhtin, *Dialogic Imagination*, 280.

34. Stanley K. Stowers, *The Diatribe and Paul's Letter to the Romans*, SBL Dissertation Series 57 (Chico, Calif.: Scholars, 1981), 175.

35. Morna Hooker, *Jesus and the Servant: The Influence of the Servant Concept of Deutero-Isaiah in the New Testament* (London: SPCK, 1959), 53–58.

36. J. F. A. Sawyer, *The Fifth Gospel: Isaiah in the History of Christianity* (Cambridge: Cambridge University Press, 1996), 112.

37. *Ibid.*, 89.

38. Cited in A. D. Neubauer and S. R. Driver, *The Fifty-third Chapter of Isaiah, according to the Jewish Interpreters*, vol. 2: *Translations* (New York: Ktav, 1969), 292.

39. Carol Newsom, "Woman and the Discourse of Patriarchal Wisdom: A Study of Proverbs 1–2," in *Gender and Difference in Ancient Israel*, ed. Peggy L. Day (Minneapolis: Fortress, 1989).

40. Stanley Stowers, *A Rereading of Romans: Justice, Jews, and Gentiles* (New Haven, Conn.: Yale University Press, 1994), 16.

41. See also Psalm 104, which shows many parallels with Genesis 1. Battle imagery is echoed in the psalm's description of the fleeing waters (v. 7). Yet, as in the Genesis account, the sea monster Leviathan is portrayed as a part of God's harmonious creation (v. 26).

42. Justin Martyr, "Dialogue with Trypho, a Jew," in *Ante-Nicene Fathers*, vol. 1, ed. A. Roberts and J. Donaldson (Peabody, Mass.: Hendrickson, 1994), chap. 62.

43. *Pentateuch with Targum Onkelos, Haphtaroth and Prayers for Sabbath and Rashi's Commentary*, vol. 1 (London: Shapiro, Vallentine & Co., 1946), 7.

For Further Reading

Aristotle. *The Art of Rhetoric*. Trans. H. E. Butler. Loeb Classical Library. Cambridge, Mass.: Harvard University Press, 1926.

Bakhtin, M. M. *The Dialogic Imagination*. Ed. Michael Holquist. Austin, Tex: University of Texas Press, 1981; Russian original, 1975.

Bal, Mieke. *Death and Dissymmetry: The Politics of Coherence in the Book of Judges*. Chicago: University of Chicago Press, 1988.

Bizzell, Patricia, and Bruce Herzberg. *The Rhetorical Tradition*. Boston: Bedford, 1990.

Fewell, Danna N., ed. *Reading between Texts: Intertextuality and the Hebrew Bible*. Louisville, Ky.: Westminster/John Knox, 1992.

Fishbane, Michael. *Biblical Interpretation in Ancient Israel*. Oxford: Clarendon Press, 1985.

Gitay, Yehoshua. *Prophecy and Persuasion*. Forum Theologicae Linguisticae 14. Bonn: Linguistica Biblica, 1981.

Hays, Richard. *Echoes of Scripture in the Letters of Paul*. New Haven, Conn.: Yale University Press, 1989.

Kennedy, George A. *New Testament Interpretation through Rhetorical Criticism*. Chapel Hill, N.C.: University of North Carolina Press, 1984.

Newsom, Carol. "Job." In *The New Interpreter's Bible*. Vol. 4. Nashville: Abingdon, 1996.

—————. "Woman and the Discourse of Patriarchal Wisdom: A Study of Proverbs 1–2." In *Gender and Difference in Ancient Israel*, ed. Peggy L. Day. Minneapolis: Fortress, 1989.

Patrick, Dale, and Allen Scult. *Rhetoric and Biblical Interpretation*. Sheffield: Almond, 1990.

Perelman, Chaim, and Lucie Olbrechts-Tyleca. *The New Rhetoric*. Notre Dame, Ind.: University of Notre Dame, 1969.

Sternberg, Meir. *The Poetics of Biblical Narrative*. Bloomington, Ind.: Indiana University Press, 1985.

Stowers, Stanley K. *A Rereading of Romans: Justice, Jews, and Gentiles*. New Haven, Conn.: Yale University Press, 1994.

Trible, Phyllis. *Rhetorical Criticism: Context, Method, and the Book of Jonah*. Minneapolis: Fortress, 1994.

Warner, Martin, ed. *The Bible as Rhetoric: Studies in Biblical Persuasion and Credibility*. New York: Routledge, 1990.

Willey, Patricia Tull. *Remember the Former Things: The Recollection of Previous Texts in Second Isaiah*. SBL Dissertation Series 161. Atlanta: Scholars, 1997.

PART THREE

OVERTURNING THE TRADITION

9

STRUCTURAL CRITICISM

DANIEL PATTE

The Origin of Structural Criticism

A Method Developed out of Semiotic and Semantic Theories

Structural criticism (or exegesis) is self-consciously developed on the basis of semiotic theories—that is, the theories that extend structural linguistic theories[1] (how meaningful communication takes place in and through language; the grammar of sentences)[2] to encompass all means of human communication (including through entire discourses and texts)[3] and semantic theories (how meaning is produced and communicated). It is called "structural" because, according to these theories, a text is meaningful for readers only insofar as they recognize (1) *different* features in this text and (2) an interrelation—a *structure*—among these different features.

The basic principles of this method can be readily understood. In the same way that one cannot truly appreciate "good health" (its meaning and value) as long as one has not experienced "sickness" (and thus does not know the difference and relation between being healthy and sick), so a word ("blue") is meaningless as long as one does not recognize that it is *different* from other words ("blew," "red") and how it is *related* to other words, either in a text (e.g., in a sentence) or in language (e.g., it belongs together with words about colors, and not with verbs of action). So it is with all the features that can be perceived in a text, from the smallest features—such as letters, syllables, words, their denotations (what they refer to), their connotations (the values associated with them)—to larger features, such as sentences, paragraphs, parts; characters, actions, situations, subplots, and plots; metaphors and other figures, allusions to other texts, figurative units, and the like. Since quite different kinds of features can be recognized in a text, different "structures" and thus different "meanings" (or "meaning-producing dimensions") are perceived in a text. Since, in a given study, one usually focuses the analysis on one or a few of these structures, structural criticism takes several different forms (see bibliography). However, in the limits of this chapter only one of its forms can be presented.

A Method for the Study of the "Faith" Expressed by a Religious Text

Among several other possibilities, structural criticism provides the means for studying the main characteristics of the "religion" or "faith"—the author's[4] "convictions"—expressed by a text. This meaning-producing dimension (which is present in any text, but is particularly important in religious texts) should not be ignored in biblical studies.

In the nineteenth century and beginning of the twentieth century, the "religion" of biblical texts was studied with a "history of religions" methodology that compared biblical texts with other religious texts of the period (e.g., Babylonian, Assyrian, Egyptian, Jewish, Hellenistic). Although such comparisons are still conducted for other purposes (cf. form and tradition criticisms), at present the method of history of religions per se is less frequently used in biblical studies because its results are often difficult to evaluate. Early practitioners of this method argued that biblical texts are comparable to, and influenced by, other religious texts and traditions of their time—both Hellenistic[5] and Jewish,[6] in the case of New Testament texts. The difficulty was how to determine which specific features of very different religious texts and traditions are truly comparable.

Structural criticism offers the possibility of reopening this quest for meaningful comparisons because semiotic theories (and especially Greimas's structural semiotics) provide the possibility of identifying several sets of features (meaning-producing dimensions) in a given text that have different functions in the communication of its religious message. These include the features that most directly express the basic religious message, which is one of the things the author "wants to convey":[7] the author's own "faith" or system of "convictions."[8] Yet these convictions should not be confused, for instance, with the "figures" (symbolism) of a text,[9] through which the author's convictions are expressed in terms of the intended readers' old views, so as to better convince them to adopt new views (the author's convictions).[10] Thus the use of Hellenistic or Jewish "figures" (e.g., "sacred meal," "Son of man") in a given New Testament text is not *necessarily* a sign that the text expresses a "religion" that is fundamentally Hellenistic or Jewish. This might be the case, as the history of religions school often insisted. But these figures might also have been used to convince readers to abandon their undue reliance on Hellenistic or Jewish views for conceiving the Christian faith. One way to adjudicate such cases is to elucidate the dimension that expresses the basic characteristics of the "religion" (system of convictions) of a text, and to compare these results with those of similar studies of Hellenistic or Jewish texts. Then one compares what is truly comparable: a dimension that, in each of these texts, has the same function.

By itself, the study of the "system of convictions" of a text reaches important exegetical results. It reveals basic characteristics of the religious message of this text, even though the full significance of these results only appears when they are compared with the results of similar studies of other texts or with those of the studies of other dimensions of the same text (something we cannot do here).

Structural Criticism and the Other Methods of Biblical Criticism

Structural criticism, in agreement with other exegetical methods, takes as its starting point the general observation that biblical texts, like other texts, were written in order to communicate something to a specific audience, and thus with the hope that they would make sense for that audience. These texts also make sense for readers in other times, including today, each time they are read. The fact that biblical texts are religious texts that, in certain instances, emphasize that their goal is to transmit "revealed" or "inspired" knowledge[11] does not prevent them from being instances of *human* communication. Even though they are, for believers, "Word of God," they remain human words.

Consequently, all exegetical methods have been developed, implicitly or explicitly, on the basis of "theories of communication,"[12] including theories about language (linguistics) and about meaning (semantics). The diversity of methods is due, in part, to differences in theories.

It makes sense to develop exegetical methods on the basis of ancient theories of communication, such as classical rhetoric, and theories about the specific forms of oral communication and literary convention that existed at the time biblical texts were composed.[13] Yet, ultimately, all exegetical methods (including the preceding ones) presuppose that communication is a human phenomenon that obeys similar rules through the centuries, despite cultural and other differences. If this were not the case, there would be no hope of understanding ancient texts.[14] Thus each method presupposes one or another general theory of human communication as a "universal" phenomenon. These general theories of communication, and their corresponding critical methods, can be viewed as belonging to two groups.

Certain theories consider what is truly significant in any given instance of communication (e.g., a text) to be what is new in it—that is, how its language, sources, traditions, and so forth, have been transformed in this given instance. This is what is presupposed by the so-called historical methods (source, form, tradition, and redaction criticisms), for which it is essential to establish the place of a given word, tradition, or text in the *linear* flow of history. This "diachronic" approach elucidates what is "new," and thus truly significant, in a given instance by showing how it differs from what precedes and follows it in time.

More recent theories[15] consider what is truly significant in any given instance of communication to be how its features are interrelated in a system, that is, how various words are interrelated with other words in the language (viewed as a system); how the different features of a text are inter-related to form a coherent whole; how a text is interrelated with its literary, social, religious, and political environment (other kinds of systems); how a text participates with its readers in producing meaning (the system being all the features of the reading process). This is what is presupposed by the newer methods (structural, narrative, and reader-response criticisms), as well as by sociological, canonical, and some rhetorical criticisms.

Structural criticism belongs to this latter set of methods, in which it distinguishes itself by making explicit the general theory of communica-tion—semiotics—upon which its methods are developed. As a conse-quence, structural exegetical studies are often unduly theoretical and methodological, and use a quite technical vocabulary (i.e., jargon). While at first this was necessary to clarify the difference with earlier methods, it is no longer necessary, as we shall see below.

A second difference between structural criticism and other exegetical methods is that even when it studies a single dimension, structural criticism is informed by semiotic theory's claim that a text involves *several* meaning-producing dimensions, which can give rise, in the process of reading, to quite different "meanings." Together with reader-response criticism, struc-tural criticism acknowledges that specific meanings are perceived in a text by certain readers because of their specific social, cultural, and religious locations. Yet it emphasizes that these meanings are not projected upon a text by these readers, except in the case of "illegitimate" readings. Because of their specific preoccupations and concerns at the time of a given reading, readers focus their attention on one or another of the several coherent meaning-producing dimensions of a text, which become the meaning of the text for them. The different "meanings" arise from the selection of different meaning-producing dimensions and their appropriation as the coherent meaning of a text for readers.

Finally, because it self-consciously uses a *theory*, structural criticism remains fully aware that it is culturally conditioned (as any theory is), a point emphasized by poststructuralist criticism.[16] This means that structural criticism views other exegetical methods, including the so-called historical methods, as complementary to itself. Different methods, based on different theories, study different meaning-producing dimensions, each of which can be legitimately perceived as the meaning of a text according to specific standpoints of readers. Thus whatever method one uses, one should not pretend that one elucidates *the* meaning of a text. This undue claim has the disastrous ethical consequences of denying, without any true examination, the legitimacy of other readings and thus the legitimacy of the interests and concerns of other readers who perceive other "meanings" in a text, because their readings are focused upon other dimensions.

A Structural Exegesis of Luke 24

Procedures for the Elucidation of Convictions Expressed by a Biblical Text

The specific method of structural criticism presented here examines a single meaning-producing dimension of a biblical text: its "system of convictions." The following twofold definition[17] provides the basis for the procedures of the exegesis.

1. Convictions as basic characteristics of the "faith" of the author are "self-evident truths," in contrast with "ideas," which are "demonstrated truths." Convictions impose themselves upon believers (and are often viewed as "revelations") instead of being learned or deduced by reasoning, as ideas are. They provide a vision of human experience that defines a believer's fundamental identity and thus orients his or her behavior.

2. Convictions form a "system" in the sense that they are organized according to a peculiar "structure"[18] (distinct from the structures of other dimensions) characterized by a fundamental pattern[19] that is repeatedly applied to the different domains of human experience. This is why, for example, one can use family language (father, children) to speak about the relationship between God and human beings; the domains of human family and of God-human relationships are perceived as being "alike" because they follow the same pattern. Consequently, although a given passage deals with only one or a few domains of human experience, its study elucidates the fundamental pattern of the entire system of convictions—that is, basic characteristics of the faith of the author.

Since, when authors express their convictions, they cannot afford to be misunderstood—their identity is at stake!—they make their convictions unambiguous by stating both what they mean to say and also what they do not mean to say. Thus the structure of a system of convictions and its fundamental pattern appears in a text as a set of *explicit* semantic oppositions.

Furthermore, since convictions govern the way believers act, and since writing a religious text is an act through which an author-believer seeks to convey his or her convictions to readers, the semantic oppositions that most directly express the author's convictions are linked with (1) the "inverted parallelisms" through which the author organizes the discourse and each of its "thematic units" so as to transform the readers' views[20] and (2) "oppositions of actions" (because actions of characters are meaningful actions according to the author's convictions).

Thus in order to elucidate basic characteristics of the system of convictions expressed in a biblical text (be it narrative, as Luke 24 is, or not), it is essential to identify a complete thematic unit and the inverted parallelisms that delimit it; to analyze its oppositions of actions; and then to interpret the results of these formal procedures by clarifying the organization of the convictions.

Luke 24:1–53 as a Complete Thematic Unit

Since we have chosen to study a thematic unit at the end of the Gospel of Luke, its end is already identified: 24:53. But does it truly begin in 24:1?

In a narrative text, thematic and narrative units do not necessarily correspond to each other. A thematic unit often contains several narrative units that function as thematic subunits; yet its beginning coincides with that of a narrative unit. Thus we first note that Luke 24:1 is the beginning of a narrative unit, since it describes the women in a new time ("on the first day of the week"),[21] going to a new space (the tomb), where they are joined by new characters (the "two men," 24:4) (note the three criteria used to identify narrative units). The narrative unit about the women that begins in 24:1 ends in 24:11. Luke 24:1–11 is also a thematic subunit defined by inverted parallelisms: The description in 24:9–11 of the women going away from the tomb and interacting with other characters (the apostles) is in inverted parallelism with the description in 24:1–4.[22] The question is, Could this subunit be the introduction of a larger unit ending in 24:53? To answer this we need to consider whether or not this subunit is in inverted parallelism with the end of the chapter.

In Luke 24:53, the apostles are "continually in the temple blessing God"; that is, they are presented as performing a Jewish (in the "temple") ritual of thanksgiving. In 24:1 the women, who had been described as resting on the Sabbath "according to the commandment" (23:56b), are also presented as attempting to perform a Jewish ritual, the ritual of mourning (with "spices and ointments"). This observation is confirmed by the presence of other inverted parallelisms. Both in 24:3 and 24:52–53, Jesus is absent (parallel features); yet it is a cause of perplexity and fear for the women at the tomb in 24:3–5, and a cause of "great joy" for the apostles at Jerusalem in 24:51–53 (inverted features). Furthermore, both in 24:6–7 and in 24:44, 46, we find, almost in the same words, a reference to what Jesus told his followers regarding his crucifixion and resurrection (parallel features), but in 24:44–49 these words are explained (inverted features).

Such multiple inverted parallelisms demonstrate that 24:1–53[23] is a complete thematic unit, which includes three subunits: 24:1–11, the introduction; 24:12–35,[24] the Emmaus story; and 24:36–53, the conclusion.[25]

The inverted parallelisms we noted between the beginning and the end of 24:1–53 allow us to identify the theme of the unit in general terms. Since they contrast people who do not believe that Jesus is risen (the mourning women going to the tomb to anoint his body, 24:1) with people who believe that he is risen (the apostles with "great joy" who "bless" God, 24:52–53), *the theme concerns the process of becoming true believers in the (crucified and) resurrected Christ*. The parallelisms show that belief in the crucified and resurrected Christ (1) is in continuity with Judaism (Jewish rituals in both 24:1 and 24:52–53), (2) is held when people remember Jesus' words (prophecies) during his ministry about his death and resurrection, and (3) is held in the absence of Jesus (24:3 and 24:51). The inversions show that in order to have such a true belief, one needs (1) to be in the right place—among the living, in society (Jerusalem, 24:52) rather than "among the dead" (the tomb, 24:5)—and (2) to understand the significance of Jesus' death and resurrection, why he "must" die and rise (cf. 24:7) with the help of the scriptures (24:45–49). In addition, the inversions show that true belief involves a positive evaluation of Jesus' absence (great joy), rather than a negative one (mourning).[26] Surprisingly, in view of the central subunit (24:12–35 and also 24:36–53, which emphasizes the recognition of the risen Jesus' presence), the inverted parallelisms underscore that true belief in Jesus' resurrection is not a belief that the risen Christ is present, since the great joy associated with this belief occurs in the absence of Jesus (after "he parted from them," 24:51).

Such seem to be the surprising convictions regarding the process of becoming believers expressed by the overall theme of Luke 24:1–53. Yet their identification is still quite general and tentative. This theme and its convictions need to be clarified through a study of the convictions expressed by each subunit.

The Convictions Expressed in Luke 24:1–11

Since the inverted parallelism between 24:1–4 and 24:9–11 (the introduction and conclusion of this subunit) concerns the women going to (24:1) and returning from (24:9) the tomb and being associated, respectively, with "two men" (24:4) and with the eleven apostles and "all the rest" (24:9), *the theme of the subunit concerns convictions about locations and relations with people*.

Two explicit oppositions of actions (here, cognitive actions) underscore and specify these convictions. The first one contrasts the women's (negative) action, being "perplexed" (lacking knowledge; 24:4), with their (positive) action, "remembering" (having knowledge; 24:8), following the two men's instruction. The underscored convictions appear when one compares the subjects (agents) and effects of the positive and negative actions. Here the question is, What distinguishes the women in 24:4 and 24:8? In brief, in 24:8 they have been instructed by the two men. Note that the validity of the women's will[27] to find Jesus is not challenged. But at first the women do not know how to find Jesus, because they lack a knowledge of Jesus' words about his death and resurrection and thus have a wrong knowledge about Jesus; they believe he is to be found among the dead, rather than among the living. *Knowing how to find Jesus involves remembering his words.*[28] Furthermore, at first the empty tomb does not make sense for the women; they are perplexed by it. In sum, *the empty tomb is meaningless as long as this extraordinary event is not interpreted in terms of Jesus' words about the necessity ("must") of this death and resurrection* (cf. 24:7).

This first set of convictions (in italics in the preceding paragraph) explains why "locations" is part of the subtheme of 24:1–11. In order to find the resurrected Jesus, one needs to be at the right place: among the living, that is, in society, rather than among the dead, at the tomb, or more generally, outside of society. This is also part of the theme of 24:1–53. Note that in 24:36–53 (see also 24:33–34), the apostles are "in society" (at Jerusalem) when they meet the resurrected Jesus. Yet the opposition also shows that the fundamental problem (which turns out to be the fundamental human predicament for Luke) is more general: People do not know how to find Jesus, or how to make sense of situations (here, the empty tomb), or as we shall see, how to recognize Jesus in these concrete situations. In order to overcome this predicament, a first condition is stipulated: One needs to remember Jesus' words. Yet this is certainly not enough; note that the text does not say either that the women believed or that they found Jesus.

The second opposition of actions contrasts the women telling "all this" to the eleven (24:9–10) and the negative response of the apostles who "did not believe them" (24:11). The conviction concerns the relationship between "women" (positive subject) and "men" (apostles, negative subject). The women accept the words of the "two men" as trustworthy, since they act accordingly. By contrast, for the apostles the women's report is not trustworthy ("an idle tale"), even though the text emphasizes that their report was complete ("all this") and thus trustworthy—a point underscored by the fact that the women are honored by being named (24:10). In brief, *the men-apostles' patriarchal attitude* (not accepting as trustworthy a report by women, even though it is trustworthy) *is marked as negative*. Yet it remains that the women's report is unable to overcome this patriarchal attitude; the women lack something so as to be in a position to be effective witnesses.

This second set of convictions explains why relationships are part of the subtheme of 24:1–11. Taking the words of witnesses as trustworthy—as the women did, and as the apostles did not do—is an essential step for believing in the resurrected Jesus. The theme of 24:1–53 also underscores this point by specifying what makes witnessing (cf. 24:48) effective: In addition to reporting the event and Jesus' words, one also needs to explain the significance of these as fulfillments of the scriptures (cf. 24:46–47) and to be "clothed with power from on high" (24:49).

Convictions Underscored in Luke 24:12–35

The theme of this second thematic subunit is marked by two sets of inverted parallelisms.

A first set concerns Simon Peter. In 24:12 he goes to the tomb, where "he saw the linen clothes by themselves" and thus does not see Jesus and is as perplexed as the women had been. After he departs from the tomb (cf. 24:12b), and thus reenters society, possibly in Jerusalem (24:33), it is reported that the risen Lord "was seen by Simon" (24:34; lit. trans.).[29] Thus once again, in order to see Jesus, one needs to be in society.

The second set of inverted parallelisms, about the two disciples of Emmaus, underscores a point concerning recognizing Jesus and believing that he has risen. In 24:13–16, while on the road with Jesus, "their eyes were kept from recognizing him." In 24:29–31, "their eyes were opened and they recognized him," and as a consequence they believe, together with the other disciples, that "the Lord has risen indeed" (24:34). This latter theme is clarified by three oppositions.

The first opposition is set by the polemical exchange between Jesus, who inquires about their conversation (24:17), and Cleopas, who rebukes him (24:18). The irony is that Cleopas and his companion accuse Jesus of not knowing what happened in Jerusalem and thus assume that they themselves truly know it. Thus the first thing that prevents them from recognizing Jesus is their false confidence in having a true and complete knowledge of the situation, although in fact their knowledge is incomplete. Such an incomplete knowledge results in a negative evaluation (they are "sad") of a situation (Jesus' crucifixion and the empty tomb) that should be assessed positively (as joyful).

The second opposition is another polemical exchange between the two disciples, who explain the situation (24:19b–24), and Jesus, who rebukes them (24:25–27). What is wrong with the two disciples and their statement is made explicit in 24:25: They are "foolish," that is, they do not understand the situation and events they describe. Why? Because they are "slow of heart to believe all that the prophets have spoken," and therefore fail to interpret these events in terms of the scriptures and the scriptures in terms of these events (24:27). As a consequence, instead of understanding that it was "necessary that the Christ should suffer these things and enter into his glory" (24:26), they view Jesus' crucifixion as the failure ("we had hoped," 24:21) of a "prophet" (24:19). And despite a more positive assessment of the women's account (because it has been partially confirmed by men, 24:24), they still take their report that Jesus is "alive" as resulting from a dubious "vision of angels" (similar to the women's "idle tale"). In sum, the main problem with the two disciples, their "foolishness," is that they do not know how to interpret the situation, because they do not interpret it in terms of scriptures; as a consequence, they do not recognize Jesus and have a negative evaluation of the situation (they are "sad"). Positively, *in order to recognize Jesus' presence and to have a positive evaluation of Jesus' crucifixion and empty tomb, one needs to interpret the situation in terms of the scriptures*, something one knows how to do if one "believe[s] all that the prophets have spoken." Yet this is not sufficient, since after Jesus has "interpreted to them in all the scriptures the things concerning himself" (24:27), they still do not recognize him.

The third opposition contrasts the (negative) action that Jesus "appeared" to want to take, going further (24:28b), and the (positive) action of staying with the two disciples (24:29b). It concerns the establishment of Jesus' will. The fact that in 24:28 Jesus is said to have "appeared" ("made as if," *prosepoesatō*) to be going further, however this term might be interpreted, shows that the text presents the disciples' perception of Jesus' will. Thus what is at stake is the role of the disciples in establishing Jesus' will to stay. For them it is important to convince this stranger ("they constrained him") not to continue his journey at night (cf. 24:29); they are concerned for his welfare. In other words, they are themselves characterized by a will to take care of the needs of this stranger for shelter and also for food; indeed, they give him the seat of honor at the table, since he is the one who says the blessing and breaks the bread (24:30). Then they recognize him. Why? It is certainly because they remembered that he had performed the same symbolic gestures before them during his ministry (cf. 9:16 and 22:19)—they have already expressed that they remembered his deeds and words (cf. 24:19).

Yet none of this would have happened if they had not taken care of the needs of the stranger and had not honored him, as Jesus taught them to do by means of parables (e.g., 10:25–37). In fact, by so doing, they initiate and participate in a symbolic act that, as the parables did, teaches them how to interpret (e.g., the parable in 10:25–37 teaches the lawyer how to interpret the law he has just recited).

In sum, what are, according to this subunit, the necessary conditions for recognizing the resurrected Christ and thus believing that "the Lord has risen indeed" (24:34)? Confidence that one understands the situation by oneself needs to be overcome by being taught to interpret it in terms of the scriptures; but according to Jesus' instruction one must also care for the needs of and honor the stranger who provides such a teaching; then, as one remembers Jesus' deeds and words during his ministry and participates in a symbolic act, one recognizes the resurrected Christ's presence.

Convictions Underscored in Luke 24:36–53

This passage is marked as a complete thematic subunit by two sets of inverted parallelisms. The first set concerns the disciples who, at first, "were startled and frightened, and supposed that they saw a spirit" (24:37), and at the end have great joy and bless God (24:52–53), an expression of true belief. The second set of inverted parallelisms concerns Jesus, who was present with the disciples in 24:36–37 but had parted from them in 24:52–53 (see 24:51).

Since there is no opposition of actions, the convictions are exclusively expressed by the inverted parallelisms. These show that the theme concerns the transformation of fear and wrong belief in Jesus' presence into great joy and true belief in his absence. Thus we need to consider closely the initial situation and how it is progressively transformed.

Initial Situation. The new subunit is linked with the preceding one by the phrase, "As they were saying this" (24:36), which refers to the disciples' preceding words, which include the declaration, "The Lord is risen indeed" (24:34). But knowing and believing that Jesus is risen do not prevent them from being startled and frightened when he stands among them, and from disbelieving (cf. 24:38). Why? Because they do not recognize Jesus and/or have a wrong understanding of what it means that he is risen. Once again, disciples do not know how to interpret a situation. More specifically, they think he is a spirit, and for them, being in the presence of a spirit is dangerous.

First Step of the Transformation. By showing them his hands and feet, Jesus dispels their misunderstanding that he is a spirit (24:38–39) and therefore cancels their fear, which is replaced by "joy" (24:41; not yet a "great joy"!).

Second Step of the Transformation. Yet they still disbelieve (24:41). In order to dispel this disbelief, Jesus eats before them the food they give him (24:41–43; cf. 24:30), reminds them of what is written about him in the scriptures, and teaches them how to interpret the scriptures ("opens their minds," 24:44–46; cf. 24:25–27, 32). The process of bringing the disciples to recognize Jesus and thus to acknowledge that he is risen is therefore the same as in the case of the disciples of Emmaus (although in reverse order).

Third Step of the Transformation. But this recognition and the belief that Jesus is risen are not enough to bring about the "great joy" that character- izes the disciples in 24:52–53 (and is not mentioned regarding the Emmaus disciples), even as Jesus departs from them. Contrary to our expectation, it is not the presence of Jesus and its recognition that give them this "great joy." What is it then? The answer lies in 24:47–51, verses that are no longer parallel to the experience of the Emmaus disciples. We find four reasons for their "great joy." First, 24:47 begins to explain the significance of Jesus' death and resurrection: These events mean that "repentance" should be and can be preached "for the forgiveness of sins" "to all the nations." Thus for- giveness of sins is now available to all the nations. Second, his death and resurrection mean that they now have a vocation as "witnesses of these things" (24:48). Third, his death and resurrection mean that the disciples will receive "the promise of the Father," "the power from on high," that is, the Holy Spirit. And finally, they are blessed (24:50); this is a true and effective blessing, since it is given by the risen Christ.

Convictions about the Process of Becoming True Believers according to Luke 24:1–53

What is the result of structural exegesis? It is the elucidation of a part of the author's system of convictions, that is, of a vision of a domain of human experience, here "the process of becoming true believers," which the author aims at sharing with readers. The events that took place during the days fol- lowing Jesus' death and that involved the women, the two disciples of Emmaus, the apostles, and the resurrected Christ are "images"[30] that together express a vision of the process of becoming true believers, whatever might be the circumstances. Would-be believers (with whom readers are invited to identify themselves) are *like* the women, *like* the two disciples of Emmaus, *like* the apostles, and the process these disciples collectively go through in order to become true believers is *like* the process any believer needs to go through.

Summarizing our findings, we seek to understand the different steps of this process. The ultimate step of the process is that true believers are effective "witnesses" of Jesus' crucifixion and resurrection (24:48) who preach repen- tance and forgiveness of sins "to all nations, beginning from Jerusalem" (24:47). The question is, What is necessary for being such a witness?

1. Like the two disciples (24:19–24) and the women (24:6–7), one needs to know (and remember) the events that took place—that is, the story of Jesus' death and of the empty tomb, as well as the story and words of

Jesus during his ministry. One can be a firsthand witness of these events, or know them through the reports of such witnesses (reports of the "two men," 24:6–7; of the women, 24:9–11, 22–24; of Peter, 24:24, 34), the latter case being like the situation of believers in the time of the church.

2. One needs to believe that the reported events mean that "the Lord has risen indeed." For this, the empty tomb and the crucifixion need to be interpreted (1) in terms of Jesus' words (24:6–7) and (2) in terms of the scriptures (24:25–27, 44–45). The fundamental problem is that would-be believers do not know how to interpret these events, even though (and because!) they self-confidently think they truly know them. They need to be taught not only that these events fulfill Jesus' words and the scriptures but also how to make this interpretation themselves (and thus how to appropriate it), by acting out what they have been taught (the women doing what the "two men" told them; 24:8–9) or by taking care of the teacher's needs and honoring the stranger (24:28–31, 41–42). This amounts to acting out Jesus' teaching and participating with him in a symbolic act.

3. This knowledge-belief that "the Lord is risen indeed" is not sufficient. Once again with the help of the scriptures and of Jesus' teaching during his ministry, one also needs to understand that Jesus' resurrection means that forgiveness of sins is available to all the nations, and that, as a believer, one has the vocation to be a "witness of all these things." One also understands that one will be given the means (power from on high and effective blessing by the risen Christ) to carry it out (24:47–50)—and not that one should expect the presence of Jesus with oneself. In order to carry out this vocation, one needs, of course, to be in society (and not to look for Jesus "among the dead").

4. As a consequence, one can have "great joy" in the absence of Jesus (who has departed for heaven); one is a true believer, in that one can continually bless God (true worship) and this in continuity with Judaism (in the temple)—continuity that is marked all along, since without the help of the Jewish scriptures one would not know that Jesus is risen and would not understand the meaning of his resurrection.

Limitations of Structural Criticism

The limitations of a structural exegesis are clear. We have left out many features of the text. Actually, our structural study was limited to the study of a single meaning-producing dimension, and thus we bracketed out its other meaning-producing dimensions. For instance, we have not studied Luke 24 as a "figurative system," a study usually concerned with the "theology" (rather than the "convictional vision," or "religion") of the text and entailing the study of each figure in terms of its "intertexts" (the texts and traditions to which the text alludes); as a story (characterized by the unfolding of its plot); as a realistic narrative (characterized by the features that give to Luke 24 a "historical" character); or as a discourse through which the author (enunciator) seeks to affect the reader (enunciatee) in certain ways. These and other dimensions can be studied by other structural methods, since each of these dimensions is characterized by a specific "structure."[31] But in most instances they can also be studied by means of other methods (e.g., historical, literary, and rhetorical methods). This is what led me to choose to focus the above presentation on a method of structural criticism aimed at elucidating the system of convictions of the text (characteristics of its "religion"), a dimension neglected by other methods, even though structural criticism has much to contribute to the study of the other dimensions.

As we have underscored above, it is essential to acknowledge the strict limitations of the method one uses. Although, as is also the case with each of the other dimensions, the meaning-producing dimension elucidated by this exegesis (its "convictional vision," "faith," or "religion") can become for certain readers *the* meaning of the text that they implement and find meaningful for their lives as believers (or for the purpose of comparing the basic characteristics of the "religion" of different religious texts), as with any type of exegesis, one must make explicit that it merely elucidates one of the possible meaning-producing dimensions of the text. Otherwise, as we have argued above, the structural exegesis will have the disastrous ethical consequences of denying, without any true examination, the legitimacy of other readings and thus the legitimacy of the interests and concerns of readers who perceive other meanings in the text, because their readings are focused upon other dimensions.

Notes

Scripture quotations in this chapter are from the Revised Standard Version.

1. The main semiotic theories are those of Charles S. Peirce (e.g., *Collected Papers*, 2d ed., ed. C. Hartshorne and P. Weiss [Cambridge, Mass.: Harvard University Press, 1960]); Umberto Eco (e.g., *A Theory of Semiotics* [Bloomington, Ind.: Indiana University Press, 1976]); and A. J. Greimas (e.g., with J. Courtes, *Semiotics and Language: An Analytical Dictionary* [Bloomington, Ind.: Indiana University Press, 1982]). This latter theory, which is more explicitly a "structural semiotics," is the basis of structural exegesis. Greimas's technical vocabulary, to which I refer in notes, is defined in this dictionary.

2. See the many linguistic theories developed out of the foundational work of F. de Saussure at the beginning of the twentieth century, published in English as *Course in General Linguistics* (New York: McGraw-Hill, 1966).

3. Actually, all cultural artifacts are means of communication, as Lévi-Strauss emphasized in his anthropological study of Native American culture. The publication of

his *Structural Anthropology* (New York: Basic Books, 1963) proved to be a decisive step in the early development of structuralism, which led to the progressive elaboration of structural semiotic theories.

4. Technically, the "enunciator's" or "implied author's" convictions. Semiotics and structural criticism emphasize in this way that, when studying a text, one only discovers the way in which the "author" presents himself or herself *in the text*—that is, one discovers the "enunciator" and not the "real author." Even if this presentation is sincere, it is always partial (incomplete and biased); the real author only presents that part of himself or herself that is appropriate for the topic at hand. Whether or not one acknowledges this distinction, it is a fact that, in biblical studies, all that is known about the author is usually derived from the text itself. Thus what is meant by "author" is the "enunciator" or "implied reader." In order to avoid distracting technical vocabulary I will use here the term "author" in that sense.

5. The history of religions school can be represented by the works of Wilhelm Bousset (see his book on the "religion of Judaism," in German, 1903, and *Kyrios Christos* [Nashville: Abingdon, 1970]; German edition, 1913), who argued that Palestinian Judaism was influenced by Hellenistic religions and that Paul and his disciples were strongly influenced by Hellenistic Oriental religions; and Richard Reitzenstein (see his book on *The Hellenistic Mystery Religions*; German edition, 1910), who claimed that Paul's Christ myth was borrowed from Hellenistic mystic and pre-Christian Gnostic redeemer myths. Both Dibelius and Bultmann were proponents of this comparative approach before using it to develop form criticism.

6. Although the designation "history of religions" is usually reserved for the studies in the preceding note, one should not overlook that this type of research also included comparisons of the New Testament with Apocalyptic Jewish literature. Thus Johannes Weiss (*Jesus' Proclamation of the Kingdom of God* [Philadelphia: Fortress, 1971; German edition,1902]) argued that late Jewish Apocalyptic expectations (of the kingdom, of the Son of man) were the framework for Jesus' proclamation.

7. Especially in a "religious" text. Note that since this "author" is the "enunciator," we are not speaking of the "intention" of the real author (which is an illusion created by readers) but technically of the "intentionality" of the text. Note also that for structural semiotics, a text is perceived as having a plurality of "intentionalities." Besides wanting to convey a religious message (one meaning-producing dimension) through a given text, the author (enunciator) might also appear to convey exhortations to moral life (another meaning-producing dimension) and the like.

8. What Greimas calls the "semantic universe" or "narrative semantics" of a text— one kind of semantic meaning-producing dimension—and what Lévi-Strauss calls the "mythical structure" or "deep structure" (this latter designation is quite misleading; for readers, this structure is not deeper than any other structure!). This structural dimension is a subject of most structural studies, although in many cases, this is only a means to elucidate another dimension. The method I will present here is greatly simplified yet still reliable, as compared with its earlier formulations, which included the use of complex models such as Greimas's "semiotic square" and Lévi-Strauss's formula and model for the mythical structure.

9. Another kind of semantic meaning-producing dimension that Greimas calls "discursive semantics."

10. Similarly, the author's "convictions" should not be confused with his or her "theological," "ethical," or narrative expressions. These are different dimensions of the

"syntax" of a text, each of which can take two different forms (in Greimas's terminology, that of a "narrative or argumentative syntax" and that of a "discursive syntax").

11. For example, the many oracles of the prophets, the teaching of Jesus as divine revelation in the Gospels, Paul's references to revelations he had received (e.g., Gal. 1:11–17).

12. This phrase is used here in a broad sense to designate all the theories concerning how people communicate meaningfully with one another, including epistemology (how we know and understand) and semantics, as well as theories concerning the means (e.g., language, text, oral speech) or conditions (e.g., social contexts, literary conventions) of communication.

13. The cases, respectively, of rhetorical criticism (although it can also be based on modern rhetorical theories), form criticism, and certain kinds of literary criticism. The same could be said about the ancient view of religious texts (implied by the formation of the canon) in canonical criticism.

14. This is one of the three basic principles of historical-critical studies that E. Troeltsch called the "principle of analogy" in his seminal essay "On the Historical Dogmatic Method in Theology" (German edition, 1898). See its discussion in Van Harvey, *The Historian and the Believer: A Confrontation between the Modern Historian's Principles of Judgement and the Christian Will-to-Believe* (New York: Macmillan, 1966), 102ff.

15. Ushered into biblical studies by James Barr, *The Semantics of Biblical Language* (London: Oxford University Press, 1961), in which the author denounced the diachronic interpretation of biblical language prevalent in exegesis, and represented by Kittel's *Theological Dictionary of the New Testament*.

16. Note that what is rejected by poststructuralism is structuralism, that is, the views of early structuralist scholars (e.g., Lévi-Strauss) who claimed universal value for the structural theory, a claim that semiotics and structural criticism also reject.

17. For a more detailed discussion and definition of "convictions," see D. Patte, *Paul's Faith and the Power of the Gospel: A Structural Introduction to Paul's Letters* (Philadelphia: Fortress, 1983), introduction, and *The Gospel according to Matthew: A Structural Commentary on Matthew's Faith* (Philadelphia: Fortress, 1987), introduction.

18. This is what Lévi-Strauss called the "mythical structure." See Lévi-Strauss, *Structural Anthropology*, chap. 11.

19. Greimas calls it an "axiology."

20. These concepts will be illustrated below through a study of Luke 24. Semiotic theory defines a "thematic unit" as a passage that (1) begins with an "inverted content," where a theme is posited so as to be readily recognizable by readers, and thus primarily expresses readers' view of that theme, and (2) ends with a "posited content," where the theme is restated in a way that most directly expresses the author's conviction. Thus a thematic unit aims at transforming the readers' vision of a theme. Its beginning and end are in "inverted parallelisms," in the sense that they have something (the topic of the theme) in common (so "parallelisms"), but also a different way of viewing this topic (so the inversions).

21. It is also possible to begin the narrative unit at 23:56b; the mention of the Sabbath can be viewed as belonging to the present unit (introducing the actual time reference, which allows one to make sense of the "first day") as well as to the preceding unit.

22. Unlike inclusions (which mark figurative units), inverted parallelisms are not necessarily expressed by the same vocabulary, and include both semantic features that are similar or parallel and other features that are different or inverted. Here, at the beginning and the end of 24:1–11, the features that are parallel include "the women in

movement (during the first day of the week)." The features that are inverted include "going to the tomb" versus "going away from the tomb" and "being with the two men" versus "being with the apostles."

23. Precisely, Luke 23:56b–24:53, so as to include the mention of resting on the Sabbath "according to the commandment." To avoid this cumbersome formulation we shall simply refer to 24:1–53.

24. We shall see that our structural exegesis provides an argument for including 24:12, which is not found in certain manuscripts.

25. The inverted parallelisms that justify the claim that these last two passages are complete thematic subunits will be discussed below.

26. Another inversion seems to be that false belief is associated with women and true belief with men. But, as we shall see, the text underscores that this distinction between women and men is irrelevant and even in contradiction with true belief (see the analysis of 24:1–11).

27. Since, in order to perform an action, a subject needs will, ability, and knowledge, the convictions that contrast two subjects necessarily concern how one or several of these are established. The question is, What is understood by the text?

28. Note that convictions are formulated in relatively general terms. As parts of a system of convictions, they reflect a general pattern that applies to the various domains of human experience.

29. The fact that two different verbs of "seeing" are used (respectively, *blepō* and *horaō*) does not invalidate an inverted parallelism! It contrasts semantic features.

30. "Images" (or "thematic expressions") should not be confused with "figures" (which form another meaning-producing textual element). These images are exclusively constituted by the features of the text that are in inverted parallelisms and in oppositions. The many other features of the text that do not participate in inverted parallelisms and oppositions contribute to form the "figures" (that are the combination of these other features with the thematic expressions, or images).

31. Respectively, what Greimas calls the structures of the "discursive semantics" (figurative system), of the "semio-narrative syntax" (story), of the "discursive syntax" (realistic narrative), and of the "enunciation" (discourse) of the text.

For Further Reading

The specific method of structural criticism introduced above is presented in the following books (the first one being focused upon the semiotic theory on which the method is based).

Patte, Daniel. *Religious Dimensions in Biblical Texts: Greimas's Structural Semiotics and Biblical Exegesis.* Society of Biblical Literature Semeia Studies. Atlanta: Scholars, 1990.

_____. *Structural Exegesis for New Testament Critics.* Guides to Biblical Scholarship. Minneapolis: Fortress, 1990.

For the use of structural criticism in the study of meaning-producing dimensions other than the system of convictions (and often several of them at once, including the system of convictions), see, for example, the following:

Boers, Hendrikus. *Neither on This Mountain nor in Jerusalem: A Study of John 4*. Society of Biblical Literature Monograph Series 35. Atlanta: Scholars, 1988.

Group of Entrevernes. *Signs and Parables: Semiotics and Gospel Texts*. Trans. G. Phillips. Pittsburgh: Pickwick, 1978.

Leach, Edmund. *Genesis as Myth and Other Essays*. London: Cape, 1969.

Malbon, Elizabeth Struthers. *Narrative Space and Mythic Meaning in Mark*. San Francisco: Harper & Row, 1986.

Polzin, Robert M. *Biblical Structuralism: Method and Subjectivity in the Study of Ancient Texts*. Semeia Supplements. Philadelphia: Fortress, 1977.

————. *Moses and the Deuteronomist: A Literary Study of the Deuteronomic History*. New York: Seabury, 1980.

10
NARRATIVE CRITICISM

DAVID M. GUNN

Definition and History

The term "narrative criticism" in biblical studies is a loose one, more found in New Testament than in Hebrew Bible studies. Since the late 1970s, it has sometimes been used broadly of literary-critical, as opposed to historical-critical, analysis of biblical narrative, from a variety of methodological standpoints. Often that has meant interpreting the existing text (in its "final form") in terms primarily of its own story world, seen as replete with meaning, rather than understanding the text by attempting to reconstruct its sources and editorial history, its original setting and audience, and its author's or editor's intention in writing. More specifically the term has been used of formalist analysis, especially in a New-Critical vein, where the critic understands the text to be an interpretable entity independent of both author and interpreter. Here meaning is to be found by close reading that identifies formal and conventional structures of the narrative, determines plot, develops characterization, distinguishes point of view, exposes language play, and relates all to some overarching, encapsulating theme. Unlike historical criticism, which in practice has segmented the text, formalist narrative criticism has often been an exercise in holism.

For more than a decade, however, narrative critics of the Bible, influenced by secular criticism, have been paying more attention to the place of the reader in the making of meaning (see chapter 11 on reader-response criticism). One important upshot of this attention is a growing recognition that no system of reading can ever guarantee the "correct" interpretation of a story, no matter how highly trained and "competent" readers may become. There will always be differing interpretive methods, just as there will always be interpreters who read from different places and who find significance in different elements of the text. Some reader-oriented approaches to narrative, particularly in Hebrew Bible studies, show the influence of secular strategies known as deconstruction (see chapter 12 on poststructuralist criticism) and ideological criticism (see chapters thirteen and fourteen). Such approaches are likely to confront seriously the view that language is infinitely unstable and so meaning always deferrable; they may radically foreground the reader's values as determinative of interpretation; they may argue that criticism is not anchored in fixed texts but in fragile communities of interpreters; and they may recognize explicitly that criticism is social construction, or persuasion, if you will.

While developments in New Testament narrative studies over the past tthree decades could be said in general terms to parallel work on the Hebrew Bible, the two fields have also remained distinct. Narrative criticism of the Gospels and Acts has tended to be relatively conservative in its methodology, concerned with observing the mechanics or artistry of literary construction, the conventions of ancient rhetoric, and often still haunted by historical criticism's need to know the author's "intention" and the text's "original" readership if it is to speak legitimately of the text's meaning. While centering interest on the story, especially its plot and characters as elements of an artistic whole, Gospel critics have been reluctant to take a literary approach that unravels unity and/or places the reader in an ideologically exposed position in relation to the text. But this is a Hebrew Bible critic speaking and, indeed, the rest of this essay is focused on Hebrew Bible criticism. I hope, however, that those primarily interested in New Testament narrative will still find here a pertinent discussion. They might also peruse the eminently readable book by David Rhoads and Donald Michie, *Mark as Story: An Introduction to the Narrative of a Gospel* (Fortress, 1982). They should then dip into a more difficult, but even more elegantly written, account of New Testament literary (narrative) criticism, namely, Stephen Moore's *Literary Criticism and the Gospels: The Theoretical Challenge* (Yale, 1989). These works mark two turning points. The former book offers accessibility to this new kind of criticism as well as comprehensibility—it shows how the method works, and it takes this approach through a whole Gospel. The latter situates New Testament studies in relation to the larger world of (secular) literary theory and criticism and challenges New Testament critics to respond.

The past decade has seen significant response. Moreover, at the cutting edge, where critical theory and biblical criticism are intersecting, there is growing convergence between New Testament and Hebrew Bible critical approaches. This may be seen most conveniently in the more recent writings of Moore (e.g., *Poststructuralism and the New Testament*, Fortress, 1994; *God's Gym: Divine Male Bodies of the Bible*, Routledge, 1996) or in the pages of the journal *Semeia* (e.g., George Aichele and Gary A. Phillips, eds., *Intertextuality and the Bible*, Semeia 69/70, 1995).

The following section offers a survey of literary-critical studies of narrative in the Hebrew Bible over the past three decades. It should also be remembered, however, that the study of poetry, though afforded much less attention than narrative, has been an integral part of literary-critical developments in connection with the Hebrew Bible throughout this period. I think, for example, of Francis Landy's brilliant work on Song of Songs, which he intimately connects with the Garden story in Genesis 2–3 (*Paradoxes of Paradise*, Almond, 1983). Indeed, for this reason alone (there are plenty of others), the narrative-oriented survey that follows relates a somewhat skewed story.

Current literary-critical study of Hebrew Bible narrative has disparate roots. As early as 1965 Edwin Good at Stanford was writing essays of literary criticism, though his book was to stay out of print for over a decade (*Irony in the Old Testament*, Westminster, 1965; 2d ed. Almond, 1981). In the crucial formative period of the 1970s a number of significant contributors worked in relative isolation from each other. Meir Sternberg, in comparative literature at Tel-Aviv University, was little known in the United States before the end of the decade and had limited impact here until the publication of his major work in English in 1985 (*The Poetics of Biblical Narrative*, Indiana University Press), though his important initial paper (with Menakhem Perry) on reading "gaps" in the story of David and Bathsheba appeared in modern Hebrew in 1968 (English translation in *Poetics Today* 7, 1986). Also teaching Hebrew and comparative literature, at the University of California at Berkeley, Robert Alter published a series of articles (mostly in *Commentary*, a journal unfamiliar to many biblical critics) between 1975 and 1980. It was not until the publication of his book in 1981 (*The Art of Biblical Narrative*, Basic) that his work came to have widespread influence. It took some time, too, before several other innovative books received due attention in North America: Jan Fokkelman's detailed study of style and structure in Genesis, published in the Netherlands in 1975 (*Narrative Art in Genesis*, Van Gorcum; reprinted by JSOT [now Sheffield Academic Press], 1992); Jonathan Magonet's analysis of Jonah, published in Switzerland in 1976 (*Form and Meaning*, Lang; 2d ed. Almond, 1983); and Shimon Bar-Efrat's extensive survey, *Narrative Art in the Bible*, published (in Hebrew) in Israel in 1979 (Sifriat Poalim; ET Almond, 1989).

On the other hand, David Clines (*The Theme of the Pentateuch*, JSOT, 1978) and I, at the University of Sheffield in England, had broader ties to the North American biblical studies guild, especially to active members of the Society of Biblical Literature (SBL), who opened valuable avenues of support and stimulation. My own first literary-critical essay on Hebrew narrative (which became a key chapter in my 1978 book, *The Story of King David*, JSOT), after the fashion of F. R. Leavis and British practical criticism learned in Australia in the late 1950s and 1960s, was commissioned by Robert Culley of McGill University in Montreal for an early issue of *Semeia*.

This journal, founded by Robert Funk in Missoula, Montana, for the SBL, has proved to be of central importance for biblical narrative criticism. That particular issue (number 3, 1975), for example, also contained papers and comment by, among others, Culley himself, George Coats (Lexington Seminary, Kentucky), Burke Long (Bowdoin College, Maine), Robert Polzin (Carleton University, Ottawa), David Robertson (University of California at Davis) and Hugh White (Rutgers University, New Brunswick, New Jersey), all of whom have played significant, though very different, roles in shaping the field of study. Later, Coats's invitation to me to speak to a consultation on narrative at the SBL in 1979 was germinal for my next book, on Saul.

From its foundation *Semeia* was a forum for innovation in biblical criticism, both Hebrew Bible and New Testament. It was an outlet for much of the discussion of structuralism that went on in the 1970s and early 1980s, particularly in the Structuralism and Exegesis Seminar at the Society of Biblical Studies, with New Testament critic Daniel Patte (Vanderbilt University) a driving force. Connections between the New-Critical or formalist types of literary criticism and the varieties of structuralism (e.g., "literary" and "anthropological") being deployed in the analysis of biblical narrative at this time were obvious. Both were inclined to see the text "synchronically" rather than "diachronically," that is, as a meaningful whole containing the essential elements of its own understanding rather than as understandable only as the product of an historically determined process of composition. On the other hand, to many structuralists the readings of those influenced by New Criticism seemed to lack rigor, more art than method, and to many of the latter critics structuralist analyses seemed arcane and rigid. An important mediating critic was David Jobling of St. Andrew's College, Saskatoon.

At Indiana University Kenneth Gros Louis, an English literature professor, and James Ackerman, in the religion department, collaborated to publish in 1974 a pioneering collection of essays (*Literary Interpretations of Biblical Narratives*, Abingdon), which would be followed in 1982 by a further volume, by this time reflecting a considerably expanded repertoire of texts and critics. Like Culley, Ackerman has been an influential figure, as much through his encouragement of others as through his own finely nuanced writing. At Union Theological Seminary in New York in the early 1960s, Ackerman had been a student of James Muilenburg, who coined the term "rhetorical criticism" for a study of literary features of texts, in New-Critical mode, that offered an alternative to traditional source and form criticisms. Muilenburg's legacy also shows in the work of other students, such as Walter Brueggemann and Phyllis Trible. Brueggemann, at Eden Theological Seminary in St. Louis (later at Columbia Theological Seminary), wrote imaginatively on the David stories in Samuel between 1968 and 1974 (and again in the 1980s). Trible, at Andover Newton Theological School and then Union Theological Seminary in New York, wrote meticulous rhetorical criticism from a feminist perspective that was groundbreaking in a profoundly new way, issuing in a book of essays of signal importance, *God and the Rhetoric of Sexuality* (Fortress, 1978).

From Canada, David Jobling published in 1978 another set of essays that reflected the first really successful attempt to convey the power of structuralist readings of biblical narrative texts to a wide audience of biblical scholars (*The Sense of Biblical Narrative*, JSOT, 1978; 2d ed. 1986). In 1978, too, Vanderbilt professor James Crenshaw wrote a book of what he termed "aesthetic criticism" (*Samson*, John Knox). From St. Thomas Seminary in Denver, Peter Miscall, influenced by Robert Alter among others, began to explore in article form the subject of "narrative analogy."

At the heart of the shift to these new explorations of narrative was a shift in publishing outlets for innovating scholars and a reorganization of the SBL. In 1974, as already noted, Robert Funk founded *Semeia*, "an experimental journal for biblical criticism" for the society. Although focused for some years on structuralist work, it yet contrived to give voice to a plurality of alternatives to conventional historical criticism. My own contribution, with colleagues David Clines and Philip Davies, was to found and edit the *Journal for the Study of the Old Testament* in 1976, which from its outset offered a home to literary-critical work. As in the case of *Semeia*, accompanying the journal was a monograph series also receptive to new methodology. At the SBL annual meeting, forums were established for cultivating contacts and discussion on the new narrative studies. Especially important were the Rhetorical Criticism Section, the Consultation on Narrative, the Structuralism and Exegesis Section, and the Biblical Criticism and Literary Criticism Section.

By about 1980 a threshold was crossed. That year Robert Polzin published *Moses and the Deuteronomist* (Seabury), a highly innovative study of Deuteronomy–Judges utilizing Bakhtin's account of narratorial voices and dialogic narrative, and I published my (more New-Critical) close reading of the Saul story, which unapologetically cut through source-critical boundaries in the interests of an extended, final-form interpretation (*The Fate of King Saul*, JSOT). Cheryl Exum of Boston College published the first of a series of papers on the Samson story; she would go on to write many other studies. The next year (1981) saw the founding of *Prooftexts*, "a journal of Jewish literary history" with serious commitment to literary-critical study of the Bible and often the vehicle for important contributions on narrative from Edward Greenstein of Jewish Theological Seminary in New York. The same year saw the publication of the inaugural volume of essays in my Bible and Literature series with newly founded Almond Press, *Images of Man and*

God: Old Testament Short Stories in Literary Focus, edited by Burke Long; also Fokkelman's massive study of King David, *Narrative Art and Poetry in the Books of Samuel*, vol. 1 (Van Gorcum). Most important, however, for the immediate impact of literary studies on the field of biblical studies, Robert Alter's *The Art of Biblical Narrative* was published and received wide and favorable publicity.

In 1982 Northrop Frye's massive analysis of the Bible from the perspective of archetypal criticism made its appearance (*The Great Code: The Bible and Literature*, Academic), though, at least among professional biblical critics, it had surprisingly limited impact for a work from a critic of such reputation in English literature scholarship. In other developments, Peter Miscall's *The Workings of Biblical Narrative* (Fortress/Scholars, 1983) took a major new step in its exploration of the "undecidability" of texts, using texts from Genesis and 1 Samuel as a proving ground, while Adele Berlin (at the University of Maryland) offered students and scholars interested in entering the new field a lucid presentation of the "mechanics" of narrative composition, especially character and point of view, in her *Poetics and Interpretation of Biblical Narrative* (Almond, 1983). Phyllis Trible brought out a second influential book of feminist readings, starting from the same New-Critical (rhetorical) reading method as before but now more reader conscious and troubled by the text (*Texts of Terror*, Fortress, 1984). At about this time Esther Fuchs began to write her hard-hitting, "text-resisting" feminist readings of Hebrew Bible narratives.

Perhaps the culmination of this phase of growth came with Meir Sternberg's book, *The Poetics of Biblical Narrative* (Indiana University Press, 1985) and the collection of essays edited by Robert Alter and English literature critic Frank Kermode, *The Literary Guide to the Bible* (Harvard, University Press, 1987). The former represented the outcome of more than a decade of work on a system of interpretation that claimed to comprehend all Hebrew Bible narrative. Central (and problematic) is Sternberg's view that God and the narrator are omniscient and that the coincidence of their omniscience helps make irresistible the meaning of the text, "the point of it all." This work basically derives from modernist assumptions about textual meaning, with clear links to formalist and New-Critical methods. (It was published, with help from James Ackerman, as the first volume of an important new series from Indiana University Press, eventually to be called Indiana Studies in Biblical Literature, and edited by Robert Polzin and Herbert Marks.) Kermode's book indicated the growing number of scholars working in the field but also, following the editors' agenda, reflected a fairly conservative, formalist approach. Several significant scholars, particularly those pursuing feminist criticism—Exum, Fuchs, and Trible, for example— were noticeably absent. This absence marked a significant failure on the part of both Alter and Sternberg in their critical method to come to terms with the power of feminist theory and critical practice. The conjunction of literary criticism and feminist criticism was already well established by the time *The Literary Guide* appeared and was not going to go away.

Alter and Kermode also eschewed structuralism and deconstruction as approaches appropriate to their volume. Not surprisingly, David Jobling was not among the contributors. He himself, however, furnished a second volume of essays in the structuralist vein (*The Sense of Biblical Narrative*, vol. 2, JSOT, 1986) that have proved prescient in the way they identify pervasive topics in a text, open up questions of readers' interests, and handle major textual disjunctions. Jobling's analysis of Judges and Deuteronomic political theory, for example, seeks a way of understanding discordances in the text without collapsing or harmonizing them. Thus, instead of dissipating the often observed pro- and antimonarchical strains in the book into redactional layers, he holds them in tension in Lévi-Straussian fashion. The book thus construes its account of polity in a way that is neither "pro" nor "anti" nor, for that matter, "balanced." This construction, Jobling argues, opens for its exilic audience possibilities for creating a new "political theology" for its own situation.

Since the mid-1980s major studies and collections have appeared with increasing frequency. Alex Preminger and Edward Greenstein edited *The Hebrew Bible in Literary Criticism* (Ungar, 1986), and Greenstein subsequently brought together some of his own work in *Essays on Biblical Method and Translation* (Scholars, 1989). Cheryl Exum edited a collection of papers, mostly on narrative, that convey well a sense of the literary-critical activity in the late 1980s (*Signs and Wonders: Biblical Texts in Literary Focus*, Scholars, 1989). David Clines, too, has a volume of very readable essays on a range of texts (*What Does Eve Do to Help? And Other Readerly Questions to the Old Testament*, JSOT, 1990).

The books of Samuel continued to be favorites in the second half of the 1980s. Joel Rosenberg (Tufts University) explored political allegory in Genesis and Samuel (*King and Kin*, Indiana University Press, 1986). Previously established critics Fokkelman (*Narrative Art*, vols. 2 and 3, Van Gorcum, 1986 and 1990), Miscall (*1 Samuel*, Indiana University Press, 1986), and Polzin (*Samuel and the Deuteronomist*, Harper & Row, 1989) all wrote extensively on this material, along with Brueggemann in a more theological vein (for example, *David's Truth* [Fortress, 1985]) and trenchant Canadian critic Lyle Eslinger (*Kingship of God in Crisis*, Almond, 1985). Eslinger also treated the Deuteronomic history as a whole (*Into the Hands of the Living God*, Almond, 1989).

The first of several book-length studies of Judges appeared in 1987 in the form of Australian Barry Webb's close reading of the whole book of Judges

(*The Book of the Judges*, JSOT, 1987; cf. e.g., Lillian R. Klein, *The Triumph of Irony in the Book of Judges*, Almond, 1989). Thomas Mann explored the "narrative integrity" of Genesis–Deuteronomy (*The Book of the Torah*, John Knox, 1988). Ezra-Nehemiah was the subject of a book-length study, *In an Age of Prose* (Scholars, 1988), by Tamara Cohn Eskenazi (Hebrew Union College, Los Angeles); and in *Circle of Sovereignty* (JSOT, 1988; 2d ed. Abingdon, 1991) Danna Nolan Fewell (Perkins School of Theology, Southern Methodist University) read Daniel 1–6 as a narrative whole rather than as discrete tales according to form-critical designations, in a close reading with deconstructive sympathies.

Using Peter Brooks's model of plot as desire (*Reading for the Plot*, Random House, 1984), Daniel Hawk (Asbury Theological Seminary, Wilmore, Kentucky) wrote on plot in Joshua (*Every Promise Fulfilled*, Westminster/John Knox 1991). His book remains one of the few to have tackled Joshua at length from a literary-critical approach. The book was also one of the first in a new series edited by Danna Fewell and myself, Literary Currents in Biblical Interpretation, designed to foster literary-critical scholarship in a variety of modes. Another title in the series, on a biblical book that has received significant attention from narrative and feminist critics (including both Mieke Bal and Phyllis Trible), was the study of characters in Ruth by Danna Fewell and myself (*Compromising Redemption*, Westminster/John Knox, 1990). The study employed the device of retelling the story as a way of giving narrative expression to an interpretation that we also present analytically. Such recourse to narrative (and poetry) in critical writing has precedents outside biblical studies and may become more common in our own field. Another early title in the same series, namely David Penchansky's *The Betrayal of God: Ideological Conflict in Job* (1990), signaled the emerging engagement of biblical literary criticism with ideological criticism and deconstruction. Drawing on the work of Pierre Macherey and Frederic Jameson, Penchansky (at the College of St. Thomas in St. Paul, Minnesota) explored dissonances of the text as a window into the social conflict that produced the text and as a means by which readers explore the dissonances in their own world.

The exploration of texts from a reader-oriented perspective (not necessarily the same as "reader-response") has been a cutting edge of Hebrew Bible narrative studies over the past decade, particularly where critics are taking account of the ideological dimensions and deconstructive possibilities of reading. A good entry point into this kind of criticism is the collection of lucid essays, not all on narratives, by David Clines in his *Interested Parties: The Ideology of Writers and Readers of the Hebrew Bible* (Sheffield, 1995), with topics such as "Haggai's Temple, Constructed, Deconstructed and Reconstructed," "God in the Pentateuch: Reading against the Grain," and "David the Man: The Construction of Masculinity in the Hebrew Bible."

A powerful influence in reader-oriented criticism since the mid-1980s has been Dutch narratologist Mieke Bal (*Narratology*, ET Toronto, 1985) working with what was then for her an unfamiliar language (Hebrew) and text (the Bible). Her books include *Lethal Love* (Indiana University Press, 1987), *Murder and Difference* (Indiana University Press, 1988), and *Death and Dissymmetry* (University of Chicago Press, 1988). In this last volume, a study of the book of Judges, she deconstructs the customary coherence, seen in a pattern of holy war, and reads for a counter-coherence, seen in a pattern of murder. With others, she sees gender-based violence shaping the book. Radically, she affirms the women who kill men. In a world where men have disproportionate power over body, life, and language, these women introduce a countervailing anger. They kill "for" the women victims.

Schooled in critical theory and wielding interpretive tools borrowed widely from semiotics, psychoanalysis, and anthropology, Bal has challenged biblical critics to broaden their disciplinary horizons. She is adamant that her own narratology, which has structuralist roots, does not produce the only "correct" interpretation. (Here she differs from another professional narratologist in the field, Sternberg.) Rather she believes that working with a given set of concepts for describing a text makes the discussion accessible to others. In a sense the distinctions that narrative theory formulates are heuristic—they have no essential reality in themselves but they enable interpretation to proceed in a consistent and discussable manner. Bal often makes particular use of the concept of point of view, what she calls "focalization," as a feminist reading strategy. Another of Bal's strategies, characteristic of deconstruction, is to build a reading around some puzzling element in the text that is usually bypassed or harmonized (cf. Penchansky). By exposing the different and the discordant she can often expose at the same time the patriarchal stamp of traditional interpretation. Perhaps most strikingly, her work is marked by illuminating shifts in disciplinary perspective. Thus in "A Body of Writing: Judges 19" (1993) she considers relationships between death, women, and representation through an analysis of narrative argumentation that includes a Rousseau short story and a sketch by Rembrandt. Her work is arguably the single most creative force at play in present studies of biblical narrative.

A growing diversity of approaches to biblical criticism is a mark of the 1990s. *Judges and Method: New Approaches in Biblical Studies* edited by Gale Yee (Fortress, 1995), for example, discusses narrative, social-scientific, feminist, structuralist, deconstructive, and ideological criticisms. At the same time, in the definition and application of these approaches there is often significant overlap: Fewell's deconstructive (but also narrative, feminist, and ideological) reading of Achsah and the "(e)razed city of writing" in the *Judges and Method* volume is a case in point. She and I have attempted to write a feminist deconstructive reading of the "subject" of Genesis–Kings as a whole, recasting the story in terms of women and children, and attending to legal texts and social situation as well as narrative (*Gender, Power, and Promise: The Subject of the Bible's First Story*, Abingdon, 1993). Both of us would still claim literary criticism as a primary category with which to describe our work. So, too, I think would ideological critic Randall Bailey (Interdenominational Theological Center, Atlanta), whose readings are imbued with questions relating to race and class, among other dimensions (e.g., pp. 165–84 in Cain Hope Felder, ed., *Stony the Road We Trod: African American Biblical Interpretation*, Fortress, 1991).

In their editorial introduction to *The New Literary Criticism* (Sheffield, 1993), Clines and Exum list deconstruction, feminist criticism, political criticism, psychoanalytic criticism, and reader-response criticism as major topics under the broad rubric "literary criticism." The list could easily be expanded. Several scholars, for example, have used folklore studies (a resource common earlier in the century) to illuminate biblical narrative, with particular interest in the trickster figure (e.g., Susan Niditch, ed., *Text and Tradition: The Hebrew Bible and Folklore*, Scholars, 1990). Elsewhere, for example, Ken Stone (Chicago Theological Seminary) employs Bal's narratology and shows the advantage of bringing an anthropological frame to bear on questions of gender, as he discusses honor and shame in narratives drawn from Judges, Samuel, and Kings (*Sex, Honor, and Power in the Deuteronomistic History*, Sheffield, 1996). All the while, formalist literary analysis has continued to be elaborated, sometimes in conjunction with redactional ("diachronic") criticism, as, for example, in Robert O'Connell's extensive account of the "rhetorical purpose" of the Judges "compiler/redactor" (*The Rhetoric of the Book of Judges*, Brill, 1996). The purpose—to enjoin readers to endorse a divinely appointed Judahite king who upholds such deuteronomistic ideals as the need to expel foreigners and to maintain YHWH's cult and covenant—O'Connell infers from formal structures and "motivic patterns" recurring throughout the book's narrative framework and from patterns of plot-structure and characterization in the plot-based deliverer stories and the book's ending.

Critics are increasingly interested in reading a text in light of its "intertextuality"—its interconnection with texts lying "outside" its immediate contextual boundaries (cf. Danna Nolan Fewell, ed., *Reading between Texts: Intertextuality and the Hebrew Bible*, Westminster/John Knox, 1992). This interest harks back to the "narrative analogies" critics such as Alter and Miscall saw earlier between story segments or "type scenes" (such as a betrothal scene), though it now embraces a much broader and more nuanced range of interrelations between texts that historical critics often have deemed to be unrelated. Thus Fewell (pp. 132–52 in Timothy K. Beal and David M. Gunn, eds., *Reading Bibles, Writing Bodies: Identity and the*

Book, Routledge, 1997) reads Judges as a rewriting of Genesis for the purpose of constructing postexilic identity—and accordingly constructs her own essay dialogically as a play of past and present voices. Ranging even more widely, Claudia Camp (*Wise and Strange: Women, Priests, and Other Biblical Boundaries*, Routledge, 1998) traces the literary and ideological connections of a large array of biblical narratives, such as the stories of Dinah, Miriam, and Samson, as part of a widespread textual web that includes law, priestly texts, and wisdom (esp. Proverbs 1–9) in addition to narrative texts. Drawing on anthropology and social history in conjunction with literary criticism, Camp seeks through the metaphorical figure of "strangeness" to achieve at least two main goals. She seeks to undermine the Bible's ostensible construction of Israelite identity, where the boundaries between "Israelite" and "non-Israelite" tend to be sharply drawn. Similarly she complicates the analysis of power—for example, how power is disposed between men and women—offered by feminist biblical criticism.

Alice Bach (Stanford) has extended the range of such "intertexts." In *Women, Seduction, and Betrayal in Biblical Narrative* (Cambridge University Press, 1997) she reads between the story of Potiphar's wife in Genesis 39 and the story's retellings in extracanonical texts such as the *Testament of Joseph* and the ancient Jewish Hellenistic romance, *Joseph and Asenath*. Nor does she privilege the biblical text as the "original," but instead shifts her readerly focus from one text to another, allowing, for example, the biblical text to be read in light of the Greek romance and the Greek romance to be read in light of the biblical text. Her goal is the elaboration of alternative stories that bring enhanced subjectivity ("life") to the characters, especially those whose perspective is given short shrift in the texts. She extends her study to include as "intertexts" other biblical narratives of "wicked" women (Bathsheba, Delilah, Salome) and in doing so moves her analysis yet a step further by bringing into play modern "retellings" in text, art, and particularly film. Biblical narrative is deeply embedded in Western art and film. Bach's analyses are symptomatic of a growing interest in such cultural appropriations, how they are to be understood in their cultural context, and how they shape our reading of the biblical texts themselves. Cheryl Exum's *Plotted, Shot, and Painted: Cultural Representations of Biblical Women* (1996) and the essays in *Biblical Glamour and Hollywood Glitz* (Alice Bach, ed.; *Semeia* 74; Scholars, 1996) offer excellent starting points for the inquiring reader.

Characteristic of much cutting edge biblical criticism is a more explicit dialogue than has previously existed between biblical critics and contemporary writers, particularly theorists, whose work lies in the main outside the conventional boundaries of biblical studies. Exemplary is the interweaving of theory and critical practice (interpretation) that emerges in the writing of Timothy Beal (Eckerd College, St. Petersburg, Florida), most recently in

The Book of Hiding: Gender, Ethnicity, Annihilation, and Esther (Routlege, 1997). Beal's analysis of Esther moves easily between the biblical narrative, on the one hand, and the texts of contemporary writers such as Judith Butler, Hélène Cixous, Luce Irigaray, and Emmanuel Levinas, on the other, illuminating both ancient and contemporary texts as he thinks through their correspondences. Characteristic, too, as has already been indicated above in relation to other recent work, is a deep engagement with questions of self and other (i.e., issues of identity) in a variety of construals—gender, ethnicity, nationality, and religion.

But while the work of biblical critics such as these may suggest distinct outlines of future narrative criticism in Hebrew Bible studies, it cannot contain the remarkable diversity of approach that we have seen over the past decade, a diversity that will, I think, continue to mark, muddy, and keep redefining the field. The lack of an obvious institutional center for a discipline of narrative criticism or literary criticism (as my location notes indicate has always been the case), is paralleled by the lack of an obvious theoretical or methodological center. That, it seems to me, has been a strength of this broad stream of critical endeavor and is still probably a healthy, if sometimes confusing, state of affairs.

An Example: Genesis 19

How do I go about reading a narrative text myself? Let me try reading the story of Lot at Sodom in Genesis 19 as an example—only an example, not a strict paradigm, for I go about the craft of interpretation in various ways, depending upon the particular text, my familiarity with it, the reason I am reading it, and who (if I am to write about it) my audience is going to be. In the present case this is not a text with which I have worked closely before, though it has been the subject of class discussion once or twice in recent years. Why choose it? Our text choices usually are not innocent, though often we may think so. In the present case it is clear to me what some of my interests are. Feminism leads me to ask questions about the interpretive possibilities for Lot's daughters and to see a deconstructive opportunity in the cursory mention of Lot's wife being turned into a pillar of salt. As part of an ongoing literary-critical project, I am also interested in the part played by God in the story. In fact, this latter interest (in the character of God) is related directly to the former interest (in feminist reading of the Bible). Thus to say that I am reading the story of *Lot* at Sodom is hardly accurate, though Lot of necessity will be a significant part of my discussion.

A crucial decision needs to be made. What are the boundaries of the text I am reading? From beginnings and endings we make meaning, no less than from middles. Chapter 19 neatly bounds the immediate account of Lot and his family, beginning with Lot sitting in the gate of Sodom and seeing the two visitors arrive and ending with him lying, unknowing, with his daughters, who subsequently give birth to two sons. On the other hand, the chapter, like Lot's story in general, is clearly interwoven with the surrounding story of Abraham. Moving back into Abraham's story, however, we reach at least 11:26, the genealogy of Terah, the patriarch's father. Moving forward into Abraham's story takes us at least to the account of his death in chapter 25. But beyond these boundaries, of course, are larger ones into which this story flows: In the final analysis the story stretches at least from Genesis to Kings, from the creation and expulsion from the garden to the monarchic state and exile from Judah. In practice, then, given the flexibility and extent of the possible boundaries to this account of Lot and his family, I shall focus mainly on chapter 19 and its immediate antecedents in chapter 18 but leave open the limits of the narrative.

Questions of plot and character are staples of the study of narrative. Some narrative criticism highlights one rather than the other. Certain structuralists and formalists, for example, regard characters as essentially functions of plot. These critics are interested in defining basic story types—the universal bones of narrative. Any complexity of characterization becomes subordinate to the character's place (as an "actant"—sender, object, receiver, helper, opponent, or subject) in a plot that is already dictated by the narrative genre. Other critics have seen character as the sine qua non of story, arguing that even when plots take readers into totally unfamiliar territory, readers reach out to identify characters in terms of their own world. Some critics try to accord no priority but rather recognize that plot and character are inseparable: We can only know characters through considering their actions and motivations, which constitute the plot; we can hardly talk of plot without considering the actions and motivations of its characters. In practice I find this last position to be true for me. Plot and character, on this understanding, are heuristic concepts, having no discrete reality in themselves but useful as starting points for making sense of narrative.

For entering this particular text, I am using plot. Here we are dealing with the organizing force or design, which we see as connecting events into some kind of comprehensible pattern. Readers are always struggling to make order out of what they read, and plot is one dimension of narrative order. We understand plot through various and incomplete sources—the voice of the narrator, the speech and actions of the characters. Often in biblical narrative the relations between events are not made explicit. Our desire for order drives us to make connections. Even so simple a link as that made by many translators and commentators between God's remembering Abraham and his rescue of Lot is not unambiguously given to us by the narrator. Literally the narrator says, "And it happened, when God destroyed the cities of the district, that he remembered Abraham and he sent Lot out of the midst of the overthrow, when he overthrew the cities in which Lot dwelt" (19:29).[1] To translate "so that he sent Lot out" is reasonable but nonetheless inferential. We read it that way in the interests of constructing the plot. That way, Abraham's earlier intercession becomes Lot's saving grace.

Plots may be conceived on a simple model of exposition, conflict, climax, and resolution. A situation is presented that is somehow disordered, incomplete, lacking, or harboring an unfulfilled desire. From this situation develops a conflict or complication that in turn produces a climactic turning point and some degree of resolution. Of course, there may be more than one conflict and more than one climax (though male writers and readers seem inclined to find satisfaction in a grand climax) and the longer stories in the Hebrew Bible are characteristically plotted in this more meandering way. Another way of asking about plot is to ask about desire. Who desires what and when? In what ways are the desires that drive the story fulfilled? Framed that way the question about plot is also more obviously a question about character. It is also a question that applies to more than one character, thus freeing the interpretation of the story from being determined entirely by a decision about who is the "main" character—not as straightforward a matter as might initially be thought. (Is the main character the one who gets the most square inches of text? In chapter 19 that would cut out YHWH, would it not?) Rather, each of the characters may be envisioned as having his or her own plot, distinct threads in a web of plots.

Since chapter 19 begins with the visitors' arrival at Sodom we could start by asking about the visitors' desire. That would require going back into chapter 18. Then we would need to ask whether their desire was the same as YHWH's desire—a question that becomes tied to another question, namely, whether we can sustain a clear distinction between the visitors and YHWH. So given a need here to be succinct, let me turn straight to the latter character.

YHWH enters the episode (18:17) persuading himself that he should disclose to Abraham "what [he is] about to do," an enigmatic intention that becomes clear when he goes on to speak of Sodom and Gomorrah and his need to know about their outcry of distress. Knowing each other is important, we learn, for both YHWH and Abraham, for upon it appears to hang the agenda that the deity has marked out for the human. As an object lesson, Abraham needs to know what YHWH is involved in. Thus the patriarch will command his sons and his house after him to keep YHWH's way by doing righteousness (ṣĕdāqāh) and justice (mišpāṭ). In turn YHWH can make good his promise that Abraham should become a great and mighty nation and a subject of blessing. YHWH's speech not only brings Abraham into the new episode in terms of Abraham's needing to know more about YHWH, but it ties the episode firmly into the larger story of YHWH and Abraham.

When the men (angels?) who are with YHWH turn and go toward Sodom, Abraham confronts the deity. Will YHWH, he asks, truly sweep away the righteous (or "innocent"—*ṣaddîq*) with the wicked? Should not the judge (*šōpēṭ*) of the earth do justice (*mišpāṭ*)? Why Abraham should assume that YHWH is going to destroy Sodom—the deity has said nothing about destroying—is unclear. Perhaps Sodom's evil reputation is known to Abraham and perhaps he knows YHWH as a god who will not hesitate to punish "great sin." Or at least he is taking no chances. (YHWH makes no effort to disabuse him of his assumption.) Some critics, reading in terms of the larger narrative, would argue that Abraham is really concerned here not with the "innocent" in general but with his nephew Lot in particular, perhaps still regarded as his heir. Certainly in chapter 14 Abraham had mounted a major expedition to rescue his nephew; hence the possibility that Lot is the subtext of Abraham's concern makes some sense, despite the fact that he is not mentioned here at all.

On this reading, YHWH enters the story desiring to deal with Sodom and Gomorrah's outcry but also desiring that Abraham learn something from what will transpire. Abraham enters the story desiring to save Lot. Precisely where YHWH is to be found in the subsequent account is hard to say, since the two visitors ("messengers" or "angels") who speak mostly as "we" and are narrated as "they" become in verse 17 "he" and in verse 19 "you" (masc. sing.) and in verse 21 "I"—"I will not overturn the city"—as though YHWH himself were speaking. (Such sliding identity is not unusual in the depiction of YHWH in Hebrew Bible narrative—see, for example, the immediately preceding story of the visitors to Abraham's tent earlier in chapter 18, or the story of Gideon in Judges 6.) Whatever the case, there is little to suggest that the divinity, despite YHWH's initial words in 18:20–21 about his needing to investigate, has any other intention than to destroy the city. The angels echo precisely Abraham's understanding of YHWH's plan and speak as though the power to destroy were theirs: "for we are destroying this place, for their cry has grown great before YHWH and YHWH sent us to destroy it" (19:13). It is not even clear that the attempted assault on the visitors is the deciding factor, though that is usually how the plot is understood. We may be left with the distinct suspicion that YHWH's speech to Abraham in 18:20–21 was less than forthright.

With the overturning of the cities, both characters' plots find resolution. For YHWH there will be no more outcries of distress from Sodom and Gomorrah, and Abraham will have learned—a salutary lesson—that his deity will not flinch from executing justice without fear or favor. For Abraham, his long journey with Lot has come to an end.

What does Lot desire? Confronted by visitors to the city, he desires to offer them hospitality in his own home. They decline. He insists. Then the complication arises: "But before they lay down, the men of the city, the men of Sodom, closed around the house, both young and old, all the people, to the last one [or 'on all sides']" (19:4) The men demand that Lot produce the visitors: "Bring them out to us that we may know [i.e., sexually] them." Perhaps premonitions about such treatment of strangers led Lot to insist in the first place that the visitors not stay in the street overnight. Perhaps he knew from his own experience something of the violence awaiting visitors to Sodom. At any rate, his response suggests that his desire to sustain his hospitality now drives his action. "Please, my brothers, do not do evil. Please, look—I have two daughters who have not known a man. Please let me bring them out to you, and do to them whatever is good in your sight. Only do not do a thing to these men, for this reason: they have come under the shelter of my roof" (19:7–8). Possibly his offer of his daughters ("do what is good in your sight") is a desperate attempt to shock the assailants into a realization of the enormity of their demand ("do not do evil"), so that they desist altogether. The simpler reading is that Lot is callously willing to sacrifice his daughters in order to uphold his honor as a provider of hospitality. Certainly he has not willingly offered *himself* in place of the strangers!

For a moment resolution, of one sort or another, hangs in the air. But for Lot the complication becomes more acute because the men of the city have their own desire, for violence. "Come on, get closer!" they mock (the Hebrew means not "draw back out of the way" as most translations have it but "get close and then some more!"). "This one came to sojourn and he's busy being a judge! Now we'll do you more evil than them." The narrator continues: "So they pressed at the man, at Lot, hard, and came close to breaking the door" (19:9). A glance at the imagery of locking and unlocking, opening, latches and doors in the Song of Songs is enough to suggest a perverse double entendre here. Rapidly Lot himself has become the rape object. With the next sentence the narrator mischievously maintains our focus on the rapists and their new victim—"And the men put out their hands and brought Lot to them"—before adding words that completely redefine the sense—"[in] to the house, and shut the door." The "men" therefore become the visitors, the reaching out a rescue instead of the inflicting of more abuse, and the door is again literally a door (though its closing against the attackers is also figuratively the closing of the door to Lot's body).

In terms of plot we could say that Lot's desire to show hospitality has been frustrated by the evil men of Sodom, to the point where Lot the sojourner is himself about to be abused along with the rules of hospitality. Put that way, plot and point of view go hand in hand. From Lot's first sight of the visitors in 19:1, the story has been narrated predominantly from Lot's point of view.

Now that changes. The visitors take charge (19:12–13). They strike blind the assailants, "both small and large," so that—a farcical touch—these wear themselves out trying to find the door. The visitors then ask whether Lot has any others with him—"sons-in-law and sons and daughters and all who belong to you in the city"—in order to take them out of the place, "for we are destroying this place, for their cry of distress [or 'cry for help'] has grown great before YHWH and YHWH sent us to destroy it." ("It" is usually taken to be the city as in verse 14, but strictly its antecedent is the cry of distress!). Here we may see the plot of chapter 18 coming back into focus.

Lot does the visitors' bidding. He goes out and says to his sons-in-law, "his daughters' takers": "'Arise, go out of this place, for YHWH is destroying the city.' But in the eyes of his sons-in-law he was just fooling around." (The word *mĕṣāḥēq* means laughing, jesting, playing the fool; perhaps there is a play on *mesāʿēq*, crying in distress.) Having failed to impress his sons-in-law he seems hardly impressed himself, for at dawn he is still at home. The visitors (now called "messengers" or "angels") urge him, "Arise, take your wife and your two daughters who happen to be here [lit.: who are found (here); cf. Gen. 19:29, 30, 31, 32 referring to the righteous/innocent], lest you be swept away up [cf. 18:23, 24] in the iniquity of the city." Yet he still lingers.

"So the men [i.e., the visitors] seized his hand and his wife's hand and his two daughters' hands, through YHWH's pity on him, and they brought him out and set him outside the city" (19:16). Having got him this far they try again to make him follow their wishes and save himself: "Flee for your life! Do not pay attention behind you, and stop nowhere in the plain! Flee to the hills, lest you be swept away!" By now we may decide that the plot, seen as the visitors' desire to destroy the city and exercise YHWH's justice and mercy/pity, is being further complicated by Lot. As Lot stalls, the visitors begin to lose charge, and Lot wrests readers' attention back to himself. Now once more he shows reluctance, though this time the reluctance begins to give shape to a new desire. Urged to flee to the hills, Lot objects "No, my lords, if you please. Look here, your [sing.] servant has found favor in your [sing.] eyes, and you have made a great commitment [*ḥesed*] to me in saving my life [lit.: causing my life (*nepeš*) to live]. But I cannot flee to the hills, lest [the] evil cling to me and I die. Look now, this city is close to escape to, and it is tiny; please let me flee there—it is tiny, is it not?—and my life [*nepeš*] will be saved [lit.: will live]."

Lot's logic seems curious to me; other commentators, where they have paused to comment, have generally found it puzzling too. What is he saying? That despite the visitors' assurance he does not trust that they can guarantee his survival if he travels to the hills? But why should a city offer him any more protection? What evil is going to cling to him? The evil practiced in Sodom or the evil (destruction) that is to befall Sodom? Or is he speaking of evil more generally as the fate likely to be his, a townsperson living without support in the hill country? What is clear alone is that he desires, if he must flee at all, that it be to this little town of Zoar. And in response his interlocutor is willing to allow him to do what he asks, and to grant Zoar a reprieve since Lot will be in the town's midst. Thus Lot's desire apparently modifies the visitors' desire to destroy all.

The narrator now tells of what would seem to be the climax to the divine plot of punishment for evil: YHWH rains brimstone and fire on Sodom and Gomorrah, "and he overturned those cities and all the plain and all dwelling in the cities, and the vegetation of the ground" (19:25). A brief comment about Lot's wife gazing behind him and being turned to a pillar of salt interposes. Then, following appropriately the account of the fulfillment of the divine desire, comes mention of Abraham, who went at dawn "to the place where he had stood before YHWH" and, looking down, beheld the whole plain smoking like a furnace (19:27–28). Abraham, who had pressed God to spare the place if any innocent people could be found therein, now has his answer. There were none found. For Abraham that must include Lot, since he has no way of knowing that Lot has escaped.

Now the narrator concludes. "So it was, when God destroyed the cities of the plain, that God remembered Abraham. . . ." As we have seen, the sentence may be read as extending into the next clause: "and [so] he sent Lot from the midst of the overturning." YHWH's remembering of Abraham turns out to be his reason for sparing Lot. The sentence as it continues, however, quickly overturns any certainty about that motivation by attaching to the Lot clause a temporal clause of its own. We may then read two separate statements about God: "So it was, when God overturned the cities of the plain, that God remembered [his conversation with] Abraham. And [so it was, too, that] he sent Lot out of the midst of the overturning, when he overturned the cities where Lot dwelt" (19:29).

If now the divine plot seems at rest (if not clear resolution), the plot as it concerns Lot turns out to be still in motion. Lot's desire to find safety in Zoar is thrown into question. Without indication of any significant time elapsing after the destruction of the plain, the narrator tells us that "Lot went up from Zoar and dwelt in the hills, and his two daughters with him, for he was afraid to dwell in Zoar. So he dwelt in a cave, he and his two daughters" (19:20). In other words, after all his delaying and prevaricating he ends up where the visitors told him to go in the first place. All sorts of questions arise. Why did he say he wanted to go to Zoar if he were afraid to dwell there? Or did the fear arise after he arrived? Why was he afraid? Did he ever actually stay in Zoar? (Verses 23 and 30 say simply that he "came to" and "went up from" Zoar.)

Let me explore one possibility among several. I suggest that all along Lot knew Zoar to be, like the other cities, a place for visitors to fear, yet he pressed to go there nonetheless because he thought he might thereby save it. Fearful places these cities; yet they were where he had lived, found sons-in-law, and survived to this point. Is the survival of Zoar, fearful though it be, Lot's gesture of humanity? Plainly unable to prevent the destruction of Sodom and Gomorrah, he tries for what he thinks is possible. Zoar is so tiny, a trifle, he insists to the divine visitors. Surely God can overlook a trifle for Lot's sake? Sensing his visitors' impatience to get on with the destruction and at the same counting on their desire to see to his own safety, Lot has played his cards well. On this reading, then, his delays are tactical in the service of a larger strategy. Lot saves a city where Abraham fails. Abraham's challenge hangs on the simple (I could say simplistic) binary categories of righteousness/innocence and evil. Lot's challenge is more subtle. It is based on his own personal involvement with his visitors: He capitalizes on what he sees (and makes sure they see he sees), namely, the *hesed* (faithfulness, commitment) they have shown him. His sons-in-law think that he is only playing the fool. If so, he is a significant fool, for he saves from destruction a whole city, tiny though it be. Whether we judge that saving to be a good thing or not is, of course, another matter.

Thus I have construed Lot's plot in terms of his desire to belong to the city, to offer hospitality, and to extend his gesture of *hesed* even to a city he fears to dwell in. Though his desire to belong is frustrated, his story is not quite finished. If we jump to its end we find him named as father of two nations. His belonging belongs to the future. A question hangs over my construal, however. What if God destroyed Zoar after all? Despite the visitor's assurance, the narrator does not single out Zoar as an exception to the depiction of destruction in verses 25 or 29, and later Lot's elder daughter seems not to know of any remnant in the land (or "on the earth"). We have no certain way of settling the matter, though commentators as early as Ibn Ezra have argued that Deut. 29:22 (which fails to mention Zoar in its list of four destroyed cities) does so. Any reading of Genesis 19 must reckon with this uncertainty.

We have followed the plots of the divinity, of Abraham, and of Lot. Now we find ourselves with another shift in point of view to that of Lot's daughters, in particular the firstborn. She convinces her sister that, as sole survivors, if they are to "make seed live" they must do so by their father. Over the next two nights they make their father drunk, and they go in and lie with him, first the elder, then the younger. Though the narrator interjects that Lot knew nothing of what happened to him those two fateful nights (vv. 33 and 35), the narrative otherwise is constructed from the daughters' perspective. Even the outcome retains that perspective, except for the phrase "to this day," which breaks the frame, as the narratologists put it, and draws attention to the narrator: "Thus they were pregnant, the two daughters of Lot, by their father. And the firstborn bore a son and she called his name Moab—he is the father of Moab to this day. And the younger, she also bore a son and she called his name Ben-Ammi—he is the father of the Bene-Ammon (Ammonites) to this day." Hence, although I have claimed resolution for Lot's plot in his fathering of the two nations, my claim is tenuous, for Lot's hold on the end of the narrative is tenuous. His older daughter (literally) "lays" him, he has no knowledge of this carnal knowledge, and the children of his ignorance who bear his name (their names play on "By-Father" and "Son-of-My-Father") are named not by him but by his daughters. The sons, not Lot, are called the fathers of their people. Thus Lot fades from the story, displaced by his daughters and by the sons he must have thought he would never have.

But I have almost displaced the daughters from view. Instead I wish to expand their plot just a little. They desire to make seed live (not "have children"). From where does their desire arise? Of course, we can say that it is part of their social construction as women in patriarchy, where men's seed is a central theme of control and inheritance. We can also look back into their story in chapter 19 and glimpse them on their father's lips as exchange for two unknown men from who knows where. Even if, as I have wondered, Lot does not mean to be taken seriously in offering his daughters to be raped, nonetheless his rhetoric places them dangerously close to disposability. If he is literal in his offer, their marginality is made amply clear. The men, the visitors, ask Lot whether he has someone else with him: "Son-in-law, sons, daughters . . ." (v. 12). The order is interesting, an indication perhaps of Lot's desire to belong to the city. A son-in-law becomes more important than a son, for he signifies the community's acceptance of the father. Daughters are only a means to an end. Lot's sons-in-law are "takers of his daughters," an unusual phrase suggesting both Lot's marginal situation and the daughters' vulnerability in the power stakes of sojourning and citizenship. And where were the sons-in-law as all the men of the city gathered to assault the strangers, and the sojourner, in their midst? The logic of the text drives us to see them among the abusive crowd. English translations customarily transform "takers of his daughters" into something like those "who were about to marry his daughters," though such a stretch of meaning has no other warrant than to smooth this text. Taking the term "son-in-law" in its usual sense, we must assume either that the sons-in-law are not living with their wives, Lot's daughters, or that they are married to other daughters who rate no mention, either by their father or their husbands.

However we look at them, these daughters are on the margins of both their father's world and the larger social world in which their father in his quest for belonging has placed them. Given such marginality, we need hardly be surprised to find them, in extremity, constructing their remaining value in terms of their ability to bring (men's) seed to life, even if that has to be the seed of their own father. As though complicit with these values, the narrator reports that the daughters bore sons, not daughters. (So, of course, Sarah, Rebekah, Rachel, Tamar, Hannah, and Naomi, to name a few, bear sons, not daughters.) Thus, given that they are the most marginal of all the story's characters, it is ironic that Lot's daughters' plot finally supplants all the others. While YHWH rains down brimstone and fire, overturns cities and wipes out whole populations, the most vulnerable and subordinated characters in the story take charge of their own lives, as they have been led to understand them, by doing what must be done to bring seed to life.

When the daughters were thrust out of Sodom their mother was with them. We may have noticed her palpable absence earlier in the chapter at the visitors' arrival. Lot, we are told, "made them a feast, and baked unleavened bread, and they ate" (v. 3). But just as in the earlier scene of hospitality in chapter 18 where Abraham is credited with preparing the visitors' food, despite the narrator's having already detailed the preparation as essentially the work of Sarah and the servant, so here we may decide that Lot is no more likely to have made the feast and baked the bread than Abraham. The narrator, in patriarchal fashion, is recounting a man's story: The host offers the visiting men hospitality; so far as the narrator, the visitors, and the implied reader are concerned, the meal is the host's. At least in the Abraham scene the narrator gave wife and servant a nod, if only perfunctorily. Here Lot's wife is visible only by inference.

We glimpse her next, seized and expelled from home and city. Then, at some undetermined point in her expulsion, she looks behind Lot and becomes a pillar of salt. Why? That is, why does she gaze behind and why is she turned to salt?

Commentators have little difficulty on the latter score. Why turned to salt? Because, they say, she disobeyed the angel's command. Few ask whether the command was heard by her, let alone addressed to her. In fact, having told us that the visitors had brought them out—Lot, wife and daughters—the narrator continues with the visitor's command: "Flee [masc. sing.] for your [masc. sing.] life; do not look back [masc. sing.]." (19:17). The divine visitors are only concerned to talk to Lot, but the woman as subsumed in her husband is expected to obey. (It is the logic of the law in Exodus–Deuteronomy.) On the other hand, the narrator is not at all specific about the agency by which she becomes salt. Given the emphatic way in which the destruction unfolding before the woman is ascribed to YHWH—"And YHWH rained on Sodom and Gomorrah brimstone and fire from YHWH in heaven"—coyness over her fate is curious. Is the narrator just a little nervous about signaling divine responsibility? Sandwiched between the big players, YHWH and Abraham, Lot's "pillaried" wife may

make for disturbing reading. As any journalist knows, an account of devastation in general (as in cities and inhabitants), no matter how massive the
scale, may shock less than an account of devastation in particular (as in Lot's
wife). Thus in the middle of the climax to both Abraham's and the divine
plot stands a pillar of salt. A disturbance? A distraction? A seasoning? For
salt surely makes a difference. We need to look further into this matter.

Why does Lot's wife turn her attention to what is behind Lot? Professional (male) critics have rarely asked the question, let alone attempted to
answer it. Their sights are set firmly on the story's men. But women, poets,
have asked and, in answering, recognized her humanity. In Kristine Batey's
poem, she is the one who cooked the meals in Sodom ("whoever is god—
the bread must still be made"), raised her daughters in Sodom ("The Lord
may kill the children tomorrow, but today they must be bathed and fed"),
and visited her women neighbors in Sodom ("weren't they there / when the
baby was born, / and when the well collapsed?"):

> It is easy for eyes that have always turned to heaven
> not to look back;
>   those that have been—by necessity—drawn to earth
>   cannot forget that life is lived from day to day.
> . . . .
> On the breast of the hill, she chooses to be human,
> and turns, in farewell—
> and never regrets the sacrifice.
>   —Kristine Batey[2]

You may say, however, that that is all very well, but in the story world of
Genesis 18–19 Sodom is evil in its totality; that these are fictions, these
neighborly, child-rearing, family-nurturing women; that they are fictions
invented against the plain sense of the text. I reply that reading this text is
not quite so simple.

In chapter 18 God speaks first of the "cry of distress" or "cry for help"
(*zĕ'āqāh*) of Sodom and Gomorrah and of their grave "sin" (18:20–21).
Implied by the term "cry for help" are many who are oppressed. Are they all
at the same time and equally oppressors deserving destruction? Neither the
narrator nor God makes any attempt to clarify the matter. The term "cry for
help" remains, disturbing the notion of total depravity. On the other hand,
when Abraham (not the narrator or YHWH) introduces the terms "innocent" (or "righteous") and "wicked" to define the fate of the cities, he forces
the issue into a rigid choice between exclusive categories. For Abraham it is
a matter of either/or: People are either innocent or wicked. Yet given his earlier treatment of Sarai (Gen. 12:10–20) and Hagar (Genesis 16) some of us

may surely be forgiven if we wonder where he would place himself on this grid. In short, however we look at this discussion of prospective corporate judgment, its terms are fraught with lack of clarity if not contradiction.

Another pointer to the text's inability to sustain a notion of total evil is a simple verbal link between chapters 18 and 19 that has the potential to disturb a reader alive to this issue. Having heard Abraham persist in asking what YHWH will do if forty righteous, or thirty or twenty or ten, "are found [there]" (*māsā'*; Gen. 18:29, 30, 31, 32), I am struck by the way the angels speak of Lot's daughters: "Arise, take your wife and your two daughters who are found [here] [*māsā'*], lest you be swept away in the iniquity of the city" (19:15). The daughters who are "found" recall the innocent/righteous who may be "found." So do the daughters signal the presence of "innocence" in the city?

The angels, however, no matter what their actions might suggest, noticeably fail to include the daughters in their spoken concern. "Arise," they say to Lot, "take your wife and your daughters . . . lest you [masc. sing.] be swept away." Likewise, the narrator's account of the angels' seizing by the hand Lot, his wife, and his daughters is punctuated by a parenthesis about YHWH's compassion for *him*. It becomes clear, therefore, that just as the narrator has rhetorically excluded Lot's wife from her kitchen, so too the angels exclude wife and daughters from their own moral space as persons. Lot's offer of his daughters to the crowd gives us sufficient clue to the identity of at least some of the oppressed in Sodom, whose cries have reached heaven. How many daughters have already been raped? How many young men? And if the young men gather to rape other men (19:4), are they all there by choice in this violent city? But now we have another way of reading this story, for the excluded are beginning to appear and the included are beginning to look different. Turn back to the crowd gathered around Lot's house and read again. "The *men* of the city, the *men* of Sodom, both young and old, all the people to the last *man*, surrounded the house." (19:4). (Even the term "people" is routinely used of men as distinguished from women—for example, "there arose a great cry of distress of the people and of their wives." [Neh. 5:1] so that this term cannot be adduced against my point.) These are the *men* of the city. So where are the *women*? Where are the young, not the young men but the *children*—the daughters and sons? Where are the *babies*? Where are all these in this facile talk of the innocent/righteous and the wicked?

I come back to the pillar of salt. Salt is seasoning for the food the woman prepares (Job 6:6), seasoning for the cereal offerings she makes ready for her man to take to the shrine (Lev. 2:13). Salt is for purifying when she finds the drinking water to be bad (2 Kings 2:20–21). The woman uses salt for preserving food; her menfolk and her god, YHWH, use it to prevent food being grown (Judg. 9:45; Deut. 29:23). Salt preserves Lot's wife as a monument that cries out in distress to heaven. For salt is tears, anguish for the women and children of Sodom.

> Who will weep for this woman?
> Isn't her death the least significant?
> But my heart will never forget the one
> Who gave her life for a single glance.[3]
> —Anna Akhmatova

Conventional readings of this story usually find in YHWH and Abraham—rarely Lot—its redeeming message and models. Instead I find in Lot's wife its seasoning.

Further Observations

This interpretation has developed from asking questions about plot, framed as questions of desire. Inevitably some sense of the characters has emerged, though I have not formally addressed the issue of characterization. Were I to do so, I would find myself starting with another set of questions. I would seek clues in the way the narrator names, describes, or evaluates a character—though both personal description and evaluation are usually sparse in biblical narrative. What characters say and how they say it tell us much about the kind of people they are. And if we pay close attention to the context of a character's speech, the circumstances in which the speech takes place, we can better decide what to make of it. Biblical characters may be seen as bending their speech to their context, speaking obliquely rather than straightforwardly, or simply lying, no less than people in "real" life. Matching speech and action (as the narrator recounts it), or observing how speech and action are retold by characters, may enable us to see below surface simplicity to underlying complexity. Comparing and contrasting characters, taking note of how they speak to and about each other, may also help our definitions.

In all of this, as in the plot-based analysis above, careful attention to point of view, or focalization, is crucial. Whose view is being presented at any given time? And what if we afford a character whose point of view has been subordinated in the narration our own focus? Mieke Bal does that by naming, for the purposes of analysis, an unnamed character—so "Jephthah's daughter" becomes "Bath" (Hebrew for "daughter") and thereby has focus in and of herself rather than being always a deflection of her father's focus. That move on the interpreter's part can make explicit what is implicit in another reading.

Three further observations need to be made on the practice of this kind of criticism. First, as I hope became clear above, any account of the text must take serious cognizance of it as a verbal construct, where words make worlds, where words lead us and tease us and plunge us into multiple possibilities of meaning. We can look for secure words, repeated or key words, for example, on which to anchor interpretation. On the other hand, we can seek to unsettle those securities by recognizing that words often participate in more than one pattern or concatenation, that words are always potentially on the move along a spectrum from literal to metaphorical. We can seek to exploit the multivalence of language. So we could talk of ambivalence, ambiguity, and irony (or of allusion and intertextuality—dialogue between texts—and so consciously see our text as a product of its relationships to other texts). Each of these discussions has the potential both to fix and disrupt our reading.

Second, speaking of reading between texts, our reading of chapter 19 paid some attention to chapter 18 but scant attention to the wider matrix spoken of when I asked about the boundaries of the narrative. Set in the larger context of the Abraham story, this episode presents us with various interesting possibilities to pursue further. I could take up a thematic question about the relationships between the Abrahamic family and foreigners. Who is the subject and who is Other in the larger story? What value is placed upon the Other? Early in the story (Genesis 12), Abraham's xenophobia turns out in the case of Pharaoh to be seriously misplaced; so, too, in the chapter immediately following the Sodom story (20), with Abimelech, king of Gerar. Lot's attempt to assimilate, on the other hand, places him in the greatest jeopardy.

Or I could delineate Lot's character by a comparison with that of Abraham and soon conclude that each character has deeply problematic attitudes towards his family. Lot's offer of his daughters may recall Abraham's prostitution of Sarah, not only at the very beginning of his story (in Genesis 12) but again, despite YHWH's insistence that Sarah is to bear the promised seed, in Genesis 20, immediately following the Sodom account. By the same token it may remind us of Abraham's preparedness to sacrifice Hagar and Ishmael (Genesis 16, 21) and, in due course, Isaac (Genesis 22). Lot can save (evil) Zoar but speak of giving his (innocent) daughters to the ravening mob. Abraham can plead for (evil) Sodom but say not a word in defense of his (innocent) son.

Or I could turn the question toward the character of YHWH and suggest that the divinity's complicity in the death of Lot's wife is no less troubling than his sustenance of Abraham the family sacrificer or his wanton disregard for Isaac's well-being when making him the pawn in a "test." I could conclude that there is little blessing for either sons or daughters in God's grand program of making Abraham a great nation (cf. Fewell and Gunn, *Gender, Power, and Promise*, Abingdon, 1993). Protecting the character of God has always been a major industry in biblical studies, and the "new" literary criticism has been slow to differ in this regard, though that is changing. When the study of character (motivation) becomes a key element of critical inquiry, it becomes difficult to avoid hard questions about a (the?) leading character in the story. For two recent studies where the dark side of YHWH is explored, see Alice Bach's *Women, Seduction, and Betrayal in Biblical Narrative* (Cambridge University Press, 1997) and Regina M. Schwartz, *The Curse of Cain: The Violent Legacy of Monotheism* (University of Chicago Press, 1997).

A further dimension of "intertextual" reading would involve bringing into interpretive play texts from further afield than the Abraham story. Robert Alter and Laurence Turner, for example, have both explored connections between the Sodom story and the account of the Flood in Genesis 6–9. It seems to me that there are also strong verbal and thematic correspondences and contrasts with the account of the plagues and deliverance from Egypt in Exodus 1–15, especially the passover account in chapter 12. From outside the corpus of Genesis–Kings, the book of Jonah, as others have observed, is an obvious candidate for a comparative reading.

My third and final point concerning my reading of biblical narrative concerns coherence. I believe that most readers, at least those who are likely to be reading this essay, have a powerful drive to form interpretations that offer an encompassing, comprehensive, and coherent account of their text. Postmodernist theory, in particular deconstruction, helps me to see that this "totalizing" drive is hardly inevitable or innocent. It places a premium on sameness (unity) and univocality and devalues difference (diversity) and multivocality. It leads to our ignoring or suppressing the very tensions and fractures in texts that may offer us enlivening insight or, indeed, escape from the tyranny of an interpretive tradition. Ironically, this is something that historical critics at the beginning of the modernist period knew and used to great effect as they sought out the verbal and conceptual discrepancies that crumbled the univocal divine voice of scripture into a very human amalgam of diverse voices and competing interests. Contemporary narrative criticism of the Bible would do well to cultivate a healthy suspicion of systematics.

A Critique of Narrative Criticism

Criticism of the new narrative studies has often taken the form of ignoring it, resisting its inclusion in curriculum or development in graduate schools, or suppressing its publication. Expressed criticism from historical critics has often been ill-conceived, argued on the basis of accusations about being subjective (as though historical criticism were not) and frequently both unwilling to acknowledge the discipline of literary criticism and unaware of the highly problematic nature of the subjective/objective distinction. "Traditional" historical critics have generally been even slower than many "new" literary critics (such as myself) to become fluent in the hugely important debate on critical theory that has gone on outside the boundaries of biblical criticism, though at least references to E. D. Hirsch (perhaps the most celebrated defender of "authorial intention"—a keystone of traditional historical criticism—as a fundamental category of criticism) seem to be on their way to becoming mandatory.

The question of literary criticism's relation to historical criticism has exercised many. A common strategy (indeed a commonplace of book reviews) of historical critics willing, albeit grudgingly, to allow the former some place in the sun has been to insist that it must build on the achievements of historical criticism, as though the latter were "basic" to biblical criticism. It remains the case, however, that much of the best literary criticism, that which carved out literary criticism's place in the field of biblical studies, was largely independent of, or in controversy with, historical criticism. Few scholars in practice have demonstrated an ability to afford literary and historical criticism equally serious consideration in any sustained study of biblical narrative. Among early exceptions are David Clines (*The Esther Scroll*, JSOT, 1984), W. Lee Humphreys (*The Tragic Vision and the Hebrew Tradition*, Fortress, 1985; and *Joseph and His Family*, South Carolina University Press, 1988), and V. Philips Long (*The Reign and Rejection of King Saul*, Scholars, 1989). Moreover, recently the growing consensus for the "late" (postexilic) dating of most Hebrew Bible narrative, including Genesis–Kings, has encouraged literary readings of narrative texts in terms of an "implied" audience in the postexilic Persian province of Yehud (Judah). The above-mentioned readings of both Fewell (in *Reading Bibles, Writing Bodies*) and Camp (*Wise and Strange*), for instance, exemplify, in different ways, this move to incorporate ancient social location once again into the construction of narrative meaning. Marxist criticism has viewed with deep suspicion theory and practice that leave out of account the production of the text. The text is a literary product of some "history," which is its "absent cause," as Frederic Jameson puts it (*The Political Unconscious: Narrative as a Socially Symbolic Act*, Cornell University Press, 1981). Jobling is one critic who has attempted to write from such a perspective, for example, on the account of Solomon's reign in 1 Kings 3–10 (in David Jobling and Stephen D. Moore, eds., *Poststructuralism as Exegesis*, Semeia 54, Scholars, 1991).

In other words, the question of the relation of literature and history is being reformulated. The assertion of historical critics that theirs is the foundational discipline is a claim for interpretive control that has become impossible to sustain on theoretical grounds. Interdisciplinary approaches now common in women's studies programs, for example, have also led critics to reconsider the interface of the disciplines involved. Old disciplinary boundaries have been breaking down, and new disciplines forming ("cultural studies" is a prime example). In biblical studies, the terms "literary critic" and "historical critic" are losing the sharp edges that seemed once to define them over against each other. Nevertheless, an acute practical problem remains in biblical studies, namely, that much of the data for any kind of historical discourse (including reconstruction of ancient social locations) must come from texts whose provenance is, despite nearly two centuries of historical investigation, a matter of mere speculation. In short, the question of literary criticism's relation to historical criticism is an important one, but it requires a more sophisticated discussion than it has generally been afforded so far.

Another argument sometimes advanced is that literary criticism of biblical narrative confuses biblical and secular literature. Biblical narrative is claimed to be unique as narrative and so not subject to the kinds of critical analysis applied to other literature. The case has usually been made by apologists for traditional Jewish or Christian views of the Bible as scripture and as such is not, in my view, susceptible of constructive debate since the position depends essentially upon an unarguable dogma or faith claim. This privileges the Bible against any kind of scrutiny that does not come from within the traditions of the faith community claiming the book as its own. Such arguments against the new criticism are basically no different from those advanced by Jewish and Christian apologists against the inroads (or threat!) of historical criticism two centuries ago.

Finally, I note a different kind of criticism that affects some narrative methods more than others. Especially in its formative, New-Critical phase, narrative criticism has often deployed observations of formal patterning to substantiate pronouncements about meaning. Thus there exist numerous studies of the "chiasm," the *abcba* pattern, whether on a few verses or a whole book (so much so that, as a friend put it several years ago, any literary critic worth his or her salt could fake a chiasm.) Nevertheless the very category of "form" is a problematic one and the interpretive move from form to meaning redolent with difficulties.

A list of criticisms could go on indefinitely, but it would involve much more discrimination between different kinds of narrative analysis than is possible here. I choose instead to urge that students of biblical narrative criticism take the trouble to learn of and reflectively apply current discussion in (secular) critical theory, exercise deep suspicion toward claims to a total or fundamental system by whomsoever, and to value imagination, intuition, joy, and pain as critical tools so that, when study of Hebrew Bible narrative becomes so technical and tedious that sleep is its only antidote, they have the courage to seek a new way.

Notes

1. Scripture translations in this chapter are the author's own.
2. From "Lot's Wife," in *Alive Now!* January/February 1988, 27.
3. From "Lot's Wife," *The Complete Poems of Anna Akhmatova*, trans. Judith Henschemeyer (Zephyr Press, 1990), vol. 1.

For Further Reading

General

Bal, Mieke. *On Story-Telling: Essays in Narratology*. Ed. David Jobling. Sonoma, Calif.: Polebridge, 1991.

Bible and Culture Collective. *The Postmodern Bible*. New Haven, Conn.: Yale University Press, 1995.

Gunn, David M., and Danna Nolan Fewell. *Narrative in the Hebrew Bible*. Oxford and New York: Oxford University Press, 1993.

Lentricchia, Frank, and Thomas McLaughlin, eds. *Critical Terms for Literary Study*. 2d ed. Chicago: University of Chicago Press, 1995.

Longman, Tremper, III. *Literary Approaches to Biblical Interpretation*. Academie Books. Grand Rapids: Zondervan, 1987.

Powell, Mark Allan. *What Is Narrative Criticism?* Minneapolis: Fortress, 1990.

Robbins, Vernon K. *Exploring the Texture of Texts: A Guide to Socio-Rhetorical Interpretation*. Valley Forge, Pa.: Trinity Press International, 1996.

Robinson, Robert B., and Robert C. Culley. *Textual Determinacy: Volume II*. Semeia 71. Atlanta: Scholars, 1995.

Trible, Phyllis. *Rhetorical Criticism: Context, Method, and the Book of Jonah*. Minneapolis: Fortress, 1994.

On Genesis 18–19

Alter, Robert. "Sodom as Nexus: The Web of Design in Biblical Narrative." In *The Book and the Text*, ed. Regina Schwartz. Oxford: Basil Blackwell, 1990.

Blenkinsopp, Joseph. "Abraham and the Righteous of Sodom." *Journal of Jewish Studies* 33 (1982): 119–32.

Jeansonne, Sharon Pace. "The Daughters of Lot: Victims of Their Father's Abuse." In *The Women of Genesis*. Minneapolis: Fortress, 1990.

Turner, Laurence A. "Lot as Jekyll and Hyde: A Reading of Genesis 18–19." In *The Bible in Three Dimensions*, ed. David J. A. Clines, Stephen E. Fowl, and Stanley E. Porter. Sheffield: JSOT, 1990.

11
READER-RESPONSE CRITICISM

EDGAR V. McKNIGHT

R eader-reponse criticism approaches biblical literature in terms of the values, attitudes, and responses of readers. The reader, therefore, plays a role in the "production" or "creation" of meaning and significance. This attitude toward the role of the reader relativizes the conventional view that the meaning of a text is like the content of a nut, simply awaiting its extraction by a reader. Radical reader-response approaches also challenge conventional views concerning the autonomy of the critic and the scientific and objective nature of the process of reading and criticism.

Diversity in Reader-Response Criticism

Reader-response criticism is not a conceptually unified criticism; it is a spectrum of positions. Specific variants are defined in part by the prior literary and philosophical assumptions of those who practice reader-response criticism. My own project is the utilization of literary criticism in general and reader-oriented approaches in particular to carry out the goal of New Testament hermeneutics by enabling the discovery and creation of meaning for the reader.[1]

Common to all reader-response approaches is the background of New Criticism with its insistence on the structural unity of a literary work and the process of close reading that uncovers that structure. The elements that were highlighted in New Criticism's close reading also remain important. In fiction, for example, Cleanth Brooks and Robert Penn Warren specify that questions such as the following should be asked:

1. What are the characters like?
2. Are they "real"?
3. What do they want? (motivation)
4. Why do they do what they do? (motivation)

230

5. Do their actions logically follow from their natures? (consistency of character)
6. What do their actions tell about their characters?
7. How are the individual pieces of action—the special incidents—related to each other? (plot development)
8. How are the characters related to one another? (subordination and emphasis among characters; conflict among characters)
9. How are the characters and incidents related to the theme?[2]

Stanley Fish and Wolfgang Iser

A summary of the approaches represented by Stanley Fish and Wolfgang Iser will provide readers with a basic vocabulary and perspective for understanding the major variants of reader-response criticism.

Stanley Fish

The background for the work of Stanley Fish was New Criticism's view of the independence and self-sufficiency of the literary work of art and its attention to close reading of the literary work itself instead of to history, biography, and so on. Fish initiated his reader-response approach when he concluded that the essential factor in meaning is not the spatial form of the text on the page but the temporal process of reading. In his early work Fish did not question assumptions of New Critics about the integrity of language and the text. Moreover, close reading and the elements of literature attended to in close reading remained important. Conventional concerns of criticism (the question of intellectual background, as well as questions of literary conventions and genre) were redefined in terms of potential and probable response of readers.

From a later perspective Fish acknowledges that his early work was not radical enough, that he had been retaining the most basic of New-Critical principles—the integrity of the text—in order to claim universality and objectivity for his method. The radical move away from New-Critical assumptions came when Fish discerned that literature is a conventional category dependent upon subjective perception. There is no basic or neutral literary language uncolored by perception and response. The conclusion is that "it is the reader who 'makes' literature." Fish qualifies this subjectivism by defining readers as members of interpretative communities (communities that differ over such matters as the nature and function of literature, for example) that determine the attention given by readers and the kind of literature made by readers.[3]

Wolfgang Iser

The work of Wolfgang Iser may be seen as mediating two positions: (1) that meaning is purely and simply a content of texts (like the content of a nut) and (2) that meaning is essentially a product of the reader. Iser sees the text as the product of an author's intention, with the reading of the text involving not only the intention of the author but also the intention of the reader. The necessary creative activity of the reader does not indicate (as with Fish) that literature and meaning are essentially dependent upon subjective perception. In fact, Iser's work continues a tradition in philosophy which denies that the relationship between things in the world (texts) and observers (readers) is such that things in themselves are unknowable.[4] In proper reading the essential structures of the text (and therefore its integrity) are maintained.

Iser emphasizes that not only the actual text but also the actions involved in responding to that text must be considered in literature. A literary text is not complete in itself. "Gaps" exist—a lack of complete continuity and/or a lack of specification of relationships between the different linguistic and literary elements. Iser makes these gaps and the completion of gaps by the reader the central factors in literary communication. In the linear process of reading there is a movement from one literary unit to another and the bridging or unifying of the units by the reader. This process of unification requires the formation of an idea or theme (a field of reference) within which the two segments make sense. In reading there is movement from one theme to another theme, with the earlier theme becoming the point of departure for the new theme. The same activity of unification must be carried out at the level of the entire literary work. That is, an idea must be formulated that will allow all of the linguistic and literary elements of the work to coexist so that the work will "make sense." Iser speaks of the development of an overarching idea as the "basic force" in literary communication. He calls it "negativity." It may be thought of in different ways: as the "frame" within which the relevant textual material is organized and subsumed; as the cause underlying the questioning of the world in the text; or as the unwritten base that conditions the formulations of the text by means of the "gaps" (from this perspective the term "negativity" makes sense). The idea does not come from the text alone, but it must be consistent with the text. The reader must ask, "What is the text all about?" Formulation of the idea requires the reader's observation of the world of the text (what is going on in the text). But just as important is the requirement of the observation of the world of the text from outside; the reader must transcend the textual world to make sense of the textual world.

The reader becomes most fully involved as the reader is forced to become aware of norms and systems that have become a part of the literary text.

These norms exist in the nonliterary life of the reader, but the reader is unaware of them—as the reader is unaware of the atmosphere in which the reader lives. In literature the norms and systems must be brought to consciousness for the text to be actually experienced by the reader. Iser sees that "the process of fulfillment is always a selective one, and any one actualization can be judged against the background of the others potentially present in the textual structure of the reader's role."[5]

Language and the Structural Tradition

The question of the integrity and determinacy of language, texts, and the subject is at the center of the different varieties of reader-response criticism. Three positions have been noted in the essay so far: (1) the position of New Criticism and the early Fish, which maintains the integrity of language and the determinacy of textual meaning, with the result that "informed readers" come to basically the same evaluation of literary texts; (2) the position of Iser, which demands the creative activity of the reader but which maintains the integrity of the text, with the result that in proper reading readers' intentions are determined by the text and are in continuity with the intention of the author; and (3) the position of the later Fish, which emphasizes the indeterminacy of language and texts and makes the perception of the reader within a community the creator of literature.

The argument between Iser and the later Fish on determinacy of language and literature is important for reader-response approaches to biblical texts. A strong view of integrity and determinacy of texts and meaning would maintain the internal and external relationships and references in such a way that the text could be treated essentially as a scientific document or a historical artifact and analyzed according to scientific or historical-critical criteria. An integrity and determinacy more suited to literature would maintain the broad classification of the text (e.g., comedy or tragedy) and the sorts of relationships that are involved in such a classification. But the text would not be forced at all points into some preconceived form. Readers would be allowed to sort out the potentiality of the text and the specific possibilities of the text in its uniqueness. Moreover, what a reader sees in one time and place would differ from what is seen in another time and place. When a biblical writing is classified as "gospel," for example, the idea of "gospel" will govern reading. But developments in world and church history, the history of interpretation of the Bible, and the history of individual readers and groups of readers influence the idea of "gospel" and the way that a particular writing is seen as instancing that idea.

A loosely defined sort of integrity is what has actually prevailed in literature. The text has been the occasion for varieties of readings influenced by different contexts (temporal, geographical, and ideological, for example). Past readers situated in specific times and places, with specific worldviews, have seen their particular readings as necessary and unrelated to context. Today, however, we are able to appreciate and utilize difference instead of being disabled by difference.[6] We are not required to choose between the establishment of the linguistic, or historical, or sociological meaning on the one hand and the forsaking of the possibility of meaning on the other hand.

"Formalism" is a term used to characterize movements emphasizing the analysis of literary works as self-sufficient objects, independent of reference to the world outside the text. New Criticism is a type of formalism, as are Russian formalism and other East European movements based on linguistic theory. These East European movements are often called "structuralist" because of their application of the linguistic theory of structuralism to literary study. The literary traditions formulated against the background of East European formalism have provided theoretical and practical resources for development and use of a view of textual unity or structure that is energetic and dynamic and capable of responding to cultural and individual development and valuation.[7] One basic argument and development in East European formalism had to do with the autonomy of the literary work of art—just as in New Criticism. A severe formalist approach took the position that only structures immanent in the text are objects of literary concern. The comparison of poetics with the art of weaving by Viktor Sklovsky (a representative of the Leningrad branch of Russian formalism) illustrates the extreme view of immanence: "I am concerned in the theory of literature only with the examination of its inner laws. To use an industrial metaphor, when studying the art of weaving, I am not interested in the situation of the world cotton market, nor in the policy of the cotton trusts, but only in the count of yarn and the techniques of weaving."[8]

The Prague formalist Jan Mukarovsky responded that the matter of weaving itself was certainly of more concern than conditions of the world market when studying the art of weaving, but he declared that the cotton market could not be entirely ignored. The needs of the market have some relation to development of the technique of weaving. The same is to be said for literature. Nonliterary factors influence literature the way that the market influences the technique of weaving, not in a direct way or in a way to change the view of literature and the literary work as a nexus of relationships. Literary structure is dynamic and not static, capable of responding to its different contexts and maintaining the nexus of internal relationships. This view of structure is adopted by Iser, for the "determinate" structure of meaning for Iser is not a static "summative whole" but "finds itself in a ceaseless stage of movement."[9]

The view of the subject (or self) is important for a hermeneutical appropriation of reader-response criticism. The view of a unified autonomous self (analogous to a unified autonomous text) capable of complete self-knowledge and knowledge of others is an Enlightenment perspective that has become problematic. The contemporary challenge to this view of the self may either bring about efforts to validate such a view or create a nihilistic attitude toward meaning and truth (how can I understand another [or the expression of another] if that other does not completely understand himself or herself?). Just as a structural view of the literary text allows a text to retain integrity and determinacy while acknowledging change and difference, a structural view of the subject allows difference and maintains integrity. The subject is defined in part by experiences and inner and outer development. Literary experience is a part of this development and definition. It is because the subject is not a static and autonomous entity that the subject may be changed in the experience of reading.[10]

Recent Developments in the Structural Tradition

Developments in structural semiotics, poststructuralism, and deconstruction associated with scholars such as Roland Barthes, Umberto Eco, and Jacques Derrida may be reconceptualized and utilized in a reader-oriented biblical hermeneutics. Barthes sees the structure of a text as dynamic and involving the reader in a process of analysis without a final synthesis or end.[11] Eco sees the process of reading as involving moves both within the text (intentional) and outside the text (extensional). The various levels and sublevels of textual and extratextual realities are interconnected, and the reader moves back and forth within and without the text to produce meaning.[12] Derrida sets knowledge, language, meaning, and interpretation not simply within a dynamic cultural context but within a larger context of power and authority. Derrida's deconstructive approach to literature is concerned with the examination of the desire for mastery—the mastery of knowledge through language and meaning through interpretation—and the subversion of that desire through the very nature of language itself. The language and logic that form the resources of an author cannot be dominated absolutely by an author. The author uses them by being governed by them. A deconstructive reader seeks to discover relationships between what the author commands and what the author does not command in the patterns of the language used by the author.[13] Reading in the conventional mode is a synthesizing process with the subjective reader being governed (as the subject/author) by language. But a deconstructive reading gives conscious attention to the impulse toward and result of the synthesizing of the conventional reading process in order to break its "domination." The reader-oriented hermeneutical approach I advocate acknowledges the dynamic and always in-process nature of reading and the subject involved in reading, but it emphasizes the making of sense for the reader—local, ad hoc, and partial as it may be. The unity and meaning found in a specific location and reading overlooks and/or excludes textual elements that cannot be assimilated in that reading, to be sure, but these elements become the basis for other unities and meanings.

Reader-Response Criticism and Biblical Study

Reader-oriented theories not only emphasize the reader's role in the process of achieving meaning but also see the result of reading in terms of an effect upon the reader. This is visualized in different ways. In his Oxford thesis, for example, Jonathan Culler suggested that the process of reading reveals the problems of the reader's condition as maker and reader of signs, and this is the meaning of the work.[14] Iser sees the process of reading as the coming together of text and imagination. It is an experience of continual modification, closely akin to our experience in life. Because of the nature of the process, the "reality" of the experience of reading illuminates the dynamic nature of real experiences.[15] Georges Poulet emphasizes the achievement of self-transcendence in reading. In reading, the object of the reader's thought is the thought of another. The reader becomes the subject of the thought (the one doing the thinking) in the act of reading. The reader thinks a thought that belongs to another mental world. "When I am absorbed in reading, a second self takes over, a self which thinks and feels for me. . . . The work lives its own life within me; in a certain sense, it thinks itself, and it even gives itself a meaning within me."[16]

Developments in Reader-Response Criticism of the Bible

Radical reader-oriented approaches are foreign to the experience of historically oriented biblical critics because of different views of the use of language and the nature of biblical literature. It is difficult to overcome this strangeness because conventional views of language and life reinforce each other. Both are governed by the Enlightenment model in which subject and object, humankind and the natural world, are distinct, with the subject—humankind—dominating. Language is a tool used by humans to refer, and the truth of the reference is validated by the human subject through establishment of correspondence between the statement and that to which it refers.

Beginnings: Literary Study of the Bible

Reader-response criticism in biblical studies began with concern for genuine literary matters, a concern that surfaced in the 1960s and 1970s and became commonplace in the 1980s. This turn in biblical studies reflected a return, in a certain sense, to concerns of the precritical period (prior to the Enlightenment). In that epoch, the cultural and intellectual distance between the biblical world and the reader's world was assumed to be small. No distinction was made between the world depicted in the Bible and the real historical world. Readers had little difficulty seeing their own actions and feelings and the events of their world in relation to the biblical world. Resources of allegory and typology assisted readers in seeing the Bible as a whole, as depicting the whole of historical reality. Old Testament stories referred directly to specific temporal events and indirectly (as figures or types) to New Testament stories, events, and realities. But these (both Old Testament and New Testament) also corresponded to the historical experiences of the reader. The biblical world extended to and impinged upon the present, upon the world of the reader of any age. The power of a precritical reading extending from the Old Testament to the readers' day without any rupture depended in part upon the fact that the world of Abraham, Isaac, and Jacob, the world of Moses and Jesus, was not the ultimate reality. Above and beyond the world extending from Adam to the present was a divine world that alone made sense of this world. The worldview of the ancient and medieval worlds did not methodologically exclude the sacred but rather made the sacred the standard.

With the Enlightenment, the historicity of literary and other cultural phenomena replaced the framework of the theological conceptualization of the ancient and medieval world. History became the standard. The realistic feature of biblical narrative was related consciously to historical reference. The role of the biblical stories was to enable readers to uncover the historical sequence of events to which they referred directly or indirectly. Undermined was the correlation between the world of the reader and the biblical world made possible when both were seen as expressions of the pre-existing divine world. This diminished the potential of the narratives to allow readers to make sense of themselves in relation to the world of the narrative in a somewhat direct fashion.

The literary turn was prepared for in the attempt of Rudolf Bultmann and the New Hermeneutic to extend the power of the biblical text into the life of contemporary readers by attention to its linguistic dimensions. Preoccupation with existential categories and the lack of interaction with secular literary criticism hindered the task. In his 1964 publication, *The Language of the Gospel,* Amos Wilder advocated a move that takes advantage of literary insights. He expounds the New Testament as "language event" (an expression used by the New Hermeneutic reflecting the idea that language and reality are inseparably connected, that reality comes into being through language) in terms of literary genre, with the conviction that "behind the particular New Testament forms [genres] lies a particular life-experience and a language-shaping faith." Wilder explicitly criticized Rudolf Bultmann's restriction of meaning to existential concepts. The view that the New Testament "tells us about ourselves, not about 'things' and the way they are and the way they happen," according to Wilder, results in a disparagement of "the whole story of man and salvation as the Bible presents it." The literary criticism appropriate for New Testament study does not ignore reference and remain confined to the structures and conventions of literature. There is reference in the biblical text, but the reference is not the same as in conventional study of the Gospels. Students of the New Testament can learn about the text's literary language and reference from students of poetry: "This kind of report of reality—as in a work of art—is more subtle and complex and concrete than in the case of a discursive statement, and therefore more adequate to the matter in hand and to things of importance."[17]

Robert Tannehill displayed concern with contemporary literary criticism of biblical texts in 1975 in *The Sword of His Mouth: Forceful and Imaginative Language in Synoptic Sayings*,[18] and in 1977 in "The Disciples in Mark: The Function of a Narrative Role."[19] In these works Tannehill integrated narrative and reader-response criticism. According to Tannehill, Mark's evaluation of the disciples is to be found in his depiction of the concordant/discordant relationships between Jesus and the disciples, which is also the key to readers' evaluation. Moreover, as the plot develops, readers are involved through the arousal of expectations that are either fulfilled or left unfulfilled by what ensues. In 1985 and 1989 issues of *Semeia* (a journal devoted to new and emergent areas and approaches in biblical criticism) were dedicated to reader-response criticism.[20]

The Role and Function of the Bible in Reader-Response Literary Criticism

Assumptions about the role and function of the Bible are important in reader-response criticism. The role of the Bible as literature is to be distinguished from the role of the Bible as historical "source" or literary "document." To read the biblical text as source is to read it as the container of some sort of information that may be extracted by objective procedures and validated by comparing the data obtained with data in the real world. To begin with the Bible as historical source and subject it to historical-critical analysis in order to discover the history behind biblical texts makes movement beyond historical-critical analysis difficult. Moreover, the matter of concern to believers cannot be obtained through this analysis as such. Robert Morgan depicts the gap that has developed between philological and historical learning on the one hand and religious engagement and theological insight on the other hand.[21] The role of the Bible as a document of ancient communication does not really bridge the gap. When the Bible is approached as both an ancient document with original meaning and a living message with contemporary significance, the bridge to a comprehensive and satisfying biblical hermeneutics may have been found. The reader's final focus is not upon the original circumstances but upon the text in the contemporary context of reading.

As literature, the Bible plays a role in the life of society and of individuals in that society. The role of the Bible (as literature) may be seen as related to knowledge that the text makes possible for the reader—knowledge extended beyond the world of the text to the world uncovered by the text. The role of the Bible is to be seen in the light of the cognitive and noncognitive affective experiences of the reader in the process of making sense of the text as knowledge. It is to be seen in the light of the development of self knowledge vis-à-vis the world and the process of reading. The Bible as literature is seen as the instrument for humankind's discovering, creating, and/or making sense of world, self, and whatever world-and-self-transcending meanings and values humankind is capable of imaging.

The Bible as *religious literature* may be distinguished from other literature in terms of role and function. One way of beginning to mark this distinction is to note that the essential shape of biblical literature is comic. That is, the Bible depicts not a reversal of fortune from good to bad (tragedy) but a movement from bad to good. Although the Bible contains examples of romance, irony, and tragedy, the thrust of the Bible is in the direction of the comic. When these other genres are present, they are to be seen in terms of the more central comic movement. Tragedy in the Bible, for example, is seen as an essential episode in the larger scheme of the divine comedy that includes restoration and resurrection.[22]

The Bible is read in the context of continuing communities of faith, and even readers who do not share the faith of those communities are influenced by that fact. The life and faith (practice and theology) of the larger communities of faith and of local expressions of those communities play their part in the experience of reading. Most of the time this is a silent, even unconscious, influence, the result of a faith perspective that is simply taken for granted. A dialectical relationship exists between the faith perspectives of religious communities and the encompassing philosophical and cultural worldview. A reader who is also a member of a religious community will operate with schemata from both worlds.

Values of Reader-Response Approaches

Whether reader-response criticism of the Bible is viewed positively or negatively depends in part upon the worldview of the reader and the role and function of the Bible in that worldview. Readers who are committed to a "modern" Enlightenment paradigm will seek to eliminate or reduce the subjective character of study. If these readers utilize reader-response criticism, it will take the form of an objective search for the implied reader or for the strategies followed by the author in influencing the reader (rhetorical criticism), which can be demonstrated as existing in the ancient world. However, this essay advocates a reader-response approach that utilizes the rich possibilities of reading for actual readers. Such an approach is valuable for a variety of reasons. First, serious interaction with the text is facilitated by reader-response criticism. This reader-response approach may do for biblical study what the New Criticism did for literature in general—free the biblical text from its domination by disciplines such as history, sociology, and psychology. Second, this reader-response approach represents a victory for the reader. Readers are freed to make sense for themselves. This method allows readers to interact with the text in light of their own context, linguistic and literary competence, and need, as well as in light of the potentialities of the text. Confidence and further competence are developed as readers are able to make sense of the text in light of their own location and "dialect." Third, such an approach allows the obvious religious concerns of the text to impinge upon reading in a way appropriate to the concerns of the reader. The world of the reader will be seen as "like" the biblical world in some way satisfying to the reader. A type of knowledge may result from the experience of reading that is different from the knowledge gained by scientific methodologies. Levels of meaning and knowledge may be experienced that were lost with the Enlightenment paradigm. Finally, reader-response approaches are capable of accommodating and utilizing approaches followed in more conventional biblical and literary studies. Historical and sociological exegeses, for example, are not precluded in reader-response criticism. They are reconceptualized and relativized but not made illegitimate as such.

Illustration: A Reading of Luke 5:1–11

A reading of Luke 5:1–11* will illustrate the sorts of moves made by the reader in making sense of a biblical text. Two basic sorts of moves are made, one giving attention to the linear arrangement of words, sentences, and so on (paralleling the close reading of New Criticism), the other giving attention to the categories of form (genre) and content that can be assigned to those units. Relationships *within* discourse enable linguistic and literary elements to have meaning as they are *combined* or chained together in a linear

---

*Scripture translations in this chapter are the author's own, unless otherwise marked.

and/or layered fashion. Perspectives outside of discourse as such are necessary for making sense of the combinations within discourse. The topic, reference, literary category, and function of the literary unit, for example, are not built up simply from within by words and sentences and their combinations. Formal, semantic, and other categories without discourse are imposed upon and complete the structures of discourse. Perspectives taken by readers influence the relationships discovered and created. Attention to relations outside discourse moves beyond New-Critical emphases.

Biblical texts say something, do something, and influence the reader affectively. The entry into the richness of cognitive and affective meaning and significance of biblical texts is by means of semantic content that involves topics, themes, or ideas. What texts do and how texts affect readers are related to what the texts say. At the level of every literary unit some topic must be discerned. Then, at the level of the total work, a comprehensive organizing principle or idea must be formulated in order for the identification of topics and relationships throughout the work, and, therefore, for the meaning of the work as a whole. Topics and ideas must be consistent with the literary data, but the interplay of literal, figurative, and often paradoxical meanings of words and other units makes the literary data susceptible to a variety of meanings. The same word, expression, or entire text can signify two or more distinct references and express and elicit different attitudes or feelings.

The reader comes to Luke 5:1–11 as a unit in the Gospel of Luke. The unit will be read in light of its definition as a part of a "Gospel" and in light of its part in defining the particular "Gospel" of which it is a part. A variety of nonliterary contexts also influence the reading of the text, and the reader may move to any of these to make sense of the text. The context within which reading takes place and the anticipated result of reading are important. These may be taken for granted and not considered consciously. Here these matters are considered, for the reading is designed to illustrate the process of reading. In this context, all of the reader's private associations will not be shared, only those that the reader/author can make understandable to readers of this book.[23]

The reader reads until some minimal unit of meaning presents itself (can be discovered or created). Luke 5:1–3 makes up a minimal unit of meaning as it is read in light of lexical and grammatical information. This unit begins with the press of the people upon Jesus to hear the word of God—and the consequent inability of Jesus to teach the word—and concludes with the successful teaching of the people from a boat. The major actor in the episode is not identified in this unit (pronouns are used instead of the name "Jesus"), so the reader must identify this actor as Jesus by moving either backward or forward in the text to a place where the proper name is used.

The reader knows that Jesus is the personal name of Jesus of Nazareth (Luke 24:19), the son of Mary (Luke 1:31), the prophet (Luke 7:39; 24:19) who is "a Savior . . . Christ the Lord" (Luke 2:11). From the words and deeds in the unit itself, a reader constructs an image of the Jesus of this unit. He is popular and is the speaker of the word of God. He is ingenious (he uses a boat to solve the problem presented by the press of the people), and his authority is compelling. The unit shows that Jesus has a mission and indicates that the mission involves being sent by God for the purpose of teaching the word of God. This indication is confirmed and made more explicit by a movement to the earlier pericope, which has a quotation from Jesus himself indicating that he has been sent to "preach the good news of the kingdom of God to the other cities also."

The text has two sentences in the first unit. The first sentence consists of two verses and gives the following information: The crowd is pressing him to hear the word of God; Jesus is standing by the lake; Jesus notices two boats left unattended while the fishermen are washing the nets. A reader has to correlate the information given: "One day as he stood by the lake of Gennesaret, with people crowding in on him to listen to the word of God, he noticed two boats lying at the water's edge; the fishermen had come ashore and were washing their nets" (NRSV). The fact that the boats are at the water's edge is explained by the fact that the fishermen have come ashore and are washing the nets. We can assume that they have completed their task of fishing and are now ready to care for their gear and rest from their labors. The fact that Jesus notices the two boats results from Jesus' need and search for some way to escape the press of the crowd and to accomplish his mission.

Can we imagine some relationship between Jesus standing along the shore and the press of the crowd? Is the relationship only temporal, or does the setting of the lake of Gennesaret have some significance? The statement of Jesus in the preceding pericope indicates that he "must preach the good news of the kingdom of God to the other cities also." He has been preaching in the synagogues of Judea just before he appears beside the lake. This reader attempts to sort out the information: Jesus is to preach in the cities (where the synagogues are located); in the cities (the synagogues) there is conflict; away from the cities (the "lonely place" of 4:42 and on the shore of the lake of Gennesaret) people are pressing upon him to keep him with them and to hear the word of God.

The presence of Jesus is the occasion of the activity of the crowd, and the activity of the crowd is precluding the very action the crowd desires and for which Jesus has been sent. A reader may mull over the relationship between the irony that Jesus is sent to teach in the city while it is in the country that the people crowd to hear him and the irony that in the country (and beside the lake) the press to hear Jesus precludes that hearing.

The disabling activity of the crowd causes Jesus to explore ways of carrying out his mission. Boats and fishermen are at hand. My limited knowledge of fishing in the New Testament period and of the experience of fishing in general causes me to image the fishermen using a large seine or draw net, with sinkers on the bottom and floats on the top. People fishing would wade in the waters near the shore and maneuver the net to shore in a wide semicircle. Two boats could be used to capture the fish on the lake, with the two boats (and the two ends of the net) closing in on one another instead of to the shore.

The second sentence in the unit has two coordinate clauses: "When he had gotten into one of the boats, which was Simon's, he asked him to put out a little from the land," and "when he sat down, he taught the people from the boat." For the reader who is familiar with the opening chapters of Luke (or who moves back to those chapters to make sense of the text), Simon is no stranger; it was to Simon's house that Jesus went after the healing of the demoniac in the synagogue in Capernaum. There he had healed Simon's mother-in-law. Simon is the other name of Peter, the most prominent of the apostles of Jesus.

With 5:3 the problem created by the press of the crowd has been solved. Jesus has distanced himself so as to be able to preach to the people. The reader images the scene simply: Jesus gets into Peter's boat and asks him to push off from the shore. At this point we see only Jesus and Peter in the boat, with the others washing nets on the shore. It was "a crowd" pressing Jesus to hear him at the beginning; as a result of Jesus' action he teaches "the crowds." The very last word in this unit is the plural form of the noun used in verse 1 in the singular. The reader for whom the reading of this unit is really a rereading knows about the marvelous catch of fish later in the narrative and may see such a catch prefigured at the very beginning with the success of Jesus. The meanings of the various episodes impinge upon one another and contribute to the rich meaning of the unit as a whole. But the relationships must be "seen" by the reader; they are not spelled out by the text.

What is the overall meaning of this unit? At the level of what the text is saying, the meaning seems simple: With the help of Simon and his boat, Jesus is enabled to solve the problem created by the press of the crowd and to carry out the mandate of God to teach the word. The reader is not yet prepared to go beyond the level of what is being said in the text, but a rich potentiality is present in relationships between Jesus and Simon, the lakeshore and the lake, and so on.

The next unit of meaning is Luke 5:4–7, and it deals with the catching of fish. Jesus first asks Simon to put out into the deep and let down his nets for a catch. It appears that the topic has changed from "teaching the word" to "catching fish." In a slow-motion process of reading, full attention will be given to the unit in terms of fishing. Why is Jesus concerned about fishing? Later in the same unit we discover that the fishermen have been busy all night and have caught nothing. There is need for food for the people and financial return for the fishermen! The command of Jesus moreover causes the reader to reimage the earlier events somewhat. Earlier, the reader imaged Jesus and Simon alone on the boat, with the other fishermen on shore with the nets. Other fishermen must now be included, along with a net. A rereading of earlier material may reenvision the fishermen on the shore alongside the boat, washing the net as it is spread on the side of the boat. Simon's taking the boat out would involve the net and apparently some of the fishermen also. The exchange between Jesus and Simon and Simon's action supports the view of Jesus as a person of confidence and authority. It also supports the view of Simon as obedient.[24] The success with catching brings a crisis. The mass of fish could mean failure in fishing, just as the mass of people earlier had threatened the hearing of the word by anyone. The need for help was met by the other fishermen and another boat. But the success of the help created another crisis. The boats began to sink. A slow-motion reading in which the reader attempts to find categories of meaning and meaning-effect that will utilize the full potential of the text will give attention to the irony and contradictions in the story.

The episode of 5:1–3 has a successful ending and some ironic touches. There is a mandate to preach the word. But something must be done before that mandate can be carried out. The very presence of the crowd to whom he was to preach created the need for some sort of prior action to be carried out by Jesus. The solution to the problem involved distancing himself from the very ones to whom the word of God is to be given. The episode beginning with Luke 5:4 is more ambiguous in terms of the mood created. Initially it appears that the same sort of sequence will be repeated. There is the need for fish to be caught for the proper operation of the social and economic order. The order of society, in which fish are caught for the people, has been interrupted, but Jesus encourages and enables Simon to catch a multitude of fish in spite of Simon's earlier failures. The reader's satisfaction is premature, however. The very success of the catch invites catastrophe. The nets begin to break. The reader may see this as a repetition of the type of thing that created the lack in the first episode. Too much of what is sought spells failure! Certainly the repetition of the very same type of threat in the sinking of the boats must be seen as comic. But repetition in a tragedy may lead to catastrophe, so the emotional response of the reader must be contained until the final denouement.

The episode of Luke 5:8–11 concludes the pericope; with this unit the reader is forced to consider the character of the whole pericope and the earlier reading in light of the decision about the meaning of the whole. Readers bring other texts with them to Luke 5:1–11, particularly those recounting Peter's call to become a disciple. Mark's account (Mark 1:16–20), followed by Matthew (4:18–22), has Jesus walking along the Sea of Galilee and calling Simon and Andrew and James and John to follow him. Jesus says to Simon and to Andrew, "Follow me and I will make you become fishers of men." Upon the call, the four leave the fishing and follow Jesus. The account of Jesus' teaching from a boat because of the pressure of a crowd along the shore (Mark 4:1) and the story of the miraculous catch of fish in John 21 also may influence the reading. From the perspective followed in this essay, the importance of these other texts is not historical; Luke 5:1–10 is not seen in light of some presumed literary development.

Some help may be given by these other texts in terms of the genre or the way that the text is to be read. Is it to be read as a tale? The catch of fish is clearly a wonder. Is it a myth (a story about the divine)? Mythic qualities are obviously present. Might "Depart from me for I am a sinful man, O Lord" be the key? What does this sentence mean? What is its function? How may a reader make sense? "Depart from me" alone would indicate that Simon sees Jesus as the cause of his problem. A purely spatial interpretation would emphasize that Simon wants Jesus out of the boat. With Jesus out of the boat, the problem might be solved. But the departure called for seems to be more radical, as is seen in the next statement where the focus is upon Simon's own situation vis-à-vis the divine and/or Jesus: "I am a sinful man." Is "sinful" a pleonasm? Is Simon acknowledging his humanity in face of the revelation of the sacred? Or is Simon acknowledging not merely that he is human but that he is a sinner in some specific way? In what way? In his skepticism at the power of Jesus to affect the catch of fish? At his cynical spread of the net in a fashion to be able to complete only the most limited catch? The title given to Jesus by Simon ("Lord") transforms the immediate episode to a completely different level; "Depart from me" and "I am a sinful man" constitute a confession similar to Isaiah's declaration of uncleanness in the presence of the Lord of hosts (Isa. 6:5). Jesus' response and commission of Simon, "Do not be afraid; henceforth you will be catching people," is read as paralleling the response to Isaiah's confession.

The reader is now able to begin to reconceptualize the earlier episodes. The statement of Jesus about catching people has the effect of instructing the reader to repeat all previous interpretative operations, at least from verse 4, with "people" replacing "fish." When rereading is done, the initial sequence becomes a pattern for the series of sequences with an interesting change of subjects, from God to Jesus to Peter (Peter and the others on the first boat beckon to the others to come and help). From the word of Jesus, "Do not be afraid, henceforth you will be catching people," there is not only a backward reference giving additional significance but also a forward thrust; readers of the Gospel are recipients of the word by means of the success of Simon and those to whom the word was preached. Do faithful believers not become involved in the forward movement of the Gospel? The forward thrust again forces a rereading of the earlier narrative segments with the readers involved.

The completion of the mission of Jesus, the major theme of the entire episode, is dependent upon the successful completion of the commission given by Jesus to his followers. The subordinate episode of the catch of fish, then, as it is reinterpreted by the christological and ecclesiastical context, serves as the model for the promise of the successful completion of both the commission given to Jesus by God and the commission given to his followers by Jesus. Luke 5:1–11 not only says something, it also accomplishes something.

The completion of the narrative finds the fishermen with their nets and boats safe on the shore. So, as a tale about successful fishing, perhaps in spite of the dangers of the success, the narrative concludes with a comic mood or tone. The reader sees this as a comic genre as opposed to the tragic genre. But this is not pure comedy. It is an ironic comedy that shows the incongruities of the world and yet holds us to the world. The emphasis is not upon the "all too human" life, which is either oppressive or ridiculous, but neither is it the ideal comedy of "whatever you will."

A reader who is religiously mature and who has a degree of symbolic competence will center upon the episode that forms the crux of the movement from the potentially catastrophic situation of those on the lake to the safe arrival on land. From this perspective, the comic ending is not only a matter of the way the plot turns out, it is also a matter of the perspective of the reader. The reader feels raised to a position above the action. The action is seen from the perspective of a better ordered and more highly elevated world. The movement of the perspective of the reader to a point above the action, the movement away from human experience, is accomplished to the extent that the reader agrees with Simon's assessment of the character of Jesus. The text and the reader are involved in this move. The story takes on mythic qualities (in the sense of a story about the divine). The narrative is not a simple story about a divine being, however. This epiphany (manifestation of the divine in the world of human experience), if it is interpreted by the reader as such, is the occasion of Jesus' mandate to Simon and the others present, which will enable Jesus to carry out the original mandate of God. The words of Jesus that establish the mandate, "henceforth you will be catching people," will be read as functioning the same way as Mark 1:17, "Follow me and I will make you fish for people." But in fact the statement is literally more of an institution of Simon and those others present than it is an invitation to follow Jesus. With the necessary view of God, providence, and Christology, the saying of Jesus may be read as both a mandate and as an authoritative pronouncement of final success of the mission of the disciples, the mission of Jesus, and, hence, reestablishment of the original divinely ordained society.

Limitations of the Method

Specific criticisms may be leveled at the use of reader-response criticism in biblical studies. An examination of these criticisms will show genuine limitations of the approach and ways that attitudes toward literature and toward the Bible may be modified for the development of a satisfying reader-response criticism.

1. Reader-response approaches, even taken as a whole, are not comprehensive. They do not do everything that can be done and ought to be done in biblical studies. They do not substitute for conventional approaches. In secular literary criticism as such many reader-response critics remain associated with other "schools" (formalism, structuralism, phenomenology, deconstruction, Marxism, feminism, and speech-act theory, for example). The same is true in biblical study. Just as in literary study, however, the reader-response shift from text as product to text as process will create changes in conventional studies.

2. Reader-response approaches to the Bible may be judged from the perspectives of both religious and historical study to be inappropriate because of the literary orientation of such approaches. The Bible is not literature in the conventional sense. A reduction of the Bible to secular literature would seem to be illegitimate. Reader-response criticism, however, does not demand the conclusion that biblical writings were composed within "literary" circles or designed to be read simply for enjoyment as "literary" works of art. The literary nature of the Bible is not due to writers' concern with belles lettres but to their utilization of the same linguistic and literary realities and principles as secular literature. It is also due to the fact that biblical writers are using language to appeal to readers who will find and create meanings that involve them, that match their needs and capacity at cognitive and noncognitive levels.

3. The fact that reader-response approaches to the Bible grow out of literary study of fictional literature, primarily novels, makes such an approach suspect to some. This fact, however, may enable us to reconceive the "reference" in biblical literature as involving a truth that historical writing as such is unable to convey. A "world" is portrayed and revealed in biblical literature. It is not necessarily unrelated to what can be rediscovered historically of Israel, Jesus Christ, and the New Testament church, but it is more than that which historical criticism as such can contain.

4. Historical-critical readers will see in reader-response criticism a lack of regard for the intention of the author. This perception is valid. The conventional concern for the intention of the author has (among other things) caused biblical criticism to remain moored at the historical level of questioning authorship and intention. And the failure to arrive at "assured results" in this regard often frustrates attention to the text itself. Reader-response criticism does not ignore the author and the intention of the author, but the construction of author and author's intention is taken to be only a penultimate strategy in reader-response criticism.[25]

5. Reader-response criticism is very unsettling and overwhelming for "modern" readers who want to control the text and discover the meaning on the basis of a secure foundation. One critic has compared historical-critical work and reader-response approaches. Historical-critical work "often left an impression of banality—monophonic interpretation of polyphonic texts." But reader-response criticism "often gave the contrary impression of an excess of critical resources . . . and of readings that outdid in complexity and creativity the texts being read."[26] This characterization is valid. But we ought to expect such complexity and creativity, given the nature and potentiality of biblical texts and the developing capacity of readers.

Notes

1. Critical theories that do not approach the theme from the perspective of the activity of contemporary readers or offer strategies of reading will not be treated in this essay. Wayne C. Booth and others speak of "implied" authors and readers as rhetorical devices of the actual author. These are to be built up by the reader on the basis of such things as the explicit commentary of the narrator, the kind of tale being told by the author, the meanings that can be extracted, and the moral and emotional content of the actions of the characters. The goal of a real reader is to become the implied reader and to find the implied author. The reader-reception criticism associated with Hans Robert Jauss is concerned with the history of readers' reception. This approach attempts to situate a literary work within the cultural context of its production and then explore the shifting relations between this context and the changing contexts of historical readers. Psychological approaches to the reader emphasize the stages of development of individual readers or (as in the case of Norman N. Holland) the role played by the "psychological set" of readers.

2. Cleanth Brooks and Robert Penn Warren, *Understanding Fiction* (New York: F. S. Crofts & Co., 1943), 28.

3. Stanley Fish, *Is There a Text in This Class? The Authority of Interpretative Communities* (Cambridge: Harvard University Press, 1980), 67.

4. The phenomenological tradition in which the work of Wolfgang Iser is situated arose as an attempt to reestablish the reality of the world by answering the philosophical theory that things in themselves are unknowable, that things are always perceived in terms of the one perceiving. The term "phenomenology" indicates that what is attempted in theory and practice is the investigation and description of the essential structures of the phenomena that appear in immediate experience. Two assumptions are

vital: that the phenomena are constituted by consciousness through intentionality and that, although the phenomena assume accidental or nonessential forms, investigation may reveal forms that are to be regarded as essential in the sense that they cannot be removed without destroying the basic intentionality of the data. In two volumes (*The Cognition of the Literary Work of Art*, trans. Ruth Ann Crowley and Kenneth R. Olson [Evanston, Ill.: Northwestern University Press, 1973] and *The Literary Work of Art: An Investigation on the Borderlines of Ontology, Logic, and Theory of Literature*, trans. George G. Grabowicz [Evanston, Ill.: Northwestern University Press, 1973]) the phenomenologist philosopher Roman Ingarden studied the formal structures common to all works of literature and the nature of cognition that is a valid and true reconstruction of the literary work. Ingarden distinguishes between the work of art itself and a concretization of the work that is constituted during reading. The complexity of a literary work is such that the reader has too much to do at the same time and cannot give himself or herself equally to all of the components of the total apprehension. Only a few of the multiplicity of simultaneously experienced and interwoven acts become central.

5. Wolfgang Iser, *The Act of Reading: A Theory of Aesthetic Response* (London: Routledge & Kegan Paul, 1978), 37.

6. In his essay "Difference" (in *Margins of Philosophy*, trans. Alan Bass [Chicago: University of Chicago Press, 1982], 8), Jacques Derrida enunciated the differential nature of language and the continual deferring of meaning. The work of Derrida has been used to support the loss of any stable meaning, linguistically and philosophically.

7. East European formalist movements ceased functioning as early as the late 1920s owing to pressure from doctrinaire Soviet Marxists, and exemplary texts of the formalists were not available in translation until the 1960s and 1970s. As movements in the structural and semiotic study of narrative, poststructuralism, and deconstruction have become influential in America, however, arguments and developments in East European formalism (structuralism) have been recapitulated.

8. Viktor Sklovsky, *O teorii prozy* [Theory of Prose] (Moscow and Leningrad, 1925). See Thomas G. Winner, "The Aesthetics and Poetics of the Prague Linguistic Circle," *Poetics* 8 (1973): 80.

9. Iser cites Jan Mukarovsky's view of the energetic and dynamic character of the structure of the literary work: "The energy of the structure is derived from the fact that each of the elements in the overall unity has a specific function which incorporates it into the structural whole and binds it to that whole; the dynamism of the structural whole arises out of the fact that these individual functions and their interacting relationships are subject, by virtue of their energetic character, to continual transformations. The structure as a whole thus finds itself in a ceaseless state of movement, in contrast to a summative whole, which is destroyed by any change" (Jan Mukarovsky, *Kapital aus der Poetik* [Frankfurt, 1967], 11). Cited in "The Repertoire" in *Critical Theory since 1965*, ed. Hazard Adams and Leroy Searle (Tallahassee, Fla.: Florida State University, 1986), 380.

10. See Edgar V. McKnight, *Meaning in Texts: The Historical Shaping of a Narrative Hermeneutics* (Philadelphia: Fortress, 1978), 24–25, 215–25, for a discussion of the role of such a dynamic structure in the hermeneutical tradition of Wilhelm Dilthey.

11. Roland Barthes, *S/Z*, trans. Richard Miller (London: Jonathan Cape, 1975).

12. Umberto Eco, *The Role of the Reader: Explorations in the Semiotics of Texts* (Bloomington, Ind.: Indiana University Press, 1979).

13. Jacques Derrida, *Of Grammatology*, trans. Gayatri C. Spivak (Baltimore: Johns Hopkins University Press, 1976), 158.

14. Jonathan Culler, "Literary Competence," *Reader-Response Criticism: From Formalism to Post-Structuralism*, ed. Jane P. Tompkins (Baltimore: Johns Hopkins University Press), 116–17.

15. Wolfgang Iser, "The Reading Process: A Phenomenological Approach," in Tompkins, *Reader-Response Criticism*, 56.

16. George Poulet, "Criticism and the Experience of Interiority," in Tompkins, *Reader-Response Criticism*, 45, 47.

17. Amos Wilder, *The Language of the Gospel: Early Christian Rhetoric* (New York: Harper & Row, 1964), 133.

18. Robert Tannehill, *The Sword of His Mouth: Forceful and Imaginative Language in Synoptic Sayings* (Missoula, Mont.: Scholars, 1975).

19. Robert Tannehill, "The Disciples in Mark: The Function of a Narrative Role," *Journal of Religion* 57 (1977): 386–405.

20. Robert Detweiler, ed., *Reader Response Approaches to Biblical and Secular Texts*, *Semeia* 31 (1985); Edgar V. McKnight, ed., *Reader Perspectives on the New Testament*, *Semeia* 48 (1989).

21. Robert Morgan with John Barton, *Biblical Interpretation* (Oxford: Oxford University Press, 1988).

22. The literary critics Richard G. Moulton and Northrop Frye have given attention to the literary unity of the Bible. Both note the narrative unity. There is a beginning and an end, with movement involving not only narrative but also a variety of other literary forms. Both Moulton and Frye emphasize the Apocalypse and the final conception of "the kingdom of the world" becoming "the kingdom of our Lord and of his Christ" (Rev. 11:15). The kerygmatic nature of the Bible as a whole is emphasized by both writers, with Frye actually using the term. See Moulton, *Modern Reader's Bible* (Macmillan, 1926), viii; see also *The Literary Study of the Bible: An Account of the Leading Forms of Literature Represented in the Sacred Writings* (Boston: D. C. Heath, 1899) and Frye, *The Great Code: The Bible and Literature* (New York: Harcourt Brace Jovanovich, 1982), 29–30, 224–25.

23. Because of this the "reader" at times seems to be the reader intended by the author or even all properly prepared readers. By "reader" in this section, however, I am referring to myself. To be sure, I hope that readers of this book will be able to make sense of my reading, but I am not attempting to establish this as the only reading. I construe meanings in light of my own experiences, knowledge, and information, and other readers must do the same.

24. The reader's earlier view of the practice of fishing creates a problem. Is the reader's view of the practice of fishing in error? Could the fishermen in one boat be expected to manipulate the seine, especially with a large catch? What does Jesus have in mind? Why did Simon do what Jesus commanded when one boat with its fishermen constituted only one half of the total resources needed for successfully landing a large catch? Was Jesus intending a situation in which more help would be needed? Was Simon simply pacifying Jesus, entertaining little or no expectation of a catch of fish? A purely private reading may benefit from such speculation, but this reader is not prepared to integrate such speculation into a comprehensive reading.

25. Intentionality from a literary perspective differs from intentionality from a historical perspective. E. D. Hirsch Jr. speaks of intentionality in terms of the "consciously willed type," and it is this that defines verbal meaning (*Validity in Interpretation* [New Haven, Conn.: Yale University Press, 1967], 53–54). In *The Aims of Interpretation* Hirsch

indicates a relationship between the reader and the "type": "That which we are understanding is itself an hypothesis constructed by ourselves, a schema, or genre, or type which provokes expectations that are confirmed by our linguistic experience, or when they are not confirmed cause us to adjust our hypothesis or schema" (*The Aims of Interpretation* [Chicago: University of Chicago Press, 1976], 33–34).

26. Ben F. Meyer, "The Challenges of Text and Reader to the Historical-Critical Method," *The Bible and Its Readers*, ed. Wim Beuken, Sean Freyne, and Anton Weiler (Valley Forge, Pa.: Trinity Press International, 1991), 10.

For Further Reading

Reader-Response Criticism in General

Eco, Umberto. *The Role of the Reader: Explorations in the Semiotics of Texts.* Bloomington, Ind.: Indiana University Press, 1979. The first chapter discusses the basic structure of the process of text interpretation in general.

Fish, Stanley E. *Is There a Text in This Class? The Authority of Interpretative Communities.* Cambridge: Harvard University Press, 1980. Collects Fish's major essays of 1970–1980 with a general introduction, a series of headnotes, and four previously unpublished essays.

Iser, Wolfgang. *The Act of Reading: A Theory of Aesthetic Response.* Baltimore: Johns Hopkins University Press, 1978. Exemplary of Iser's practice of close reading in a phenomenological mode.

Suleiman, Susan, and Inge Crosman, eds. *The Reader in the Text: Essays on Audience and Interpretation.* Princeton, N.J.: Princeton University Press, 1980. Contains sixteen original articles. In her introduction, Suleiman surveys six approaches to "audience-oriented criticism": rhetorical, structuralist-semiotic, phenomenological, psychoanalytic, sociological-historical, and hermeneutical. She (unlike Tompkins) treats European critics who were important in the development of reader-oriented theory and practice.

Tompkins, Jane P., ed. *Reader-Response Criticism: From Formalism to Post-Structuralism.* Baltimore: Johns Hopkins University Press, 1980. Contains eleven key texts signifying the culmination of the move from text-centered to reader-oriented criticism in literary study in American universities. Also contains an introduction and conclusion by Tompkins herself.

Reader-Response Criticism in Biblical Studies

Brown, Schuyler. "Reader Response: Demythologizing the Text." *New Testament Studies* 34 (1988): 232–37.

Detweiler, Robert, ed. *Reader Response Approaches to Biblical and Secular Texts. Semeia* 31 (1985). Offers a theoretical orientation and examples of reader-response criticism, illustrating that reader-response criticism is an aggregate of approaches that interact with one another.

Fowler, Robert M. *Let the Reader Understand: Reader-Response Criticism and the Gospel of Mark*. Minneapolis: Fortress, 1991. A synthesis of over a decade of work directed toward the actual experience of reading.

McKnight, Edgar V. *Postmodern Use of the Bible: The Emergence of Reader-Oriented Criticism*. Nashville: Abingdon, 1988.

McKnight, Edgar V., ed. *Reader Perspectives on the New Testament*. *Semeia* 48 (1989). Contains essays growing out of the work of a seminar of the Society of New Testament Studies inaugurated in 1984 to deal with the theme of "The Role of the Reader in the Interpretation of the New Testament."

Moore, Stephen D. *Literary Criticism and the Gospels: The Theoretical Challenge*. New Haven, Conn.: Yale University Press, 1989. Surveys the field of biblical literary scholarship with particular attention to narrative criticism and reading of the Gospels.

Van Iersel, B. *Reading Mark*. Edinburgh: T. & T. Clark, 1989. A commentary on Mark that gives particular attention to the insights of structural linguistics, especially to the nature of narrative structures and the way they function in communication.

12

POSTSTRUCTURALIST CRITICISM

WILLIAM A. BEARDSLEE

I

Poststructuralist criticism includes several ways of reading a text. We concentrate here on deconstructive criticism or deconstruction, since other poststructuralist methods appear elsewhere in this book. Deconstructive criticism is a way of reading that involves both discovering the incompleteness of the text and finding a fresh, if transient, insight made possible by the "free play" or indeterminacy of the text. These formal moves are not arbitrarily chosen as simply one possible form of criticism; they are dictated by the sense that "not only is 'Truth' fatally embroiled with power; it is inseparable from and dependent on historical change."[1] Deconstruction is distinguished from other sorts of poststructuralist criticism by its focus on the dismantling of existing patterns. Other poststructuralist approaches such as much feminist and Third World criticism, in contrast to deconstruction, offer a positive program to counter the structures they criticize.

The first move of deconstructive criticism, the strategy of uncovering the inconsistencies or gaps in the vision or argument of a text, has quite understandably been the focus of most of the attention in the attempt to evaluate its contribution. Deconstructive criticism insists that if we are to read any text fruitfully, we need to be aware of several aspects of language: its incompleteness, that is, the way in which the hearer or reader has to fill in the picture that is suggested by speech or writing; its enclosure within itself, that is, the way in which the immediate connection of words is not with "reality," but with other words in a pattern that gives them meaning; and the unfixed, flowing quality of language, that is, the way in which meanings are continually being enlarged or shifted as a reader moves through a text. Hence the emphasis on "deconstruction," which is the most characteristic form of poststructuralist criticism, with its disassembling of the structure of language, even language that seems to convey a clear and unequivocal meaning.

But the deeper importance of this kind of reading is in its second move, which affirms that significant reading is not "reproduction," not reactualizing of a meaning that was once expressed by the author of the text or that is resident in the pattern of the text. Rather it is reading that challenges the reader, throws open the reader's world to creative discovery, to new associations that may be suggested as much by irrational or chance associations as by the logical relations so carefully studied, for instance, by the structuralists. A central example of this kind of reading is discovery through the pun, or paronomasia, which juxtaposes two elements of language that have no logical relation, and not necessarily any emotive relation either, but are brought close simply by similarity of sound. Thus Jacques Derrida plays with the similarity between "Hegel" and "eagle" (even closer in French, *aigle*),[2] and we might play with the pun between "here" and "hear" to shock the reader into awareness of the ambiguity of "presence," that is, present meaning in spoken language. But the emphasis on "play," so well illustrated by the pun, should not distract attention from the function of this kind of poststructuralist interpretation: to deliver the interpreter from the repression of limits and traditions so that fresh interpretation may take place.

Poststructuralist criticism and its specific and most rigorous form, deconstruction, are at home in the culture of Western Europe. Kant and Hegel provide the remoter background—Kant with his argument that we cannot know the "thing in itself," since the forms of our knowing are so deeply shaped by the processes of thought themselves, and Hegel, with his conception of spirit as unfolding in the history of the human mind. But there is a long path from Kant and Hegel to deconstruction. Deconstruction represents one of the various currents of thought that have eroded what Kant and Hegel, after their critical work, believed they could still affirm as the bases on which culture and society were founded. Gone now are Kant's conviction that a sense of obligation is a universal component of human existence and Hegel's view that the history of the unfolding of Spirit is marked by a teleology, a purposive direction. Both of these fundamental convictions, which guided so much nineteenth-century European thought, have been abandoned by much late twentieth-century European culture, and this abandonment marks deconstructive criticism's approach to language and texts. This sort of critique of the bases for stability in culture was first sharply formulated by Friedrich Nietzsche. Marx and Freud in their different ways were also important forerunners of deconstruction, for they showed that the deceptively consistent surface-level logic of discourse actually functioned to express power relations at the economic (Marx) or psychological (Freud) level.

Martin Heidegger, with his critique of Western metaphysics, is another important forerunner of deconstruction. But Heidegger, for all his criticism of metaphysics, was reaching for an ontology, a statement about "Being." Deconstruction recognizes that we are perpetually entwined in the quest for an order that stands behind our language and experience but holds that no "closure," no final, and indeed, no real result is possible in this quest. Rather we work with "traces," marks left by earlier quests, none of which can lead us out of our imprisonment in language and the worlds that language creates, to any higher or transcendent vision.

Existentialism, well-known in biblical studies especially through the work of Rudolf Bultmann, provides an important background for poststructuralism and deconstruction, since existentialism abandoned the belief that there is an ordering in the world. But existentialism retained a vision of a centered self, a self that was still very Kantian in its sense of obligation. In the face of the destructive social forces of our century, the existentialists were able to affirm the "centered" self, which they drew from a long Western tradition, by seeing the self as isolated, as creating its own meaning and world. In poststructuralism in general and specifically in deconstruction, the centered self is replaced by a self that is a node in a network of relations. At times, in this perspective, the relatedness of the self tends to erode the sense of responsibility.

Structuralism is also deeply important for understanding deconstruction. Structuralism is a turn away from the referential or descriptive view of language to a picture of language as a system of relations, so that each part is defined by its role in the linguistic network; this role is also taken up by deconstructive poststructuralism. Structuralism and poststructuralism are both, in different ways, suspicious of the seemingly clear surface meaning of a text. The difference is that most structuralism looks for a determinate deeper structure in the linguistic network, while deconstructive poststructuralism emphasizes the openness, the play, of the network of relations, the imperfections in the text that disallow any thoroughly consistent patterns, with the aim of freeing the reader or hearer to make her or his own creative discovery of transient meaning.

Michel Foucault and Jacques Derrida are the two figures particularly associated with deconstructive poststructuralist criticism. Foucault's emphasis on the ways in which texts express power relations is taken up in much poststructuralist criticism.[3] But the figure usually in mind when one speaks of deconstruction is Jacques Derrida. To introduce this difficult thinker, we will cite from an excellent introduction to his thought:

> If in this process of deciphering a text in the traditional way we come across a word that seems to harbor an unresolvable contradiction, and by virtue of being one word is made sometimes to work in one way and sometimes in another and thus is made to point away from the

absence of a unified meaning, we shall catch at [attentively seek out
the nuances and connections of] that word. If a metaphor seems to
suppress its implications, we shall catch at that metaphor. We shall
follow its adventures through the text and see the text coming undone
as a structure of concealment, revealing its self-transgression, its
undecidability. It must be emphasized that I am not speaking simply of
locating a moment of ambiguity or irony ultimately incorporated into
the text's system of unified meaning but rather a moment that gen-
uinely threatens to collapse the system.[4]

Often deconstructive writing uses a formidable special vocabulary in the
attempt to stimulate us to think differently. Some key terms are *undecidability*, the openness of meaning that is often concealed by the seeming closure
of the text; *differance*, a revised spelling of "difference" (originally, of course,
in French), which indicates, in a form that appears only in writing, both
differing and deferring (meaning is found in difference, but it is never really
found, it is deferred; the quest is endless), and *deconstruction* (see below).
Another key term is *logocentrism*, which is criticized and dismissed as the
assumption that language communicates the presence of an order or logos
that is beyond language.

The often hidden assumption of a metaphysical consistency at least
partly expressed by language is abetted by the assumption that spoken language, with its seeming immediacy of "presence," the presence of the
speaker's meaning through the presence of the speaker, is the primary form
of language. On the contrary, according to deconstruction, *writing* is primary, since writing makes clear the impossibility of full presence in
communication, and also makes much more evident that all language is a
reworking of previous language, not a fresh and impartial presentation of a
translinguistic referent. Thus *intertextuality* is a fundamental feature of writing; any given "text" or structured communication either simply repeats or
else modifies (perhaps "deforms") earlier conventionally established patterns in forming its own structure. Deconstruction considers any form of
communication as a text, a configuration interwoven ("textured") with previous communications, in contrast to a book, which is thought of as a
coherent whole, an organized statement in which the parts support one
another because they are all supported by a coherent system that comes to
a conclusion, a closure. And contrary to what has often been assumed,
deconstruction asserts that there is no connected pattern in the historical
shifts of meaning that intertextuality produces.

Deconstruction, the commonest term in this vocabulary, means dismantling the seeming coherence of the text and reading it in a way that resists
"closure." In contrast to most earlier forms of interpretation, including

structuralism, poststructuralist reading looks for the "gaps," the incoherences, the points where aspects of the text pass by one another, in order to show that the text does not communicate a definitive or closed meaning.

Deconstructive criticism does not speak much about ethics; traditional ethics is seen as narrow and repressive. But this kind of criticism is no detached intellectual exercise. It has strong ethical implications. The reaction against traditional ethics of obligation is grounded in the assumption that rule-making is a form of violence or coercion. The emphasis on undecidability, on the plural meaning of texts, is intended to challenge reigning orthodoxies and dominant social groups. Deconstruction is an attack upon the social and institutional powers that justify their power and authority by appeal precisely to a structured world in which they hold a recognized and often dominating place. From this point of view the various forms of Marxist critique of culture form an important background to and preliminary form of deconstruction, by virtue of their pointing to the ideological functions of theoretical systems and of religion. The difference between the various Marxist critiques and deconstruction is that classical Marxism, at least, offered a "true" vision to supplant the false and power-driven ideological visions it criticized. (The "true" vision was qualified in some forms of later Marxist thought.) Deconstruction, on the other hand, offers no such resolution. Each dismantling of a cultural or religious expression can be a valid critique of social power, but it cannot provide a clear-cut alternative. Its function is rather to lead readers to live without absolutes, in a world of process that is not directed to a goal.

Thus poststructuralism identifies with the "marginal." At times there may be a romantic glorification of the martyr position of the marginally situated critic. And the resistance to choice, the emphasis on keeping one's options open, is difficult to maintain indefinitely. Yet this resistance has to be recognized as itself an ethical claim, a protest against the power of established interpretations.[5]

Deconstruction is highly critical of traditional religion and theology, which are seen as falsely believing in the "presence" of a transcendent reality. Though the approach can well be combined with a variety of religious and theological positions (and thereby relativized), its affinities are with "negative theology."[6]

II

A major way in which New Testament scholarship was prepared for deconstructive criticism was the fresh approach to the parables of Jesus that is especially associated with the names of Robert W. Funk and John Dominic Crossan. Traditionally, parables have been read as reinforcing some aspect of the overall Christian story, but Funk and Crossan reread key parables to show that they are better understood as challenging or subverting the world of the hearer (including the way in which that world is shaped by the tradition of faith). Funk emphasized the element of risk in listening to a parable; one has to let go of the structured world that one brings to hearing it.[7] Crossan contrasted organizing stories with disorganizing stories; the parable is the classic type of the latter. It shatters the hearer's world. As Crossan put it, parabolic religion (he could have said, "parabolic language") "continually and deliberately subverts the final words about 'reality' and thereby introduces the possibility of transcendence."[8] Others, including the present writer, have seen a similar function in some of the proverbial sayings in the Gospels.[9]

These interpreters looked within the text for moves toward dismantling the reader's world, and thus they anticipated deconstructive criticism. They were not agreed about the key point of whether the parables or proverbs of the Gospels also implied the possibility of rebuilding a vision of the whole after it had been jolted by the saying's immediate impact. Crossan was closest to deconstructive interpretation with his recognition that the force of parabolic language ran counter to the force of what he called "mythic" language that structured the world of the hearer—"myth" (including Gospel narrative) establishes world, while "parable" subverts world.[10]

From this example, it is clear that one may approach a text in a deconstructive way with an eye to finding how aspects of the text that are "intended" by the text work against one another—in the illustration of the parable, how the organizing narrative of a Gospel is countered by the shattering of world by a parable. Equally characteristic of such criticism is the effort to work with oppositions in the text that are not "intended" by the text or the author, as in Derrida's breaking traditional connections and making unexpected new ones through the use of the pun, as noted above.

A direct encounter between biblical studies and deconstruction is a mark of contemporary New Testament studies. We need cite only one work: Stephen D. Moore's *Literary Criticism and the Gospels: The Theoretical Challenge*.[11] Moore carefully analyzes narrative criticism, which is perhaps the most widely used form of literary criticism in biblical studies, looking especially at those forms of narrative criticism that deal with the response of the reader. One of his techniques is to show how varied and even contradictory are the results that different scholars achieve by using the same or very similar methods. His conclusion is that the texts do not sufficiently determine the interpretation for traditional narrative criticism to be successful. Moore offers a challenge to those forms of literary criticism that look for coherent meanings in a text by showing that in order to achieve such an interpretation one has to find a privileged position "above" the text or above the world created by the text. Poststructuralism or deconstructive criticism is the rejection of the attempt to find such a position. Since the reader or critic has no such superior position, the results of criticism are necessarily part of the flux.[12] Moore gives an example of a deconstructive reading of a symbol in the Gospel of John, but he also discusses at length the narrative criticism of Luke.

Luke-Acts, or, for that matter, despite their interrelationships, either Luke or Acts taken separately, is very much a rounded whole, a "book," in the language of deconstruction. So we have a text that cries out for deconstruction. We should remember that a kind of dismantling of the internal order of biblical books has been practiced for a long time, namely, historical source criticism. In method and perspective coming from an immensely different world from that of deconstruction, this more traditional criticism nonetheless has a similar effect on a text: breaking up its seeming unity. The very important difference is that traditional source criticism, though often finding a complete work to be a patchwork of points of view, nonetheless assumes that the scholar could work from a coherent point of view, "above" the text, so to speak.[13]

Our deconstructive reading will focus on the first of Luke's beatitudes: "Blessed [perhaps better, 'Happy'] are you who are poor, for yours is the kingdom of God" (Luke 6:20).

The first beatitude is a powerful focal statement of what in Luke-Acts is at the heart of the "new" that Jesus brings—a "new" that remains active in the new community of the church. Jesus' inclusion of outsiders, outcasts, or marginal people among those whom he draws into community with himself is a central thread of Luke-Acts. Correspondingly, Jesus challenges the rich, not only because of the danger of riches for the wealthy but also because of the need of the poor. The rich, it should be said, are not simply condemned but are sharply challenged (Luke 6:24; 12:13–21; 16:13; 18:18–25).[14]

This theme runs throughout Luke-Acts. From the Magnificat ("[God] has brought down the powerful from their thrones, and lifted up the lowly; [God] has filled the hungry with good things, and sent the rich away empty," Luke 1:52–53), into the central part of the Gospel, with the early scene of Jesus in the synagogue at Nazareth speaking of bringing "good news to the poor" (Luke 4:18), and with its many encounters of Jesus with the poor and marginal, and his sayings about them on into Acts, according to which in the Jerusalem community "no one claimed private ownership of any possessions, but everything they owned was held in common" (Acts 4:32), to Paul's last visit to Jerusalem, which included the purpose of "bringing alms to my nation" (Acts 24:17), the theme of openness to the "otherness" of the poor is a major theme of the two-volume work.

Robert Tannehill summarizes the position of Luke-Acts well:

We see, then, that Jesus preaches good news to the poor not only by announcing that they will share in God's reign and by healing the poor beggars but also by creating disciples who are pledged to share with the poor and by seeking to transform grasping rich people into persons who will give their wealth to the poor. Later the narrator will suggest that Jesus' call has the power to create a community that cares for the poor so that there are no longer needy persons among them (Acts 4:34). Jesus' mission to the poor, claimed by him in the Nazareth synagogue, becomes a major theme in the narrative of Jesus' words and deeds in Luke.[15]

Later, in commenting on Acts 4:34, Tannehill adds:

> The community of goods is mentioned only in connection with the early Jerusalem church. It is part of the narrator's picture of the ideal church at the beginning. Already at the time of writing there was probably a clear difference between this ideal picture and the actual practice of Christians. Nevertheless, this ideal is emphasized. We need not suppose that the narrator expected later churches to be transformed into the ideal community described. Such an expectation is not required for the ideal to be relevant. The ideal can function as a critique of a complacent church with narrow vision, content with its own obedience, and this constructive criticism may find a response among individuals, if not in a church as a whole. If Jesus' call and this ideal picture of the church lead some Christians with assets to recognize that they can and should give those assets to the poor, something important has happened. Such responses by individuals may not in themselves produce the ideal community of the narrator's vision, but they do recognize the needs of the poor as a moral claim, as did the early church, according to Acts.[16]

The immediate thrust of the text of Luke-Acts is to integrate the concern for the poor into the practice of the community. The global concern for "the poor" and the bold proclamation that they are "happy" because the kingdom of God is theirs, is structured into the practice of the church, and even there it becomes an ideal that, we may agree with Tannehill, was at best only very imperfectly practiced. The pressure of the saying, with its reversal of our ordinary standards, can be bent to fit the narrative pattern if one keeps in mind that for this text (1) there was a stronger presence of salvation during the time of Jesus than later and (2) a final eschatological resolution would bring about that aspect of God's will that is not realized in the present.

We do not have to ask any historical questions to become aware of the tension between the saying and its context. In our actual study of the

Gospels, we may indeed assume that the strong power of the beatitude represents the early stage, the time of Jesus, while the more calmly organized text of Luke reflects a later, more institutional time. But deconstructionist criticism brackets such questions and looks at the tensions in the text as it stands. It asks, Can the parabolic, reversing power of "Happy are you who are poor" be so smoothly integrated into the story of the church that Luke created? Can the hearers' identification with the poor, which the beatitude calls for, be so readily expressed in the limited action for the poor that Acts describes? In our discussion above we have emphasized the integration of the saying into the narrative pattern. But it resists integration! Tannehill recognizes that this is a saying of reversal,[17] but he correctly sees that the text intends to domesticate this reversal into the narrative. The narrative pattern does just what the saying resists. It organizes a structure into which life fits, in the sense that one can expect a meaningful result from one's acts. In this case the structure is one in which limited acts on behalf of a specific small segment of the poor are enough and are all that can be expected, and in which the poor tend to become the objects of generosity rather than being themselves subjects. This is true even though the church has many times brought people of differing social strata together effectively, so that marginal people could indeed become subjects. Of course, we suppose that an author ("Luke," whoever he was) drew the beatitude from tradition and worked to fit it into the overall story of the book. But deconstructive criticism as such is not concerned with the question of the author's intention, or with the historical question whether the beatitude represents Jesus better than the Lucan narrative does. We will have to add that the distinction between the text— the proper focus of deconstructive criticism—and the author and the author's world is harder to maintain than many deconstructive critics admit. When Derrida writes about Rousseau's work, a vivid Rousseau appears.

To return to the beatitude about the poor, the radical thrust of the saying has often been noted. For instance, James Dawsey comments about the Lucan Sermon on the Plain as a whole, that it has "much more the flavor of a statement about how God is reversing the order of society."[18] If we bracket out the eschatological framework of the saying, the statement is deeply disconcerting, since it seems to be out of touch with reality as we know it. And how can we not bracket out or at least transform the eschatology that the saying presupposes, since the poverty of the poor, after so many centuries, is still so unbearable? Deconstructive criticism starts with the present reader, not with an attempt to reconstruct a historical picture of an "original meaning."

What happens when we listen seriously to the statement "Happy are you who are poor" is exactly the opposite of finding a place for the poor in a structured society. The structure is broken; the line between the hearer and the poor is erased; we find ourselves open to, at times perhaps even identified with, the subjects of the saying. A vivid, shattering awareness of the possibility that there, among the poor, is the place of happiness or blessedness does not produce a plan of action (not even giving away all that one possesses, to say nothing of a plan for restructuring the means of production or the rules of property ownership). It does break the established lines of relatedness by opening up a new and hitherto unrecognized relatedness to the poor. It challenges the structure of power that establishes a place for the poor. Such a listening is a deconstruction of the way in which the text integrates the saying into its overall narrative pattern, a pattern admirably interpreted by Tannehill in the quotations that we have cited above and in his chapter, "Jesus' Ministry to the Oppressed and Excluded."[19]

The broken structure and our exposure to identification with the poor are not timeless insights. They are the fragile opening to a glimpse, or to use a favorite deconstructive word, a "trace" of that which we cannot grasp. The encounter leaves us shaken, but we will have to turn elsewhere if we are to do precisely what deconstruction is so loath to do, namely, find a new pattern in which to act in order to try to do something purposeful as a response to the glimpse.

III

Since Jacques Derrida, the leading thinker of deconstruction, has insisted that he does not present a method and that he does not want people simply to copy what he is doing, it would be mechanical to set out rules for developing a deconstructive way of reading. What is required is a way of listening. If the perspective sketched at the beginning of this chapter makes sense, one can listen to texts from that perspective. We do not have to accept the total historical relativity of truth, or hold that its involvement with power deprives truth of any assertiveness, to find that there is a large persuasive element in the convictions that are the presuppositions of deconstructive criticism. We do not have simply to jettison the coherent readings of a text, such as Tannehill so ably works out in the case of Luke-Acts. What we do have to do to read deconstructively is to set beside a traditional way of reading a radical questioning of the pattern into which the text seems to fit.

One could test one's reading with another important theme in Luke-Acts: the text's view of the Jewish people. As Luke-Acts presents the matter, is it too late for the Jewish people? Are they included in the ongoing work of God, or has their time passed?

Fortunately for the student, a very useful volume of essays on this question is available: *Luke-Acts and the Jewish People,* edited by Joseph B. Tyson.[20] A student could review Luke-Acts with an eye to how it deals with the relation between Jesus and the emerging church on the one hand, and the Jewish people on the other. Then one would sample the essays in Tyson's book, for instance contrasting Jack T. Sanders's contention that the Jewish people are consistently rejected with Robert C. Tannehill's view that salvation is still open to them.[21] (But the whole volume is well worth attention.) Then one would confront the question, Does the text succeed in being consistent on this point? If not, can the contradiction be dealt with under a mediating heading like irony, in which two points of view are held in tension, or is a more radical deconstruction appropriate, which would show that the approach of Luke-Acts on this point is incoherent and unsatisfactory?

IV

Poststructuralism in general is a way of recognizing that our visions of reality are historically situated and that the exercise of power plays a large, though often unnoticed, role in shaping what we think of as truth. Deconstruction is a particularly rigorous form of poststructuralism because taken by itself it does not offer any alternative structure to the pattern it deconstructs, other than a transient flash of new insight. The thrust of deconstruction is critical, disclosing the incoherences and the implications of domination in accepted patterns and thus depriving them of their power.

The discussion above has shown that deconstruction has a very important role to play in biblical studies. Many biblical books and many, if not most, modern readers and scholars tend to accept uncritically the move of organizing the world, and to a degree at least, also God, into an at least partly comprehensible pattern, an ordered whole. Most commonly, in the Bible, the world is "organized" by telling a story in which the community and the believer can find a place. All of the Gospels serve this function in different ways. For instance, Matthew's emphasis on the believer's place in the church and John's exploration of what it means to believe in a hostile world are what is here termed organizing the world. Yet the deconstructive move is also found in biblical texts, as our references to the parables and to Luke's first beatitude have shown. Deconstruction shows how broken and imperfect the organizing patterns are, as in the example chosen above of the poor. In this function it is related to a major thrust of prophetic faith. But taken by itself, deconstruction does not effectively move toward the kind of "application" that has long been recognized as an important part of interpretation. This is equally true whether one focuses on the sheer deconstructive act or whether, as in the example of the first Lucan beatitude worked out above, the emphasis shifts to the rhetoric of discovery, the shock of the unexpected.

Thus deconstruction does not have the self-sufficient adequacy as a critical method that is often claimed for it. Or rather, it can be taken as adequate only if one agrees that human existence and the world as a whole are as directionless as the wandering or "erring" that is sometimes presented as the sober postmodern alternative to the dominating purposiveness of the modern world.[22] That this is not the whole story is shown by the way in which the shock of insight often requires a subsequent move to act, a move that in turn needs a framework, if not an absolute one. A recognition of this is part of the reason that college and university departments of literature and philosophy are moving away from deconstruction toward neopragmatism. We cannot here discuss neopragmatism. Like deconstruction it is thoroughly relativistic, but it makes a place for purposive action.

One way of using deconstruction would be to deconstruct the "public" or "natural" patterns of religion and society and then affirm a "confessional" or revealed pattern that, it would be claimed, was self-authenticating and did not need to be subjected to deconstruction. We may expect to see this route followed, but it is ultimately unsatisfactory, since it leaves the competing confessional perspectives with no way of communicating with one another. No perspective is exempt from deconstruction. But that does not undermine the strength of religious faith or of religious communities; it requires that they see that they, too, are part of the process.

If deconstruction is taken to be an academic method, unfriendly to the life of religious communities, its prophetic potential may easily be lost. Serious interpretation of biblical texts must engage both the religious and the academic communities. The illustration of "the poor" shows how the method of deconstruction can be relevant to both. Academic reflection about how language "works" (such as we have suggested above, showing how the beatitude about the poor is in conflict with the setting in which it is found) can lead the reader beyond academic circles to an actual engagement with the poor such as religious communities often speak for. Also, from the other side, as base communities in Latin America have found, the intuitive insights of religious communities, as their members reflect about them, call for a dialogue with the work of biblical scholars; in this case, the kind of study of the first Lucan beatitude that we have explored here can lead a religious community to see that the ways in which we fit "the poor" into our institutional structures is not enough. But as noted above, the disassembling of a structure, in this case a way of fitting the poor into the picture, is a prelude to a fresh engagement with all the ways in which the reader deals with this issue. Deconstruction calls for a reengagement in a more inclusive frame. That requires a search for a new structure and work to make it actual. The reluctance of some deconstructionist thinkers to deal with this stage can be understood as a reaction against the "totalizing" nature of so many "solutions."[23]

Thus the presuppositions of deconstruction are not to be accepted uncritically.[24] We can indeed accept its "nonfoundationalism," that is, the claim that we do not have a clear and certain way of knowing by which we can build up our knowledge and our values. But that does not mean that our language is as fully out of touch with the larger reality within which we live and speak, or as fluid and bereft of any determinate meaning, as deconstructionists have claimed.

For one thing, despite their indeterminacy, which deconstruction has emphasized, texts nonetheless do set limits to interpretation. The very form and language of a lament, for instance, prevents its being taken as a joyful lyric. Here the structuralists, who strive to be more rigorous in establishing an ancient and widely held insight, are right. The structures in a text may indeed be in conflict, but this is not always a destructive conflict. The interplay of structures may keep conflict within such limits that it does not become destructive, or it may also release new creative insight.[25] For example, the central illustration on which this chapter focuses, the conflict between the "Lucan" structure that incorporates the poor into a pattern of institutional life and the disruptive structure of the first beatitude, is at the heart of the creative life of the Christian community. No final resolution of this conflict is possible, yet it has repeatedly released new energies and new activities in the life of the church.

More than that, the reach of language beyond its own network—the referential dimension of language—is not as formless as it is often pictured. Our commonsense intuition that language is "about" something, something that is at least partially given, has not been canceled by deconstruction. On the contrary, starting in the midst and without any fixed foundational method of knowing, we nevertheless can know something about reality, including values and the reality with which religious language deals. What deconstruction does is to remind us of the limitations of any particular perspective. That recognition can open the way to a reengagement with the quest to know, in a more inclusive frame.[26]

Thus this writer sees promise for deconstruction as it is used as one tool and not the sole way of reading. A good example would be David Jobling's combination of deconstruction with liberation theology; Jobling also indicates how deconstruction and feminist theology work together.[27] The present author has practiced a kind of deconstruction while reframing a patterned way of viewing the scripture made possible in part by process theology.[28] An evaluation of deconstructive reading that is more positive about making it the central focus can be found in Stephen D. Moore's *Literary Criticism and the Gospels*.[29]

Notes

1. Helen Vendler, commenting on the postmodern vision of the poet Frank Bidart in the *New Yorker,* June 10, 1991.

2. Jacques Derrida, *Glas,* 7, cited in Gayatri Chakravarti Spivak, "Translator's Preface," in Jacques Derrida, *Of Grammatology* (Baltimore: Johns Hopkins University Press, 1974), lxxxiv.

3. See, for instance, Michel Foucault, *Power/Knowledge: Selected Interviews and Other Writings, 1972–1977* (New York: Pantheon, 1980).

4. Spivak, "Translator's Preface," in Derrida, *Of Grammatology,* lxxv.

5. On ethics in poststructuralist criticism, see especially Tobin Seebers, *The Ethics of Criticism* (Ithaca, N.Y.: Cornell University Press, 1988).

6. See John Dominic Crossan, "Difference and Divinity," *Semeia* 23 (1982): 29–40.

7. Robert W. Funk, "The Good Samaritan as Metaphor," *Semeia* 2 (1974): 76. See also Robert W. Funk, *Language, Hermeneutic, and Word of God* (New York: Harper & Row, 1966), 124–222; and *Parables and Presence* (Philadelphia: Fortress, 1982).

8. John Dominic Crossan, *The Dark Interval: Towards a Theology of Story* (Allen, Tex.: Argus Communications, 1975), 128.

9. William A. Beardslee, "Uses of the Proverb in the Synoptic Gospels," *Interpretation* 24 (1970): 61–71, reprinted in Beardslee, *Margins of Belonging: Essays on the New Testament and Theology* (Atlanta: Scholars, 1991), 13–24.

10. Crossan, *Dark Interval,* 57–62, referring to the work of Sheldon Sacks.

11. Stephen D. Moore, *Literary Criticism and the Gospels: The Theoretical Challenge* (New Haven, Conn.: Yale University Press, 1989).

12. Ibid., 174–75.

13. See the comments of Moore, *Literary Criticism and the Gospels,* 165.

14. Robert C. Tannehill, *The Narrative Unity of Luke-Acts* (Philadelphia: Fortress, 1986–1990), 1:129.

15. Ibid.

16. Ibid., 2:46.

17. Ibid., 1:109–10.

18. James M. Dawsey, *The Lucan Voice: Confusion and Irony in the Gospel of Luke* (Macon, Ga.: Mercer University Press, 1986), 146.

19. Tannehill, *Narrative Unity of Luke-Acts,* vol. 1, 101–39.

20. Joseph B. Tyson, ed., *Luke-Acts and the Jewish People* (Minneapolis: Augsburg, 1988).

21. Jack T. Sanders, "The Jewish People in Luke-Acts," in Tyson, *Luke-Acts and the Jewish People,* 51–75; Robert C. Tannehill, "Rejection by Jews and Turning to Gentiles: The Pattern of Paul's Mission in Acts," in Tyson, *Luke-Acts and the Jewish People,* 83–101.

22. As by Mark C. Taylor, *Erring: A Postmodern A/theology* (Chicago: University of Chicago Press, 1984).

23. For a startlingly fresh approach to our economic structures, see Herman E. Daly and John B. Cobb Jr., *For the Common Good: Redirecting the Economy toward Community, the Environment, and a Sustainable Future* (Boston: Beacon, 1989). For many, a shock of "deconstruction" of our present system will be needed before they can confront the new possibilities that Daly and Cobb offer.

24. See, from a somewhat different point of view, the similar point of Wesley C. Kort,

"'Religion and Literature' in Postmodern Contexts," *Journal of the American Academy of Religion* 53 (1990): 575–88.

25. See the article by Daniel Patte in this volume and Henrikus Boers, *Neither on This Mountain nor in Jerusalem: A Study of John 4* (Atlanta: Scholars, 1988).

26. See the important but difficult book of Robert C. Neville, *Recovery of the Measure: Interpretation and Nature* (Albany, N.Y.: State University of New York, 1989); for an introduction to this topic, see my review of Neville in *Process Studies* 19 (1990): 138–40.

27. David Jobling, "Writing the Wrongs of the World: The Deconstruction of the Biblical Text in the Context of Liberation Theologies," *Semeia* 51 (1990): 81–118.

28. William A. Beardslee, "Vital Ruins: Biblical Narrative and the Story Frameworks of Our Lives," *Southern Humanities Review* 24 (1990): 101–16, reprinted in Beardslee, *Margins of Belonging*, 219–36.

29. Moore, *Literary Criticism of the Gospels*, 171–78.

For Further Reading

Derrida, Jacques. *Of Grammatology*. Trans. Gayatri Chakravarti Spivak. Baltimore: Johns Hopkins University Press, 1974. An important work, translated with a long and perceptive introduction by Spivak.

Detweiler, Robert, ed. *Derrida and Biblical Studies*. *Semeia* 23 (1982). Essays in the interpretation of biblical texts by reading them "as systems of difference rather than privileged channels of an extra-textual transcendent" (p. 1).

Moore, Stephen D. *Literary Criticism of the Gospels: The Theoretical Challenge*. New Haven, Conn.: Yale University Press, 1989. Moore's survey of literary criticism moves toward showing the limits of coherence in New Testament texts and concludes with a presentation of deconstruction.

Phillips, Gary A., ed. *Poststructuralist Criticism and the Bible: Text/History/ Discourse*. *Semeia* 51 (1990). A variety of poststructuralist approaches, "concerned with institutional control and power" (p. 2).

Taylor, Mark C. *Erring: A Postmodern A/theology*. Chicago: University of Chicago Press, 1984. A major work of theological deconstruction.

Ulmer, Gregory. *Applied Grammatology: Post(e), Pedagogy from Jacques Derrida to Joseph Beuys*. Baltimore: Johns Hopkins University Press, 1985. Ulmer moves poststructuralism to a focus on the rhetoric of discovery, contrasting linear thought to discovery quickened by unexpected juxtapositions.

13

READING THE BIBLE IDEOLOGICALLY: FEMINIST CRITICISM

DANNA NOLAN FEWELL

I MYSELF HAVE NEVER BEEN ABLE TO FIND OUT PRECISELY
WHAT FEMINISM IS. I ONLY KNOW THAT PEOPLE CALL ME A
FEMINIST WHENEVER I EXPRESS SENTIMENTS THAT DIFFERENTIATE
ME FROM A DOORMAT OR A PROSTITUTE. —REBECCA WEST[1]

INDEED, IF I WERE TO TRY TO ARTICULATE VERY SUCCINCTLY
WHAT FEMINIST CRITICISM, AS A WAY OF THINKING ABOUT
LITERARY TEXTS, WANTS PHILOSOPHICALLY, I WOULD SAY THAT
AT ITS MOST AMBITIOUS IT WANTS TO DECODE AND DEMYSTIFY
ALL THE DISGUISED QUESTIONS AND ANSWERS THAT HAVE ALWAYS
SHADOWED THE CONNECTIONS BETWEEN TEXTUALITY AND
SEXUALITY, GENRE AND GENDER, PSYCHOSEXUAL IDENTITY
AND CULTURAL AUTHORITY. —SANDRA M. GILBERT[2]

IT WAS AS HER LIFE WAS DEPARTING—FOR SHE WAS DYING—
SHE CALLED HIS NAME SON OF MY SORROW. BUT HIS FATHER
CALLED HIM SON OF THE SOUTH. —GENESIS 35:18[3]

STEIN SAYS WE NO LONGER HAVE THE WORDS PEOPLE
USED TO HAVE SO WE HAVE TO MAKE THEM NEW IN SOME
WAY BUT WOMEN HAVEN'T HAD THEM AT ALL AND HOW CAN
YOU DECONSTRUCT A LANGUAGE YOU NEVER CONSTRUCTED
OR IT WAS NEVER CONSTRUCTED BY OTHERS LIKE YOU,
OR WITH YOU IN MIND? —FRANCES JAFFER[4]

B ecause feminist theory insists that singular definitions are misleading and limiting, I confess to a certain amount of confusion about
how to explain what feminist criticism is. Basically feminist criticism concentrates on the political, social, and economic rights of women.

Beyond that description I dare not venture to speak for all. Instead I begin with the above quotations to make several interrelated observations about feminist criticism.

First, feminism as an ideology is difficult to date since women's historical records tend to be in short supply. As a critical discipline, however, feminism came into its own with the rise of the women's movement in the 1960s. It is a secular discipline, unapologetically political, that is gradually infiltrating all areas of the humanities and the sciences.

Like all new critical approaches, feminist criticism is born of a dissatisfaction with other means of inquiry and, like most new critical approaches, it has been greeted with skepticism and, in some quarters, even condescension. Feminist criticism, however, has met with more hostility than most, probably because it questions the very presuppositions of the Western scholarly tradition, a tradition that has been, until quite recently, exclusively male-oriented in posture. Like other ideological criticisms (Marxist or African-American criticisms, for example) and unlike traditional forms of analysis, feminist criticism makes no pretense to objectivity; it challenges the notion of universals; it is more interested in relevance than in so-called absolute truth. In short, it resists the categories and definitions that male scholars and artists have set forth, in particular their definitions of women. When women speak "uncategorically," when they, as West so adroitly puts it, fail to fit the mold of doormat or prostitute, many men become uncomfortable, partly because such resistance to categorization signifies a deficit in the male reservoir of knowledge (in other words, the world is not as men have pictured and depicted it) and partly because the issue of gender difference is as personal as it is academic.

Second, feminist critics work in a number of fields and use an assortment of methods to pursue their subjects. Their specific goals, their self-identities, are as varied as the critics themselves. Diversity is considered to be a major strength of the movement. If there is, however, any one thing that most feminist critics are likely to agree on, it is that texts of all kinds, whether creative or critical, are gendered. It has commonly been thought that women's writings are clearly feminized while men's writings are neutral. Feminist critics would claim rather that all of Western culture's classics—the literature, the histories, the paradigmatic philosophical, psychological, and sociological theories—reflect and promote a gendered perspective. There is no universal norm from which women writers deviate. The writings of men are just as masculinized as those of women are feminized.

Gender, however, is more than simply a matter of sexual difference. Gender is a matter of power. There are few, if any, cultures today where men and women are equal. Men have power over women socially, politically, and economically. Race and class further complicate the hierarchy of dominance. Such hierarchy is inscribed in our classic texts, presupposed as if it were natural law rather than cultural construct. One of the tasks of feminist criticism is to expose the culturally based presuppositions embodied in classic discourse.

Third, throughout the course of history, women have rarely been allowed to name their experiences. Just as Rachel's child and Rachel's ordeal are renamed by her husband, so women's experiences have countless times been inscribed or reinscribed by men. Women's sufferings, joys, and concerns have been "written over," altered, and even negated in subservience to what has been of significance to men. What has the world looked like to women? How have women felt about their assigned roles in society? How have women perceived men? How have they viewed one another? The history, the perceptions, the wisdom of half the human race have been lost. Another of feminism's critical tasks is to recover and to reclaim these lost lives and voices and values.

Fourth, while the task of reclaiming often involves rediscovering women's texts and encouraging women to experiment with and to produce new texts, more often the task and its results in the historical disciplines are less promising. Sometimes, as in the case of biblical studies, there are no new texts to be rediscovered. We must, instead, read behind what men have written. We must deal with texts that are not ours, texts that were not written for us or by others like us. We work with a feeling of estrangement, reading between the lines of alien texts, looking for invisible women, listening for muted voices.

The Bible, for the most part, is an alien text, not written by women or with women in mind. Some feminist critics have asked why we should be reading the Bible at all. For some, reading is a matter of religious tradition. For others, the issue is more diffuse. The Bible has prescribed our gender, dictated our sexuality, and defined our social roles even to this day and this culture. Genesis 2–3, perhaps more than any other biblical text, has been the biggest influence on the way men and women relate to one another in the Western world. Cited most often as "proof" that women are inferior to men and as support for male dominance over women, Genesis 2–3 has hardly been a liberating text. Consequently, this story has attracted a wide variety of feminist critiques.

Some would contend that *readings* of Genesis 2–3—not the text itself—have contributed to the present inequality between the sexes. Closer attention to the details of the text, some feminist critics argue, yields a more positive portrait of woman and woman's plight.

Phyllis Trible, among the first to publish on this story in contemporary feminist criticism, points out that the history of interpretation has shown more misogynist tendencies than does the actual text.[5] Rather than a justification of woman's inferiority, Trible discerns in the text a remarkable equality between the sexes in the original creation of humankind, arguing that it is only after the "fall" that hierarchy becomes a part of human existence as a consequence (not a punishment) of the disobedience.

Using rhetorical analysis, she argues that God created the first human without gender. Her interpretation has merit. The '*ādām*, literally, the "human," is created from the '*ădāmāh*, the "humus," the earth. Though a masculine pronoun is used for this "earth creature" (Hebrew has no neuter pronoun), it is not until the woman is differentiated from this creature (made from its side) that the original human being acquires a gender. (This line of interpretation is actually not new. The famous tenth-century Jewish commentator, Rashi, suggested that the first human was male on one side and female on the other and that God simply divided the creature in half.) The interpretation may not be supported by the grammar of the text, but it appeals to our sense of binary logic. We know things by their opposites: We only know light because we know darkness; we know hot because we know cold; we know male because we know female.

Trible offers further arguments. She interprets the woman as the crown of creation rather than God's afterthought. She argues that the word "helper" ('*ēzer*) used to describe the woman is most often used in reference to God and therefore denotes a superior rather than an inferior being, and she observes that the woman is assertive and decisive while the man is passive and compliant. Read in this light, the text affirms women in ways the history of interpretation never imagined.

More recent work on Genesis 2–3 has been less idealistic about the egalitarian nature of the text but has nonetheless attempted to rehabilitate the character of Eve. For Mieke Bal, another feminist literary critic, Eve develops into a character of great power.[6] Her decision to eat the fruit from the tree of the knowledge of good and evil is the first act of human independence and puts the human creatures on a more equal footing with God. For Bal this is not a negative thing because now the human and the divine are in a real relationship of give and take rather than an artificial relationship of puppet and puppeteer. Eve did not "sin"; she opted for reality. She chose real life, and her choice marks the emergence of human character.

Text-affirming or character-affirming readings are not exclusive to literary criticism. Carol Meyers, a feminist historical critic, in an attempt to reconstruct the social situations of ancient Israelite women, has also understood this text to be less misogynist than its subsequent interpretations have allowed.[7] For Meyers the story of Eden must be set against the backdrop of the premonarchical agrarian society of the Palestinian highlands. Eden is indeed paradise because it depicts an existence very different from that of the ancient Israelite farming family. The garden's trees are already well established, there is no need to plant backbreaking field crops, and water is in steady supply. The repetition of the words "food" and "eat" suggest that the people who would have told this story, the farm community in the highlands of Palestine, understood the sustenance of life to be a central concern, overriding the theme of disobedience and its consequences. For Meyers, Genesis 2–3 is not a story of "the fall" (no word for "fall" or "sin" is ever mentioned) but a wisdom tale dealing "with the meaning of the paradoxes and harsh facts of life" (91).

Crucial to her argument is a retranslation of Gen. 3:16, God's judgment upon the woman, which she renders as follows:

> I will greatly increase your toil and your pregnancies;
> [along] with travail shall you beget children.
> For to your man is your desire, and he shall predominate over you.
> (Meyers, 118)

The plight of women described is not pain in childbirth but increased agrarian toil in addition to multiple pregnancies. The ancient Israelite woman, due to the mortality rate of women in their childbearing years (life expectancy for a woman was around thirty years, while a man could expect to live to forty), would have understandably been reluctant to endure repeated childbirths. But because of her own sexual desire and the propensity of men to insist on sexual intercourse, she would have faced the additional risks of pregnancies and childbirths along with the hard work she would have shared with her man.

For Meyers, then, the text's emphasis on female subordination lies only in the realm of sexual activity. The reference is to the man's overpowering sex drive rather than to any general social hierarchy. Men and women in an agricultural society would have, according to Meyers, lived a more egalitarian existence than would have been the case in later urban culture.

While the preceding critics have attempted to rehabilitate the text's gender code, making the story more palatable to modern women, others have viewed the biblical text with more suspicion. Could the ancient writer(s) have intended for Eve to be so equal and admirable? Was Eve truly meant to be portrayed as bold, decisive, and wise? Can the centuries of interpreters who have read her to be gullible and stupid be so far off the mark? Suppose the text is implying that she is inferior, the first to sin, and responsible for the fallen state of humankind—who has cast her in this light?

In other words, some critics are asking, if all writing is gendered, then what about the sexual politics of biblical composers? Who has defined positive and negative female qualities? Are the womanly assets commended in the Bible (beauty, submissiveness, obedience, fecundity, industriousness, for example) merely those characteristics deemed valuable by the patriarchy? And what about less than admirable female characters—the Jezebels and the Delilahs? Are they being portrayed thus because of some political strategy at work to control women's self-understanding?

Gender is, after all, a social construction. Unlike biological sexual difference, gender identity is socially defined. People are born male or female, but they become men and women through adhering to cultural constructions of what men and women are supposed to be like. As Myra Jehlen[8] writes, "Femininity is a performance and not a natural mode of being" (269).

Genesis 2–3, as a story of origins, is, among other things, in the business of constructing gender roles and fitting them into accepted social hierarchy. The man does name both genders—and according to him, the woman is derivative of the man. God relates the woman to the man as his "helper." The narrator defines their sexual orientation to be heterosexual. God designates the labors assigned to each gender. The man stipulates that the woman's primary role in life is to be the "mother of all living." The narrative establishes a particular kind of lifestyle for men and women. In whose interests is this description? Who would have promoted this construction of gender?

The appeal to authorial intention has led recent commentators to counter the reading of sexual equality. Susan Lanser, applying the principles of speech-act theory to the text, argues that inference and context are as important to the production of meaning as the formal characteristics of language.[9] When a character is introduced into a story, that character is assumed to have a gender. Even though the first human is not identified as male, argues Lanser, *hā'ādām* would have been, and should be understood to be, a male human. There is nothing in the text to indicate otherwise. Furthermore, inference and context suggest that when the man calls the new creature "woman," this, like the naming of the animals, is an act that defines her. It is not, as Trible would contend, simply a recognition of sexual difference. Finally, context dictates that the accusatory formula "Because you did this," addressed to the serpent in 3:14, also carries over to the woman. Thus God's pronouncement in 3:16 is in fact punishment and not simply a statement of consequences as Trible and Bal would allow. When the context of production is foregrounded against the context of reading or reproduction, Genesis 2–3 remains very much a text of the patriarchy.

David Clines has argued at length that the word "helper" does not, as Trible has suggested, designate a superior being.[10] While a helper may have superior status, she or he is, nevertheless, secondary to the project of the one who is being helped. Eve is, in Clines's reading, unalterably subordinate to Adam. Citing Gen. 1:28 and finding support among the church fathers, Clines concludes that Eve is necessary to help Adam do the only task he cannot accomplish by himself, namely, procreate.[11]

Despite its androcentricity ("man-centeredness"), however, the text is not completely a lost cause. Clines insists that it still has much to offer us:

> The authority of a text has to do with its nature; we want to be saying things about the Bible that have to do with its *function*. We want to be saying, not so much that the Bible is right, not even that the Bible is wrong, but that it impacts for good upon people. Despite its handicaps, despite the fact that it has misled people and promoted patriarchy, it has an unquenchable capacity—when taken in conjunction with a commitment to personal integrity—to inspire people, bring out the best in them and suggest a vision they could never have dreamed of for themselves. Think of it as dogma and you will at times, as over the matter of men and women, either be wrong or get it wrong. Think of it rather as a resource for living which has no authority but which nevertheless manages to impose itself powerfully upon people. (Clines, 48)

Recognizing the androcentric nature of the text but taking a more compromising tack is Phyllis Bird's attempt to examine Genesis 1–3 as a source for a theology of sexuality.[12] The first human is admittedly male, but though "he bears the appellation of the species, he does not fully represent it" (38). The remainder of the chapter, suggests Bird, is devoted to overcoming this problem of singularity. As far as woman's status as helper is concerned, Bird considers closely the narrative context: "Although the help which the woman is meant to give to the man is undoubtedly help in procreation, the account in Genesis 2 subordinates function to passion. The attraction of the sexes is the author's primary interest, the sexual drive whose consummation is conceived as a re-union" (38).

The subordination of woman to man is not part of the created order. Rather, says Bird, the equality of the sexes in Genesis 2 is the "prelude to its negation in Genesis 3" (39). Alienation and estrangement are the result of sin. This is still a message of relevance: "It is the Yahwist's contribution to remind us that the good gift of sexuality may become the means and the sign of alienation within the species, that what was intended for fulfillment and self-transcendence may become the occasion and instrument of deprivation and oppression" (44).

Pamela Milne is less optimistic about any helpful message coming from Genesis 2–3.[13] If men created the text, then Adam will always dominate Eve. And as long as men read the text, Eve comes out the loser. No feminist reformation of surface elements, suggests Milne, is going to disguise the fact that Genesis 2–3 is essentially male mythology and has been consistently perceived as such by male scholars who have analyzed it. She somewhat despairingly points to the fact that feminist work on Genesis 2–3 has consistently been ignored by male scholars dealing with this text.

Readers who look to the Bible for spiritual direction and yet disagree with the values found there face a dilemma. In Milne's judgment our alternatives are few:

> We can either accept the patriarchal biblical text as sacred and content ourselves with exposing its patriarchy . . . or we can expose its patriarchy and reject it as sacred and authoritative. But if we are looking for a sacred scripture that is not patriarchal, that does not construct woman as "other" and that does not support patriarchal interpretations based on this otherness, we are not likely to find it or to recover it in texts such as Genesis 2–3. If we want an authoritative sacred scripture that does not make it possible to believe that women are secondary and inferior humans, it appears that we need to make new wine to fill our new wineskins. (Milne, 22)

Feminist criticism has had the tendency to focus on the roles and characterization of women in the biblical text. While inevitable and crucial to the project, such study is not without its drawbacks. Paradoxically, the focus on women has, to some extent, slipped into the patriarchal syndrome of defining women as "other." Women, because they differ from men, are the subject of investigation. Whether women emerge as positive figures, as in the analysis of Trible, or are hopelessly minimal, as in Clines's view of the text, the implication is the same. Men and men's interests somehow remain the unquestioned standard. Even the recognition that writing itself is gendered—that is, that it reflects gendered experience—has often occasioned little more than observation in biblical criticism.

As has been noted above, gender is not simply a matter of difference but a matter of power. Thus to say that a text is androcentric or racist, as if that were an ideological perspective equal to any other, and to leave it at that, may sound scholarly, but it is not neutral. It is according some value, if only by default, to certain oppressive relations of power between people. How critics write of gender, then, is a matter of grave responsibility. Categories such as gender, race, and class hierarchically structure our lives and our texts, but not without troubling tensions and contradictions. To say that a text is androcentric, even when taking a clear stand on the question of value, and to leave it at that, may be missing an opportunity to deal with inherent tensions and contradictions in androcentrism's disposition of power.[14]

Scholars who are scrutinizing the power relations both within texts and in the writing of texts are producing readings in which tension and contradiction are part of the text's meaning. David Jobling, employing structuralist methodology clearly informed by Marxist and feminist ideology, finds several conflicts at work in Genesis 2–3.[15] First, there is the conflict between two narrative programs. On the one hand, the story explains the creation and fall of humankind—this is the program traditionally recognized. On the other hand, this plot agenda competes with a more basic agenda—explaining how there came to be a man to till the earth, the problem or need set forth at the beginning of the story.[16] Conflict also exists on the ideological level. The patriarchal tendency of the story is to subordinate the woman in the social order and to blame the woman for the misfortune that has befallen humankind. In tension with this agenda are the undeniable positive characteristics of the woman in the text.

There is, Jobling insists, asymmetry in the creation of the man and the woman and in their subsequent offenses. Yet while the patriarchal culture that produced and received this text would have assumed the first human to be male, an assumption grounded in the grammar of the text, the logic, Jobling admits, is on Trible's side: "Male" is meaningless without "female." While the woman sins first and is implicated in the man's sin, the woman is (as Trible has also observed) active and intelligent while the man is passive and oblivious. How do such characterizations come to be in a patriarchal text?

> They are inevitable expressions of the logic of the myth: woman and sexuality belong to the same semantic configuration as knowledge. Part of the price the male mindset pays is the admission that woman is more aware of the complexity of the world, more in touch with "all living." And finally, at the deepest level of the text, where the fall myth as a whole is in tension with "a man to till the earth," the possibility is evoked that the human transformation in which the woman took powerful initiative was positive, rather than negative, that the complex human world is to be preferred over any male ideal.
>
> But these "positive" features are not the direct expression of a feminist consciousness. . . . Rather, they are the effects of the patriarchal mindset tying itself in knots trying to account for woman and femaleness in a way which *both* makes sense *and* supports patriarchal assumptions. (Jobling, 42–43)

Bal recognizes the same phenomenon. The text reveals a problem with man's priority and domination.

> The reason for this situation is obvious. The burden of domination is hard to bear. Dominators have, first, to establish their position, then to safeguard it. Subsequently, they must make both the dominated *and* themselves believe in it. Insecurity is not a prerogative exclusively of the dominated. The establishing of a justifying "myth of origin," which has to be sufficiently credible and realistic to account for common experience, is not that simple a performance. Traces of the

painful process of gaining control can therefore be perceived in those very myths. They serve to limit repression to acceptable, viable proportions. (Bal, 1987:110)

Consequently, the story may be designed to communicate male priority and natural superiority over women and to justify thereby the social dominance of men over women, but the more vehement their claim, the more fragile their case. Texts do more than they say. In fact, they often do quite the opposite of what they intend to say.[17]

We are dealing here, however, not simply with instability or indeterminacy within texts but with a particular way of reading. "Reading against the grain" is, in Gerald Graff's terms, "a method which does not take the texts' apparent contexts and intentions at face value, but looks at the doubts they repress or leave unsaid and how this repressed or 'absent' element can undermine or undo what the text says" (171). It is, in short, choosing to question the priorities and hierarchies of a text, to deconstruct the text, if you will.

In the case of Genesis 2–3, the questioning of hierarchies might extend beyond the roles of man and woman. The divine, the human, and the animal realms also fall into a prioritized order. The divine character, YHWH Elohim, not surprisingly, is heavily engaged in the business of authority. He is the "author" of the garden and all that is in it. He creates not only the man but also the woman and the serpent, who are traditionally blamed for the "fall." And it is he who places that momentous tree in the midst of the garden and circumscribes it with arbitrary prohibition.

Most commentators, for obvious theological reasons, want to "protect" God, to remove this character from scrutiny, much as God pronounces the tree of the knowledge of good and evil to be off-limits to the humans in the garden. Some readers, however, are willing to pluck the fruit, eager to learn what the knowledge of good and evil is all about. Tensions and contradictions within the text, and between text and reader, may challenge us to reenter the garden with our eyes opened, even if that means eventually running up against the contradictory, unstable character of God.

David Jobling's structural analysis reveals that YHWH Elohim is both the initiator and the opponent of the action. God creates what the earth needs, a man to till it, but then acts as villain by retaining the man to keep his own private garden. Furthermore, YHWH counteracts his own villainy by creating the tree of knowledge, the serpent, and the woman, who converge to foil the divine conspiracy.

In a more recent attempt to "read against the grain," David Gunn has suggested that certain characteristics of God, established in Genesis 1 and transferred to the humans who were created in the divine image, keep the text from completely succeeding in shifting the blame for the fall onto the

woman and the serpent.[18] God's desire for dominion (evident in such language as "rule" [1:16], "subjugate" [1:26], and "subdue" [1:28]), for dividing
and naming, for creating self-likeness, and for discovery color both God and
humans with a mixture of control and freedom. Domination, categorization, labeling, and ensuring sameness or conformity are all manifestations
of the need to control. The capacity for discovery, however ("And God saw
that it was good"), undermines control, valuing exploration and venture.
Furthermore, as the divine pronouncements of "good" reveal, God can differentiate between good and evil. In the slippage between plural self-reference
and singular verbs ("Elohim [plural] said [singular], 'Let us make humankind
in our image'"), God admits differentiation within the divine self.

The contradictions in the creator are manifested in the creature. We see
the first human categorizing and naming the animals. We see the man labeling the woman, declaring her likeness and yet her difference. We see the
woman's curiosity and love of discovery, her desire to be "like" God, to know
good and evil. And we see humankind divided among itself, aware of and
attempting to conceal its differences. The man blames the "other" one and
eventually subjugates her.

The language of the text allows the blame to shift from man to woman
to serpent, and there the buck-passing stops, because "the serpent's mouth
is stopped with dust." But as hard as the words try to locate fault in humans
in general, and women and their animal counterparts specifically, the
silences, the tensions, the contradictions whisper that, ultimately, God is
responsible for the "fallen," or perhaps more to the point, the "realistic"
state of creation.

It should be clear by this catalog of readings that feminist criticism is not a
monolithic enterprise. Granted, all of these critics, in one way or another,
are asking about the status of women in Genesis 2–3. They are nonetheless
also asking other questions, using a variety of methods, and arriving at different answers. Although I have suggested some affinities and dissimilarities
among these readings, it should be quickly noted that feminist work on
other biblical texts may or may not fit these heuristic categories. Even these
particular critics do not always employ the same critical stance. As I have
tried to indicate in this outline, there are many explicit and implicit inter-
changes taking place among scholars working in this critical mode. An
energetic internal critique is occurring among feminist readers.

These dynamics raise some troubling questions about the nature of the
Bible and its authority. Should we be looking with Bal and Trible for role
models (whether male or female) in the Bible?[19] Is the Bible really in the
business of providing us characters to emulate, people after whom we can
pattern our lives? Or are biblical messages more complex than that?

If interpretation is to be guided by context and inference, as Lanser suggests, how precise can we be? Is "precision" even the right word to describe the goals of reading? If we all are to "infer" the same things, to understand contexts in the same way, do we not run the risk of returning to the univocality of patriarchy?

Can we depend on reconstructed historical and sociological contexts to inform our reading? Do the Bible's stories simply reflect the lifestyles of a particular community, as Meyers contends? Or are there some sexual politics at work that are meant to promote a specific way of life?

If we conclude that the Bible is androcentric, should we completely reject it as sacred scripture, as Milne suggests? If we hang on to it as sacred scripture, what do we do with its androcentrism? Is the androcentrism, as Clines argues, an unfortunate but not necessarily an insurmountable problem? Can we truly distinguish between a text having authority and a text "imposing itself powerfully upon people"? Can we indeed rely on "personal integrity," knowing that church fathers such as Augustine and Aquinas no doubt read with integrity, yet constructed *and promoted* debasingly misogynist interpretations?

Given that the text is androcentric, is there not always a danger in using it as a resource for a theology of sexuality, even for careful readers like Phyllis Bird? Can we accept how the Bible defines gender roles? And what about the deconstructionists—how comfortable are we when the character of God becomes the subject of deconstruction? After all, in the biblical story world God allows, if not promotes, patriarchal hierarchy. What are Jewish and Christian believers to do with that?

While some might construe these questions and others like them to indicate weaknesses in the critical approach, I tend to think they are a sign of great vitality. More voices are engaging the question of gender, helping to create a language, a body of critical discourse. What we are discovering is that the conversation cannot stay in or with the text. Inevitably, it leads to questions about how we live and how we should live. It cuts through to the heart of our values, challenging us to dismantle oppressive structures in our world.

Postscript

Because of its diversity I find it difficult to pinpoint major weaknesses in feminist criticism in general. Nevertheless, I do think that anyone wishing to employ feminist criticism should be forewarned: Feminist criticism is not always taken seriously. Considered by some to be "faddish" or "trendy" or downright trivial, it is often ignored, or in some situations even ridiculed. Its results sometimes make people angry, and that anger is almost always directed toward the interpreter.

One need not be surprised by this response. Feminist criticism undermines ingrained worldviews and cherished beliefs. It suggests that the Bible
offers something other than universal truth, and for many Jewish and
Christian believers that is a difficult notion to accept.

Nevertheless, for readers who are open to the complexity, the plurality,
and even the indeterminacy of the biblical witness, for readers who are comfortable with the notion that the Bible shows us a broken world more often
than it does an exemplary one, for readers who recognize that not all people
experience life in the same way, feminist criticism is an effective and stimulating mode of analysis for men as well as women. Not only does it have the
potential to transform the way we look at the Bible, it also has the power to
transform the way we look at ourselves and the way we live in our society.

Notes

1. Rebecca West, *The Young Rebecca*. ed. J. Marcus (London: Macmillan, 1982), 219.

2. Sandra M. Gilbert, "What Do Feminist Critics Want? A Postcard from the
Volcano," in *The New Feminist Criticism: Essays on Women, Literature, and Theory*, ed.
Elaine Showalter (New York: Pantheon, 1985), 36.

3. All scripture translations in this chapter are the author's own.

4. Unpublished lecture. Quoted by Rachel Blau DuPlessis in "For the Etruscans" in
The New Feminist Criticism: Essays on Women, Literature, and Theory, ed. Elaine
Showalter (New York: Pantheon, 1985), 271–91.

5. First argued by Trible in "Depatriarchalizing in Biblical Interpretation," *Journal of
the American Academy of Religion* 41 (1973): 30–48 and "Eve and Adam, Genesis 2–3
Reread," *Andover Newton Quarterly* 13 (1975): 251–58. Later appearing in "Genesis 2–3
Revisited" in *Womanspirit Rising: A Feminist Reader on Religion*, ed. Carol Christ and
Judith Plaskow (New York: Harper & Row, 1975) and in *God and the Rhetoric of Sexuality*
(Philadelphia: Fortress, 1978).

6. Mieke Bal, "Sexuality, Sin and Sorrow: The Emergence of Female Character [A
Reading of Genesis 2–3]," in *The Female Body in Western Culture*, ed. Susan Rubin
Suleiman (Cambridge: Harvard University Press, 1986), 317–38; reprinted in *Lethal
Love: Feminist Literary Readings of Biblical Love Stories* (Bloomington, Ind.: Indiana
University Press, 1987), 104–130.

7. Carol Meyers, *Discovering Eve: Ancient Israelite Women in Context* (New York:
Oxford University Press, 1988).

8. Myra Jehlen, "Gender," in *Critical Terms for Literary Study*, ed. Frank Lentricchia
and Thomas McLaughlin (Chicago: University of Chicago Press, 1990), 263–73.

9. Susan Lanser, "(Feminist) Criticism in the Garden: Inferring Genesis 2–3," *Semeia*
41 (1988): 67–84.

10. David Clines, "What Does Eve Do to Help? and Other Irredeemably
Androcentric Orientations in Genesis 1–3," in *What Does Eve Do to Help? and Other
Readerly Questions to the Old Testament* (Sheffield: Journal for the Study of the Old
Testament, 1990), 25–48. It should be noted that though Clines shows sympathy for
feminist concerns and a "mastery" of the discussion regarding this particular text, he also
maintains a certain detachment and is careful not to refer to himself as a feminist. For

some pertinent observations on male feminist criticism, see Elaine Showalter's "The Rise of Gender," in *Speaking of Gender*, ed. E. Showalter (London: Routledge, 1989), 1–16, especially 5–8 and 10.

11. Note that Meyers would, in all likelihood, dispute this claim. She would have no problem seeing Eve (Everywoman) helping with gardening/farming duties.

12. Phyllis Bird, "Genesis 1–3 as a Source for a Contemporary Theology of Sexuality," *Ex Auditu* (1987): 31–44.

13. Pamela Milne, "The Patriarchal Stamp of Scripture: The Implications of Structuralist Analyses for Feminist Hermeneutics," *Journal of Feminist Studies in Religion* 5 (1989): 11–22.

14. Susan Lanser is moving in this direction when she asks, "Might not the tension between inference and form signify a deep ambivalence on the part of the Jahwist writer or his society about the place of woman? Might such a disease not signify the dissonance within early Judaism between the status of woman in traditional patriarchal society and the theologically egalitarian impulse manifested more openly in the later Genesis 1? Might this not make Genesis 2–3 the document of a patriarchy already beginning to be uncomfortable with itself?" (79).

15. David Jobling, "Myth and Its Limits in Genesis 2.4b–3.24," in *The Sense of Biblical Narrative II* (Sheffield: Journal for the Study of the Old Testament, 1986), 17–43. Many of his arguments were first published in "The Myth Semantics of Genesis 2:4b–3:24," *Semeia* 18 (1980): 41–49.

16. Note here the similarity to Meyers's position that the real issue in the story is not "the fall" but sustenance of life.

17. Gerald Graff writes, "The point here is that language attempts to build up positions of authority which language itself calls into question. . . . The very expressions by which we claim . . . credibility betray how fragile and challengeable [that credibility] is" ("Determinacy/Indeterminacy," in Lentricchia and McLaughlin, *Critical Terms for Literary Study*, 170).

18. David Gunn, "Shifting the Blame: God and Patriarchy in the Garden," unpublished paper presented at the midwest regional meeting of the Society of Biblical Literature (1990). This paper provides the basis for a jointly authored chapter entitled "Shifting the Blame," in Danna Nolan Fewell and David M. Gunn, *Gender, Power, and Promise: The Subject of the Bible's First Story* (Nashville: Abingdon, 1993), 22–38.

19. Let me reiterate that Bal and Trible do not take such a stance in all their work. See, for example, Trible's more recent *Texts of Terror: Feminist Literary Readings of Biblical Narrative* (Philadelphia: Fortress, 1984) and Bal's *Death and Dissymmetry: The Politics of Coherence in Judges* (Chicago: University of Chicago Press, 1988).

For Further Reading

Collins, Adela Yarbro, ed. *Feminist Perspectives on Biblical Scholarship*. Chico, Calif.: Scholars, 1985.

Day, Peggy L., ed. *Gender and Difference in Ancient Israel*. Minneapolis: Fortress, 1989.

Exum, J. Cheryl, and Johanna W. H. Bos, eds. *Reasoning with the Foxes: Female Wit in a World of Male Power. Semeia* 42. Atlanta: Scholars, 1988.

Newsom, Carol A., and Sharon H. Ringe, eds. *The Women's Bible Commentary*. Louisville, Ky.: Westminster/John Knox, 1992.

Russell, Letty M., ed. *Feminist Interpretation of the Bible*. Philadelphia: Westminster, 1985.

Tolbert, Mary Ann, ed. *The Bible and Feminist Hermeneutics*. *Semeia* 28. Chico, Calif.: Scholars, 1983.

Trible, Phyllis, ed. "The Effects of Women's Studies on Biblical Studies." *Journal for the Study of the Old Testament* 22 (1992).

14

READING THE BIBLE IDEOLOGICALLY: SOCIOECONOMIC CRITICISM

FERNANDO F. SEGOVIA

L iberation hermeneutics is the interpretation of biblical and related texts from a self-conscious perspective and program of social transformation. It is understood and practiced in any number of ways, depending on how the situation of oppression and the agenda of liberation are formulated and addressed. As such, a full introduction to the topic would call for an account of liberationist interpretation as conceived and practiced from the point of view of class, culture, ethnicity and race, gender, and politics. Such an introduction would also require an account of how such different angles of vision relate to and interact with one another, historically as well as theoretically. Imperative and instructive as such a task would be, it lies well beyond the scope of the present chapter.

The size of the topic as well as its complexity render it impossible for me to pursue such a comprehensive introduction here. Besides, a number of similar approaches are touched upon elsewhere in this volume. My aims and parameters must, perforce, be more modest. In effect, what I want to do in this article is to explore that particular strand of liberationist hermeneutics that focuses on socioeconomic matters. This focus is readily identified with the emergence of liberation theology in Latin America in the 1960s and 1970s. To be sure, the emphasis on oppression as material poverty finds its way into most if not all other liberationist discourses, but as it does it is also gradually expanded and hence decentered as other dimensions of oppression are problematized and theorized as well.

Given the breadth of the socioeconomic approach itself, I shall focus on the work of two figures who have played a prominent role in the formulation and grounding of this reading strategy, Clodovis and Leonardo Boff.[1] It will be useful, however, to begin with an overview of the irruption and impact of this type of liberation hermeneutics within the discipline of biblical studies.

Biblical Criticism and Liberation Hermeneutics

Like feminist hermeneutics, liberationist hermeneutics of the socioeconomic type was a harbinger of things to come in the discipline, pointing to and helping to bring about the collapse of the methodological and theoretical consensus that had been operative in biblical criticism for a long time. To understand this, it is necessary to trace the course of the discipline from its inception in the early nineteenth century through its present configuration. Elsewhere I have described this disciplinary history in terms of four paradigms or grand models of interpretation, each with its own distinctive mode of discourse and broad spectrum of approaches. These models are reproduced here by way of summary.[2]

From the early 1800s through the mid-1970s, historical criticism was the paradigm that reigned supreme in biblical studies. Its main opposition came from outside the academy in the form of antimodernist responses such as traditional ecclesiastical theologism, fundamentalist literalism, and pentecostal spiritualism. Historical criticism called for the reconstruction of the ancient (biblical) world and the recreation of the original message of the (biblical) texts as intended by the authors, and for the adoption of a universal and objective reader beyond contextualization and perspective—the scientific reader construct.

It was not until the mid-1970s that the historical consensus began to be challenged and disrupted from the inside. Growing frustration with this longstanding historical paradigm led a number of voices within the discipline to look for inspiration and guidance elsewhere in the academy, especially in the human and social sciences. In the process two new paradigms began to coalesce. On the one hand, literary criticism turned to such fields as linguistics, narratology, rhetoric, and psychoanalysis; on the other hand, sociocultural criticism looked to sociology and anthropology. While literary critics focused on the internal dynamics of texts, sociocultural critics emphasized the external dynamics of the world behind a text and encoded in it. In both cases, however, the operative reader-construct remained, by and large, that of the universal and objective reader beyond contextuality and perspective. Both paradigms underwent swift expansion, broad internal diversification, and increasing sophistication through the 1980s and 1990s, ultimately establishing themselves within the discipline of biblical studies as alternative approaches to historical criticism.

Toward the end of the 1980s, the first signs of yet another paradigm— known as cultural studies—began to appear. As literary criticism and sociocultural criticism focused more and more on the role of the reader in interpretation, the discipline of biblical studies was eventually forced to come face to face with the real or flesh-and-blood reader—a reader-construct that was no longer universal and objective, no longer beyond contextualization and perspective but inextricably situated and ideological. Within this model the reader was no longer above history and culture but fully implicated in the various layers of human life and fully interested at all times—a reader immersed and engaged in history and culture. Interpretation within this paradigm was regarded as construction on the part of such readers, with respect to the world of (biblical) antiquity (re-constructions of history) and the world of the text (re-creations of meaning). For cultural studies, therefore, the interpreter became as important as the text. While this model is still very much in the making, it has already become a viable alternative to historical criticism. Moreover, the model has already spawned a series of rapidly expanding and highly sophisticated discourses, often in dialogue with one another.

In the course of the last quarter century, therefore, the fairly unitary conception and practice of the discipline of biblical studies has yielded to a situation of radical diversity in method and theory. A further point is in order: Over this same period, the discipline has experienced another and not unrelated sort of diversity. Biblical criticism has become much more socioculturally diverse as more and more critics from the outside have joined its ranks—voices from the non-Western world, the world of Western women, and the world of non-Western minorities in the West. It is in the light of this twofold scenario that the irruption and impact of Liberation Hermeneutics should be situated and analyzed.

In effect, the presence and influence of liberation hermeneutics began to be felt in the discipline in the 1970s. It was introduced into the discipline from the outside and by outsiders on two fronts: on the one hand, from the point of view of Latin American critics and theologians in the form of socioeconomic criticism; on the other hand, from the point of view of Western women in the form of feminist criticism. Although the relationship between these liberationist strands of biblical criticism is certainly worth tracing, my focus here is on socioeconomic criticism. Its irruption and impact I would describe as follows: First, a concern with biblical hermeneutics in general and socioeconomic hermeneutics in particular followed naturally upon the formation of liberation theology in the 1960s and early 1970s; second, such a concern led to an increasingly systematic and sustained exposition of socioeconomic criticism through the 1970s and 1980s; third, this concern with matters socioeconomic foreshadowed the much later focus of the discipline on real readers in the late 1980s and early 1990s.

For Latin American theologians and biblical critics, the fundamental question of massive material poverty, with its roots in the conflict between socioeconomic classes, became the point of departure for a new way of doing theology. This was readily extended to the realm of biblical studies in the form of a search for the stance of the Bible and its proper interpretation. As this search unfolded, a consensus gradually emerged. On the one hand, the Bible was seen as a text against oppression and for liberation; on the other hand, a twofold interpretation was posited: The Bible can be read either from the perspective of continuing oppression, as it has been, or from the perspective of liberation, as it should be. Consequently, the interpreter was called upon to read the Bible on the side of the oppressed and thus for their liberation from socioeconomic oppression.

Liberationist interpretation of the socioeconomic sort appeared on the disciplinary horizon just as the discipline of biblical studies itself was undergoing certain radical changes from within, changes that would ultimately lead to a thorough overhauling of its conception and practice. As such, socioeconomic criticism, along with feminist criticism, played an early and crucial role in undermining the existing methodological and theoretical consensus of the time. It challenged in particular the established myth of the scientific reader-construct: first, on account of its assumptions regarding the relationship between socioeconomic standing and interpretation; second, because of charges leveled at the academic tradition in general as bourgeois and elitist, buried in the past and divorced from the present needs of Christian communities.

Socioeconomic criticism foreshadowed the later position of cultural studies regarding the character of all reading as contextualized and perspectival. It argued that socioeconomic class had a direct and decisive impact upon interpretation—there was an interpretation of the poor-oppressed and an interpretation of the bourgeois-oppressor. However, the position taken by socioeconomic criticism was, in the end, but a variation of the historical-critical position. This is because for socioeconomic criticism it remained feasible (1) to recapture the past, to reconstruct (biblical) history and recreate the meaning of (biblical) texts; (2) to do so by adopting a privileged hermeneutical perspective, no longer that of the scientific reader-construct but rather that of the informed and committed reader-construct, in consonance with the people and the oppressed; (3) to bring such meaning and such history to bear on the present in the face of their long consignment to the past on the part of traditional historical criticism. Socioeconomic criticism amounted, therefore, to historical criticism from the ground up—from the underside of history, from the perspective of the oppressed, advanced as the perspective of the Bible itself.

To illumine these basic principles of socioeconomic criticism I have opted to use the work of Clodovis and Leonardo Boff, which is both thorough and clear. In what follows, then, I shall unfold their position on socioeconomic criticism in three steps: I begin with the theoretical grounding provided for a hermeneutics of liberation, as advanced by Clodovis Boff;

continue with the basic principles of critical practice, as formulated by both Clodovis and Leonardo Boff; and conclude with the view of the historical Jesus that emerges from such an approach, as presented by Leonardo Boff.

Socioeconomic Criticism: Theoretical Grounding

By far the most extensive theoretical grounding for socioeconomic criticism is provided by Clodovis Boff in his major work of 1978, *Teologia e prática*.[3] In this work Boff sets out to correct what he perceives as the serious lack of a proper and informed theoretical grounding for liberation theology.[4] Boff observes that in seeking to provide a new way of doing theology, liberation theology has advanced a series of postulates meant to guide and inform theological practice. Yet these principles have remained at the level of pronouncements and, hence, of rhetoric. Consequently, Boff argues, it is necessary to move beyond this initial phase of formulation in order to provide a sound critical basis for the postulates of liberation theology.[5] Among such postulates lies the practice of biblical interpretation; thus the discussion of hermeneutics is to be located within this much broader reflection on theological practice.

This reflection encompasses three main "question areas" identified within liberation theology (C. Boff, xxi-xxii). The first, *socioanalytic mediation*, concerns the relationship of theology to the social sciences: its demand for a contextual knowledge of society and hence for interaction with social theories. This area addresses the *material* object of such a theology—the realm of the political—through the use of the social sciences. The second area, *hermeneutic mediation*, addresses the relationship of theology to scripture: theology's call for a contextual reading of scripture with emphasis on the political character of salvific events and the subversive nature of the biblical message. This second area addresses the *formal* object of this theology—the realm of theology—through an interpretation of the material object, the political, in the light of the scriptures. The third area, *practical mediation*, deals with the relationship between theology and praxis: its call for an engaged and liberating theology, a theology with a political option that is subordinated to praxis. This third area addresses the *concrete* object of liberation theology—the praxis of faith[6]—through an analysis of the multiple interfacing between theory and practice.

From the point of view of hermeneutics, it is the second area that proves crucial, for it is here that the "political" receives a proper "theological" reading, that the "material" object becomes a "formal" object, that the findings of the social sciences are appropriated theologically. This process of theological appropriation, or pertinency, is carried out on the basis of the Christian scriptures and calls for a discussion of biblical hermeneutics. The discussion involves three steps: (1) a definition of the hermeneutics involved in hermeneutic mediation; (2) an exposition of the theoretical model proper to such hermeneutics; (3) a delineation of the reading strategy proper to such hermeneutics.

Definition of Hermeneutics

Boff defines the hermeneutics involved in the process of hermeneutic mediation in terms of three fundamental principles (132–33). First, theological pertinency, the process of theological appropriation, implies the notion of a Christian "positivity"—a realm of the given in matters dogmatic or historical. Second, such positivity resides in the Christian scriptures, in the canon of the church, which constitute the "font" of all other Christian writings. Third, the meaning of these foundational texts requires a process of interpretation given the distance between these texts and present readers. The process of overcoming this distance—the process of decoding and reappropriating the original meaning of the scriptures—is what constitutes hermeneutics proper. For Boff such a hermeneutic is "an interpretive activity bearing on *written* texts" (133). Moreover, such a hermeneutic is also profoundly theological in nature, circumscribed as it is in both object and method. It applies only to the Christian scriptures and has to do only with the interpretation of the scriptures.

Proper Hermeneutic Model

So understood, the process of hermeneutic mediation calls for the adoption of a specific theoretical model: the hermeneutic circle, which is best described by contrasting it with other models (135–39). One such model is that of hermeneutic improvisation, whereby the text is subordinated to the self-interest of the reader, yielding a "riotous carnival" of readings (136); in this model biblical passages are approached as prooftexts for any given project or practice. Another model is that of semantic positivism, whereby the text is confined to the past, yielding a depository of meaning in history; in this model biblical passages are approached as frozen items in a "refrigerator," exhibition pieces in a "museum," or bodily remains in a "cemetery" (136). The hermeneutic circle moves beyond such pragmatism and positivism, respectively, by positing a sustained dialectical relationship between texts and readers.

The hermeneutic circle posits a fundamental difference between two concepts that are generally considered identical—scripture and Word of God. According to this model, the Word of God is to be found neither in the letter of scripture (as positivism would have it) nor in the spirit of the hearing or reading community (as pragmatism would have it), but rather in the mutual relationship between community and scripture. Thus the meaning of scripture—the Word of God—can be apprehended only within the context of the "living spirit of the living community"—the church (136).[7]

The hermeneutic circle advances a middle way, therefore, between the options of pragmatism and positivism. Against positivism the text is regarded as open, always directed toward the present—interpreted by the reader but also interpreting the reader. Consequently, hermeneutic technique can never establish the meaning of scripture once and for all. Against pragmatism the text is not viewed as wide open, subject to any interpretation by the reader. To the contrary, hermeneutic technique can establish boundaries of meaning beyond which interpretation cannot proceed.[8] What hermeneutic technique cannot do, however, according to the model, is determine which is the "right" meaning within the boundaries in question. That is a decision calling for a creative act on the part of the reader, a response to scripture within the context of the hermeneutic circle. For Boff, therefore, interpretation is always "innovative, more or less arbitrary, and always personal" (138), but certainly not without limits or constraints. In other words, while the overall boundaries of interpretation can be set, the particular stance to be adopted within such boundaries—what one might call the discernment of the Word of God in the present situation—is not.

The hermeneutic circle clearly involves a very particular view of revelation and scripture: Revelation is regarded as canonized but never closed; scripture (the canonization of revelation) is viewed as an "exemplar, model, or code" (140), a "spring" of meaning (141), a "font" for all later Christian reflection and writing (132). Thus revelation is canonized, but only for the sake of making possible a multiplicity of readings in subsequent historical periods. Consequently, scripture as canonized revelation contains not a prescriptive meaning for all time but a meaning that may be characterized either as "negative" (ruling out a certain range of meanings) or "inductive" (alluding to a certain range of meanings) (140). According to the hermeneutic circle, scripture becomes what one might call a guiding horizon for interpretation or, as Boff puts it, a "model interpretation," an "interpreting interpretation," a "paradigmatic message" (140). As such, scripture allows the ongoing hermeneutic tradition of the church to become ever richer through the manifold interpretations offered over time within the hermeneutic circle. According to the model, furthermore, revelation takes place in the present, and it does so by means of and in the light of scripture, as the church looks for the Word of God within the parameters established by scripture and its tradition of interpretation in the church.

Proper Reading Strategy

Given its adoption of the hermeneutic circle, the process of hermeneutic mediation calls for the acceptance of a proper methodological approach to or reading strategy for the Scriptures, a strategy that allows readers to determine the "right" meaning of scripture (the Word of God) in the present, in their respective political situations. Such a strategy is illuminated by way of contrast with two other competing strategies (142–46).

On the one hand, there is the *gospel/politics strategy*, which regards the relationship between gospel and politics (scripture and community) as one of rule to application, with the gospel as a code of norms to be applied to the situation at hand. Such a strategy of "application" is deemed defective on two counts: first, because the relationship between scripture and situation appears quite mechanical; second, because it completely bypasses both historical contexts in question. It is a strategy, Boff argues, that leaves itself wide open to improvisation and positivism, and hence to both manipulation of the gospel and mystification of the political.

On the other hand, there is the *correspondence-of-terms strategy*, which looks upon the relationship between gospel and politics in terms of an equation involving two ratios, with equivalence posited between the terms in question: Scripture is to its political situation as the theology of the political stands to its present political context. What applies in scripture, therefore, applies directly in the present. The position of Jesus then, however conceived, should be the position of the church today. Unlike the gospel/politics strategy, this strategy does have the virtue of taking historical context into account; nonetheless, it is deemed defective, insofar as the distance in historical context between gospel and politics is neither sufficiently acknowledged nor problematized.

In the face of such competing methodological approaches, Boff argues for a *correspondence-of-relationships strategy*, which he believes is evident in the hermeneutic practice of early Christian communities as well as of Christian communities in general (146–50).

Historical criticism has shown that the canonical writings are the result of a process of redaction and accretion, so that in them one finds already a distance between the words and deeds of Jesus and the biblical texts, which contain reflections or commentaries on Jesus' words and deeds in the light of the community's own situation and exigencies. The attitude governing this process was "creative fidelity": Following the principle of identity between the Jesus of history and the Christ of faith, later developments of Jesus' message and work were attributed to Jesus (147–48). Such a practice of reflection and commentary has continued within Christian communities to the present time. Christian communities have thus sought to apply the gospel to their situation, just as the early communities did. In this process the operative attitude continues to be one of creative fidelity; all such applications are characterized as Word of God.

The basic principles of the process are clear. First, both text and situation preserve their respective autonomy; neither is completely subsumed by the other. Second, together they yield a "spiritual" meaning, "a basic identity of signification" (148). Such a sense of "spiritual" identity between text and reader is what Boff proposes to capture by way of the correspondence-of-relationships strategy.

This strategy looks upon the relationship between gospel and politics in terms of an equation involving two ratios; however, equivalence is posited not between the terms but between the relationships within pairs of terms. In other words, the relationship of scripture to its context is equivalent to the relationship of the theology of the political to its context. Identity is sought, therefore, not at the level of context nor at the level of message but at the level of the relationship between context and message on each side of the equation, at the level of "spirit." What applies in scripture, therefore, does not apply directly in the present. Scripture is not a "what" but a "how," a horizon of meaning that allows for interpretation in the present in creative fidelity to the gospel. In the end, this strategy does not dispense with the normal procedures of hermeneutics, but calls for a "spiritual" reading of scripture.

In sum, the socioeconomic type of liberation hermeneutics, as advanced by Clodovis Boff, presupposes the use of a correspondence-of-relationships strategy, the deployment of a hermeneutic circle model, and the exercise of hermeneutic mediation. From the theoretical grounding supplied for liberation hermeneutics, I turn to the basic principles at work in the practice of socioeconomic criticism.

Socioeconomic Criticism: Principles of Critical Practice

In 1986, eight years after the publication of *Teologia e prática*, Clodovis Boff coauthored with his brother Leonardo a small volume entitled, *Como fazer Teologia de Libertação* (ET: *Introducing Liberation Theology*).[9] As the title indicates, this volume was intended as a beginning manual for "doing" liberation theology.[10] It touches upon the various constitutive dimensions and components of this theological movement: its driving question—how to be Christian in a world of destitution (chap. 1); the levels of activity within liberation theology—the professional, the pastoral, the popular (chap. 2); its method of analysis—the three critical mediations at work (chap. 3); its resultant key themes (chap. 4); a concise history of the movement (chap. 5); a sense of its worldwide reach (chap. 6); and its vision of the future—a new humanity (chap. 8).

The volume also provides an account of the principles involved in the liberationist approach to biblical texts, but these must be culled from the overall description of the movement. What follows, then, is my comprehensive construction of these critical principles on the basis of information provided in the various chapters of the Boffs' book.

1. The fundamental or grounding principle—indeed the point of departure for the entire enterprise of liberationist biblical interpretation—is the perception of massive poverty, the scandal of crushing oppression and consequent suffering, present not only in Latin America but in the whole of the Third World (Boff and Boff, 2–3). This scandal, which affects the vast majority of Christians in Latin America and the vast majority of the world's population, has three interrelated dimensions: From a social point of view, it involves collective oppression, exclusion, and marginalization; from an individual point of view, it involves injustice and the denial of human rights; from a religious point of view, it involves social sinfulness. Liberation reacts in vigorous protest to this scandal and commits itself to the life, cause, and struggle of the oppressed and marginalized. It seeks thereby to suffer with the poor in their present situation of injustice and to work with them to put an end to such inequity and suffering.

Liberation theology looks upon such protest and commitment as a confrontation between the injustice perpetrated on the poor and the Christian faith. Liberation sees in the suffering poor the face of Jesus Christ, its own crucified who weeps and cries out in the faces of these newly crucified, and as a result of this vision commits itself to the struggle for their liberation through service in solidarity with the poor and as an act of love for the suffering Christ. Since the scandal of massive poverty lies at the core of the liberation theology movement, it will have pride of place as well in the hermeneutics of liberation. Thus the socioeconomic interpretation of the scriptures has as its driving impulse the scandal of poverty that affects and afflicts most of humanity. It is from such a vantage point that socioeconomic criticism approaches the Bible.

2. A second principle follows immediately from the first. Since massive poverty constitutes the driving force behind the liberation theology movement, it becomes imperative to define the actual parameters of "the poor." For the Boffs this category consists of two different though related groupings, one of which is primary and the other secondary.

In keeping with the socioeconomic tenor of the liberation movement, the primary grouping consists of the materially poor (46–47), in whose ranks the authors include several groups: the traditional proletariat—the industrial workers who, without capital or productive means of their own, have nothing to offer but their labor in exchange for wages; all workers exploited by the capitalist system; the underemployed, pushed aside by the production process but always available to take the place of employed workers; those who labor in the countryside; and migrant workers, for whom there exists only seasonal work (3–4).[11]

The second grouping encompasses those discriminated against on the basis of race, culture, and sex—blacks, indigenous and other minority groups, women (47)—or age—children, juveniles, and the elderly (29). The Boffs immediately add that those who belong to the second grouping more often than not also qualify under the first grouping, since they generally belong among the socioeconomically destitute as well. Indeed they are often the poorest of the poor, since they suffer under the weight of multiple oppressions (47). They further argue that while conflicts of a sociocultural character are in principle reconcilable, conflicts of a socioeconomic nature are beyond resolution, rooted as they are in a class-divided society marked by exploitation (29). Within such a context socioeconomic oppression constitutes the infrastructural expression of oppression, while noneconomic forms of oppression represent its superstructural expressions. In the end, however, socioeconomic criticism of the Bible provides no critical apparatus for the analysis of noneconomic forms of oppression, even though it argues that such forms require their own specific forms of liberation.

3. The emphasis on socioeconomic matters in general and on material poverty in particular immediately raises the question of the relationship between liberation and Marxism. The question is not whether such a relationship exists, for it does and is openly acknowledged, but rather the nature of this relationship, which I would characterize as a third principle of socioeconomic criticism.

In an earlier essay I located socioeconomic criticism within the paradigm of cultural studies, arguing that critics within this paradigm of interpretation are influenced not only by sociology and anthropology but also economics.[12] Historically, socioeconomic criticism also emphasized the external dynamics of the world behind the text and encoded in the text, though from a strictly socioeconomic point of view and with a neo-Marxist view of the text as an ideological product and a site of struggle. However, socioeconomic criticism also went on to see the critics themselves as contextualized and perspectival, again from a strictly socioeconomic point of view and with a specific neo-Marxist view of the critic as an ideological product and hence as a site of struggle. As a result, critics were called upon to become sophisticated in economic theory (informed critics) as well as committed or engaged (interested critics), able to recognize the ideological character of biblical texts and to read them for liberation and against oppression.

I proceeded to characterize this vein of cultural criticism not as "economic"—alongside "sociological" and "anthropological"—but as "neo-Marxist." Such a designation merits further explication, since the relationship between Marxism and liberation has always been far more subtle and complex than generally acknowledged. The Boffs themselves go out of their way to place considerable distance between Marxism and liberation.

Three basic principles define this relationship (Boff and Boff, 27–28). First, Marxism is to be treated not as a subject on its own but as always subject to the perspective of the poor; in other words, liberation must submit Marxism to the judgment of the poor and their cause. Second, Marxism is to be used only as an instrument, not as an end in itself; liberation may borrow from Marxism whatever should prove useful from a theoretical or methodological point of view. Third, Marxism must be viewed critically as a companion on the way. The end result, ironically, is a rather triumphalist view of liberation vis-à-vis Marxism. Liberation, the Boffs argue, has not only displaced Marxism from its position of monopoly with regard to social commitment and historical change but has done so with enormous success among the religious masses. In so doing, moreover, it has shown tremendous appeal at a time when Marxism, like all traditional revolutionary ideologies, has found it increasingly difficult to communicate. For the Boffs, liberation, with its view of religion as an agent for social change rather than as a source of alienation (87), stands as a sharp refutation of the modern atheism represented by Marxism.

From the fundamental vantage point of material poverty, the socioeconomic interpretation of the scriptures turns to Marxism as a primary tool in its reading strategy, borrowing from it a good many of its guiding theoretical concepts and methodological moves. At the same time, this neo-Marxist angle of vision and analysis remains a tool, to be employed critically, subject at all times not only to the needs and interests of the poor themselves but also to the Bible, the message of God for the poor.

4. Mention of the Bible and its message leads to a fourth principle of socioeconomic criticism—the actual approach employed by liberation in its reading and interpretation of biblical texts. This principle has to do with the second mediation of liberation theology as a political theology—the hermeneutic mediation. Upon examining the scandal of material poverty in the world through the critical lens of the social sciences and prior to adopting a praxis of faith in the face of such poverty, liberation turns to the scriptures for inspiration and guidance—for theological *pertinency*, validation, and appropriation—regarding God's plan for the poor. This turning gives rise to socioeconomic criticism proper, which in itself involves a variety of constitutive dimensions.

a. The first of these, an indispensable prolegomenon for socioeconomic criticism, has to do with the lifestyle of the theologian in the society at large. Liberation theologians must not only have the scandal of poverty in mind when turning to the scriptures but must also experience in some way this scandal in their own life (22–24). It is not sufficient to reflect on material poverty from the outside, as it were; it is essential to live it from within, to share with the poor their experience of oppression and their struggle for liberation. If not from among the poor, theologians must join the ranks of the "evangelically poor"—those who, regardless of social class, opt to join the poor in bringing about change.

It would be fair to say that the principle of living commitment to the poor proves far more important than the actual mode or extent of its application. Thus theologians may work alongside the poor in organizations such as base communities, Bible societies, evangelization groups, human rights movements, or social agencies. Similarly, their activities may vary widely, from sporadic visits to base communities, to regular pastoral work on weekends, to alternating periods of scholarly and practical work, to living permanently with the people.

b. A second indispensable prolegomenon for socioeconomic criticism pertains to the lifestyle of the theologian in the church at large. Theologians within the liberation movement must not regard themselves as a separate class—isolated in academic centers, removed from the people in conflict with the institutional church. They must not view themselves as a privileged circle of readers, responsible for determining the meaning of the scriptures. On the contrary, theologians must see themselves as comprising but one level of activity in the church, alongside and closely tied to two other levels (11–16).

At the base or popular level of the church are the poor, gathered in base communities and Bible study groups; at the top, or professional level, are those with academic training and expertise in the theological disciplines; the middle, or pastoral level, encompasses the entire gamut of the institutional church. At all three levels the ideal is close contact as well as a constant interflow of ideas. To be sure, liberation theology's official formulation occurs at the top but only as ultimately grounded in the base and in harmony with the center. Indeed, the main movement must be from the base up, with the poor or popular classes as the basic constituent and spring of liberation theology, as they seek to live their faith by confronting oppression and struggling for liberation, aided by both professional theologians and pastoral representatives.

For the Boffs, therefore, theologians emerge as "organic" and "militant" intellectuals, with deep roots in and active links with the church (19). They must listen to and, above all, participate in the life of the popular church. Consequently, "doing" liberation theology presupposes a fundamental ecclesiastical dimension: Theologizing becomes an academic activity carried out for the sake of the church, informed by the popular church, and permeating the church, in all of its venues and activities. Thus theologians must be present and active in their local communities (where they serve in a variety of roles, from pastors to fellow pilgrims), in all other gatherings of the people of God (from retreats to discussion groups, as advisors), in interdisciplinary contexts and discussion groups (as advocates), and at their own desks (in their role as lecturers, writers, researchers). Their multifaceted role as organic and militant intellectuals serves to reinforce the collective nature of the theological enterprise.

c. A third and final dimension of socioeconomic criticism has to do with the theologians' approach to the scriptures, as they search for the message of God to the poor, profoundly rooted in both the life of the poor and the life of the church (32–35). This approach puts into practice the model of the hermeneutic circle set forth above and calls for a reading strategy with a variety of constitutive components.

First and foremost, the scriptures are to be read from the perspective of the materially poor. Such a reading must focus on those themes in the Bible that are most relevant to the poor—for example, God as the father of life and advocate of the oppressed, the liberation of Israel from bondage, the predictions and visions of a new world, Jesus' giving of the kingdom to the poor, and the church as a community of total sharing. Then, since the poor also seek life to the full, this reading strategy must take into account the transcendental themes of the Bible—such as conversion, grace, and resurrection—and proceed to reread them in the light of poverty so that these themes are rendered directly relevant to the life and cause of the poor. The Boffs add that, quite in keeping with the hermeneutic circle, such a reading remains subject to the Word of God. The Bible always retains the lead in this (dialectical) process of reading, although experience has shown that its message will be one of radical consolation and liberation for the poor.

Second, the reading strategy issuing from the hermeneutic circle strongly privileges application over explanation. This strategy is not as concerned with meaning as with the ramifications of meaning. It reads the Bible not as a book of strange stories but as a book of life, seeking to interpret life according to the text; it is intent on discovering and activating the energy of the Bible, both in terms of individual conversion and historical revolution; and it emphasizes the social content of the message, situating the text within its historical context in order to construct (through the correspondence-of-relationships model delineated above) an appropriate translation into the contemporary context.

Third, such a reading strategy favors certain biblical texts over others. Thus special emphasis is placed on Exodus as the epic of liberation, with its narrative of the transformation of a mass of slaves into the people of God;

on the prophets, for their denunciation of injustice, their defense of the poor, and their proclamation of the messianic world; on the Gospels, for their focus on the divine person of Jesus; on Acts, for its portrayal of the ideal Christian community, free and liberating; and on Revelation, for its description of the struggles of God's people. Even among such favored texts there is a further hierarchy: Writings of the New Testament rank above writings of the Old Testament, and within the New Testament itself the gospels have pride of place.

Finally, such a reading strategy must always be conducted in a christological key, with every book of the Bible read from the perspective of the high point of revelation in the Gospels. Through the figure of Jesus in the Gospels, the perspective of the poor is placed within the wider perspective of the Lord of history, from whom "the Word of God derives its consistency and strength" (35).

5. These references to the centrality of the Gospels and to the need for a christological reading of the Bible serve to introduce a final principle of socioeconomic criticism—the foundational role ascribed to the figure of the historical Jesus. As the Boffs note (49–63), liberation has given rise to a large number of distinctive claims: (1) a living and true faith includes the practice of liberation; (2) the living God sides with the oppressed against the pharaohs of this world; (3) the kingdom of God is God's project in history and eternity; (4) Jesus, the Son of God, took on oppression in order to set us free; (5) the Holy Spirit is the "Father of the poor" and is present in the struggles of the oppressed; (6) Mary is the prophetic and liberating woman of the people; (7) the church is a sign and instrument of liberation; (8) the rights of the poor are God's rights; and (9) liberated human potential becomes liberative. Among these, none is as important for socioeconomic criticism as the belief that the historical Jesus is the great liberator, a belief that is both the result of and foundation for critical inquiry.

In addressing the principle of massive poverty, I pointed out that liberation sees in the faces of the poor, the crucified of today, the face of its own crucified, Jesus Christ. Thus it commits itself to the poor not only by way of service in solidarity but also as an act of love for the suffering Christ. This christological focus is evident throughout the Boffs' volume, yielding a twofold image of the historical Jesus (53–55). On the one hand, this christological image is quite high: Jesus as the second person of the Trinity, the Son of God, and the revealer of the kingdom of God—the divine plan for the full and total liberation of all creation. On the other hand, this image is quite low: Jesus as taking on human misery and oppression; making an option for the poor, assuming their hopes and announcing their fulfillment both in the present and in the future; preaching the liberation of the kingdom outside all boundaries and thus calling for radical conversion; paying for this option and message with his own death. For liberation theology, the kingdom and the poor are indissolubly joined together in and through Jesus. As a result, the poor become for liberation much more than the social category of those oppressed and marginalized by material poverty; they take on the image of the Son of God made suffering servant and rejected, and serve as a memorial of the poor and persecuted Jesus (31).

Thus for the socioeconomic interpretation of the Scriptures, the figure of the historical Jesus plays a foundational role: first, because it is in Jesus' life and message that liberation finds the grounding and exemplar for its own option for the poor; second, because it is through Jesus that liberation theology proceeds to read the whole of the Bible from the thematic of poverty. In what follows I shall amplify this reading of the historical Jesus on the part of socioeconomic criticism.

Socioeconomic Criticism: The Historical Jesus

In 1972, quite early on in the development of the liberation movement, Leonardo Boff published a major work entitled *Jesus Cristo Libertador*. This was six years before the appearance of Clodovis Boff's *Teologia e prática* and fourteen years before the publication of their joint manual on doing liberation theology.[13] Although this discussion of the figure of Jesus appeared prior to the other two volumes under consideration, I include it at this point for two reasons. First, its portrayal of the historical Jesus serves as a clear illustration of the critical practice of socioeconomic criticism. Second, this portrayal provides an expanded account of the foundational role assigned to the historical Jesus in the hermeneutics of liberation.

Jesus as Preacher of the Kingdom

Boff begins his portrayal of the historical Jesus with the matter of Jesus' intention (L. Boff, 49–62), summarized as follows: "Jesus Christ wants to be in his own person God's answer to the human condition" (50). Across all cultures and civilizations human beings experience profound alienation as well as radical hope. This alienation affects all of reality—individual, social, and cosmic; this hope is correspondingly utopian in character. Within this universal human context, Jesus of Nazareth reveals himself as God in human condition and discloses God's own plan for such alienation and hope—the kingdom of God. As God made human, Jesus is the savior of the world, the one awaited by all nations. As God's own plan, the kingdom of God is a message of absolute meaning for the world.

The kingdom preached by Jesus signifies "the manifestation of the sovereignty and lordship of God over this world" (52)—a world ruled by demonic forces and locked in combat with the forces of good—through which all alienation and all evil, physical or moral, is overcome and all the consequences of sin are destroyed. This kingdom transcends any particular agenda of liberation to encompass the transformation of the old world into a new world. This transformation, moreover, is ongoing, with a present as well as a future dimension. The kingdom has already been inaugurated by Jesus himself, as his miracles clearly demonstrate, and will be brought to fulfillment at the end of history. As the one who preaches the kingdom, Jesus presents himself as the liberator of all reality.

For Boff, therefore, one finds in Jesus of Nazareth not just the presence of God in the human condition but a God-made-human who participated fully in it, taking on its deepest aspirations and announcing its total liberation. Jesus preached not himself but the kingdom. It was only after the resurrection that his disciples raised the question of his identity, making explicit by way of the christological titles bestowed upon him what had been implicit in Jesus' own words and works—Jesus was Son of God, Messiah, God.

Jesus as Liberator

As he preached the kingdom of God in full awareness of his role as liberator of all reality, Jesus made two fundamental demands for participation in this new order—personal conversion and social reconstruction. First, the kingdom called for a revolution within, a radical change in human ways of thinking and living in accordance with God's plan of liberation. In addition, the kingdom called for a societal revolution, a similarly radical transformation in purpose and structure, again in keeping with God's plan of liberation. Through these demands Jesus pointedly showed that the established order could not serve as a basis for the kingdom and set out to create the conditions necessary for the kingdom's new order.

These demands entailed a total transfiguration of human and social existence. The internal revolution demanded a sharp rejection of the established order among human beings: All were called upon to sell their property, to abandon their families, to risk their lives. In doing these things, human beings would open themselves to God and become God's children. A new way of life and thought—unconditional love—would be the result. This love calls for giving oneself to the service of others and is far superior to any concept of justice, for the latter always presupposes giving to each their due within a given social system and hence a sanctioning of the status quo. This love is also universal, embracing all brothers and sisters. The external revolution demanded just as sharp a rejection of the established order in human societies: away from all forms of legalism, conventionalism, and authoritarianism, and toward liberty and equality.

Such demands coincide with Jesus' own option for the poor. Within the present order it is the poor who stand nearest to the kingdom and who will enter the kingdom first. Since they have nothing and are nothing, they stand to lose nothing and are thus much more likely to listen to and follow the message of the kingdom. For their sake, therefore, Jesus transgresses all social conventions of the established order, breaking all class distinctions and approaching those who are despised and shunned. In so doing, he shows that he is free of all preconceptions and is willing to give himself in unconditional love to others, especially the oppressed and the marginalized.

Jesus, Boff concludes, calls a new type of human being into existence, one who belongs to the family of the world; labors in the world and assists in its construction and direction; is not content with the world as it is; and works, as a "stranger en route" (78), toward the creation of a more human and happier world. Such human beings of the new order are the ones who ultimately overcome the sense of alienation afflicting humankind and find true fulfillment for the hope of liberation. Such human beings, of course, constitute the Christians of all generations, of all cultures and civilizations, insofar as the historical Jesus is the risen Christ and the demands of the former continue to be the demands of the latter.

Jesus as Extraordinary Person

As he preached this message of total liberation, with its radical demands for personal and social transformation, Jesus presented himself as the image of God's new order, new human being, and new creation. He revealed himself to be a person of good sense, creative imagination, and authentic originality. Indeed, in all three respects Jesus ranks far above any other human being, past or future, and remains unparalleled in the history of religion, for now or to come. The preacher of liberation was himself totally liberated.

Having good sense means possessing a concrete knowledge of reality, knowing how to distinguish what is essential from what is secondary and being able to see things in their proper perspective. Jesus showed extraordinary good sense: He drew his teaching from common experience and appealed to sound reason; he formulated anew the moral wisdom of old; he looked at the world precisely as it was, without preconceptions of any sort; he was a person of profound human sentiment. Having creative imagination implies being free to think and speak otherwise. Jesus revealed extraordinary imagination: He stood up and spoke differently; he called for liberty and love rather than order and obedience; he respected all human beings in their originality and asked for openness to others and to God. Having originality means speaking of things with absolute immediacy and superiority. Jesus displayed extraordinary originality: He went to the core of human nature; he broke down all barriers, sacred and profane; he allowed access to God for all, regarding all as children of the same Father.

For Boff, therefore, all those who belong to the kingdom must follow the example of the historical Jesus, the image of God's new order. They too must be liberated persons in the service of love, remaining completely open to God and others, exercising indiscriminate love, critically confronting the current social, cultural, and religious orders, giving primacy to persons over things.

Concluding Comments

It should be clear from this portrayal of the historical Jesus that for Boff there is an unbroken continuity between Jesus of Nazareth and the Jesus of the Gospels. Although Jesus did not preach himself as Son of God, Messiah, or God, he *was* Son of God, Messiah, and God before as well as after the resurrection. For Boff there is no rupture between the Jesus of history and the Christ of faith, only a transition from the implicit to the explicit, and this by way of the disciples' subsequent understanding and formulation of Jesus' intention, Jesus' message, and Jesus' personality. Consequently, the portrayal of Jesus Christ in the Gospels functions as the foundation (that is, both grounding and exemplar) for the protest and commitment of liberation theology in the face of massive poverty, as well as for its reading and interpretation of the scriptures from the perspective of poverty. In its protest, commitment, and reading (and here one can see the correspondence-of-relationships model at work), liberation seeks to comply with the preaching, demands, and image of God's new order introduced by Jesus.

Socioeconomic Criticism: Critical Comments

Socioeconomic criticism is as important for the development of biblical criticism at the end of the twentieth century as literary criticism and cultural criticism; what the latter movements do from inside the discipline, the former accomplishes from outside. Thus there can be no proper understanding of biblical criticism—its recent history, its present configuration, or its future development—without a proper understanding of the hermeneutics of liberation. By way of conclusion, a few critical comments are in order.

First, in my opinion no critical movement has been as uniformly forthcoming regarding its context and perspective as socioeconomic criticism. From the outset it has pointed to material poverty as its driving force and its reading lens, all the while emphasizing the need for the critic to share in the life of the poor. In the 1960s and 1970s, socioeconomic criticism beheld the pervasive, inescapable, and overwhelming presence of human misery, socioeconomic oppression and discrimination in Latin America and the Third World, and turned such poverty into a fundamental lens for reading and interpreting the scriptures. Not only did it pursue the thematic of poverty in the Bible in a sustained and systematic way, it also proceeded to re-read and reinterpret the whole of the Bible in light of this thematic.

In retrospect, such constancy of focus has proven both a blessing and a burden. While a new reading of the scriptures emerged in the process—the first true reading from the periphery—this reading has remained unduly monolithic. Initially, the complexity and diversity of the Bible in matters social, political, and economic remained unaddressed. The Bible as a whole emerged as an undisputed and undivided manifesto of liberation for the masses experiencing material oppression. It was a text not to be challenged but to be followed. The ideological edge of the movement came to a halt at the Bible; in the struggle, the text was seen as standing fully and without question on the side of liberation.

Second, such constancy of focus has proven problematic in another respect as well. While acknowledging other forms of oppression and discrimination, socioeconomic criticism persisted in regarding material poverty as the primary expression of oppression. Such a perspective remained both limited and limiting. This failure meant that the relationship between socioeconomic oppression and other forms of oppression would remain unproblematized and untheorized in socioeconomic criticism. Analysis of this relationship would in time be undertaken elsewhere in the name of liberation—in other parts of the Third World as well as within the West, among women and among ethnic and racial minorities. However, in this regard socioeconomic criticism proved singularly unable to lead and to develop in new directions.

Third, although quite radical in social matters, early socioeconomic criticism proved quite conservative in theological matters, as the following examples make abundantly clear:

It posited no difference between the Jesus of history and the Christ of faith—the Christ of the Gospels was the Jesus of Nazareth. The critic was to have complete trust in the rhetoric and ideology of the biblical texts.

It regarded the Bible as the fundamental criterion for all theological activity. The results yielded by the critical analysis of society were to be brought to the Bible for evaluation and validation (theological pertinency). The critic was to be a constructive theologian in dialogue with the scriptures, in search of the Word of God for the present.

It regarded the Bible as the fundamental basis for all practical activity, the praxis of faith in human society being determined in the light of the evaluation and validation provided by the Bible (correspondence-of-relationships). The critic was to be a practical theologian in search of a concrete political way of life in the world, sanctioned by the Bible and in the light of the Word of God for the present.

It called for a reading of the whole Bible, Hebrew and Christian writings, in a christological key. The summit of God's revelation was to be found in the New Testament, in the Gospels, and in the figure of Jesus Christ as portrayed in the Gospels. The critic was to be a Christian believer.

It regarded interpretation as a thoroughly ecclesiastical exercise. The scriptures were to be read and interpreted within the context of the church and in solidarity with other levels of theological activity in the church. The critic was to be a member of the church, in close contact with the popular church and in close harmony with the pastoral church.

Thus the call for a socioeconomic approach to the scriptures, despite its daring dependence on neo-Marxist criticism, ultimately presupposed a very traditional view of the authority of the scriptures, of the theological dimensions of interpretation, and of the ecclesiastical character of criticism.

Finally, the picture of Jesus that emerged from within socioeconomic criticism proved quite triumphalist as well. It is in Jesus that human beings come to know God's plan of liberation for all humankind; it is in Jesus that all human beings and all religions find their apex; it is in Jesus that the alienation of all humankind is resolved and the hope of all human beings is fulfilled. Thus early socioeconomic criticism proved completely blind to the histories and realities, the sensibilities and concerns, the beliefs and practices of non-Christians. Indeed, in keeping with its unquestioned commitment to the rhetoric and the ideology of the Bible, liberation could easily and quite unabashedly paraphrase the declaration of Jesus in John 4:22, "for salvation is from the Christians." The result could hardly be liberative for those outside the Christian fold.

Many of these questions and problems were eventually pursued by hosts of critics who expanded and decentered socioeconomic criticism. In so doing, critics looked back to the initial outburst of liberationist criticism in Latin America for inspiration and guidance and proudly situated themselves within its legacy. In large part because of socioeconomic criticism, biblical studies will never be the same. In this regard, liberationist criticism of the socioeconomic type has proven thoroughly liberating for the discipline as well.

Notes

1. For other introductions in English to liberationist hermeneutics see Christopher Rowland and Mark Corner, "The Foundation and Form of Liberation Exegesis," chap. 2 in *Liberating Exegesis: The Challenge of Liberation Theology to Biblical Studies* (Louisville,

Ky.: Westminster/John Knox, 1989); Arthur F. McGovern, *Liberation Theology and Its Critics: Toward an Assessment* (Maryknoll, N.Y.: Orbis, 1990), 62–82; and David Tombs, "The Hermeneutics of Liberation," in *Approaches to New Testament Study*, ed. Stanley E. Porter and David Tombs, JSNT Supplement Series 120 (Sheffield: Sheffield Academic Press, 1995), 310–55.

2. See Fernando F. Segovia, "'And They Began to Speak in Other Tongues': Competing Modes of Discourse in Contemporary Biblical Criticism," in *Reading from This Place*, vol. 1: *Social Location and Biblical Interpretation in the United States*, ed. Fernando F. Segovia and Mary Ann Tolbert (Minneapolis: Fortress, 1995), 1–32; "Cultural Studies and Contemporary Biblical Criticism: Ideological Criticism as Mode of Discourse," in *Reading from This Place*, vol. 2: *Social Location and Biblical Interpretation in Global Perspective*, ed. Fernando F. Segovia and Mary Ann Tolbert (Minneapolis: Fortress, 1995), 1–17.

3. C. Boff, *Teologia e prática: Teologia do político e suas mediações* (Petrópolis: Editora Vozes, 1978). English translation by Robert Barr, *Theology and Praxis: Epistemological Foundations* (Maryknoll, N.Y.: Orbis, 1987). All references are to the English edition.

4. See the book's preface, xxi-xxx.

5. The volume actually seeks to provide a theoretical foundation for a "theology of the political" in general, encompassing not only the theology of liberation as such but also all possible political theologies, including the theology of captivity, the theology of revolution, and the theology of violence. The result is a highly theoretical work, a critical reflection on method from the point of view of a theology of the political in conversation with a full array of dialogue partners, including European social and hermeneutical theory, European Roman Catholic theological epistemology, and Latin American liberation theology.

6. Praxis, Boff explains, constitutes the starting point, the venue, and the goal of liberation theology. In the ongoing dialectic posited between theory and praxis, praxis emerges as the fundamental locus of theology and has primacy over theory. It is precisely this emphasis on the praxis of faith that calls for contextual social analysis as a first mediation against any type of speculative and abstract thought, for contextual biblical interpretation as a second mediation against any sort of spiritual hermeneutics, and for an engaged theology of the political as a third mediation.

7. Here one can readily see the concept of the *sensus fidelium* at work. Scripture is bound to the church in another way as well (136, 146–48). Just as the meaning of scripture is to be had only within the context of the church, so scripture itself emerges from within this context.

8. Boff adds that one can only search for the original meaning of scripture by way of Christian tradition, insofar as a hermeneutic practice always stands within a tradition and takes a position within such a tradition (139). Thus, while hermeneutic technique establishes boundaries within the text, it is clear that tradition also establishes boundaries.

9. C. Boff and L. Boff, *Como fazer Teologia da Libertação* (Petrópolis: Editora Vozes, 1986). English translation by Paul Burns, *Introducing Liberation Theology* (Tunbridge Wells, Kent: Burns & Oates/Search Press; Maryknoll, N.Y.: Orbis, 1987). All references are to the English edition.

10. As the preface puts it (xi), its aim is to give "an overall, non-technical, and objective account of this new way of 'doing theology.'"

11. The materially poor constitute "all those who lack or are deprived of the necessary means of subsistence—food, clothing, shelter, basic health care, elementary education, and work" (46–47). The Boffs opt for a dialectical explanation of poverty: Poverty is the result of neither vice nor backwardness but of oppression (25–27). To be sure, there is a type of poverty ("innocent" poverty) that is due to natural conditions or disasters and is thus not connected to any system as such (47). For the most part, however, poverty is the direct result of the economic organization of society itself, with the capitalist system directly responsible for its existence and continuation (47–48). Such poverty is brought about both by exclusion and by exploitation.

12. Segovia, "'And They Began to Speak in Other Tongues,'" 7.

13. L. Boff, *Jesus Cristo Libertador: Ensaio de cristologia crítica para o nosso tempo* (Petrópolis: Editora Vozes, 1972). English translation by Patrick Hughes, *Jesus Christ Liberator: A Critical Christology for Our Time* (Maryknoll, N.Y.: Orbis, 1978). All references are to the English edition. A year earlier Clodovis Boff published an article on the historical Jesus, "Foi Jésus um Revolucionário?" *Revista Eclesiástica Brasileira* 31 (1971): 97–118. The preface to the English edition explains that the volume had been put together at a time of severe political repression in Brazil, a time when even the word "liberation" itself had been banned from all the communications media, thus preventing the author from saying all that he had wanted to say with respect to Jesus. In the English edition an epilogue is added ("A Christological View from the Periphery") in which the author pursues, at a time of much greater political tolerance, the liberative dimension of Jesus in quite explicit fashion.

For Further Reading

Liberation Theology

Ellacuría, I., and J. Sobrino, eds. *Mysterium Liberationis: Fundamental Concepts of Liberation Theology.* Maryknoll, N.Y.: Orbis, 1993.

Gutiérrez, G. *A Theology of Liberation: History, Politics, and Salvation.* Rev. ed. Trans. Sr. C. Inda and J. Eagleson. Maryknoll, N.Y.: Orbis, 1988.

Hennelly, A., ed. *Liberation Theology: A Documentary History.* Maryknoll, N.Y.: Orbis, 1990.

McGovern, A. F. *Liberation Theology and Its Critics: Toward an Assessment.* Maryknoll, N.Y.: Orbis, 1989.

Smith, C. *The Emergence of Liberation Theology: Radical Religion and Social Movement Theory.* Chicago: University of Chicago Press, 1991.

Liberation Hermeneutics

Croatto, J. S. *Biblical Hermeneutics: Toward a Theory of Reading in the Production of Meaning.* Trans. R. R. Barr. Maryknoll, N.Y.: Orbis, 1987.

Mesters, C. *Defenseless Flower: A New Reading of the Bible.* Trans. Francis McDonagh. Maryknoll, N.Y.: Orbis, 1989.

Richard, P. "The Hermeneutics of Liberation: Theoretical Grounding for the Communitarian Reading of the Bible." In *Reading from This Place,*

vol. 2: *Social Location and Biblical Interpretation in Global Perspective*, ed.
F. F. Segovia and M. A. Tolbert, 263–80. Minneapolis: Fortress, 1995.
_____. "The Hermeneutics of Liberation: A Hermeneutics of the Spirit."
In *Teaching the Bible: The Discourses and Politics of Biblical Pedagogy*, ed. F.
F. Segovia and M. A. Tolbert, 272–82. Maryknoll, N.Y.: Orbis, 1998.
Rowland, C. and M. Corner. *Liberating Exegesis: The Challenge of Liberation
Theology to Biblical Studies*. Louisville, Ky.: Westminster/John Knox, 1989.
Tombs, D. "The Hermeneutics of Liberation." In *Approaches to New
Testament Study*, ed. S. E. Porter and D. Tombs, 310–55. Journal for the
Study of the New Testament Supplement Series 120. Sheffield: Sheffield
Academic Press, 1995.

Clodovis and Leonardo Boff

Boff, C., and L. Boff. *Salvation and Liberation: In Search of a Balance between
Faith and Politics*. Trans. R. Barr. Maryknoll, N.Y.: Orbis, 1984.
_____. *Introducing Liberation Theology*. Trans. P. Burns. Tunbridge Wells,
Kent: Burns & Oates/Search Press; Maryknoll, N.Y.: Orbis, 1987.
Boff, C. *Theology and Praxis: Epistemological Foundations*. Trans. R. Barr.
Maryknoll, N.Y.: Orbis, 1987.
Boff, L. *Jesus Christ Liberator: A Critical Theology for Our Time*. Trans. P.
Hughes. Maryknoll, N.Y.: Orbis, 1978.

Form

RHETORICAL

Source

REDACTION

TRADITION